# Macmillan Law Masters

## Social Security Law

# Macmillan Law Masters

*Series editor* Marise Cremona

# Social Security Law

**Robert East**
*Principal Lecturer, School of Law, University of Glamorgan*

## Law series editor: Marise Cremona
*Senior Fellow, Centre for Commercial Law Studies*
*Queen Mary and Westfield College, University of London*

MACMILLAN

Published by
MACMILLAN PRESS LTD
Houndmills, Basingstoke, Hampshire RG21 6XS
and London
Companies and representatives
throughout the world

ISBN 0-333-71577-2

A catalogue record for this book is available
from the British Library.

This book is printed on paper suitable for recycling
and made from fully managed and sustained forest sources.

Printed and bound in Great Britain by
Creative Print and Design (Wales), Ebbw Vale

10  9    8    7    6    5    4    3    2    1
08 07   06   05   04   03   02   01   00   99

# Contents

# Preface

The provision of social security is currently a contentious issue. Following 18 years of Conservative administration where successive governments sought to impose their imprint on the provision of social security in Great Britain, the return of a Labour government in 1997 has seen social security reform at the very centre of political debate. In fact, since the creation of the post-war British social security system, substantially based on the proposals in the Beveridge Report of 1942, successive post-war governments introduced new legislation and new regulations to bring about reform. One consequence of this is that the legal framework for the provision of social security benefits in the United Kingdom is bewilderingly complex.

The aims of this book are twofold. First, it seeks to provide a clear account of the law relating to social security benefits in Great Britain. The main target audience consists of students, both undergraduates and others, who are studying this area of law, although the book should assist anyone seeking to gain an insight into the legal framework of the British social security system and an understanding of the features of the main social security benefits. The book attempts to strike a balance between providing a detailed account of these benefits and their legal rules yet retains a clarity of explanation so that readers new to the subject area can obtain an understanding that remains unconfused by the plethora of rules. Secondly, there is more to the study of any area of law than merely to know the legal rules. To make sense of those rules, it is also necessary to understand how and why they were created as well as to explore how effective they are and what reforms might be available. The study of legal rules, in other words, must be placed in context. The second aim of the book, therefore, is to provide such context. This is provided in a number of ways:

(i)   A major objective of social security is to seek to address the issue of poverty. The first chapter, therefore, explores the various ways that poverty is defined and what its causes might be.

(ii)  Chapter 3 specifically seeks to place the British social security system in context in a number of ways. Post-war changes, from the Beveridge Report to 1997, are explored in the context of the political and philosophical ideas that influenced such developments. The British system of social security is also examined in an international context, most obviously by comparing it with that of other European Community member states.

(iii) Many of the chapters that examine individual social security benefits include sections entitled 'context and commentary'. These sections seek to provide an account of the creation and development of individual social security benefits along with critical analysis of their current operation. Many of these also include discussion of current reform proposals.

(iv) The last chapter contains a critical examination of the reforms introduced in the period of Conservative administration between 1979 and 1997 as well as an exploration of the reform strategy of the current Labour government.

The division of many of the chapters on individual social security benefits into sections entitled 'context and commentary' and 'the legal rules', in fact, is designed to assist readers in manoeuvring around the book. Those who wish to obtain information on current benefits, their features and their legal framework should turn to 'the legal rules' sections. Those who are seeking an understanding of the historical and political context, along with current reform proposals, should address the 'context and commentary' sections.

While the book is intended to provide a comprehensive account of the British social security system, some benefits have not been included. These include guardian's allowance, war pensions, widow's benefit and statutory maternity pay, while disablement benefit is the only industrial injuries benefit that is examined. The book aims to state the law as at 1 May 1999. Any errors that may have arisen in this respect, as is the case of any other mistakes throughout the book, are solely my responsibility. One difficulty has been that there are currently rapid changes to social security law. Towards the end of 1999, as a result of the Social Security Act 1998, the title of 'adjudicating officer' is to be changed. I have, nevertheless, used the phrase 'adjudicating officer' throughout the book. October 1999 sees the replacement of family credit and disability working allowance with working families tax credit and disabled person's tax credit respectively. While detailed rules were not available at the time of writing, chapter 9 provides an account of the new 'tax credit' benefits, and the rest of the book assumes that the new benefits are in operation rather than their predecessors.

My thanks extend to the students who, over the last fifteen years or so, have studied social security law at the University of Glamorgan Law School and who, largely unknowingly, have helped in the genesis of this book. Express appreciation is also extended to Clare Lewis whose research throughout the summer of 1998 was of invaluable assistance in writing this book.

# Table of Cases

# Table of Statutes and Regulations

# 1   Social Security and Poverty

*'A decent provision for the poor is the true test of civilisation'* (Samuel Johnson 1770)

## Social Security

Social security is concerned with the provision of financial support to those with problems of financial hardship. Twentieth-century Britain has seen the emergence of the welfare state whereby the government plays an active role in promoting social welfare by providing cash benefits and benefits in kind. The latter include the provision of health and medical facilities as well as schooling, whereas cash benefits most obviously embrace social security benefits provided to those deemed to require them. The objectives of social security, like those of the welfare state in general, are diverse with different protagonists advocating different aspirations. These objectives range from promoting greater economic equality by redistributing resources from the rich, via taxation, to the poor in the form of social security benefits to facilitating people to provide more effectively for their own needs by requiring contributions to be paid by working individuals in order to finance benefits when they are not working, e.g. when sick, unemployed or in old age. However, the most widely supported objective of a system of social security is to provide a minimum standard of living below which no one should fall. Support for this, although their motives for so doing differed, has ranged from Anthony Crosland on the left to Sir William Beveridge and on to right-wing thinkers such as Hayek. As such, the provision of social security benefits has had, as a central aim, the relief of poverty. This is not to deny that other aspects of the welfare state, e.g. housing, are concerned with poverty but that the most important policies in the relief of poverty come within the ambit of social security. Also, it is important to recognise that the main reason that the state has intervened to provide cash benefits to meet this minimum standard is because it could not be guaranteed by a market economy. Thus, most individuals who cannot work, because of old age, disability, sickness, unemployment, etc. have little or no alternative sources of income. Governments of diverging political persuasions, again with different motives and differing views on what the minimum standard should be, have therefore sought to provide a system of social security cash benefits so that claimants and their dependants have resources sufficient to meet this minimum standard.

In examining the role of social security and its legal framework, it is necessary to appreciate this fundamental objective of social security, namely that it is that part of a society's welfare provision that is aimed at providing financial support, usually in the form of a benefit payment, to those deemed to be poor or facing the threat of poverty. Like many advanced industrialised countries, Britain has a social security system provided by the state that provides social security payments to the unemployed, sick, disabled, elderly and others on the grounds that these are the groups that are most likely to be under threat of poverty and therefore in need of such financial support. A major difficulty, however, lies with the fact that, while there is general agreement on the need to provide cash benefits at a minimum standard in order to alleviate poverty, there is no consensus on what this minimum standard should be. One of the main reasons for this is that there is no agreement on what is poverty or how it is caused. Central to understanding the role of social security therefore is an understanding of how poverty is defined.

## Poverty

On the face of it, the issue of what is poverty and who are the poor seems fairly straightforward, though in reality it has been highly problematic with no consensus emerging on a definition. Yet this definitional issue is vital for at least two reasons. First, how poverty is defined will affect the issue of how many people are deemed to be poor and hence the size of the perceived problem. Secondly, the perception of the scope of the 'problem' of poverty will clearly have an impact on what policies are deemed necessary to deal with that problem. Thus Townsend states:

> 'The definition of poverty has implications for the numbers measured to be in poverty according to that definition as well as the policies required to combat poverty.' (Townsend, 1983, p. 59)

Yet the task of defining poverty has been, and still is, a difficult and controversial exercise, as indicated in the following statement:

> 'Measuring poverty is an exercise in demarcation. Lines have to be drawn where none are visible and they have to be made bold. Where one draws the line is itself a battlefield... Those who are suspicious of the notion of poverty insist both on there being a precise definition of what poverty consists of and then on blurring the exercise by pointing to a diversity of needs, circumstances, tastes, propensities, etc. The notion of a poverty threshold, a demarcation line between the poor and the not-poor, is a fraught exercise for just such reasons. A simple

threshold figure, easy to grasp and on which to base an anti-poverty policy would be invaluable, but to be that it also has to be (nearly) universally acceptable. It is in the nature of the social perceptions of poverty in unequal societies that such simple figures are demanded only to be debated.' (Desai, 1986, p. 1)

It is with these difficulties in mind that the various attempts that have been made to provide a definition of poverty can be examined. Particularly influential early steps in this task were Charles Booth's study of poverty in London in 1887 (Booth, 1902) and Seebohm Rowntree's detailed studies of poverty in York in 1889, 1936 and 1950 (Rowntree, 1901; Rowntree and Lavers, 1951) leading to the notion of *absolute poverty*.

# Defining Poverty

## Absolute definitions of poverty

Rowntree, in his study of poverty in York in 1889, considered the problems involved in defining poverty. Based on this study, Rowntree sought to define poverty on the basis of a minimum level of income necessary for individuals to subsist or survive. Thus poverty was based on the idea of a subsistence level, and those individuals and families whose finances fell below this level were deemed to be in poverty. This was known as *primary* or *absolute poverty* and could be contrasted with *secondary poverty*.

*Primary poverty* applied to families whose income was 'insufficient to obtain the minimum necessaries for the maintenance of merely physical efficiency', i.e. income too low to purchase the basic necessities of life. In order to calculate the subsistence level of income to obtain these basic necessities (and hence establish absolute poverty) Rowntree calculated a weekly sum. This was an irreducible minimum expenditure, which for food purchases involved using estimates by the American nutritionist Atwater to calculate the minimum requirements of protein and calories and then translating these into a 'diet containing the necessary nutrients at the lowest cost compatible with a certain amount of variety'. Calculations were also made for the minimum expenditure for the other necessary elements for subsistence or survival such as clothing and shelter.

An absolute (or primary) definition of poverty seeks, therefore, to define poverty on the basis of a minimum standard of living based on an individual's biological and physiological needs for food, water, shelter and clothing, and people are in poverty when their income falls below a level to maintain this. A contemporary definition of poverty using an absolute approach is that of Sir Keith Joseph (the former Conservative minister) and J. Sumption (1979) which is set out on p. 6.

Advocates of defining poverty in this way also identify *secondary poverty*. This is a state of affairs where income is deemed to be initially just sufficient to avoid absolute poverty but the recipient of the income then mismanages some of that income on the purchase of items (e.g. alcohol and tobacco) which do not contribute to physical efficiency, the result being that the recipient and family fall into the state of absolute poverty.

## Relative definitions of poverty

Advocates of adopting a relative approach argue that, in defining who are in poverty in a society, one has to take account of the living standards that prevail in that society. Poverty is not a static state of affairs based on some fixed standard of subsistence or whatever, it is related or *relative* to the rest of society and the range of incomes enjoyed by members of that society. The role of contemporary living standards in seeking to define poverty has long been established. The famous Scottish political economist Adam Smith, for example, stated in *The Wealth of Nations* (1776) that:

'By necessaries I understand not only the commodities which are indispensably necessary for the support of life but whatever the custom of the country renders it indecent for creditable people, even of the lowest order, to be without.'

Poverty, then, is defined on the basis of *relative deprivation*, i.e. those deemed to be in poverty are deprived of certain living conditions and amenities generally enjoyed in the society within which they live. Such a definition was famously adopted in 1985 in a Church of England report that was highly critical of the policies of the then Thatcher government; this report proving to be the high water mark in the strained relations of that government and the hierarchy of the Anglican Church. Its definition of poverty was:

'Poor people in Britain are not, of course, as poor as those in the Third World. But their poverty is real enough nonetheless. For poverty is a relative, as well as an absolute concept. It exists, even in a relatively rich Western society, if people are denied access to what is generally regarded as a reasonable standard and quality of life in that society.' (Commission on Urban Priority, 1985)

Peter Townsend has emerged as the leading contemporary British exponent of this approach. In his weighty *Poverty in the United Kingdom: a survey of household resources and standards of living* (1979), he developed a detailed definition of poverty based on relative deprivation:

'Poverty can be defined objectively and applied consistently in terms of the concept of relative deprivation... The term is understood objectively rather than subjectively. Individuals, families and groups in the population can be said to be in poverty when they lack the resources to obtain the types of diet, participate in the activities and have the living standards and amenities which are customary, or at least widely encouraged or approved in the societies to which they belong. Their resources are so seriously below those commanded by the average individual or family that they are, in effect, excluded from ordinary living patterns, customs and activities.' (Townsend, 1979, chapter 1)

From this approach, poverty is more than a lack of financial resources, it is also about *social exclusion*. Relative poverty involves being excluded, as a result of inadequate income, from the types of social activities that the rest of society enjoys, e.g. not being able to enjoy an adequate diet or damp-free accommodation; lacking the ability to purchase those consumer goods widespread in society, e.g. refrigerator, television; not participating in activities widely enjoyed by others, e.g. going out with friends, sending children on school trips, etc.

## Comments on absolute and relative definitions of poverty

The absolute poverty approach has a number of conceptual difficulties. There is no single subsistence level that can be used as a basis for the poverty line. An individual's nutritional needs depend on his or her level of physical activity, the office worker thus requiring less than a miner or a farm worker. Even within such groups, individual requirements are difficult to define precisely. Thus where a line is drawn depends on the judgement of the investigator and the idea of a purely physiological basis for the poverty criterion is lost. Even if nutritional requirements could be determined there would still be problems arising from the disparity between expert judgement and actual consumption behaviour as exemplified in the following quote:

'Not only do housewives lack the dietary knowledge required to calculate the least-cost foods, not only are poor families forced to purchase food in uneconomical ways, but also eating habits are profoundly influenced by social conventions.' (Atkinson, 1983, p. 226)

In fact Rowntree himself recognised the validity of this view when he stated:

'My primary poverty line represented the minimum sum on which physical efficiency could be maintained. It was a bare standard of *subsistence* rather than living...such a minimum does not by any means constitute a reasonable *living* wage.' (Rowntree quoted in Veit-Wilson, 1986)

Defining an 'irreducible minimum' expenditure level for non-food items such as shelter and clothing is even more problematic and subject to individual opinion. As Atkinson points out:

'In the case of non-food items, there is an even greater degree of arbitrariness. Rowntree's 1950 standard included 2 p a week for wireless, 3 p for a daily newspaper, and 34 p a week for beer, tobacco, presents, holidays and books. It is hard to justify the inclusion of these items on an absolute subsistence definition. As Townsend (1962) has pointed out, "a family might maintain its physical efficiency just as well in a caravan...as in a three-bedroom house. It could go to bed early and spend nothing on electricity".' (Atkinson, 1983, chapter 10)

Such criticism has led to a direct attack on the idea of secondary poverty, which suggests that individuals living in secondary poverty are in such a position because of their own inadequate behaviour. Such an assertion has been criticised on grounds of consumer rationality. It assumes that those with incomes at or near poverty levels are able to be as rational or as efficient as those higher up the income scale in purchasing food and other items. Aside from the claim that advertising is geared to inducing consumer irrationality amongst us all, those on low incomes are not, as Atkinson points out, in a position to benefit from 'economies of scale' when purchasing food and other items.

Relative definitions of poverty have also had their critics. A major criticism is that such definitions confuse poverty with inequality. To say that an individual lacks resources in comparison to someone else living in the same society is to make a statement about unequal resources or inequality, it is not a statement about poverty. Thus Joseph and Sumption state that:

'A family is poor if it cannot afford to eat. It is not poor if it cannot afford endless smokes and *it does not become poor by the mere fact that other people can afford them.*' (Joseph and Sumption, 1979, p. 27) [my emphasis]

From this perspective, claims by those embracing a relative definition that poverty should be measured on the basis of a line constituting 50% of a country's average income (and other similar proposals) means little as this measures the level of inequality in that country and does not measure poverty, the latter being defined by a level of income merely needed to maintain subsistence. Advocates of an absolute definition of poverty thus often conclude that poverty no longer exists in the United Kingdom, leading to the claim that relative definitions overestimate the number of people in poverty. From an *absolute* perspective, therefore, the fact that in 1992/3 14.1 million people (25% of the population) were living below 50% of average income (Oppenheim and Harker, 1996, p. 24) is no indicator of the number of poor people in the United Kingdom today. In contrast, from a *relative* definition, it can be presented as an accurate indicator of the scope of poverty in this country.

Relative definitions are also attacked on the grounds that, from such a perspective, poverty can never be eradicated until total economic equality is achieved, and that is itself an unachievable goal. Such a criticism is, however, challenged by Atkinson:

> '...the adoption of a relative poverty standard does NOT mean that the poor are necessarily always with us. It is sometimes suggested that if, for example, we define the poverty line as half the average income, moving up with the general standard of living, then poverty cannot be abolished. On the contrary, it is quite possible to imagine a society in which no one has less than half the average income – in which there is no poverty according to this definition.' (Atkinson, 1983, p. 228)

However, while a relative definition of poverty may be forwarded in respect of advanced industrialised societies such as the United Kingdom, even its most earnest advocates recognise its limitations when applied to Third World countries particularly when they are compared with more affluent countries. Thus, George and Howards argue that a relative definition:[1]

> '...cannot be used by itself to measure poverty in third world countries. It can lead to such unacceptable conclusions that since the vast majority of the population in a country is ill-fed, ill-housed, ill-clothed, ill-educated etc., the majority of the population cannot be in poverty...Moreover, it can lead to the equally unacceptable conclusion that the extent of...poverty in Britain and India is similar. It is for this reason that in third world countries the more austere [i.e. absolute] definitions of poverty are more useful. As Sen (1981, p. 22) has argued, the notion of relative poverty 'supplements (but cannot supplant) the earlier approach of absolute dispossession.' If the majority of the population of a country lack the basic needs of life then the majority of the population is in poverty.' (George and Howards, 1991, p. 10)

# Causes of Poverty

The issue of identifying the causes of poverty is as controversial as that of defining poverty. A number of radically different explanations and theories of why poverty exists have been developed. The most important of these are set out below.

## Theories relating to moral inadequacy

A view widely held in early nineteenth-century England was that the reason why people were living in poverty was that it was due to their own fault. As Berthoud et al. state, the prevalent view was that:

> 'poverty was caused by idleness, improvidence and intemperance, defects of character which the individual could, if he chose, overcome.' (Berthoud, Brown and Copper, 1981, pp. 7–8)

This view was held particularly in respect of the able-bodied poor. In contrast to the disabled, sick or old, it was argued that the able-bodied could obtain employment if only they were prepared to do so. This approach was the dominant influence behind the Poor Law Report 1832 and the subsequent Poor Law Act 1834. This established workhouses as the basis for parishes providing support (or 'relief') for the poor. The level of relief was to be at a lower standard of living than if those seeking it were working. This was known as the *less eligibility principle*:

> 'The situation of the individual relieved should not be made really or apparently so eligible as the situation of the independent labourer of the lowest class' (Poor Law Act 1834)

The provision of relief in the workhouses was thus at a very basic level, being designed to deter those who claimed relief from continuing to remain dependent upon it as well as to discourage others from acting in a way that might result in the need to claim poor relief. This prompted Disraeli to remark that the Poor Law Act of 1834 '[a]nnounces to the world that in England poverty is a crime.'

A major problem with this approach was that while in theory the able-bodied poor were distinguished from others in poverty, in practice the provision of relief in the workhouses did not discriminate between the able-bodied and others, all received the minimal 'less eligibility' level of relief. Towards the end of the nineteenth century, however:

> '...this theory was modified by the recognition that among those in

poverty were decent, hardworking, good living, provident people who, in spite of personal effort, were defeated by successive or prolonged crises beyond their control.' (Berthoud, Brown and Copper, 1981, p. 8)

In academic – if not popular – circles, the view that the poor were poor because of their own weaknesses or defects became unfashionable but has re-emerged in recent years as a means of explaining the existence of persistent poverty in otherwise affluent societies. Tied closely to merito-cratic explanations of income distribution, this character deficiency ap-proach is explained in a comparative analysis of poverty in the United Kingdom and the United States by George and Howards. While ultimately highly critical of this explanation of poverty, they set out its main features as follows:

'...in the same way that high income is the result of high ability, high motivation and high qualifications, poverty, too, is the result of low ability, low motivation and low qualifications. What is more these individual deficiencies are...the result of...individual, familial factors. It is for this reason that many have referred to this group of individual factors as character deficiency, personal fault or flawed character explanations [of poverty].' (George and Howards, 1991, p. 96)

Criticism of this approach centres around its assumption that wealth and high income are attained on the meritocratic grounds of high intelligence and educational achievement whereas poverty is a consequence of low intelligence and low educational achievement. Critics argue that other factors are more influential. Most obviously, there is a lack of equality of opportunity which stems, inter alia, from the ability of the wealthy to pass on their wealth, and the advantages it provides, to the next generation. Similarly inequalities in the provision of education, most obviously (but not solely) as manifested in the existence of private schools, means that individuals of the same ability may, because of factors outside their control, experience differing quality education.

A highly influential version of this character deficiency approach is the *culture of poverty* thesis. This suggests that poverty is passed from one generation to another by the cultural attitudes and life style of the poor. Oscar Lewis put forward the theory that poverty, once developed, per-petuated itself through the socialisation of the children within it, and both adults and children became immune to the influence of improved socio-economic conditions, and thus were not psychologically geared to take full advantage of changing conditions or increased opportunities which might occur (Lewis, 1965). A variant of this was propounded in 1972 by Sir Keith Joseph who, at the time, was Secretary of State for Health and Social

Security in the then Conservative government. His theory of a *cycle of deprivation* in which deprivation or poverty is transmitted from one generation to another in certain families stresses the effect of material factors, such as poor housing and low income, in undermining prospects for self-improvement from generation to generation. With regard to cultural factors, he particularly emphasised the inadequacy of parental upbringing and the home background. Parents who were themselves deprived provide inadequate socialisation for their children who consequently do not acquire the motivation, skills and capacities necessary to avail themselves of educational and job opportunities. The outcome, therefore, is that they remain poor in a society which otherwise offers them prosperity.

The notion of the *dependency culture* slightly alters the above ideas by attributing responsibility for such a state of affairs upon the social security system rather than on the recipients of social security. Popularised by the UK Conservative government in the late 1980s, for example in 1987, Margaret Thatcher, then Prime Minister, 'announced her determination to end the "dependency culture" ' (Lister, 1990, pp. 7–8), the idea of a dependency culture is that recipients of social security became dependent on such state benefits as their source of income. They lose the initiative or responsibility to seek employment. While their long-term economic well being would be better served in obtaining a job, they lose the enterprise to seek one because of the access to benefits while out of work. This approach therefore claims that those on benefits, and therefore on a low income, are in such a position because of this lack of personal initiative. However, it lays much of the blame on the social security system for not providing the incentive for benefit recipients to seek work, thereby creating a 'dependency culture'. The welfare state, in other words, has created poverty by generating such attitudes in the recipients of social security benefits. Such a view has been influenced by the work of two right-wing American academics. The first of these was Charles Murray who, in 1984, published his book *Losing Ground*. Here, he argued that welfare programmes in the USA had created rather than relieved poverty, as the benefit system in the USA gave poor people incentives to behave in ways that were contrary to their long-term interests. Aid to Families with Dependent Children (AFDC), which provided cash assistance to low-income families, was identified as the chief culprit. Increases in the level of such payments, together with the relaxation of the rules governing their receipt, resulted, so Murray argued, in young women choosing lone parenthood rather than low-paid work. Murray's solution to this perceived problem was to abolish welfare payments. In 1986 a second American book, *Beyond Entitlement* by Lawrence Mead (1986), argued that the dependency culture was encouraged by making social security benefits too easily available in terms of the lack of conditions required in order to be eligible for such benefits. Mead's view was that the harm was done, not by the provision of welfare benefits themselves, but by the fact that they were entitlements, provided regardless of the behaviour of claimants. Mead's solution was not to recommend abolition of welfare payments but to make it more difficult to be eligible for such payments. In particular he suggested a work obligation for recipients of social security. This could take the form of a 'workfare' requirement whereby benefit recipients must undertake certain stipulated work or some employment training as a condition of receiving benefit. In this way, it was argued, the poor could recognise, and thus acquire, values that emphasised the virtues of hard work. The dependency culture would then be destroyed and the poor would develop a willingness to undertake a job however unpleasant or low paid.

## Structural explanations of poverty

A radically different set of theories on the causes of poverty is based on the assumption that poverty is inherent in the structure of a society based on a market economy. One consequence of this is that the poor are not to be blamed for their poverty. This assumption is shared by both advocates and critics of market economics. Advocates of the market argue that in such an economic order there will inevitably be changes in the demand for goods due to factors outside the control of a business or the endeavours of its workforce, e.g. when there is a technological development this may lead to a change in demand for different goods. Those who have produced the original goods that are now obsolete might see a decline in the demand for those goods and, as a consequence, they may suffer unemployment leading to poverty for at least some of them. From this perspective, it can be argued that the state should therefore be prepared to provide benefits for such short-term periods of unemployment while a new job is obtained.

Critics of the market system, on the other hand, consider the cause of poverty to be in the structure of the market, or capitalist, system itself; that profit not human need is the basic principle of capitalism. The most obvious of such critics are Marxists:

> 'In brief, Marx saw inequality in capitalist societies as the inevitable result of the exploitation of the working class by the capitalist class. This state of affairs is perpetuated because of the superior economic and political power of the capitalist class and because of the development of a dominant ideology that justifies and legitimizes inequality. Moreover, workers' exploitation is the very basis of profit making and hence of the capitalist system...The clear implication is that workers' exploitation and hence poverty can only be abolished after the abolition of the capitalist system.' (George and Howards, 1991, pp. 89–90)

Another structural explanation of poverty forwarded by supporters of a market economy stresses the role of economic inequality by claiming that such an economy functions on the basis of economic inequality. The able, the entrepreneurial, the hardworking, the risk takers and the lucky will have their abilities rewarded by becoming wealthy. The less able, indolent, unlucky, etc. will be less well off. In other words, capitalism is based on economic inequality whereby there will be winners and losers. As Berthoud et al. point out:

> '...the system requires inequality to function correctly. Jobs of markedly different levels of skills must be filled and must receive different rewards in order to attract personnel of the correct calibre. In any case, some persons are more able than others and the system will naturally pay them in accordance with their abilities and productivity.' (Berthoud, Brown and Copper, 1981, p. 10)

Inequality in the distribution of economic rewards is, thus, seen as necessary for the economy to function. It is not a form of exploitation; rather it benefits all in society, even those at the bottom end of the income scale. The argument is that a market economy functions on the basis of economic inequality so that such inequality is both inevitable and necessary. And anyway, if poverty is defined in absolute terms, then, in many such societies, it does not exist. In fact those at the bottom end of the income scale are better off in a market economy that rewards ability, hard work, etc. than any other type of society. This approach is based on what is sometimes called the 'trickle down' theory and sometimes the 'bigger cake' theory. 'Trickle down' means that the wealth of the wealthy few will trickle down for the benefit of the rest as their initiative and hard work leads to jobs being created and they also spend their money, generating work within the economy, etc. The 'bigger cake' theory argues that by allowing the able or hardworking to become wealthy and to retain that wealth will act as an incentive to them. They will thus generate a more successful economy, with more jobs – in other words a larger economic cake – than in a society without such incentives. According to this approach, interference by the state, e.g. in controlling the economy or by imposing too much taxation, particularly redistributive taxation which seeks to tax the rich heavily, will be economically disastrous – for the poor as much as, if not more than, for the rest of society.

## Concluding Comments

There is clearly no unanimity of view both in respect of defining poverty and of establishing the causes of poverty. Nevertheless, for those wishing to gain an understanding of social security and its legal arrangements, it is important to be aware of the differing views on these issues. Social security aims to deal directly with the problem of poverty. The divergent opinions on poverty and its causes puts social security law into its social and political context, helping to understand the different attitudes to what social security is achieving as well as what it should seek to achieve.

## Notes

**1.** George and Howards are here expressly referring to the *social participation* definition of poverty. However, this is a type of relative definition of poverty and their comments can be applied generally to such definitions.

## Bibliography

Atkinson, A. B. (1983) *The Economics of Inequality*, 2nd edition, Oxford University Press.

Becker, S. (1991) *Windows of Opportunity*, Child Poverty Action Group.

Berthoud, R., Brown, J. C. and Copper, S. (1981) *Poverty and the Development of Anti-Poverty Policy in the United Kingdom*, Heinemann.

Booth, C. (1902) *Life and Labour of the People in London*.

Commission on Urban Priority (1985) *Faith in the City, a Call for Action by Church and Nation*, Church House.

Deacon, A. (1991) 'The retreat from state welfare'. In D. Becker.

Desai, M. (1986) Drawing the line: defining the poverty threshold. In P. Golding (ed.) *Excluding the Poor*, Child Poverty Action Group, p. 1.

George, V. (1973) *Social Security and Society*, Routledge and Kegan Paul.

George, V. and Howards, I. (1991) *Poverty amidst Affluence: Britain and the United States*, Edward Elgar.

Golding, P. (1986) *Excluding the Poor*, Child Poverty Action Group.

Joseph, K. and Sumption, J. (1979) *Equality*, Murray.

Lister, R. (1990) *The Exclusive Society: Citizenship and the Poor,* Child Poverty Action Group.

Lewis, O. (1961) *The Children of Sanchez,* Random House.

Loney, M., Boswell, D. and Clarke, J. (1983) *Social Policy and Social Welfare*, Open University Press.

Mead, L. (1986) *Beyond Entitlement*, Free Press.

Murray, C. (1984) *Losing Ground*, Basic Books.

Oppenheim, C. and Harker, L. (1996) *Poverty: The Facts*, Child Poverty Action Group.

Rowntree, B. S. (1901) *Poverty: A Study of Town Life*, Macmillan.

Rowntree, B. S. and Lavers, G. (1951) *Poverty and the Welfare State*, Longmans.

Sen, A. K. (1981) *Poverty and Famines*, Clarendon Press.

Smith, A. (1776) *The Wealth of Nations*.

Spicker, P. (1993) *Poverty and Social Security*, Routledge.

Townsend, P. (1962) The meaning of poverty, *British Journal of Sociology*, **13**.

Townsend, P. (1979) *Poverty in the United Kingdom: a survey of household resources and standards of living*, Penguin.

Townsend, P. (1983) 'A theory of poverty and the role of social policy'. In M. Loney, D. Boswell and J. Clarke, *Social Policy and Social Welfare*, Open University Press.

Veit-Wilson, J. (1986) 'Paradigms of poverty', *Journal of Social Policy*, January.

# 2 An Introduction to the British Social Security System

## Different Methods of Social Security

Social security has, as one of its primary aims, the provision of financial support, usually in the form of a benefit payment, to those deemed to be poor or facing the threat of poverty. It provides assistance to compensate for a lack of financial resources, most obviously where an individual is not able to work because of such factors as sickness, disability, unemployment or old age. Social security can also be paid as a 'top up' for individuals who are working but are in receipt of low wages, while some social security provision targets particular groups in society, such as disabled individuals or families with children, who are deemed to have specific needs that warrant financial assistance. In Britain, in the twentieth century, the state has played a major role in the provision of social security with, for example, the first social security provision in the event of unemployment being established in 1911. Such state provision of social security can take a number of forms depending on two features: first, the way in which the resources to finance the benefits are acquired and secondly, the criteria by which entitlement to a social security benefit is determined. Turning to the first of these, the British social security system has been dominated by the difference between *contributory* and *non-contributory* social security benefits.

## Contributory and non-contributory social security schemes

A *contributory* scheme of social security is based on the principle of social insurance whereby the scheme is financed by contributions made when people are working so that they are eligible for benefit during periods of their life when they are not working e.g. because of unemployment, sickness or old age. Thus an important aim of a contributory scheme is that it seeks to redistribute resources over a person's lifetime by deducting income when employed and paying it back when not employed. The scheme is clearly based on the notion of insurance in the sense that contributions are made (e.g. by the employer deducting the amount of the contribution from employees' wages and transferring it to the state's contribution fund) as a form of insurance premium to cover the possible risk that the contributor will not be able to obtain wages via employment at some future period in his or her lifetime. It also redistributes resources in another way in that such a scheme can also be seen as a pooling of resources by all those participating in the scheme whereby, at any point in time, there is a redistribution of resources from those who are paying contributions to those who are receiving benefits.

Known as national, or social, insurance, this approach to the provision of social security makes eligibility for benefit consequent on a claimant having achieved the necessary contributions record. If a claimant lacks such a record, then he or she is ineligible for benefit. Consequently, this approach cannot be totally comprehensive in terms of ensuring that all those who fall into a category of eligibility, for example those who become unemployed, will receive benefit. Those who are excluded are largely those who are unable to work and include chronically sick and disabled people, the long-term unemployed, school leavers and young mothers.

This weakness has been particularly relevant in the 1980s and 1990s when Britain, like much of Western Europe, has experienced high levels of unemployment. Many people have been unable to obtain employment in order to make the necessary contributions to be eligible for a contributory benefit. Contributory schemes can never, therefore, be comprehensive in the sense of guaranteeing financial assistance to all who might be deemed in need of it. High levels of unemployment also create practical problems in the funding of contributory schemes. It means that as fewer people are employed then fewer people are making contributions while there will also be more claimants. Another feature of contributory schemes has been the need for a large bureaucracy to maintain a record of the contributions made by all who participate in the scheme, although computerisation is likely to reduce the amount of bureaucracy.

*Non-contributory* schemes do not determine eligibility for benefit on the basis of having previously satisfied a contributions record. Rather, these schemes are funded in the United Kingdom out of general taxation with eligibility being based on an individual satisfying a test of need, e.g. disability or that a claimant's financial resources fall below a predetermined means test. The current use of non-contributory benefits in the British social security system reflects a great diversity. While all are paid out of general taxation rather than from the National Insurance Fund, some (such as income support and income-based jobseekers allowance) are administered centrally, some (housing benefit and council tax benefit) locally. Some are mandatory (such as those referred to above), others are discretionary (such as a number of Social Fund loans).

While the difference between contributory and non-contributory benefits refers to how different benefits are resourced, there is also another way in which benefits can be categorised, namely how entitlement to receive the benefit is determined. In this respect, the following distinction is important.

## Means-tested and non-means-tested benefits

The means-test approach is to limit entitlement to those whose income and, usually, capital fall below a certain prescribed level. Income-based jobseeker's allowance (JSA), which came into existence in October 1996, is an example of a means-tested benefit. Individuals who are required to be available for work are eligible for the benefit if their means fall below the prescribed limits. Income-based JSA also highlights another feature of means-tested benefits in that such benefits tend to be 'safety net' benefits, providing residual support to people who lack other sources of financial support. Along with income support, which is the means-tested benefit available to people who do not have to be available for work, income-based JSA is, in principle, a supplement to other benefits in that it brings claimants up to a level of income, acting as a guaranteed minimum income for a wide range of claimants. Claimants whose income, whether from other social security benefits or alternative sources of income, is above this guaranteed income level are not eligible for these means-tested benefits. In contrast, non-means-tested benefits base entitlement on a claimant satisfying certain conditions of entitlement such as being unemployed, widowed, disabled or pregnant, not on whether a claimant's income falls below some prescribed level.

Often the distinction between non-means-tested and means-tested benefits is described as the difference between *universal* and *selective* benefits. Selective benefits are those provided to people who are deemed to be in need whereas universal benefits are available to all, a hypothetical example of a universal benefit being a 'social dividend' benefit that might be paid to every adult. Means-tested benefits are sometimes referred to as selective benefits as only those claimants who can show need in that their financial resources fall below the predetermined means level are 'selected' for benefit. Nevertheless, to call means-tested benefits selective and non-means-tested benefits universal is, in fact, erroneous. Basing eligibility on means is merely one way of determining need. Equally selective is to base eligibility to a benefit on grounds of disability or pregnancy or, as with child benefit, on having children in the household or, in fact, on any ground. Thus Spicker argues that non-means-tested benefits:

> '...are better considered as categorical benefits, relying on membership of a demographic category–like children or old age. This implies that social security is provided universally for certain classes of people...' (Spicker, 1993, p. 144)

The comparative advantages and disadvantages of means-tested and non-means-tested (or categorical) benefits have generated much debate.

The main arguments can be summarised as follows:

## Non-means-tested benefits

Advantages:

1. Non-means-tested benefits are claimed to be very simple to administer, particularly if eligibility is not based on contributions. The heavy administrative costs involved in means-testing potential claimants do not exist while, if a benefit is also non-contributory, there is an equal absence of the need to maintain an administrative record of the contribution record of individuals.
2. Another major advantage is the claim that such benefits do not create a poverty trap (which is explained below).
3. Thirdly, non-means tested benefits reach their target. There is unlikely to be any substantial 'take-up' problem whereby those who are eligible fail to receive (or 'take up') the benefit.

Disadvantages:

1. The major criticism of non-means-tested benefits is that they are claimed to be 'inefficient'. If a major objective is to provide financial assistance to the poor or those under threat of poverty, this is a very wasteful method in that all in a category, irrespective of their financial position, receive the benefit. This often results in the benefit being paid at a lower rate than if it were only to be paid to low income groups. The principal categorical benefit in the British social security system, child benefit has suffered from such criticism. In other words, universal benefits do not 'target' resources towards those most in need of them. Three-quarters of child benefit, for example, goes to people above the income-based JSA/income support level.
2. A second criticism comes from those who see social security as having an additional function of redistributing financial resources from the rich to the poor. From this perspective, taxing the rich and then redistributing the resources obtained back to the poor in the form of benefits is a way of achieving greater economic equality. Benefits that are paid to all in a category, irrespective of financial position, cannot achieve that objective whereas, in principle, means-tested benefits can, as they are only paid to those whose income falls below the means test level.
3. Another criticism directed at categorical or non-means-tested benefits is that, because they are not directed solely at those who fall below a threshold of need or test of means, they are more costly than means-tested benefits and therefore necessitate greater tax revenues to pay for them.

## Means-tested benefits

Advantages:

1. Means-tested benefits can be used to supplement contributory benefits

as the latter only provide benefit to those who have made the necessary contributions. Thus, in the post-war period, the British social security system has utilised a means-tested 'safety net' benefit for those claimants who are not eligible for contributory benefits. Currently, for example, income-based JSA is used in this way for those claimants ineligible for contributory JSA and other contributory benefits.

2. Advocates of means-tested benefits argue that they direct financial resources to those most in need. Such benefits target resources to those people who need it most, rather than, with non-means-tested benefits, spreading them thinly to many who are not in need of state benefit.

3. In contrast to categorical benefits, means-tested benefits can, as mentioned above, achieve some degree of redistribution of economic resources from the rich to the poor.

4. While means-testing tends to be associated with safety net provision to low income groups, it can be inverted to screen out high income groups. Thus, while child benefit is currently not means-tested, it could become so by making it taxable. Those not paying income tax would receive it in full, those paying income tax at the basic rate would receive a net amount with basic rate deducted, while higher rate payers would retain a smaller net amount, minus whatever higher rate of income tax they were paying. Taxing child benefit would therefore mean that the state would 'claw back' some of the benefit initially paid out to those whose income is subject to income tax. Such a strategy was endorsed by the DSS in the March 1998 Green Paper *New Ambitions for our Country: A New Contract for Welfare* (Cm3805):

> 'We have...underlined our commitment to Child Benefit in the Budget. Child Benefit should and will remain universal where it is already universal...[Yet i]t must be right in principle that if Child Benefit is raised in future, then there is a case for higher rate taxpayers paying tax on it.' (p. 58)

Disadvantages:

1. A major criticism of means testing is that it is administratively complex. A large bureaucracy has traditionally been necessary to determine whether claimants' means make them eligible for the benefit or not. This inevitably makes means-tested benefits more expensive to administer than categorical benefits, although computerisation may well reduce administrative costs in the future.

2. Another important criticism of means testing is that it leads to a 'poverty trap'. This refers to situations where a claimant's income increases so that he or she ceases to be eligible for the means-tested benefit. The combination of the withdrawal of the benefit with a likely increase in the amount of income tax paid on the higher income means that the claimant is little better off than before the income rise.

People in such a situation find it very difficult, therefore, to increase their level of income such that they can break out of poverty.

3.   Stigma is often identified as a feature of means-tested benefits. Claimants are required to admit both to themselves and to the world at large that their financial resources are below the prescribed income level. This is both humiliating and also leaves them vulnerable to publicly voiced opinions about benefit claimants being scroungers, lazy, etc. This is not, however, an inherent feature of means testing but rather means testing in relation to providing a 'safety net' provision at the bottom of the income scale. Means testing using taxation of income to 'claw back' a categorical benefit, e.g., need not stigmatise.

4.   The final criticism traditionally made of means-tested benefits is that they are often ineffective in reaching their target. Designed specifically to reach those deemed to be in need, means-tested benefits often fail to reach this target group because of problems of 'take up', that is those eligible for the benefit do not apply for it and therefore do not receive it. Means-tested benefits in the British social security system such as housing benefit, income support, income-based JSA and working families tax credit all suffer from lack of take up in that they are not claimed by all those who are eligible. Reasons for lack of take up include the aforementioned stigma of claiming this type of 'safety net' means-tested benefit while some claimants may not be aware of their entitlement to such a benefit. Thus, in 1998 over one million pensioners eligible for income support were not receiving it.

## Earnings replacement benefits and other non-means-tested benefits

While the function of means-tested benefits is primarily to alleviate poverty by providing a basic income or topping up low earnings or other benefits, non-means-tested benefits tend to fulfil one of two functions. Some non-means-tested benefits are designed as a direct replacement for earnings. Paid when a person is unable to work because of unemployment, sickness, pregnancy or old age, these earnings replacement benefits seek to compensate a claimant because of this inability to work. They include contributory JSA, incapacity benefit, severe disablement allowance, maternity allowance, invalid care allowance and retirement pension. Other non-means-tested benefits, however, exist as a recognition that certain people have specific needs that generate extra costs because they are sick, disabled or have children. These benefits exist to provide extra resources for a claimant because he or she has a particular need, e.g. disability or children and not as a direct replacement of earnings. The sole requirement is that the claimant falls into a category of people deemed to warrant a benefit. They include disability living allowance, attendance allowance, industrial injuries benefit, child benefit and guardian's allowance. Normally, a claimant can only receive one earnings replacement benefit but can receive any number of the other benefits depending on his or her particular needs.

Having identified the different ways both of resourcing social security and determining eligibility for benefit, it is appropriate to categorise the different benefits within the British social security system.

## Categories of Benefit

On the basis of the two criteria examined in the last section, namely the way in which the resources to finance the benefits are acquired and the criteria by which entitlement to a social security benefit is determined, it is possible to divide the main benefits of the British social security system into the following categories.

### Contributory non-means-tested benefits

Eligibility for these benefits is principally based on a claimant's National Insurance contributions record (or, in some cases, that of his or her spouse):

Contributory Jobseeker's Allowance
Incapacity Benefit
Categories A and B Retirement Pension
Widows Pension, Widowed Mother's Allowance and Widow's Payment
Maternity Allowance

### Non-contributory non-means-tested benefits

Otherwise known as categorical benefits, eligibility is established when a claimant (or a member of his or her family unit) falls into a category of people deemed to be in need of benefit which is provided to all who fall into that category:

Child Benefit
Severe Disablement Allowance
Invalid Care Allowance
Disability Living Allowance
Attendance Allowance
Category D Retirement Pension
Industrial Injuries Benefits, including Disablement Benefit
Statutory Sick Pay
Statutory Maternity Pay

## Income-related benefits

'Income related' is a statutorily defined substitute phrase for means-tested first used in the Social Security Act 1986 (when, inter alia, income support was introduced to replace supplementary benefit). Strictly inaccurate, as these benefits are also 'capital related', 'income-related' benefits are paid to claimants whose means fall below a prescribed level. The main income-related benefits are:

Income-based Jobseeker's Allowance
Income Support
Working Families Tax Credit (and its predecessor Family Credit)
Disabled Person's Tax Credit (and its predecessor Disability Working
    Allowance)
Social Fund Payments
Housing Benefit
Council Tax Benefit

It is important to note that a claimant can be in receipt of a number of different benefits from each category, e.g. an unemployed parent may be in receipt of contributory JSA, income-based JSA, child benefit, housing benefit and council tax benefit, while a disabled pensioner might be receiving retirement pension, attendance allowance, income support, housing benefit and council tax benefit. Another significant issue is that eligibility for certain income-related benefits automatically brings entitlement to other benefits. Some benefits do not have their own means test; eligibility for the benefit is determined merely by receiving another benefit. The latter benefit provides a 'passport' of entitlement to the other benefit(s). The extent of this in the British social security system is set out below:

| *Passporting benefit* | *Passported benefit* |
| --- | --- |
| Income-based JSA | Free school meals; housing renovation grants; free prescriptions and other health benefits; Social Fund cold weather, funeral expenses and maternity expenses payments and community care and budgeting loans payments |
| Income support | Free school meals; housing renovation grants; free prescriptions and other health benefits; a number of Social Fund payments |
| Working families tax credit and Disabled Person's tax credit | Health benefits; Social Fund funeral expenses and maternity expenses payments |
| Housing benefit and council tax benefit | Social Fund funeral expenses payments |

# Legal Framework

The law relating to social security benefits comes from a number of sources. Unlike many other areas of law, however, there is a very heavy reliance on regulations, while the social security appeal system also generates legally binding decisions. The various sources of the law relating to social security benefits are set out as follows:

## Legislation

The main statutes that currently apply to social security benefits are the Social Security Contributions and Benefits Act 1992, Social Security Administration Act 1992, Social Security Consequential Provisions Act 1992, the Jobseekers Act 1995 and the Social Security Act 1998. The three 1992 statutes are consolidating pieces of legislation replacing a plethora of legislation largely created by the wide ranging reforms introduced up to that point in time by successive Conservative governments since 1979. These Acts produced no substantial change in the law but gave effect to 'a much-needed consolidation of social security law' (Poynter and Martin, 1992/93, p. xi). In contrast, the Jobseekers Act 1995 produced arguably the greatest change to the British social security system since the implementation of the Beveridge proposals. The Social Security Act 1998 was the first major piece of social security legislation introduced by the Labour government elected on 1 May 1997. The Act includes a number of important changes such as altering the appeals system, modifying the system of National Insurance contributions by introducing a new Class 1B contribution and ending the higher lone parent rates for child benefit and a number of means-tested benefits.

## Regulations

The statutes are largely 'enabling', which means that they merely set out the general legal framework, allowing (or enabling) the details to be introduced by the Department of Social Security. Most of the detailed rules governing each benefit are therefore contained in sets of regulations, for example, the details in respect of jobseeker's allowance are set out in The Jobseekers Allowance Regulations 1996 No. 207. These regulations create a bewildering array of rules, not least because there are sometimes more than one set of regulations for a benefit (e.g. income support) while some sets of regulations are general, applying to more than one type of benefit.

## Case law

As is explained later in this chapter, there is a two-tier appeal system operating for most benefits. Appeals from the decision of a social security appeal tribunal (the first tier of appeal) can be made to the second level of appeal, a Social Security Commissioner (or Commissioners) on a point of law or on decisions on medical and disability issues. Most tribunal decisions on points of fact are not, therefore, the basis of appeal to a Commissioner. Since the case of *R(I) 12/75*, a system of binding precedent operates. The most important decisions of a Commissioner have, since 1982, been 'reported' and such decisions are binding on tribunals and adjudication officers. They are also bound by unreported decisions although, in the event of a clash, reported decisions prevail over unreported ones. The courts exercise control over this appeal process in two ways. First, appeals can be made in respect of Commissioner's decisions to the Court of Appeal and, thus, to the House of Lords. Secondly, the High Court exercises a supervisory jurisdiction over all decision making in the sphere of social security via judicial review. This applies even to those benefits where there is no independent appeal system such as housing benefit and some parts of the operation of the Social Fund.

## Administration

Since 1988, the Department of Social Security (DSS) has been responsible for the administration of social security benefits. However, the early 1990s saw a policy of transferring DSS functions to agencies, headed by chief executives, often recruited from outside the Civil Service. While remaining part of the DSS with staff continuing to be civil servants, the rationale for the creation of these semi-autonomous agencies was to separate the policy functions of government departments from their operational functions. Thus the agencies are required to enter into agreements with central government to operate schemes, such as the benefits system, which had formerly been run by central government departments, who remain responsible for policy decisions. The aim is that the agencies administer schemes in a more business-like way than was previously the case. As a result six agencies were created to carry out the DSS's executive operations.

The *Benefits Agency* is the largest of the agencies, coming into operation in April 1991. It administers payment of most social security payments. It operates via district offices throughout the country, which are each responsible for a number of local offices. Each office is divided into sections, which are responsible for a specific benefit or for contributions or for fraud. An executive officer supervises each section, under whom are administrative officers (from whom, until 1999, adjudication officers were appointed) and administrative assistants. Some of the work of the Benefits Agency is undertaken by central offices. These include the Pensions Directorate, Overseas Benefit Directorate and the Child Benefit Centre located at Newcastle-upon-Tyne. The *Contributions Agency* is also based at Newcastle and is responsible for the operation of the national insurance scheme. It also has local collection and enforcement offices throughout the country. Since April 1999, however, this agency is under the authority of the Inland Revenue as part of a policy to harmonise the collection of income tax and national insurance contributions. Aside from the *Resettlement Agency*, *War Pensions Agency* and *Information Services Technology Agency*, the other agency is the *Child Support Agency*, responsible for the child support scheme. As well as these, there is the *Employment Service*, a similar agency operating at arms length from the Department for Education and Employment. Employment officers of the Employment Service are located in Jobcentres throughout the country. The introduction of the jobseeker's allowance in 1996 saw Benefits Agency staff moving into Jobcentres in order to administer that benefit in conjunction with the Employment Service.

In February 1996, Peter Lilley, then Secretary of State for Social Security, introduced a further change to the operation of the benefits system. He launched the *DSS Change Programme*, which was designed to reduce the costs of all the DSS agencies, with the Benefits Agency given a target of saving £750 million (or a quarter of its administrative costs) within three years. This was largely to be achieved by using private sector companies to undertake certain tasks then performed by the six agencies. Harriet Harman, from May 1997 to July 1998 the Labour government's first Secretary of State for Social Security, decided, soon after appointment, to continue with the projects involving the private sector. Thus, the ownership and management of Benefits Agency offices was transferred, as part of the DSS Estates Project (known as PRIME–the Private Sector Resource Initiative for Management of the Estate), to Partnership Property Management Ltd (PPM), a private consortium that included the investment bank, Goldman Sachs International. The Contributions Agency contracted out the responsibility for maintaining contributions records to a private company while the Benefits Agency Medical Service (BAMS), responsible, inter alia, for determining medical entitlement to incapacity benefit under the 'all work test', was also transferred to the private sector.

The reasoning behind these reforms was part of the governments attempts to modernise the social security system by seeking to make it simpler, streamlined and more efficient. As mentioned earlier, further changes have been implemented in the Social Security Act 1998. Harriet Harman announced, when publishing the Bill, that:

'[The government]...have to modernise the way social security is delivered. We must have a more efficient social security system which is more accessible, which people can understand, which is streamlined and which paves the way for future improvement. At present, people dealing with the Department have to give the same information over and over again. That is frustrating for them and for our staff. They want to be able to give the information just once and leave us to deal with it. And that is what our reforms will achieve. We currently have a system which has thirteen different sorts of decision maker, five different tribunal systems and around twenty different appeal routes. This is not sensible–we must do better. ...We will deliver an active and secure social security system. We will aim to provide an integrated and simple service for those we deal with and employ. This Bill sets us on the right track.' ('Bill to modernise the social security system', *Department of Social Security Press Release*, 7 October 1997)

Prior to the Act, claims for benefit were decided by those executive officers or administrative officers within the Benefits Agency who, under s.20 of the Social Security Administration Act 1992, had been designated 'adjudication officers'. A 'Chief Adjudication Officer' was responsible for advising adjudication officers and keeping their work under review and he was also required to submit an annual report to the Secretary of State for Social Security on adjudication standards. The Chief Adjudication Officer (CAO) also decided whether appeals from a tribunal decision should be made to a Commissioner as well as whether appeals were to be made to the Court of Appeal from a Commissioner's decision. This structure was based on the idea that 'adjudication' on issues of eligibility for benefit is a 'quasi judicial' function that is different from administration. Thus, it is necessary to provide a level of independence in decision making from the administrative concerns of the Benefits Agency. The CAO's role was to maintain that independence. However, a major difficulty for both the previous Conservative government and its Labour successor was that while such decisions continue to be regarded as 'adjudicatory' rather than 'administrative', it was not be possible to contract them out to the private sector, yet this was seen as an essential part of streamlining the social security system. Thus, to facilitate such a change, the Social Security Act 1998 abolished the positions both of adjudication officers and Chief Adjudication Officer. Section 1 transfers the decision-making powers of adjudication officers to the Secretary of State which, in practice, means that, while the same administrative and executive officers make the decisions on benefit eligibility as before the implementation of the Act, the reform ends the distinction between adjudication and administration along with the resulting independence. The Chief Adjudication Officer's responsibility for monitoring standards and seeking to improve the quality of decision making is replaced by a variety of strategies. First, there are a number of Chief Executives who are accountable to the

Secretary of State both for the general quality of decision making and for individual decisions made. Secondly, the Audit Office has the remit to provide reports on the operation of the benefits system and the performance of the various agencies. Thirdly, performance targets and quality standards are set within agencies.

Reservations have been expressed about the reforms contained in the Social Security Act 1998. Most notably, concern has been raised that the overwhelming motivation for these changes has been to save money and this does not necessarily go hand in hand with improving the standard of decision making. Thus Mary Scott comments:

> 'Chief Executives will be responsible for both monitoring standards and controlling budgets, and could therefore be seen as having conflicting interests.' (Scott, 1998, p. 6)

# Adjudication and Appeals

There is a two-tier system of appeal operating in respect of social security. The first level of appeal is to the social security appeal tribunal. Appeals against any decision of the tribunal on points of law can be made to a Social Security Commissioner.

## Tribunals

*Context and commentary*

The provision for allowing claimants to appeal against a decision concerning eligibility for benefit is a well-established feature of social security and ties in with notions of due process and the rule of law in that an independent mechanism should be available for individuals to appeal against decisions that they feel have been incorrectly made. The housing benefit scheme, however, has been heavily criticised in that, from its outset, such arrangements have not existed, rather there is a much less robust system of 'review' that, critics argue, lacks the essential independence required. For most benefits, however, an independent appeals mechanism has been a central feature of the British post-war social security system, though the appeals system has not been without its critics and has been subject to a number of reforms. Prior to the reforms of the 1980s, for example, there were separate appeal tribunals for contributory benefits (*national insurance local tribunals*) and for supplementary benefits (*supplementary benefit appeal tribunals*). In 1975, Professor Kathleen Bell of the University of Newcastle produced an important report on the operation of supplementary benefit appeal tribunals (*Research Study on Supplementary Benefit Appeals Tribunals*). This was critical of certain aspects of tribunal operation and suggested a number of reforms designed to improve the quality of decision making within these tribunals. In 1984 reform, in fact, took place, when as a result of the Health and Social Services and Social Security Adjudications Act 1983, social security appeal tribunals were created to replace national insurance local tribunals and supplementary benefit appeal tribunals, so that appeals in respect of both contributory benefits and means-tested benefits were heard by the same tribunal. As a result of Professor Bell's report, this Act also introduced the requirement that all tribunal chairmen must be legally qualified as she concluded that the main reason for the poor quality of adjudication in supplementary benefit appeal tribunals was that, in contrast to national insurance local tribunals, many chairmen were lay. At the same time the administration of tribunals became the responsibility of the Office of the President of the Social Security Appeal Tribunals which, in 1991, was renamed the *Independent Tribunal Service*. This was designed to ensure the independence of the tribunal system. The Independent Tribunal Service (ITS), though funded by the DSS, was free from any direct departmental control. It had responsibility not only for social security appeal tribunals but also other tribunals such as medical appeal tribunals and disability appeal tribunals. Its duties extended to appointing lay members of tribunals, training tribunal chairmen, clerks and other tribunal members as well as being responsible for the general administration of tribunals. The ITS was organised into six regions each headed by a regional chairman and above these was the president of the Independent Tribunal Service.

The tribunal system in respect of social security has in recent years, however, been the subject of further reforms. In July 1996 the Department of Social Security issued a consultation paper entitled *Improving Decision Making and Appeals in Social Security*. This advocated fundamental changes to the tribunal system and was part of the then Conservative government's 'Change Programme' which was designed to cut costs within the tribunal service as a part of saving 25% of the Department of Social Security's administration budget. The consultation document proposed radical changes, those that did not require new legislation being speedily introduced. Other of its reforms that did require changes to the law were largely implemented by the incoming Labour government's Social Security Act 1998 and the Social Security (Fraud) Act 1998.

Prior to the changes introduced by the Social Security Act 1998, if a claimant lodged an appeal against a decision, it would, in the first instance, be reviewed by an adjudication officer before being forwarded to the Independent Tribunal Service. Most issues that went to appeal would be dealt with by the social security appeals tribunal. However, some issues concerning social security benefits were dealt with by other tribunals. Thus, under ss.46, 50 and 96 and Schedule 2 of the Social Security

Administration Act 1992 a medical appeal tribunal, comprising a legally qualified chairman and two consultant doctors, heard appeals on disablement questions in respect of disablement benefit and severe disablement allowance. Similar issues in respect of disability living allowance, disability working allowance and attendance allowance were dealt with, under s.33, by a disability appeal tribunal which consists of a legally qualified chairman, a medical practitioner and someone with experience of the needs of disabled people. Both these tribunals were also administered by the Independent Tribunal Service. Changes to the structure and number of tribunals were, however, part of the reforms introduced by the Social Security Act 1998.

## Appeals: current arrangements

As part of its aspirations to modernise the social security system, the government argued that the appeal process was too cumbersome and, in particular, was far too slow:

'If people want a decision changed they often get drawn into the appeal process. They face a daunting, formal process and a long wait to have their case heard–the average wait is six months–far too long. They want their cases heard quickly.' ('Bill to modernise the social security system', *Department of Social Security Press Release*, 7 October 1997)

Changes to the appeal structure were introduced in the Social Security Act 1998, fundamentally altering the appeal process. In the first place, the tribunal structure has been changed. The Act has introduced a unified appeal structure where there is only one appeal tribunal that hears all appeals. In effect, this means the abolition of medical appeal tribunals, disability appeal tribunals, child support appeal tribunals and vaccine damage tribunals. Appeals will be sifted according to their complexity and dealt with by a one-member, two-member or three-member panel or even struck out as lacking any prospect of success. This particular reform raises two important issues. First, prior to the 1998 Act, s.41 of the Social Security Administration Act 1992 required a social security appeal tribunal to consist of three members, two lay wing members and a legally qualified chairman. Now ss.6 and 7 of the 1998 Act, while leaving the details to be contained in regulations, allow for tribunals of a smaller composition to decide cases. Also, while the chairman is no longer required to be legally qualified, under s.7(2), one of the members of the tribunal (or the sole member deciding the appeal), though not necessarily the chairman, must be legally qualified. This was an amendment to the Act introduced, against the government's wishes, in the House of Lords, during its parliamentary passage. In practice, the result of these changes is that many appeals are now considered by a single, legally qualified person. Another important change concerns the procedure operated by tribunals when hearing appeals. The underlying approach, before the reforms contained in the 1998 Act was inquisitorial whereby the tribunal, particularly the chairman, played an active role in examining all relevant issues, establishing the facts and identifying the appropriate law. Under s.12(8) of the 1998 Act, however, a tribunal 'need not consider any issue that is not raised by the appeal'. In other words, the onus is on the parties to identify the relevant issues. This means that the inquisitorial role of the tribunal is fundamentally reduced so that if, for example, an appellant fails to raise issues relevant to his appeal the tribunal is not required to consider them. It is difficult to deny that this radically undermines the quality of the decision making of tribunals. Another important issue is the provision to strike out weak cases. These changes lead to Mary Scott stating:

> 'On the face of it, such a system seems fraught with pitfalls. Applicants will need to ensure that they have good advice from the outset or a clear understanding of the law and even if they have both, they will still have only one month to lodge their appeal.' (Scott, 1998, p. 6)

Another associated reform, implemented in October 1996 in the aftermath of the publication of the June 1996 consultation paper, is that an oral hearing now takes place only if one of the parties has requested it or the chairman feels that it is necessary to enable the tribunal to reach a decision. Previously a tribunal could not decide an appeal without an oral hearing, but reg. 22 of the Social Security Adjudication Regulations now allows for 'paper appeals' whereby a tribunal (of one, two or three members, one of which must be legally qualified) considers the appeal on the basis of any written submissions provided. For critics, this is a major diminution in the quality of the appeal process. It relies heavily on the quality of the written evidence provided. Yet many claimants may lack the detailed knowledge of both social security law and of the type of evidence necessary to be able to frame an effective written appeal. Concern has, therefore, been expressed in respect of this change:

> 'The move towards paper appeals is a worrying development. The statistics show clearly that claimants who attend the hearing have a much better chance of success than those who do not. However, many claimants, particularly those who are not represented, will not appreciate the importance of an oral hearing, or will, quite understandably, wish to avoid the trauma of giving evidence.' (Robertson and Thomas, 1997, p. 20)

Similarly concerns have been made by Tony Lynes:

> 'The justification for this change was that nearly one in three appellants failed to attend an oral hearing, causing considerable waste of time and resources. It seems probable, however, that many appellants who in the past would have attended, as well as those who would not, will agree to a "paper hearing". By doing so, they will seriously diminish their chances of success, despite the consultation paper's assertion that "there must be no prejudice to appellants' cases if they choose not to be seen"...SSAT statistics for April-June 1996 (before the amended regulations came into force) show that, where the appellant was present or represented at the hearing, the success rate was 53.6%. Even unrepresented appellants who attended achieved a success rate of 46%. For unattended hearings the success rate was only 12.5%.' (Lynes, 1997, p. 24)

A major consequence of the above-mentioned reforms is clearly to place much greater responsibility on the parties in respect of appeals. While the Benefits Agency and the Department of Social Security are likely to be equipped to perform their role satisfactorily, the essential issue is whether individual claimants will be similarly equipped. The government's view is that all relevant information is provided to appellants on the appeals procedure so that they can make decisions such as whether to seek an oral hearing as well as ensuring that appellants effectively conduct their appeal. There must, however, be grave doubt as to whether these arrangements provide the necessary equality between the two parties and raises the view that the demand to reduce costs in respect of the appeals procedure has proved to be a greater motivation for reform than the concern to maintain and enhance the quality of decision making. This view is further fuelled by the fact that the Independent Tribunal Service has been abolished. The administration of appeals now comes under the direct control of the Secretary of State for Social Security which, in practice, means that the administration is undertaken by an executive agency within the Department of Social Security. It is claimed that independence from DSS control remains, for example the Lord Chancellor continues to appoint tribunal members. However, under paras 10 and 11 of Schedule 1 of the Social Security Act 1998, the Secretary of State has the power to appoint clerks and officers of tribunals, this being transferred from the former Independent Tribunal Service. Concern that the essential independence of the appeal process has been substantially eroded by these changes is made in the following statement, which was made while the Bill was proceeding through Parliament:

> 'There is concern that the "independence" of the system will be seriously undermined by the abolition of the ITS. It is proposed that

clerks will decide the allocation of cases and the constitution of tribunals. The clerks...will now come under DSS control. They will have tough targets to meet. Tribunal members and clerks know that the best and most thorough chairs [i.e. chairmen] are not necessarily the fastest, but there is an obvious risk that the pressure to meet targets will influence decisions on allocations. Thoroughness and fairness are not always compatible with speed; it is in the interests of claimants that the law and the facts are properly considered.' ('Appeal tribunals to lose independence', October 1997, *Welfare Rights Bulletin*, p. 6)

## Social Security Commissioners

Headed by a Chief Social Security Commissioner, Social Security Commissioners are the second tier of appeal on social security matters. Under ss.23, 34 and 48 of the Social Security Administration Act 1992, they hear appeals from social security appeal tribunals on points of law. An error of law, forming the basis of such an appeal, can be made, per *R(A)1/72*, if a tribunal has:

(a)  misinterpreted what the law is;
(b)  made a decision on a finding of fact on which there is no evidence;
(c)  made a decision which is claimed to be one that no tribunal could reasonably have made;
(d)  breached the rules of natural justice in failing to act fairly.

Commissioners are full-time judges with the same standing as circuit judges. Leave to appeal needs to be obtained. This is usually obtained from the tribunal chairman within three months of the tribunal's decision. If this is refused, leave to appeal can be made, within six weeks of the chairman's refusal, to a commissioner. Usually a single commissioner hears an appeal, although the Chief Social Security Commissioner may convene a tribunal of three commissioners to hear an appeal involving a point of law of particular difficulty.

## Citation of cases

The 2,500 or so cases heard annually by commissioners constitute precedents that bind tribunals and adjudicating officers. A decision is 'starred' by the commissioner deciding the case and is then reported if the Chief Commissioner, after consultation with his colleagues, thinks it raises a point of legal importance. A decision which is not 'starred' remains unreported as it is deemed not to contain any important legal point. Both types of decision are binding, although reported decisions have priority over unreported ones while the decisions of a tribunal of three commissioners are binding on individual commissioners.

The citation of the decisions of Social Security Commissioners differs from the conventional methods of case citation utilised in the English legal system in that the names of the parties are not used. Instead a system of letters and numbers are used. Most cases commence with the letter *R*. This indicates that this decision has been reported. It is then followed by other letters in brackets which refer to the series of commissioners' decisions where the case is located. Thus *R(P)* refers to a decision on pensions and *R(IS)* to an income support decision. These letters are followed by numbers such as *12/86*. The first figure refers to the report number and the second to the year in question. Therefore *R(P)12/86* is the twelfth reported decision in the pension series of commissioners' decisions for the year 1986. Not all commissioners' decisions are, however, reported and, when this is the case, the first letter is a *C* rather than an *R*. Thus *C(UB)3/57* is the third unreported decision in the unemployment series of commissioners' decisions for the year 1957.

## The National Insurance Contribution System

Eligibility for many benefits within the British social security system is based on claimants paying contributions into the National Insurance Fund. This Fund is made up of the contributions made by employees, employers, the self-employed and others who make certain voluntary contributions as well as by payments made by the Treasury. Until April 1999, the Inland Revenue collected most contributions for the Department of Social Security and the Contributions Agency was responsible for keeping the contributions records of contributors. Originally announced in the March 1998 Budget, from April 1999 the Contribution Agency comes under the authority of the Inland Revenue. National Insurance contributions go to the National Insurance Fund, out of which are made payments for the contributory benefits – those for unemployment, sickness, invalidity, widowhood, retirement pensions (Categories A and B) and the maternity allowance. All other benefits are paid for out of general taxation.

### Classes of contribution

Under s.1(2) of the Social Security Contributions and Benefits Act 1992, as modified by s.51 of the Social Security Act 1998, there are, from April 1999, six different classes of contribution. *Class 1* contributions are payable by employed earners topped up by a contribution by their employers. They give entitlement to all contributory benefits. *Class 1A* contributions are paid by employers in respect of those employees who have company cars. They do not provide entitlement to any benefit. Section 53 of the

Social Security Act 1998 introduces *Class 1B* as a new class of contribution from April 1999. This is paid where a person is accountable to the Inland Revenue for payment of income tax on any emoluments (i.e. any salary or other financial benefits) in respect of a PAYE settlement for income tax. Contributions do not establish entitlement to any social security benefit. *Class 2* contributions are flat-rate contributions by self-employed earners which give entitlement to all benefits except contributory jobseeker's allowance. *Class 3* contributions are voluntary contributions mainly paid by those who have deficiencies in their contribution record. They give entitlement to widows' benefits and retirement pensions. *Class 4* contributions are paid by self-employed earners and are earnings-related contributions that are payable by those paying Class 2 contributions.

Under ss.6(1)(a) and 13(1) of the Social Security Contributions Act 1992 and reg. 60 of the Social Security (Contributions) Regulations, contributions are not payable by those under 16 or, under s.6(2) and reg. 58, by those over pensionable age. Class 1 contributions are paid, under s.2(1)(a), by employees who are employed in Great Britain and who are present, resident or ordinarily resident in Great Britain (s.2(1)(a) and reg. 119(1)(A)). Section 2(1)(b) and reg. 119(1)(d) make class 2 contributions compulsory for those who are self-employed and are either ordinarily resident in Great Britain or have been resident here for at least 26 weeks during the last year, the year being the tax year commencing on 6 April. Class 3 contributions are voluntary while class 4 contributions are payable, under reg. 58(b), by those resident in the UK for tax purposes.

## Class 1 contributions

Under ss.6 and 7 of the Social Security Contributions and Benefits Act 1992, class 1 contributions are paid by employed earners, known as primary contributors, and by their employers, known as secondary contributors. Section 2 (1)(a) defines an employed earner as:

> 'a person who is gainfully employed in Great Britain either under a contract of service, or in an office (including elective office) with emoluments chargeable to income tax under Schedule E.'

### Amount of Class 1 National Insurance contributions

The amount of both the primary and secondary contributions is based on the earnings of the employed earner. There is both a lower earnings limit (LEL) and an upper earnings limit (UEL). For the year commencing 6 April 1998, the lower earnings limit was £64 per week and the upper earnings limit was £485 per week, these figures have risen to £66 and £500, respectively from 6 April 1999. Under regs 8(2) and 8A(2) of the Social Security (Contributions) Regulations, monthly earnings are determined by multiplying these weekly figures by four and a third. Anyone whose weekly earnings are below the lower earnings limit makes no contributions and no entitlement is earned towards contributory benefits such as contributory JSA, incapacity benefit or retirement pension. This is particularly problematic for those who have more than one job as, under regs 10,11, 12, 12(A) and 17, the basic rule is that liability to pay Class 1 contributions is calculated for each job as if the other(s) did not exist. In a climate of increasing casualisation of the labour market with large numbers of part-time and low-paid jobs, many individuals may not be earning enough to make sufficient contributions in a year in order to establish eligibility for these benefits, although proposals contained in the report by Martin Taylor for the Treasury which are discussed below have led to changes in entitlement to contributory benefits. For those whose income is greater than the higher earnings limit, any earnings above the limit is ignored in calculating the amount of contribution to be paid.

The exact amount of contribution paid depends on whether an employee has contracted out of the State Earnings Related Pension Scheme (SERPS), which is discussed in Chapter 6. Prior to April 1999, if an individual had not contracted out of SERPS, under ss. 8(1) and (2) of the Social Security Contributions and Benefits Act 1992, the contribution is 2% of earnings below the lower earnings limit (known as the entry fee) plus 10% of earnings between the lower and upper earnings limits. If an employee had contracted out of SERPS (e.g. he or she contributed instead to an occupational or private pension scheme outside SERPS) then, under s.27 of the Social Security Pensions Act 1975, a 2% contribution of earnings below the lower earnings limit was paid along with 8.4% of earnings between the lower and upper earnings limits. Under s.9 of the Social Security Contributions and Benefits Act 1992, the employer's secondary contribution was calculated differently. For employees in SERPS, an employer paid a contribution calculated on an employee's total earnings which, for the year commencing 6 April 1998, was as follows:

| Weekly earnings | Contribution rate |
| --- | --- |
| £64–£109.99 | 3% |
| £110–£154.99 | 5% |
| £155–£209.99 | 7% |
| £210+ | 10% |

No contribution was made for employees whose wages were less than £64 per week. Under s.27(2) of the Social Security Pensions Act 1975, for employees contracted out of SERPS, an employer paid 3% less on an employee's earnings between the upper and lower earnings limits if he or she was in a *salary-related* pension scheme and 1.5% less if in a *money purchase* scheme.

April 1999 saw changes to the way the amount of class 1 contributions are calculated. In the summer of 1997, the incoming Labour government had set up a task force to review the tax and benefits systems and their interrelationship, and its main proposals were endorsed by Gordon Brown in the Budget of 17 March 1998. On the same day, the report of the task force, headed by Martin Taylor then of Barclays Bank, was published (*The Modernisation of Britain's Tax and Benefit System: Work Incentives*). This budget and its successor on 9 March 1999 saw Gordon Brown announce fundamental changes to the National Insurance system. As well as the previously mentioned reform whereby the Contributions Agency became the responsibility of the Inland Revenue, he announced changes to align the lower earnings limit with the income tax personal allowance. While, from April 1999, the lower earnings limit for National Insurance contributions was merely raised to £66 per week, the following two years see steps towards this alignment. In April 2000, the lower earnings limit rises to £76 per week with full alignment with income tax personal allowances being reached in April 2001 when the lower earnings level becomes £87 per week in respect of National Insurance Contributions (NICs). The statutory authority for these changes is contained in s.51 of the Social Security Act 1998. Claimed to be the part of biggest reform to National Insurance contributions since the mid-1970s, an important consequence of raising the lower earnings limit (LEL) is to reduce the amount of contribution payments by many lower paid employees and their employers with many of the lowest paid ceasing to be required to make contributions, although this may also affect entitlement to contributory benefits, an issue that was not addressed in Gordon Brown's budget speeches. These points are explained as follows:

> 'Aligning the LEL with the personal allowance would take up to 1 million people out of NICs altogether. However, it would also affect their entitlement to contributory benefits. This could be resolved by moving to a new definition of the contributory principle, which might be desirable in its own right, as a replacement for rules dating back to sticking national insurance stamps on cards. However, both employers and the government would need some lead time before the changes could be brought in.' (Taylor 1998, p. 14)

A second important reform is that the 2% 'entry fee' payments on earnings below the lower earnings limit was abolished from April 1999, contributions being determined only on the amount of earnings of any individual above the lower earnings limit, up to the upper earnings limit. The March 1999 budget, however, also saw Gordon Brown announce that this upper earnings limit would rise to £500 per week in April 1999 and then to £535 in April 2000 and, 12 months later, to £575. Another change, announced in the 1998 budget, sees the abolition of the different rates of contribution for different earnings bands between the two earnings limits. Following Martin Taylor's recommendations, contributions are at a single rate of, for 1999/2000, 12.2%. The deductions for those who have opted out of SERPS, however, remain the same as previously (see p. 35). These changes have been implemented under section 51 of the Social Security Act 1998. Their overall effect is that for most people earning below £450 a week the employer's contribution is reduced.

## Class 1A contributions

Under s.1(2) of the Social Security Contributions and Benefits Act 1992, Class 1A contributions are paid exclusively by employers and are only payable for employees who have a company car. Introduced in 1992 to close a loophole in the provision of company cars and subsidised petrol to many, largely managerial, employees, the contribution, for 1998/99, was paid at 10% of the cash equivalent of the car and/or petrol provided for the employee and, in 1999/2000, the rate is 12.2%.

## Class 1B contributions

These are paid where an employer has entered into a PAYE Settlement Agreement with the Inland Revenue for tax and are designed to ease the administration of National Insurance contributions for employers by simplifying the payment of contributions and aligning it more closely with payment of income tax via the PAYE system. Class 1B contributions are payable only by employers and no entitlement to benefit derives from their payment. Introduced by s.53 of the Social Security Act 1998, the Social Security (Contributions) Regulations 1979 have been amended to accommodate Class 1B contributions by the Social Security (Contributions), Statutory Maternity Pay and Statutory Sick Pay (Miscellaneous Amendments) Regulations 1998.

## Class 2 contributions

Under s.21(2) of the Social Security Contributions and Benefits Act 1992, these bestow entitlement to all contributory benefits other than contribution-based JSA and any earnings-related additional components in pensions. They are paid by self-employed earners and are paid at a flat rate. Section 2(1)(b) of the Social Security Contributions and Benefits Act 1992 defines a self-employed earner as anyone who is 'gainfully employed in Great Britain otherwise than in employed earner's employment'. For the year commencing 6 April 1998 the rate of contribution was £6.35 per week (for the previous year it was £6.15 per week) and, in 1999/2000, it was provisionally set at £6.55. However, the March 1999 Budget saw Gordon Brown announce that, in line with the abolition of the 2% 'entry fee' for employed earners paying a Class 1 contribution, the weekly flat-rate payment is £2 for Class 2 contributions. Self-employed earners with low earnings are exempt from paying if, under s.11 of the Social Security Contributions and Benefits Act 1992, a certificate of exemption is obtained which confirms that earnings were below £3,590 in 1998–99 (£3,480 in 1997–98 and £3,430 in 1996–97). All self-employed earners without a certificate must pay a Class 2 contribution while those with a certificate can pay the contribution. Most self-employed people are also required to pay Class 4 contributions which are explained below, as are the proposals of Martin Taylor's task force to abolish Class 2 contributions.

## Class 3 contributions

These are entirely voluntary and, under s.13 of the Social Security Contributions and Benefits Act 1992, only give entitlement to widow's benefit and retirement pension. They are flat rate, at £6.55 per week for 1999–2000 (for 1998–99 £6.05), and are usually paid if other contributions that an individual has paid or been credited with in any tax year are insufficient for that year to count as a 'qualifying year' for these two benefits. This is more fully explained in the sections on contribution credits and contribution conditions.

## Class 4 contributions

These contributions are paid, under ss.15(1) and (3) of the Social Security Contributions and Benefits Act 1992, by self-employed earners but do not establish entitlement to any benefit. They are the payment by a self-employed person of a fixed proportion of any profits and other gains between a prescribed lower profit level and an upper profit level. Class 4 contributions are, therefore, a means of obtaining earnings-related contributions from those paying the flat-rate Class 2 contribution. The rate for 1999–2000 is 7% of profits or gains between the lower profits level (LPL) of £7,540 and the upper profits level (UPL) of £26,000. In 1998–99 the rate was 6% of profits between £7,130 and of £25,220.

The report of Martin Taylor's taskforce examined the system of contributions to the National Insurance Fund by the self-employed and proposed the abolition of Class 2 contributions for self-employed earners. The report argued that the self-employed under-contribute to the National Insurance Fund, via the flat-rate Class 2 contribution combined with Class 4 contributions on profits between the lower and upper profit levels, with the Class 4 contributions being substantially lower than Class 1 contributions made in respect of employed earners:

'...[I]t would be consistent with my proposals for employees:
(a) to abolish the Class 2 charge (which means inventing a new benefit entitlement test, such as a minimum profits test or a minimum Class 4 payment, for contributory benefits);
(b) to align the LPL with the LEL;
(c) to increase the Class 4 rate nearer to the employee rate, so as at least to restore the Class 2 yield...
Although the self-employed have less entitlement than employees to contributory benefits, they substantially under-contribute to the National Insurance Fund, even allowing for their reduced entitlements.'
(Taylor, 1998, p. 16)

This reform was not implemented by the Social Security Act 1998 and, in fact, Gordon Brown's 1999 budget saw the Chancellor introduce reforms that did not see the contributions of most self-employed people rise, as proposed by Martin Taylor a year earlier. Thus, as well as reducing the flat-rate Class 2 payment from £6.35 to £2 per week for 1999/2000, he announced that while the lower profits level threshold for Class 4 payments should rise by 1% in 1999–2000 to 7% of profits or gains between the lower profits level (LPL) of £7,540 and the upper profits level (UPL) of £26,000:

'...I will set contributions at a lower rate than envisaged by the Taylor Report, at 7 per cent in contrast with the 10 per cent employees pay.'
(Budget Speech, 9 March 1999)

As well as understanding the different classes of contributions, it is necessary to comprehend the following features of the contribution system.

## Contribution credits

Governed by the Social Security (Credits) Regulations 1975, credits apply in certain situations where a claimant does not, in fact, make a contribution. Under reg. 9(1), a person will be 'credited' with a Class 1 contribution for every complete week he or she signs on as unemployed or is covered by a medical certificate. Such credits are relevant in determining the second of the two contribution conditions set out in the next section.

## Contribution conditions

In order to be eligible for contributory benefits, other than maternity allowance and widow's payment, a claimant must satisfy two contribution conditions. The first condition, under s.21 and paras 1 and 2 of Schedule

1 of the Social Security Contributions and Benefits Act 1992, is that, in at least one qualifying year, the appropriate contributions must actually have been paid on earnings with an 'earnings factor' of at least 25 times the lower earnings limit. The lower earnings limit for the year from April 1999 is £66 per week. Under s.22(1)(a), the earnings factor is merely the amount of earnings on which contributions are paid. Thus, for 1999–2000, to satisfy this condition, contribution has to be paid on £1,650 of earnings (25 x £66). In 1998–99, the figure was £1,600 (25 x £64). In the case of many contributors, this minimum amount of income for which contributions are made is often earned in quite a short number of weeks or months. For incapacity benefit the contributions must be Class 1 or 2 while for contributory JSA only Class 1 contributions establish eligibility. For contribution purposes the year commences on 6 April and a qualifying year for incapacity benefit is any tax year whereas, for contributory JSA, it is one of the last two complete tax years before the 'relevant benefit' year. As the benefit year commences on the first Sunday in January, this can complicate calculating entitlement. For retirement pensions and widow's pension the earnings factor is 52 times the lower earnings limit. What constitutes 'qualifying years' can also differ for these benefits.

It is in regard to the second condition that contribution *credits* are relevant. This condition stipulates, again under s.21 and paras 1 and 2 of Sch.3, that a claimant must, in certain specified years, have paid *or been credited* with contributions producing an earnings factor of 50 times the lower earnings limit. The earnings factor for earnings in 1999–2000 is thus £3,300 (50 x £66) while, for 1998–99, it is £3,200 (50 x £64). For contributory JSA, for example, this second condition must be met in each of the last two complete contribution years ending before the relevant benefit. Again the fact that the contribution year and the benefit year start on dates three months apart can sometimes create difficulties.

Credits thus help to satisfy this second contribution condition for those contributory benefits with two contribution conditions. These include contributory JSA, incapacity benefit and Category A and B retirement pension. Credits cannot, however, be used to establish the first contribution condition nor can they be used to qualify for maternity allowance or widow's payment which both have a single contribution condition. This means that to satisfy this first condition, for retirement pension or widowed mother's allowance or widow's pension, the claimant (or deceased spouse) must have actually paid a full year's contribution (i.e. 52 weeks) at some stage in his or her working life. For incapacity benefit and contributory JSA, the first condition means that a claimant must actually have paid contributions with an earnings factor of at least 25 times of the lower earnings limit for the year in question which, for contributory JSA, must be one of the two years before the benefit year when the claim is made.

# Bibliography

Bell, K. (1975) *Research Study on Supplementary Benefit Appeals Tribunals*, HMSO.

Lynes, T. (1997) 'Social security tribunals: new procedures', *Legal Action*, June.

Poynter, R. and Martin, C. (1992/93) *Rights Guide to Non-means-tested Benefits*, 15th edition.

Robertson, S. and Thomas, D. (1997) 'Recent developments in social security law', *Legal Action*, February.

Scott, M. (1998) 'The Social Security Bill', *Disability Rights Bulletin*.

Spicker, P. (1993) *Poverty and Social Security*, Routledge.

Taylor, M. (1998) *The Modernisation of Britain's Tax and Benefit System: Work Incentives*.

# 3 The British Social Security System in Context

## Introduction

Placing the contemporary British social security system in a wider context helps to gain a fuller understanding of its functioning. This is undertaken in this chapter in two ways. The first way is to place the current social security system in its historical context by tracing its evolution in the post-war period. One problem with adopting an historical perspective is deciding on the starting date, as any such date is somewhat arbitrary. Certainly a system of social security can be traced back many centuries, to the sixteenth century and even earlier. Other important developments include the Poor Law Act 1834, which established the workhouse system, and Lloyd George's reforms before the First World War introducing old-age pensions and unemployment benefit. Some of these events have already been mentioned in Chapter 1. The publication of the Beveridge Report in 1942 and subsequent implementing of most of its proposals in the immediate aftermath of the Second World War, however, constitute a seminal episode in the development not only of the British social security system but also in the international, particularly European, development of social security provision. It is, therefore, also important in respect of the second aspect of placing the British social security system in context, namely examining it in relation to social security in other countries, particularly in other member states of the European Community.

## The British Social Security System in a Historical Context: Post-war to 1997

The current British social security system and many of its most important features can best be understood by appreciating how and why the system was created. The first step in establishing the post-war social security system is usually seen as the publication of the Beveridge Report in 1942.

### The Beveridge Report

As a condition of membership of the coalition government of the Second World War, the Labour Party insisted on particular attention being paid to social policies. One consequence of this was that the government set up an inquiry in June 1941 to examine social insurance and allied services under the chairmanship of Sir William Beveridge. The inquiry was not, however, seen by the government as a vehicle to lead to radical reform, merely having civil servants (and no politicians) as members. Thus Jose Harris (1979) points out:

> 'The Beveridge committee was in no sense designed by the wartime coalition government as an instrument of radical reform. It was intended mainly to shield ministers from parliamentary embarrassment, and was not expected even to report until the end of the war. The fact that these expectations were not realised was entirely due to Beveridge himself.'

The Beveridge Report came out in 1942, the year following the establishment of the Beveridge committee and its proposals formed the basis for the 1945–51 Labour government's radical reforms, which created the framework of the post-war social security system. Beveridge had recognised from the beginning of the investigations that a reform of all social services designed to provide a minimum of subsistence and care for the whole population should be implemented. He also argued that as all individuals ran the risk of unforeseen poverty any provision should be universal (i.e. the provision should apply to all citizens).

The Beveridge Report recommended the adoption of a *contributory social security system* which improved on the existing system by protecting all citizens against sickness, unemployment and old age. The contribution principles would be insurance ones continuing to involve the employee, the employer and the state, with both contributions and benefits being flat rate. Benefits, where necessary, would be unlimited in duration though subject to conditions – like compulsory retraining in cases of long-term unemployment.

Beveridge envisaged such a system covering all predictable needs from the cradle to the grave though residual assistance would be retained for marginal cases and unforeseeable emergencies. He also believed it was impossible to provide the basic minimum unless:

(a)  a national health service was established;
(b)  there was a system of family allowances;
(c)  there was provision of adequate housing for all.

He also believed that the maintenance of full employment would be essential to enable social insurance to work properly. Social insurance would provide income security so that, along with the above points as well as reforms in the education system and the maintenance of policies for full employment, it would form an attack on what Beveridge saw as five *Giant Evils*. These were *want, disease, ignorance, squalor* and *idleness*.

Beveridge proceeded to examine the means of establishing a unified, universal social insurance system designed to cover all groups in actual or potential need. He identified six groups:

(i)   employees;
(ii)  self-employed;
(iii) housewives;
(iv)  age not gainfully occupied' including the unemployed, the sick and the disabled;
(v)   those below working age;
(vi)  those retired, above working age.

To cover the above groups he suggested seven different kinds of cash benefits:

(a)   unemployment and sickness benefits;
(b)   the self-employed who suffered threat of bankruptcy;
(c)   special provision for the marriage needs of women;
(d)   disability benefit which would embrace industrial injuries;
(e)   funeral benefits;
(f)   family allowances;
(g)   old-age pensions.

All the benefits would have the following features:

1.   They would be flat rate and not graduated according to income when employed.
2.   They would all be calculated on the basis of *subsistence*. This calculation would follow Rowntree's 1936 'Human Needs' stringent scale.

All these schemes would be financed through weekly contributions from employer and employee plus an exchequer contribution, i.e. the schemes would be *contributory*, based on the insurance principle. Those eligible for benefits would be those who had paid contributions when working and would receive benefit when unable, for whatever reason, to obtain remuneration from work.

Eligibility for such benefits would be based on contributions paid. It would not be based on a means test. There would, however, need to be a 'safety net' means-tested benefit for those small number who were not covered by the comprehensive system of contributory benefits.

The essential features of Beveridge's scheme are set out in the following quote:

'The significance of Beveridge's vision was his assumption that any reconstruction of social security must take place within a context of full employment, universal medical care and the payment of family allowances at subsistence level. The emphasis on benefits fixed at subsistence level was crucial to the entire plan. Based on insurance contributions, it was intended to be self-financing through a redistribution of national income.' (MacGregor, 1992, p. 10)

## Implementation of the Beveridge proposals

The wartime coalition government was slow to respond to the Beveridge Report and it was 1944 before a white paper was produced. No further action was taken until July 1945 when a Labour government was elected. There was then rapid implementation of the Beveridge Report, though with some important deviations from his original proposals.

The National Insurance Act 1946 established a system of flat-rate universal pensions, sickness and unemployment benefits for those insured, i.e. those who contributed. Along with the National Insurance (Industrial Injuries) Act 1946 and the NHS Act 1946 it formed the basis of our present system of social insurance. For those who were not eligible under the contributory schemes, the National Assistance Act 1948 established a means-tested national assistance payment or a 'safety net'. This safety net scheme was financed, not by National Insurance contributions, but out of general taxation. With the implementation of these reforms, the remaining elements of the pre-war schemes with the vestiges of the Poor Law, heavy reliance on means tests, deterrence and discretionary official inquiry into private lives, were abolished.

However, while the Beveridge proposals were largely implemented in the legislation of the Labour government in the late 1940s, it deviated in some important respects from Beveridge's ideas, e.g. many of the social insurance benefits (such as unemployment benefit) were not paid for an unlimited duration. Consequently if people still needed a benefit after the end of their entitlement to a contributory benefit, they had to claim the means-tested 'national assistance' benefit. Thus, from the outset, national assistance assumed a greater importance in the post-war social security system than had originally been envisaged by Sir William Beveridge.

## Post-war developments to 1979

A major feature throughout the post-war period was that the level of the contributory, non-means-tested benefits failed to keep pace with inflation. In contrast, national assistance was so increased, largely because it was cheaper as only those below the means-tested level of income received the benefit. The consequence was that the means-tested benefit soon assumed (and continues to assume) the central role in the system of social security benefits, which is clearly contrary to what Beveridge envisaged. This trend is exemplified in the following quote:

'...between 1946 and 1957 prices of basic commodities rose by 50% and wages by 80%. Under the legislation of 1945–48 [national] assistance benefits were regularly adjusted to take account of this rise, but insurance benefits were reviewed only at five year intervals. This meant there was a continuing decline in the purchase power of insurance benefits...So, far from withering away, the means-tested sector continued to play a major role in meeting financial need. By 1950 nearly three million people a year were applying for assistance....' (Harris, 1979)

One of the main consequences of this was that the National Insurance benefits failed to provide the level of minimum subsistence that had been promised. This meant that Beveridge's idea that the contributory benefits would be paid at subsistence level was quickly replaced by the fact that they would be paid at a lower level and those recipients of national insurance benefits (e.g. unemployment benefit and old-age pensions) whose lack of other resources brought them under the national assistance means test could 'top up' with national assistance.

In fact, by the end of the 1950s, evidence started to emerge indicating that the social security system was not providing effective financial support to those in need. This culminated in the publication in 1965 of *The Poor and Poorest* by Brian Abel-Smith and Peter Townsend in which the authors claimed to have 'rediscovered poverty' by highlighting the large number of people living on incomes below the national assistance rate. These included those working on low wages, who were ineligible for national assistance, as well as a number of people who were not taking up national assistance even though entitled to it. Another theme that emerged during this time was the call for the development of earnings-related benefits to top up the flat-rate nature of certain contributory benefits. Thus, in 1959, the then Conservative government introduced a small earnings-related pension. The Labour government elected in 1964 was committed to introducing a 'national superannuation scheme' aimed at establishing a comprehensive system of state-graduated (i.e. earnings-related) pensions comparable to private pensions. It failed to implement its grand proposals due to political pressures, in its place much less substantial reform was contained in the National Insurance Act 1966 and the Ministry of Social Security Act 1966. The first of these brought in earnings-related supplements for the first six months of a claim of sickness and unemployment benefit schemes. This Act also extended the scope of earnings-related contributions originally introduced in 1959 to replace the flat-rate contributions proposed by Beveridge and implemented after the war. The Ministry of

Social Security Act 1966 brought the contributory and non-contributory schemes under the control of one ministry – the Ministry of Social Security (previously there had been two different ministries). It also replaced the national assistance scheme by a new supplementary benefits scheme (though this was basically a 'cosmetic' change, e.g. of terminology). However, the new scheme came under the control of a body independent of the ministry – the Supplementary Benefits Commission (SBC) – although the day-to-day administration was carried out by officials from the Ministry of Social Security (from 1968 this was combined with the Ministry of Health to become the Department of Health and Social Security). Both the SBC and the earnings-related top-ups to sickness and unemployment benefit were abolished in 1982.

The aspiration to provide graduated additions to state pensions, to be paid for by earnings-related contributions, was also an issue addressed by the 1970–74 Conservative government and its successor, the 1974–79 Labour government. As the elderly population grew in size, it created increasing costs for the social security system. The Conservative proposals, contained in the Social Security Act 1973, were never implemented as the government fell from power before it could do so. This piece of legislation was replaced by the Social Security Pensions Act 1975, which created the State Earnings-Related Pension Scheme (SERPS). This is an earnings-related superannuation scheme whereby graduated contributions determined the size of the state pension ultimately received. It allowed people already in a private pension scheme to opt out of the state scheme if the government deemed the scheme to meet certain minimum standards. This is discussed in greater detail in Chapter 8.

## Reforms of the Conservative governments of 1979 to 1997

In May 1979 a Conservative government was returned to power. Between 1979 and 1997 successive Conservative administrations sought to introduce a number of reforms that reflected a philosophy radically different to that underpinning the Beveridge Report. The Beveridge philosophy, despite the moves away from Beveridge's ideas in the immediate post-war period, largely reflected a consensus between the Labour and Conservative parties during that period. Some of the most radical changes reflecting the new Conservative ideology took place in the spheres of education and the National Health Service. In social security, a radical philosophy was espoused though the changes implemented did not always achieve the objectives based on that philosophy.

A fundamental belief underpinning the approach of the successive Conservative governments of 1979, 1983, 1987 and 1992 was that existing provision of social security was distorting the labour market by acting as a disincentive for people to take jobs at lower wage levels. This view was based on the ideological perspective that the role of the state in a market economy needs to be limited as the market is the correct mechanism for distributing economic resources. From this viewpoint, the existing role of the state was too great and, thus, needed to be substantially reduced. As a consequence, a central aspiration of these governments was a reduction in the level of public expenditure on social security.

It was, therefore, these beliefs that provided the basis for the approach to social security provision of the successive Conservative administrations during this period. This most notably manifested itself in the first years by benefit rates being raised in line with prices rather than with wages, thereby reducing their real value. Section 1 of the Social Security Act 1980, for example, implemented this policy in respect of pensions, which resulted in a steady deterioration in the real value of the state pension. This strategy meant that more and more claimants of contributory benefits such as pensions and unemployment benefit increasingly had to resort to topping up these benefits with means tested supplementary benefit. Thus the trend of moving away from Beveridge's ideas that had pervaded the post-war period continued but with two major changes. First, there was a greater ideological commitment to such a strategy, in contrast to earlier post-war governments from both political parties, which allowed such developments because of political expediency. Secondly, as a consequence, the fervour for such developments was greater. The conscious decisions not to maintain both contributory and means-tested benefit levels in line with wages were a reflection of this. This fervour was further exemplified in the mid-1980s when a major review of social security was instigated by the then Secretary for Social Security, Norman Fowler, which led to the Social Security Act 1986. This Act replaced supplementary benefit with income support, tightening up eligibility and reducing entitlement. The Act also sought to reduce the level of benefit to many income support recipients. For example, in comparison with supplementary benefit, lower weekly rates were introduced for income support for claimants under 25 while the age of entitlement for income support was raised from 16 to 18. Changes were also made to unemployment benefit that eroded entitlement. Further reforms to the benefit entitlement of the unemployed were introduced in the Social Security Act 1988. The changes to unemployment benefit during this period directed reforms at reducing entitlement to unemployment benefit, restricting contribution conditions, tightening arrangements for ensuring that the claimant was available for employment, ensuring that the claimant was actively seeking employment; extending the period of disqualification from benefit for voluntary unemployment and related reasons and curtailing the rights of students and occupational pensioners to benefit.

The consequences for the social security system of the Conservative reforms between 1979 and 1997 involved both the tightening of eligibility requirements for non-means-tested benefits and the increasing of weekly benefit rates at a lower rate than prevailed before 1980. This led to an ever-greater reliance on means-tested benefits, whose weekly rates were also increased at a lower rate than before 1980. Thus means-tested income support was the main benefit for the unemployed, rather than unemployment benefit. This is highlighted by the fact that in 1992/93, of persons registered for employment, 24% received unemployment benefit without income support, 72% received income support without unemployment benefit while 4% had unemployment benefit topped up by income support (see Ogus, Barendt and Wikeley, p.76).

The final major social security reform during the 1979–97 period of Conservative government was the replacement of unemployment benefit by jobseeker's allowance which was initially outlined in a White Paper in October 1994. Following the introduction of incapacity benefit in April 1995, jobseeker's allowance came into operation on 7 October 1996 and within seven months, the 1992 Conservative government, with John Major as Prime Minister, suffered a crushing defeat in the General Election of 1 May 1997 and were swept from power.

The 1994 White Paper on jobseeker's allowance, nevertheless, highlighted the approach of the 1992 Conservative government towards social security. As part of its espoused objective of reducing public expenditure on social security, thereby 'targeting' benefits only towards those deemed to be seeking employment, the philosophy behind the White Paper placed an emphasis on a deregulated labour market. Central to this was a belief in the need for a low-wage economy in order to compete against rival economies. Social security benefits that were deemed to be too easy to obtain or paid at levels which mean that the unemployed may lack enthusiasm to take low-paid jobs were seen as unacceptable. The White Paper thus emphasised the need for the unemployed to 'compete effectively for jobs'. This required a social security benefits system which 'encourages people to make efforts to find work' while benefits were seen as 'a means of support while an unemployed person looks for work, not an income for a lifestyle divorced from work'. Claimed to save £70 million in the first year, some of the consequences of the subsequent implementation of the White Paper's proposals were that the contributory replacement of unemployment benefit now only lasts for 26 weeks rather than the previous 52 weeks. As a consequence, official estimates were that 165,000 claimants lost entitlement to contributory benefit after 26 weeks. Of these, 95,000 remained eligible for the means-tested benefit but the other 70,000 lost all entitlement as they failed the means test. Also, for claimants with a partner, the weekly rate of contributory benefit was reduced by almost £30 as a result of the abolition of the adult dependant addition previously paid to recipients of unemployment benefit. The Jobseekers Act, implementing the central features of the White Paper, received the Royal Assent in July 1995 and, as a consequence, the new jobseeker's allowance replaced unemployment benefit and income support in October 1996 as the social security benefit for the unemployed.

Despite the large number of reforms to social security introduced during 1979–97, which sought to reduce both entitlement to benefit and benefit rates, thereby aiming to reduce public expenditure on social security, the fact was that the level of social security public expenditure consistently increased during this period. The annual rate of real growth (i.e. excluding the effects of inflation) increased by over 3% each year. In 1978/79, social security expenditure stood at £15.9 billion, rising to £74.1 billion in 1992/93 and culminating at over £92 billion by the last year of the Conservative government (1996/97). The reasons for this are explored in Chapter 14 where the approach to social security of the Labour government of 1997 is also examined.

## The British Social Security System in a Comparative Context

While we are primarily concerned with the operation of the British social security system, its legal framework and the main issues surrounding the provision of social security, it is important to bear in mind that many of the factors that have influenced, and that continue to influence, the development of the British social security system have also affected the provision of social security in many other countries. It is instructive, therefore, to adopt a comparative approach. One important aspect of this is that UK membership of the European Community has both influenced the nature of social security within this country as well as providing substantial comparative statistical evidence.

### Types of social security systems in EC member states

Historically, an important distinction has traditionally been drawn in terms of the provision of social security in Western European countries between the *Beveridge* and *Bismarck* approaches. The Beveridge approach bases social security provision on social insurance whereby the state provides comprehensive social security protection for all citizens, which is primarily financed by compulsory payments or contributions when, for example, individuals are in employment which are topped up by other forms of finance such as general taxation. Benefits tend to be paid at a flat rate whereby all recipients receive the same amount of benefit and are aimed at providing a minimum standard of income protection for the entire population. Some form of provision of benefit is, however, also available to people who have not made the relevant financial contributions, these benefits being examples of financing from general taxation, etc. Obviously seen as providing the framework for British social security provision after the Second World War, it was also influential in determining social security in the Scandinavian countries and is otherwise known as the Atlantic approach. In contrast, the Bismarck approach, otherwise known as the Continental approach and pioneered by the German Chancellor at the end of the nineteenth century, bases eligibility for state provision of social security benefits more directly on the labour market. This approach determines provision of benefit on contributions paid when working but does not seek to provide as comprehensive a range of social security benefits to all. Benefit is provided to those who have been present and past workers, the aim being largely to maintain individuals' income levels for a period of time and, therefore, the level of benefits tends to be earnings-related. This more employment-linked approach has a much more limited role for state provision of social security, with an assumption that private 'social security' provision allied to family and voluntary agencies can provide support for other groups in financial need. This approach has been influential in many European countries. Thus Roebroek states, in respect of EC member states, that:

'Existing national systems can more or less be characterised by one of these two types of social security systems. The Belgian, French and German systems were modelled along Bismarckian lines, and the Danish and British systems along a Beveridgean route. And even a *third* option exists. These are systems that are characterised by a *mixture* of both types, as for instance the Dutch and Italian systems.' (Roebroek, 1991, p. 63)

One obvious consequence of this distinction is that in examining social security it can be misleading to concentrate solely on state provision, particularly when seeking to provide a comparative understanding as some countries have substantial private provision of social security outside the state structure. In fact, state provision of resources for social security purposes, itself, may often not be easily visible. For example, tax relief given to individuals taking out a private pension is a form of public financing of a social security nature yet can be less conspicuous than overt expenditure on state provision of social security benefits. Recognition of different approaches involving both state and private social security provision, based on the Beveridge/Bismarck dichotomy, highlights that the

British approach is more state centred, or 'statist', than many other Western European countries.

In recent years, however, the categorisation of social security provision on the basis of the Beveridge/Bismarck distinction has been criticised as being too simplistic. Aside from failing to accommodate a wide variety of approaches to social security throughout the world, it has been deemed inadequate even in explaining comparative social security in Western Europe. Within the Beveridge tradition, for example, Scandinavian social security provision is much more comprehensive and universal than is the case in Britain, and explains why social security expenditure tends to be higher in Scandinavia. Under the Bismarck approach, the types of protection provided and the groups covered varies quite substantially from country to country while the entry of Greece, Portugal and Spain into the European Union has highlighted that social security provision in these countries is much more elementary (see Alcock, 1996, pp.172–78 for a useful discussion of the other ways that social security approaches can be categorised). On the basis of the above observations, the European Commission itself has sought to characterise *four* groupings of EC social security systems (European Commission, 1995):

1.   The three Scandinavian countries (Denmark, Sweden and Finland) where benefit levels are high and everyone is entitled to the same basic amount, with those in employment receiving earnings-related benefits (e.g. in respect of sickness, maternity and occupational injury benefits). Unemployment insurance is, however, separate from the state-run system of benefits and is run by mutual bodies or trade unions, being voluntary rather than compulsory.
2.   The UK and Ireland where the social security system provides virtually universal coverage. Benefits tend to be flat rate and provided at a lower level than in the Scandinavian countries and means testing plays a major role.
3.   Germany Austria, France and the Benelux countries where, in line with the Bismarckian tradition, the insurance principle plays the dominant role so that benefits are less universal, being based to a great extent on employment and linked to contributions. Entitlement to benefit can vary between different occupations and benefits tend be earnings-related.
4.   Italy, Spain, Greece and Portugal where social security provision is much more rudimentary. Social security systems tend to be a mixture of fragmented occupational and insurance-based income maintenance schemes with substantial gaps in coverage.

Nevertheless, even within each grouping, there are differences as regards the rules of eligibility, e.g. pensionable age varies between countries as does the length of time for which individual benefits are paid.

# A brief comparison of the provision of social security in the EC with the USA and Japan

The previous section highlighted a number of differences in the social security provision of EC member states. However, in comparison with other, even First World, countries such as the USA and Japan, it is possible to identify common features which unite the systems of social security amongst EC member states. Thus the European Commission, talking of social protection in general, which includes not only social security but also spending in other areas such as health services, argues that:

'Viewed from within Europe, the social protection systems of Member States of the [European] Union appear to be very different: indeed so different that it may seem impossible to identify common traits and pointless to speak of the European welfare model...[However], from a broader perspective, it is not difficult to discern the common nature of European social protection systems which distinguish them from other parts of the world, especially the US and Japan. In most respects, social protection systems in Europe are more different from systems in these latter two countries than they are from each other.' (European Commission, 1995, p. 25)

The most obvious factor to support such a claim is the level of expenditure in EC countries on social protection, including social security provision, in comparison to other countries. Whereas, in 1990, public expenditure on social protection averaged 22% of gross domestic product across the (then) 12 EC member states, it was 15% in the USA, 13% in Australia and under 12% in Japan (European Commission, 1995, pp. 25–26). The main reasons, in the sphere of social security, for this greater level of spending are that the coverage provided by benefits is much more comprehensive and the level of the rates of benefit is more generous. In Japan and the USA, in particular, there is an 'occupational welfare system' where much greater reliance is placed on individuals protecting themselves against risks such as unemployment, medical needs and provision for old age. This is largely achieved either by taking private measures, such as medical insurance or payments into a private pension scheme, or coverage on an occupational basis, such as occupational pension schemes. Both in the USA and Japan, there is much less compulsory provision, with the state, for example, tending to provide a very limited system of social protection with a minimal level of support for the residual poor. The consequences of this are that state measures to protect the population against the risks and exigencies of life are less extensive and less comprehensive than under the European model. This tends to provide a much less universal system and the role of the state system is to provide a very limited system of social protection to those on the margins of the labour market. In contrast, 'private welfare states' exist for better off individuals and occupations amongst the working population who can afford to pay for, and receive, much higher quality provision. In other words, those that can afford to take out private medical insurance or private pension schemes do so and the state provides a very minimal and much more inferior system for those who cannot.

## General demographic changes within the EC affecting the provision of social security

While debate exists on the scope of similarity of the provision of social security, and social protection measures generally, amongst EC member states, there are clear pressures towards convergence of the social security arrangements of EC member countries. The Maastricht Treaty 1992 and its Social Chapter, for example, seek to encourage EC member countries to standardise social security provision. Similarly, the European Commission has, since 1991, proposed a strategy of convergence of objectives and policies. This is partly due to the fact that, as with many other countries, all member states have been required to grapple with the social security implications of similar important demographic developments. Some of the most important of these are discussed below.

### An ageing population

The first demographic change affecting many countries, both within and outside the EC, is the ageing of the population. Quite simply, people in most developed countries are living longer and this has substantial implications not only for expenditure on social security but also on health and social care as well. Figures provided by Eurostat (the statistical office of the European Communities) indicate that, across the EC, the largest share of social protection expenditure is assigned to the elderly at, in 1992, 44.8% of total social protection expenditure. The second highest category was health at 36%, this also being influenced by the consequences of an increasingly elderly population. In contrast, the proportion of expenditure relating to other social protection needs include 7.8% for family/maternity and 7.2% for unemployment. In Great Britain, one of the main forms of social protection expenditure is payment of social security benefits and, in 1996–97, benefits for the elderly, most obviously retirement pension and income support, constituted 46% of total benefit expenditure. This reflects the general trend within EC countries over the last decade where national percentages of social protection expenditure on the elderly consistently hover around 40–47% of the total for all member states except the more generous Italians and more frugal Dutch and Irish (figures from Eurostat, 1995; HMSO, 1998).

However, highlighting some divergence of approach in different EC countries, is the fact that while, in real terms, the amount of resources expended on benefits for the old aged has increased within the EC throughout the 1980s and 1990s, for example between 1980 and 1992 by 50.8%, individual countries have responded differently:

> 'In the individual countries, this [EC] trend was repeated in Italy, Belgium, Greece, the Netherlands and Luxembourg, while in Germany, Ireland and the UK, real expenditure on old age/survivors' benefits rose considerably more slowly...' (Eurostat, 1995)

## Unemployment

A second important demographic development that is prevalent in many industrial countries is the growth in unemployment. While specific trends and the timing of increased levels of unemployment has varied between countries, the general trend has been that:

> 'Since the economic crisis of the mid-1970s most industrial societies have not succeeded in maintaining full employment. Rates of unemployment have increased steeply and have reached the level of 8, 10 and even 12 per cent or more of the labour force. It is estimated that the level of unemployment will continue to remain high and most industrial societies are faced with the reality of having to cope with a large and permanent pool of unemployed people.'(Doron, 1991, pp. 72–73)

The consequences for social security have been twofold: an increase in the number of recipients of social security and a reduction in the level of work-based contributions towards financing the provision of social security. Different countries, though, have responded differently. In the UK, for example, successive Conservative governments between 1979 and 1997, as part of a philosophy that aspired to reduce both the role of the state generally as well as public expenditure, sought to limit the criteria of benefit eligibility and the financial level at which benefit for the unemployed was provided. Other countries adopted different strategies, channelling more resources towards dealing with the social security consequences of increased levels of unemployment. Thus, within the European Community, while some countries, such as the Netherlands, Germany, Spain, France, Greece and Denmark, have reduced benefit rates, they have also extended the period of benefit duration. This contrasts with the reduction from 52 to 26 weeks for entitlement to non-means-tested benefit for the unemployed introduced in 1996 in the UK:

> '[Thus in 1992 i]n Denmark, the Netherlands and Belgium, expenditure on unemployment was very high (3.7, 3.2 and 2.6% of GDP respectively), while the unemployment rate was close to the European Union average, or 9.4% of the active population. In contrast, Italy spent less than 0.5% of its GDP on unemployment benefits, while recording an unemployment rate higher than the European average. Expenditure per unemployed person...was highest in Denmark, the Netherlands and Belgium. It was lowest in Italy and well below the average in Greece, Portugal and the UK. (Eurostat, 1995)

### Single parent families

Another important development affecting the provision of social security has been the change in family structures with the substantial increase in the number of family units headed by a single parent. In most EC countries, around 90% of single parents are women, the majority of whom are divorced or were in a previous cohabiting relationship. Thus, whereas there were just over half a million one-parent families in Britain in 1971, rising to one million in 1986, by 1995 there were 1.56 million lone parents, 93% of whom were women (MacDermott et al., 1998, p. 13).

The social security consequences of this include the fact that many of these single parents have not been in employment and thus are precluded from employment-based benefits while the responsibilities of single parenthood inhibit the opportunity of taking up employment. Research commissioned for the Department of Social Security in 1997 thus found that, in the UK, lone parents' incomes were typically less than half those of two parent families (Marsh, Ford and Finlayson, 1997). One result of this is that lone parents are much more likely to suffer poverty:

> 'In 1995, 41% of one parent families had a weekly household income of £100 or less compared with 4% of married couples.' (MacDermott et al., 1998, p. 14)

## Social Security Expenditure

Having explored some of the most important current demographic developments affecting the provision of social security, particularly in EC member states, it is appropriate to examine the level of expenditure on social security benefits, first in the UK and then in other EC countries.

## Social security spending in the UK

Expenditure on social security benefits in the UK in 1998/99 was £96.7 billion rising from £94.1 billion in 1997/98 while it is predicted to rise to £102.4 billion in 1999/2000. These figures constitute around one-third of total government expenditure. For the period to 1997/98, there was an annual growth in social security spending, during the five-year period from 1992/93, of 1.9%, the 1992/93 figure being £85.5 billion. During this period, social security expenditure remained between 12% and 13% of gross domestic product. Between 1978/79 and 1992/93 the annual growth in spending was 3.7%, being 9.1% of gross domestic product in 1978/79 rising to 12.3% in 1992/93. The main recipient groups have been:

(a) *The elderly*  The elderly are the group that receives the greatest amount of benefit expenditure, and this has been the case for over two decades. Total benefit expenditure on the elderly in 1996/97 was £40.8 billion (or 46% of total benefit expenditure). The largest amount of this was in respect of the state retirement pension with over 10.5 billion recipients. As discussed in Chapter 8, what has emerged in the UK has been two groupings amongst the elderly. Those reliant exclusively or mainly on state retirement pension increasingly face the prospect of poverty as state pensions have declined in value. For example, since 1980, pensions have been raised in line with prices rather then, as previously, on the more generous basis of increasing wage levels. In contrast, beneficiaries of private and occupational pension schemes in addition to the basic state pension are in a much more healthy financial position.

(b) *The sick and disabled*  This is the second largest recipient group of social security spending, with total spending on benefits for the sick and disabled constituting £23.5 billion in 1996/97. This group has seen a substantial increase in expenditure since the earlier 1980s with a trebling of spending between 1981/82 and 1996/97. Constituting 25% of total benefit expenditure in 1996/97, there are, for example, 1.9 million claimants of disability living allowance and 1.6 million who receive incapacity benefit. The increased expenditure since the early 1980s is explained as follows:

> 'In 1995–96 just over 2 million people were in receipt of incapacity benefit or severe disablement allowance. This represents more than double the number on the equivalent benefits in 1981–82. The rise in the number of those receiving these invalidity benefits is partly due to an increase in the duration of claims rather than an increase in new claims. The number of claimants receiving these benefits for more than ten years in 1994–95 was 246,000 compared with 70,000...in 1981–82.' (HMSO, 1998, p. 148)

(c) *The family*   £18.05 billion was spent on family benefits in 1996/97, constituting 20% of total benefit spending. Child benefit constitutes the largest category of recipients. Virtually all families with dependent children receive this universally available benefit, with the number of children receiving child benefit being over 12.8 million spread among 7 million families. £10 billion of family expenditure goes to families with one parent. As well as receiving child benefit, a high proportion of lone parent families receive income-related benefits such as income support, housing benefit and council tax. Until April 1998, when these additions were abolished by the recently installed Labour government, both child benefit and income support provided additional amounts for lone parent families. Family credit and its successor, working families tax credit, are other important family benefits paid to parents who are in employment but on low wages. In 1996/97 there were 831,000 claimants of family credit.

(d) *The unemployed*   Expenditure on benefits for the unemployed was £8.2 billion in 1996/97, which represented a reduction in comparison to the previous five years. Throughout the 1980s and early 1990s, expenditure on benefits for the unemployed increased substantially from £4.7 billion in 1982/83 to £9.7 billion in 1993/94. This reflected the general trend in increasing unemployment levels rising to a peak of almost 3.5 million in 1986 and, following a drop in the late 1980s, returning to over 3 million in 1993. Since 1993, spending on benefits for the unemployed has declined as the number of unemployed has decreased. Against this background, the unemployed's eligibility for benefit has been curtailed, with new conditions being imposed on benefit entitlement such as being required to be 'actively seeking work', reducing the level of benefit provision. The length of time that non-means-tested benefit can be received has also been cut back, from 52 weeks to 26 weeks while the eligibility for benefit of those aged 16 to 24 has also been reduced.

(The UK social security statistics are taken from *Social Trends 1998, Social Security Statistics 1998* and *Social Security Departmental Report – The Government's Expenditure Plans 1998/99*, all of which are HMSO publications.)

## UK social security spending in comparison to other EC member states

When comparing UK expenditure on social security with other EC countries, the most striking feature is that expenditure is substantially lower than many other member states. Eurostat provides information on government expenditure programmes, including benefits in kind as well as cash benefits, on social protection designed to protect people against common sources of hardship such as old age, sickness, disability and unemployment. Figures for 11 member countries in 1995 (data for the Irish Republic, Greece, Luxembourg and Spain was not available) show that the UK was ninth in the table, with only Italy and Portugal spending less on social protection. Denmark spent more on social protection per head of population than any other EC country at almost £7,000, which was over five times that of Portugal, the lowest spender. The UK spent just over £3,000, while Sweden, Germany and Austria spent over £5,000 and Finland, the Netherlands, France and Belgium over £4,000. As a percentage of gross domestic product, this placed the UK seventh. This reflects a constant trend as far back as 1980, throughout which period UK social protection expenditure has been below the EC average.

Specific evidence in respect of expenditure on social security benefits also indicates that the UK is not a high spender in comparison to its EC colleagues, which is particularly significant as, in the UK, social security benefits constitute the major form of social protection expenditure. This is indicated in respect of *social assistance* benefits, which most member states make available to provide a minimum guarantee for those whose financial resources are not adequate for their basic needs. In the UK this takes the form of income support (and, since 1996, income-based job-seeker's allowance) while, for example, in France the social assistance benefit is the 'revenue minimum d'insertion' (RMI) and, in Belgium, 'Minimex'. Of the 12 member states for which appropriate statistics are available for 1995 (excluding Greece, Portugal, Italy and the Irish Republic), the level of benefit paid to a couple with two children placed the UK eighth and, to single persons, fifth. Similarly, the level of benefits for the elderly placed the UK eighth out of the 12 member states for which statistics were available (Statistics taken from the *Eurostat Yearbook 1997*).

## Impact of European Community Law

The UK's membership of the European Community has had an impact on the British social security system, yet it is important to note that, despite pressures for the convergence of the social security systems of EC member states, European Community law primarily seeks to *co-ordinate*, rather than *harmonise*, social security provision in member states. One of the main aims of the EC has always been the free movement of workers and, in order to facilitate this, it has proved necessary to protect the social security rights of the persons concerned. Therefore, the main emphasis of EC legislation on social security aims to ensure that the social security systems of member states are co-ordinated to the extent that individuals are not penalised, in terms of social security eligibility, when moving from one member state to another. In contrast, there is little attempt to harmonise social security in the sense that all member countries are required to provide a uniform system of social security. Thus O'Neill and Coppel comment:

> '...Community law seeks to co-ordinate national social security systems, so as to ensure that no disadvantage as regards social security ensues from the right of free movement. Community law does not provide for uniform rates and conditions for benefit. Instead, questions of the structure and range of benefits, which benefit to provide for whom and under what conditions are all matters left to the Member States' existing social security systems.' (O'Neill and Coppel, 1994, pp. 259–60)

In fact, the co-ordination of social security systems extends beyond the 15 member states of the European Community to include Norway, Iceland and Liechtenstein. Collectively, this is known as the *European Economic Area* (EEA).

## Migrant workers

In order to facilitate the free movement of workers, Article 51 of the Treaty of Rome imposed measures that all member states had to adopt in the sphere of social security in order to achieve greater co-ordination. Regulation 1408/71 was introduced, implemented and supplemented by Regulation 574/72, requiring member states to adopt these measures. In order to appreciate the extent of co-ordination in respect of social security benefits, a distinction must be drawn between those benefits that are categorised as *social security* and those that are deemed to be of a *social assistance* nature.

### Social security benefits

Article 51 of the Treaty of Rome 1957 sets out that EC member countries must implement measures in respect of social security benefits to ensure that there is no discrimination against migrant workers and their dependants. To achieve this, in the early 1970s, EC Regulations 1408/71 and 574/72 (as amended, inter alia, by EC Regulation 2864/72) were introduced:

> 'Article 51 of the EEC Treaty and the EEC regulations Nos. 1408/71 and 574/72 implementing this provision are based on the fundamental principle of non-discrimination. This means that in social security matters there must be no difference in the treatment of nationals and non-nationals from other Member States.' (Schulte, 1991, p. 164)

***Benefits within the scope of Article 51 and regulations 1408/71 and 574/72***
These provisions relate only to social security benefits and not to those defined as social assistance benefits. This means that not all of the benefits within the British social security system are affected by EC Regulations 1408/71 and 574/72 (as amended, inter alia, by EC Regulation 2864/72). Article 4 of Regulation 1408/71 determines which benefits come within the scope of the regulation, the benefits covered being those to which there is a legally defined right to benefit. Thus, under Article 4(1) of Regulation 1408/71, benefits of the British social security system that are regarded as social security benefits and are, therefore, within the scope of the regulation include sickness and maternity benefits, invalidity benefits (e.g. incapacity benefit), old-age benefits, survivors' benefits, benefits in relation to accidents at work and occupational diseases, death grants, unemployment benefits (e.g. contributory jobseeker's allowance) and family benefits. All similar benefits in each member state, whether contributory or non-contributory, are covered. Also Article 4(2a), which was originally introduced as a result of an amending regulation 1247/92, has (since June 1992) extended EC law jurisdiction to include, inter alia, those benefits that provide specific protection to the disabled, such as disability living allowance and disabled person's tax credit.

***People covered by Article 51 and regulations 1408/71 and 574/72*** This regulation covers employed workers, the self-employed and their families and survivors. Article 1(a), as amended by Article 1(2)(a) of Regulation 1390/81, defines employed worker and self-employed as:

> '...any person who is insured, compulsorily or on an optional continued basis, for one or more of the contingencies covered by the branches of a social security scheme for employed or self-employed persons.'

What this means is that any individual must have been insured as an employed worker or self-employed under the National Insurance scheme of a member state in order to be covered by these EC regulations. A 'member of the family' is, under Article 1(f), defined according to the legislation of the member state under which the benefit is provided or claimed, although the European Court of Justice has sought to interpret this in line with the general principles set out in the preamble of Regulation 1408/71 or by reference to Regulation 1612/68 by extending a State's definition of family where it was necessary to promote freedom of movement for workers (see Case 7/75 *Mr and Mrs F.* v. *Belgian State*)

***Impact of Article 51 and regulations 1408/71 and 574/72 on social security provision*** The significance of these elements of EC law is that they are designed to guarantee social protection for people who move from one

EEA member country to another. Consequently they require the co-ordination of social security amongst EC (and EEA) member countries so that workers who migrate from one EC (and EEA) country to another shall benefit from two fundamental principles:

1.   aggregation;
2.   exporting benefits.

*Aggregation*   This means that in order to satisfy any condition of benefit entitlement in a member country, such as paying contributions, then periods spent in different member countries where such a condition is satisfied must be aggregated together. Aggregation thus aims to compensate for deficiencies in people's insurance record arising from their employment in a number of member states. It seeks to ensure that individuals who acquire social security rights in a member state who then move to another member state do not lose their rights in consequence of the move. Thus, in order to satisfy any condition of entitlement to benefit, reference must be made to periods spent, and contributions paid, in other EEA countries, Article 18(1) of EC Regulation 1408/71 (as amended by Article 1(3) of EC Regulation 2864/72) stating that:

> 'The competent institution of a Member State whose legislation makes the acquisition, retention or recovery of the right to benefit conditional upon the completion of insurance periods or periods of employment or residence shall, to the extent necessary, take account of insurance periods or periods of employment or residence completed under the legislation of any other member state as if they were periods completed under the legislation which it administers.'

*Exporting benefits*   The principle of exportability means that a social security benefit can be paid to a claimant who is not resident in the member state in question. Under Article 51(b) of the Treaty of Rome, social security benefits should be paid in full regardless of where in the Community the claimant is living. The principle of exportability applies, however, to a more restricted number of benefits than those coming within the scope of the aggregation requirement, as outlined in the last section. Thus O'Neill and Coppel state that:

> 'Article 10(1) of regulation 1408/71 explicitly applies this principle to invalidity, old-age or survivors' cash benefits, pensions for accidents at work or occupational diseases and death grants. Sickness benefits, family benefits and unemployment benefits are subject to more specific provisions.' (O'Neill and Coppel, 1994, p. 262)

With reference to more specific provisions for some benefits, Arts 67–69, e.g., provide that unemployment benefits, such as contributory jobseeker's allowance, can be paid for a period of three months while an individual is seeking a job in another member state. In the context of the British social security system, disability living allowance, attendance allowance and invalid care allowance, as non-contributory cash benefits, do not come within the scope of Art 10(1) and, therefore, the principle of exportability does not apply to them. The case of *Snares* v. *Adjudication Officer* (case C-20/96 The Times 10 December 1997) confirmed that disability living allowance was not an allowance that was exportable. The European Court of Justice stated that a recipient of disability living allowance was no longer entitled to receive this benefit after he took up residence in another member state of the European Community. Section 71(6) of the Social Security Contributions and Benefits Act 1992 and reg. 2 of the Social Security (Disability Living Allowance) Regulations stipulated that disability living allowance was only payable to a person ordinarily resident in Great Britain and present there apart from temporary absences. This requirement was deemed not to be in breach of reg. 1408/72 as the benefit was one of a number of 'special non-contributory benefits' expressly excluded in Annex IIa of reg. 408/71.

## Social assistance benefits

Social assistance benefits remain largely unaffected by Article 15 and accompany regulations. The notion of social assistance has been deemed by the European Court of Justice, in Case 249/83 *Hoecx* [1985] ECR 973 and Case 122/84 *Scrivner* [1985] ECR 1027, to cover benefits that are provided on a discretionary basis and where financial need is an essential condition of entitlement. Clearly means-tested benefits base eligibility on financial need, so that benefits in the British social security system such as income support, income based jobseeker's allowance and housing benefit would appear to be unaffected by Article 51 and regulations 1408/71 and 574/72. However, in Case C-78/91 *Hughes* [1992] 3 CMLR 490, the European Court of Justice decided that Family Credit, the means-tested benefit within the British social security system which, prior to Working Families' Tax Credit, was designed to provide additional income to low-wage earners who have a family, did come within the scope of the regulation. This was due to the fact that, although a means-tested benefit, it was regarded as a 'family benefit' and thus comes within the scope of Article 4(1) of regulation 1408/71. In fact, since 1992 this regulation has been extended to cover 'special non-contributory benefits' which include income support and income-based JSA.

  One consequence of this was the recent case of *Swaddling* v. *Adjudication Officer* (*The Times* 4 March 1999), where the European Court of

Justice interpreted the 'habitual residence' condition of income support in light of regulation 1408/71. The court considered the 'habitual residence' condition of income support in relation to a British national who had recently returned to the UK (for greater discussion of the issue of habitual residence see Chapter 6). 'Habitual residence' had previously been subject to a number of British judicial pronouncements. In CIS/1067/1995, the Social Security Commissioner had established that a claimant must reside for an *appreciable period of time* in order to become habitually resident and what constitutes an 'appreciable period of time' must depend on the facts of each case. In CIS 2326/1995, the Commissioner had emphasised that, in determining an 'appreciable length of time', no minimum period is necessary and to give illustrative examples, such as three to six months, is inadvisable as these may be read as the minimum or normal periods necessary to satisfy this requirement. The Court of Appeal, in *Nessa* v. *Chief Adjudication Officer* (*The Times* 11 Feb 1998), gave judicial approval to this requirement that habitual residence necessitated a claimant to be in the British Isles for an 'appreciable amount of time'. However, in *Swaddling* the habitual residence requirement for receipt of income support was addressed by the European Court of Justice in respect of a British national who had largely worked in France between 1980 and 1995 and who, on his return, had claimed income support. The court confirmed that, in respect of employed persons returning to their state of origin after working in another EU member state, the length of the period of residence was irrelevant in determining habitual residence. In this case, Mr Swaddling had made it clear at the time of applying for the benefit that he intended to remain in the UK, his state of origin and where his close relatives lived, although, if the opportunity arose, he may seek to obtain work in another member state. The ECJ determined that, in these circumstances, he could not be refused income support on the basis that he had not yet resided in the UK long enough.

It is also important to appreciate that, while social assistance benefits generally do not come within the scope of regulation 1408/71, nevertheless, due to the decision making of the European Court of Justice, they have not remained unaffected by EC law. The Court has treated social assistance benefits as 'social advantages' under Article 7(2) of Regulation 1612/68. In both *Hoeckx* and *Scrivner*, for example, the claimants were nationals from other countries and were deemed to be entitled to the Belgian minimum income allowance (the 'minimex'), a social assistance benefit. The Court decided that, as they were 'lawfully resident' in Belgium, the claimants were entitled to be treated equally with Belgian nationals under Article 7(2) of Regulation 1612/68, despite strict nationality and residence requirements on entitlement to receive the benefit. The European Court of Justice is, therefore, prepared to intervene to declare aspects of social assistance benefits of member countries to be in breach of Regulation 1618/68. However, the scope of Regulation 1618/68 is much more limited than that of Regulation 1408/71. Most importantly, only benefits that come within Regulation 1408/71 can be exported, whereas 'social advantages' under Regulation 1618/68 cannot be exported. Similarly, the principle of aggregation only applies to benefits that come within Regulation 1408/71.

## Equal treatment and social security

The second way that the European Community has influenced British social security law is in respect of equal treatment of men and women. In contrast to the provisions in respect of migrant workers, which only concern individuals who move from one EEA state to another, Directive 79/7, dealing with equal treatment in matters of social security, operates in respect of all social security matters, including those that are wholly internal to each member state. To this extent, Directive 79/7 has more of a harmonisation, rather than a co-ordination, objective as it seeks to improve the social security systems of member states. The directive, which first came into direct effect in all EC member states on 23 December 1984, implements the principle of equal treatment for men and women in social security matters. Article 4(1) states that:

> 'there shall be no discrimination whatsoever on grounds of sex, either directly or indirectly, by reference in particular to marital or family status, in particular as concerns:
> – the scope of [social security] schemes and the conditions of access thereto,
> – the obligation to contribute and the calculation of contributions,
> – the calculation of benefits including increases due in respect of a spouse and for dependants, and
> – the conditions governing the duration and retention of entitlement to benefits.'

Article 3 establishes that the Directive covers statutory social security schemes in relation to sickness, invalidity, old age, accidents at work and occupational diseases and unemployment as well as 'social assistance' schemes to the extent that they supplement or replace benefits meeting any of the aforementioned requirements. Directive 79/7 does not apply to social security provision in respect of maternity nor does it apply to survivors' benefits or family benefits. Article 2 sets out what is called the 'personal scope' of the directive, namely the categories of person to whom it applies. First, it covers the 'working population' which consists of people who are employed or self-employed along with those whose work is interrupted by illness, accident or involuntary unemployment and those who are seeking employment. Secondly, it covers retired or invalided employees and self-employed people.

The general consequences of Directive 79/7 for the British social security system are spelled out by O'Neill and Coppel as follows:

'[T]he entitlement and contribution to, as well as the rate and the duration of statutory social benefits, should be the same as between men and women regardless of, in particular, their marital or family status, in so far as the claimants of these benefits can be regarded as part of the 'working population.

Translating the Community categories into UK social security terms, it would seem that any sex discrimination in the claims of workers for severe disablement allowance, [incapacity] benefit, disability living allowance, attendance allowance, invalidity care allowance, industrial injury benefit or retirement pensions is prohibited under Community law.'(O'Neill and Coppel, 1994, pp. 263–64)

In respect of 'social assistance' schemes that supplement or replace other benefits under Article 4(1), the European Court of Justice, in *R.* v. *Secretary of State for Social Security, ex parte Smithson* (case C 243/90), refused to extend the right of equal treatment under Directive 79/7 to the UK housing benefit scheme because it was not 'directly and effectively' linked to protection against any one of the risks set out in Article 3(1). A similar decision was reached by the Court in respect of income support in *Jackson* v. *Chief Adjudication Officer* (case C 63/ 64/91).

Another important point to note in respect of Directive 79/7 is that Article 7(1) expressly allows member states to exclude the following matters from the scope of the directive:

(a)   the determination of pensionable age for the purposes of old-age and retirement pensions and possible consequences thereof for other benefits;
(b)   benefits or entitlements granted to persons who have brought up children;
(c)   wives' derived old-age or invalidity benefits; and
(d)   increases granted in respect of dependent wives related to long-term invalidity, old-age, accidents at work and occupational disease benefits.

The first of these exemptions has, in particular, generated litigation before the European Court of Justice. Thus, in *R.* v. *Secretary of State for Social Security, ex parte the Equal Opportunities Commission* (case C 9/91), the

Court held that the different pension ages for men (65) and women (60) in the UK did not contravene the directive even though it meant that men were required to continue to pay National Insurance contributions for five years longer than women and yet receive the same pension. The Court said that to alter such arrangements would disrupt the complex financial 'equilibrium' of the state pension system. Similarly, in *Secretary of State for Social Security and Chief Adjudication Officer* v. *Graham and Others* (case C 92/94) the Court declared that for the purposes of invalidity benefit (which has now been replaced by incapacity benefit) it was lawful to discriminate against women aged over 60. The decision centred on the exemption from the scope of the directive, under Article 7(1), of *the possible consequences for other benefits* of the setting of pensionable age for the purposes of old-age and retirement pensions. The appellant, Rose Graham, was discriminated against in comparison to a male recipient of invalidity benefit on a number of grounds based on the fact that the female retirement age was five years earlier than for men, which meant that the amount of benefit she received was less than a man would have received in the same circumstances. Despite the Advocate General providing an opinion in favour of Ms Graham, the Court of Justice decided that this provision came within the scope of the exemption in Article 7(1).

---

## Bibliography

Abel-Smith, B. and Townsend, P. (1965) *The Poor and Poorest*, Bell.

Alcock, P. (1996) *Social Policy in Britain: Themes and Issues*, Macmillan.

Doron, A. (1991) 'Alternative futures for social security'. In M. Adler et al. (eds) *The Sociology of Social Security*, Edinburgh University Press.

European Commission (1995) *Europe: Social Protection*.

Eurostat (1995) *Eurostat Yearbook '97: A statistical eye on Europe 1986–1996; Europe in figures*, 4th Edition, Eurostat.

Harris, J. (1979) 'From Cradle to Grave: the rise of the Welfare State', *New Society*, 18 January.

HMSO (1998) *Social Trends*, HMSO.

MacDermott, T. et al. (1998) *Real Choices for Lone Parent and their Children*, Child Poverty Action Group.

MacGregor, S. (1992) 'Come back Beveridge: all is forgiven? *Poverty*, 82, p. 10.

Marsh, A., Ford, R. and Finlayson, L. (1997) *Lone Parents, Work and Benefits*, York Publishing Services.

Ogus, A. I., Barendt, E. M. and Wikeley, N. J. (1995) *The Law of Social Security*, 4th Edition, Butterworths.

O'Neill, A. and Coppel, J. (1994) *EC Law for UK Lawyers*, Butterworths.

Roebroek, J.M. (1991) 'Social policy diversions in Europe'. In D. Pieters, *Social Security in Europe*, Bruylant. Brussels.

Schulte, B. (1991) 'Social security legislation in the European Communities: co-ordination, harmonization and convergence'. In D. Pieters, *Social Security in Europe*, Bruylant. Brussels.

# 4 Jobseeker's Allowance

## Context and Commentary

Jobseeker's allowance is a social security benefit which was introduced by the Jobseekers Act 1995 and is paid to people who are unemployed or working fewer than 16 hours per week and who are seeking work. It is a benefit with two distinct parts. Contributory jobseeker's allowance is a contributory non-means-tested benefit payable for the first 26 weeks of unemployment and has replaced unemployment benefit. Income-based jobseeker's allowance is a non-contributory means-tested benefit payable after 26 weeks of unemployment, or during the first 26 weeks either for claimants not eligible for contributory jobseeker's allowance or as an additional 'top up' to contributory jobseeker's allowance. Income-based jobseeker's allowance has replaced income support for people who have to look for work in order to qualify for benefit although, unlike unemployment benefit, income support still exists. It is now a benefit that can only be claimed by those incapable of work due to sickness or illness, who are not required to seek work.

## Historical introduction

The payment of a social security benefit to the unemployed was first provided by Part II of the National Insurance Act 1911. It adopted an insurance or contributory approach with a tri-partite system of contributors: the employee, the employer and the state contributing in equal proportion. Applying only to a small number of workers, this scheme never embraced all employed workers, even when its scope was extended in 1916 and in the early post First World War years. In fact, the economic crisis of the early 1930s saw the level of benefit cut in 1931 by 10%, requiring the employed to increasingly resort to means-tested forms of assistance, variously known as *uncovenanted benefits*, *extended* or *transitional benefit*, *unemployment assistance* or the *dole* which had been introduced in an ad hoc fashion in the 1920s and 1930s to deal with claimants who either were not eligible for unemployment benefit or had exhausted their entitlement to it by remaining unemployed beyond the period of payment of benefit. A major review of the system was undertaken by the Royal Commission on Unemployment Insurance (1932, Cmd 4185), with its recommendations largely implemented in the Unemployment Act 1934. This formalised the basic pattern of state support for the unemployed that has continued to remain in place. This involves the provision of the two above-mentioned types of benefit. The first type is contributory and non-means-tested and lasts for a fixed period of unemployment which, until 1996, was 52 weeks. After this period, this form of benefit ceases, the only benefit for which the unemployed are then eligible being a non-contributory means-tested benefit which consequently is available only to those whose financial circumstances or 'means' are low enough. Thus, by the end of the 1930s, state provision of benefit as a substitute for income loss due to unemployment was largely based on social insurance. Benefit was flat rate and was paid at a survival level. This was supplemented by a means-tested benefit for those who were either ineligible for the social insurance benefit or had exhausted their entitlement to it.

1942 saw the publication of the Beveridge Report (Beveridge, 1942). The comprehensive plan for social security put forward in this report, as discussed in Chapter 3, also envisaged a system of social security benefits based on the social insurance principle. While retaining the two types of benefit, Beveridge nevertheless saw a much reduced role for means-tested benefits than that developed in the 1920s and 1930s. Rather, benefits would be paid for by a system of compulsory contributions paid when people were employed, these contributions determining subsequent eligibility for benefits. The Beveridge Report thus laid much greater stress on the social insurance principle as the basis for the provision of benefits for those deemed to be in need, particularly in respect of the unemployed. Sympathetic to the hostility to the much hated 'means test' to which the unemployed were forced to submit in the 1930s in order to obtain *unemployment assistance*, Beveridge envisaged a contributory-based system of *unemployment benefit* that would not be means tested and he envisaged that this benefit would be paid at subsistence level and be of unlimited duration.

Unemployment benefit was seen by Beveridge as part of a comprehensive system of contributory benefits covering nearly all eventualities where state financial assistance would be required. There would, nevertheless, be a limited role for a means-tested *national assistance* benefit as a safety net for the small number of claimants not eligible for a contributory benefit because, for example, not enough contributions had been made.

The proposals contained in the Beveridge Report were largely implemented by the Labour government of 1945–51. The National Insurance Act 1946 created a comprehensive contributory unemployment benefit scheme and the National Assistance Act 1948 established the means-tested 'national assistance' benefit which Beveridge envisaged would be payable to a small number of claimants who 'fell through' the system of contributory schemes, including unemployment benefit. However, from the outset, national assistance assumed a far larger role than Beveridge envisaged, becoming, in fact, the major benefit in the post-war social security system. One reason for this was that not all Beveridge's proposals were implemented. Most notably, unemployment benefit was not paid for an unlimited duration, meaning that the long-termed unemployed were eligible only for means-tested national assistance (or its successors supplementary benefit and income support) when eligibility for unemployment benefit ended after 52 weeks. Even more significantly, the levels of contributory benefits, such as unemployment benefit and old-age pension, were not increased in pace with inflation to the same extent as means-tested national assistance. This was largely due to the fact that it was cheaper to increase means-tested benefits. However, a major consequence was that a large number of recipients of social insurance benefits (such as unemployment benefit and pensions) had to 'top up' that benefit with national assistance (and later its replacements, supplementary benefit and then income support). This was clearly a break with Beveridge's idea that the level at which each contributory benefit should be paid should in itself 'be sufficient without further resources to provide the minimum income for subsistence in all normal cases' (Beveridge, 1942, p. 122).

The Labour government of 1964–70 implemented further changes to the system of social security benefits for the unemployed. In 1966, an earnings-related supplement was added to unemployment benefit which previously had been paid at a flat rate to all recipients. This earnings-related supplement lasted for 16 years until abolished by the Conservative government that had been returned in 1979. The Ministry of Social Security Act 1966 also replaced national assistance with supplementary benefit. The administration of the new scheme was placed in the hands of the Ministry of Social Security and later the Department of Health and Social Security though a body independent of government, the Supplementary Benefits Commission, was set up to monitor the operation of the supplementary benefits scheme, accordingly producing Annual Reports suggesting possible reforms and improvements.

May 1979 saw the election of a Conservative government committed to reducing public expenditure levels. Allied to its belief that existing provision of social security distorts the labour market by acting as a disincentive for people to take jobs at lower wage levels, this provided the basis for successive Conservative governments' approach to social security provision for the unemployed throughout their long period in office up to 1997. As discussed in Chapter 3, this led in the early 1980s to benefit rates being raised in line with prices rather than, as previously, with wages, thereby reducing their real value. Then, following the Fowler Review of social security in the mid-1980s, the Social Security Act 1986, inter alia, replaced supplementary benefit with income support, tightening up eligibility and reducing entitlement along with implementing changes to unemployment

benefit that also eroded entitlement. The Social Security Act 1988 introduced further changes to benefit entitlement for the unemployed, e.g. the
basic age of entitlement for income support was raised from 16 to 18. The
overall reforms introduced during this period to benefits for the unemployed included tightening up what constitutes 'available for employment', introducing a new requirement of 'actively seeking work' and
extending the period of disqualification from benefit for voluntary unemployment.

Further restrictions on the eligibility of the unemployed to claim benefit
were set out in a White Paper in October 1994, which proposed the
introduction of jobseeker's allowance. The ideology behind the White
Paper continued to embrace a deregulated labour market in the belief that
this was necessary for Britain to remain competitive. This approach,
therefore, emphasised that social security benefits should not be too easy
to obtain or paid at levels which mean that the unemployed may lack
enthusiasm to take low paid jobs. The White Paper (and subsequently, the
Jobseekers Act 1995) embraced further restrictions designed to make the
unemployed 'compete effectively for jobs', benefits being 'a means of
support while an unemployed person looks for work, not an income for a
lifestyle divorced from work'. Whereas non-means-tested benefit was paid
for a period of 52 weeks in respect of unemployment benefit, after which
only means-tested benefits were available, jobseeker's allowance reduces
the non-means-tested period of benefit entitlement to 26 weeks. In all, the
official estimates predicted that, on its implementation, 70,000 claimants
lost entitlement to benefit after 26 weeks.

The Jobseekers Act obtained the Royal Assent in July 1995 so that
jobseeker's allowance replaced unemployment benefit and income support in October 1996 as the social security benefit for the unemployed.
Some of the consequences of the new benefit were spelt out at the time
as follows:

> 'The already tough requirements on claimants to demonstrate that
> they are available for and actively seeking work are to be made even
> tougher with the introduction of JSA...[W]e [also] appear to be wit-
> nessing a wholesale withdrawal of state support for long-termed un-
> employed people and the undermining of the contributory principle
> more generally.' (Barnes and Witcher, 1995, pp. 13 and 16)

Before 7 October 1996 the main benefits for people who were out of work
were unemployment benefit and income support. Unemployment benefit
was a contributory, non-means-tested taxable benefit payable for 312 days
(i.e. 52 weeks). Under s.25 of the Social Security Contributions and
Benefits Act 1992 a claimant was required to be available for, and actively
seeking, work in order to be eligible for unemployment benefit. Under

s.28(1) of the Act a claimant could be disqualified from receiving unemployment benefit if he or she had voluntarily left the job or had lost employment through misconduct. Such disqualification could be for up to a maximum of 26 weeks, deferring entitlement to the benefit.

Under reg. 7B of the Unemployment, Sickness and Incapacity Benefit Regulations (USIB Regs) a claimant was *not* treated as being available for work if he or she placed restrictions on the type of job he or she was prepared to accept (e.g. the rate of pay, the type of job) unless it could be proved that the claimant still had a reasonable chance of getting a job despite the restrictions. Under reg. 7B(4) a claimant was, however, permitted a period of a maximum of 13 weeks (the exact amount of time in each case was determined by a Department of Employment advisor) when a claimant was allowed only to consider jobs in his or her 'usual occupation'. After the end of this 'permitted period', claimants had to be available for, and actively seeking, work in occupations other than their usual occupation.

Income support is a non-contributory, means-tested, non-taxable benefit. It is payable to people who are not in full-time work (full time being defined as 16 hours or more per week) and was, prior to 7 October 1996, the principal benefit for unemployed people on low incomes. Still payable to a smaller number of claimants *not* required to be available for work, before 7 October 1996 it was also payable to unemployed people who were available for, and actively seeking, work. Thus, for the unemployed, it could be paid in addition to unemployment benefit because, in many circumstances, unemployment benefit was paid at a lower rate than income support. It was also the principal benefit for the long-term unemployed as unemployment benefit ceased after 52 weeks.

Jobseeker's allowance, implemented on 6 October 1996, actually consists of two different types of benefit. *Contributory jobseeker's allowance* is a contributory non-means-tested, non-taxable benefit that has replaced unemployment benefit and *income-based jobseeker's allowance* is a non-contributory, means-tested, non-taxable benefit that has replaced income support for claimants who are required to be available for work. The details of each type of jobseeker's allowance are set out in the next section.

Changes to jobseeker's allowance were introduced following the return of the Labour government in May 1997, when the new Chancellor of the Exchequer Gordon Brown, in his first Budget in July, announced the 'New Deal', a government initiative that seeks to help people find work. Funded by a 'windfall levy' on the profits of privatised utility companies, and initially targeted at 18–24 year olds, it has been extended to people aged over 25 who have been employed for more than two years and to lone parents as well as to the sick and disabled. The New Deal aims to provide a much more proactive strategy by the Employment Service in assisting benefit claimants to obtain work. It is not restricted to claimants of jobseeker's allowance, although many of those on the New Deal scheme are recipients of JSA on whom certain conditions for entitlement to receive the benefit are imposed. Claimants who breach any such condition can be disqualified from receiving any benefit they are claiming, including JSA. The regulations concerning the New Deal and its effects on benefit entitlement are set out in Chapter 6 while the policy developments behind the scheme are discussed in Chapter 14.

## The Legal Rules

The Jobseekers Act 1995 introduced the jobseeker's allowance (JSA). This is a benefit paid to unemployed people between 18 and retirement age that has two forms. Contributory JSA has many similarities to the former unemployment benefit in that eligibility depends on whether a person has paid sufficient national insurance contributions, the contributions conditions being largely the same as for unemployment benefit. Income-based JSA is very similar to its predecessor, income support, continuing to use the same means test as income support did (and which, in fact, income support continues to use for claimants not required to be available for, and actively seeking, work). As a single benefit, JSA has the same claim form for both forms of the benefit. Also, the main rates of both contributory and income-based JSA are the same, as is the three-day waiting period before either form of benefit can be paid. The requirements to be available for, and actively seeking, work are also identical though there are also important differences between the two forms of benefit.

The jobseeker's allowance was a new benefit in the British social security system. However, like much social security legislation, the Jobseekers Act 1995 is an enabling Act, setting out the basic framework of the new benefit but enabling the details to be contained in the regulations. The detailed provisions for both forms of JSA are thus contained in a number of sets of regulations, the most important of which is the Jobseekers Allowance Regulations 1996. Other relevant sets of regulations include the Jobseekers Allowance (Transitional Provisions) Regulations 1995 and the Social Security (Back to Work Bonus) Regulations 1996. As well as these, the Employment Service has produced guidance for employment officers to decide if the claimant is available for, and actively seeking, employment and whether the jobseeker's agreement requirement is being met, while the Central Adjudication Services has also produced guidance on other factors determining eligibility.

### Common conditions of entitlement

Under ss.1–3 of the Jobseekers Act 1995, to qualify for either form of JSA, a claimant must:

(a) be capable of work;
(b) be available for work;
(c) be actively seeking work;
(d) have signed a jobseeker's agreement with the Employment Service;
(e) not be in remunerative work;
(f) be at least 18 years old (with some exceptions) and below pensionable age;
(g) not be in full-time education; and
(h) be in Great Britain.

As well as these the 'New Deal' initiative, first introduced in 1997, requires that some claimants must take part in the New Deal programmes otherwise entitlement to benefit, including jobseeker's allowance, is affected. This is discussed in Chapter 6.

## Capable of work

Whether a claimant is deemed to be capable of work or not determines which benefit he or she is entitled to. Incapacity for work is established by either the 'own occupation' or the 'all work' test (see Chapter 5 for a detailed explanation of these tests) and is used to determine eligibility for incapacity benefit, severe disablement allowance and income support. A claimant who is found to be capable of work under the appropriate test is, however, per ss.171A–G of the Social Security Contributions and Benefits Act 1992 and paragraph 2 of Schedule 1 of the Jobseekers Act 1995, treated as capable of work for the purposes of JSA.

## Available for work

Section 6(1) of the Jobseekers Act 1995 stipulates that '...a person is available for employment if he is willing and able to take up immediately any employed earner's employment.' This marks an important change from eligibility for unemployment benefit where a claimant had to be available for *suitable* employment whereas claimants must now be available for *any* employment. Section 6(3) and JSA reg. 8, however, allow claimants to place restrictions on the type of job that they are prepared to accept as long as there is a reasonable prospect of obtaining a job despite such restriction(s). Restrictions on the type of work, the hours of work, conditions of employment, the location of a job and the rate of pay can, for example be imposed by a claimant although the reasonableness of any restriction is determined by the following:

1. JSA reg. 9 stipulates that, after JSA has been claimed for six months, no restriction can be placed on the rate of pay that a claimant is prepared to consider.
2. Under ss.6(5) and (7) of the JSA 1995 and JSA reg. 16 claimants may be allowed to restrict availability to their usual occupation and/or

level of pay for a 'permitted period' of between 1 and 13 weeks. Not all claimants will be granted a permitted period by an employment officer and whether a claimant is granted such a period, as well as its duration, will be set out in the jobseeker's agreement, this decision being based on such factors as the claimant's qualifications and skills, what his/her normal occupation is, the length of time he/she has worked in that occupation and the availability and location of jobs in that area of work.

3.  JSA regs 6(1) and 7(1) establish the general rule that claimants of both forms of JSA must be willing and able to to work at least 40 hours a week yet also be willing and able to work fewer than 40 hours a week. In other words, claimants must be available for a full-time job but should also be prepared to accept a part-time job. Regulation 13 provides that some claimants may restrict availability for employment to fewer than 40 hours a week, e.g. if it is reasonable in light of the claimant's physical or mental condition, or if the claimant has caring responsibilities.

4.  A claimant who is deemed capable of work but who has a physical or mental disability may be able to place restrictions on the type of work for which he/she is available. Under reg. 13(3) of the Jobseekers Allowance Regulations 1996 (JSA Regs) *any* restrictions can be placed on availability for work as long as they are deemed *reasonable* in the light of the claimant's physical or mental condition, even if it means that the claimant has no reasonable prospect of obtaining employment. To establish this, a claimant is normally required to provide medical evidence and may be referred to a Disability Employment Adviser.

In certain situations, a claimant is treated as being available for work (or *deemed* available) where, strictly speaking, this may not be the case. Thus reg. 14 stipulates that where a claimant takes a child abroad for medical treatment, he/she will be deemed available for work for up to 8 weeks. Similarly, for the first and last weeks of a claim for JSA, a claimant can be deemed to be available for work even if, e.g., the claimant is engaged during such period in preparing for the new job or sorting matters out vis-à-vis the recently ended job and therefore is, strictly speaking, unavailable for work.

All the relevant tribunal and commissioners' decisions and case law in respect of similar features of unemployment benefit also apply to JSA. Thus, for example, under *R(U) 44/53* the Employment Service can deem a claimant not to be available for work without having to be required to prove that an offer of work has actually been turned down.

## Actively seeking work

Originally introduced by the Social Security Act 1989, the requirement to be 'actively seeking work' is set out in s.7(1) JSA 1995:

'...a person is actively seeking employment in any week if he takes in that week such steps as he can reasonably be expected to have to take in order to have the best prospects of securing employment.'

JSA reg. 18 stipulates that taking a single step during a week will not be enough unless taking only one step is reasonable. In deciding what can be reasonably expected of a claimant, reg. 18(3) establishes that all the circumstances must be taken into account including the claimant's skills, qualifications and abilities, any physical and mental limitations, the length of time unemployed, previous steps undertaken and time spent improving job prospects. Regulation 18(2)(a)–(d) contains a list of the type of steps that claimants should be undertaking. These include making job applications; seeking information from advertisers; registering with an employment agency and appointing someone else to assist in seeking employment. Regulation 18(2)(f)–(j) sets out preparatory steps that also count, such as preparing a c.v. and asking a previous employer for a reference. Regulation 18(2) does not, however, provide an exhaustive list of steps that could be taken in the search for employment.

Under reg. 20, if a claimant has been allowed a permitted period, he/she is only required to take steps to find a job in his or her usual occupation or at a level of pay not lower than the claimant is accustomed, or both. Finally, reg. 19 sets out a number of situations where a claimant can be deemed to be actively seeking work in circumstances where, strictly speaking, he or she is not. This includes the last week of a claim for JSA and for up to 8 weeks where a claimant takes a child abroad for medical treatment.

## A jobseeker's agreement with the Employment Service

The requirement for claimants to enter into a jobseeker's agreement constitutes the major new feature introduced by the 1995 Act. This agreement is drawn up at the first interview a claimant has with an Employment Officer (EO) after making a claim for JSA. Until the contents of the jobseeker's agreement have been agreed by the claimant and the EO, no claim for either type of JSA will be passed to the Benefits Agency.

Under s.9(1) JSA 1995 and JSA reg. 31 the jobseeker's agreement contains the following information:

(a) the claimant's name;
(b) the number of hours he/she is prepared to work per week (with a daily breakdown of these hours);
(c) any restrictions the claimant is placing on work he/she is prepared to undertake (e.g. type of work, level of pay, distance prepared to travel to work);

(d)   the type of job the claimant is prepared to consider;
(e)   what steps the claimant will take to actively seek work;
(f)   whether the claimant has been granted a 'permitted period' and, if so, its duration, and the start and end dates;
(g)   the date of the agreement.

If the claimant and EO cannot reach an agreement, then the claimant must be given a statement of his or her rights. If agreement is reached, this will be backdated to the first day of claim. Under s.9(5) JSA 1995 the EO will, however, only sign an agreement if he/she agrees that any restrictions placed on availability for work are reasonable and still provide the claimant with a reasonable prospect of finding a job. The EO will also have to be satisfied that the terms of the agreement mean that the claimant is both available for and actively seeking work (these two conditions being termed the *labour market conditions*). If no agreement is reached between the claimant and the EO, then the case is referred to an Adjudication Officer (like the Employment Officer, an employee of the Employment Service) who, under s.9(7)(a), must make a decision within 14 days. If a claimant is unhappy with the AO's decision, then he/she has a right of appeal to a Social Security Appeal Tribunal. A second level of appeal is available, on points of law only, to a Social Security Commissioner.

## Remunerative work

In order to be eligible for JSA, a claimant must not be in remunerative work. This is defined as working 16 hours or more a week. A claimant can, thus, work for up to 16 hours and still claim JSA. This definition of remunerative work is the same as for other benefits such as working families tax credit and disabled person's tax credit and reflects the definition adopted for unemployment benefit before October 1995. However, an important change introduced by the Jobseeker's Act is that a claimant's partner can work up to 24 hours a week (where previously it was 16 hours) without ending entitlement to income-based JSA, although any amount earned can affect the amount of benefit received. A person's entitlement to contributory JSA is unaffected by a partner's employment.

## Aged 18 years old and under pensionable age

Most claimants of JSA are required to be 18 years old or over. However, under s.3(1)(f)(ii) and (iii) JSA 1995 a person aged 16 or 17 years old is eligible for JSA if, as well as satisfying the basic entitlement rules, he/she falls into one of a number of categories which include:

(i)   Under JSA reg. 66(1)(b), the claimant is one of a couple with a child for whom he/she is eligible to claim.

(ii) Under JSA reg. 66(1)(a), the claimant has been laid off or on short time work.

(iii) Where claimants are not eligible for income support, they are eligible for JSA if, inter alia, they are a single parent or single foster parent with a child under 16; looking after a child under 16 while the child's parents are ill or temporarily away; the claimant is pregnant and is either unable to work or within 11 weeks before the baby is due or 7 weeks after the birth; the claimant is blind or incapable of work because of illness or disability (see JSA reg. 66(1)(c), s.124(1) JSA 1995 and Income Support reg. 4ZA and sch.1B).

A claimant must be under pensionable age to be eligible for JSA, pensionable age currently being 65 for men and 60 for women. However, under s.126 and Sch. 4 of the Pensions Act 1995 the pensionable age of women will be increased from 60 to 65 between 2010 and 2020. Thus, women born before 6 April 1950 will continue to retire at 60 and those born after 5 April 1955 will retire at 65. For those born between these two dates, the retirement age is between 60 and 65 depending on their exact date of birth.

## Full-time education

Under s.1(2)(g) JSA 1995, students in full time education are not normally eligible for JSA, although there are some exceptions. Students under 19 are not eligible for JSA if engaged in full-time study in school or college. For studies up to A level, OND or similar, 'full time' is defined under reg. 54(2) as involving more than 12 hours' instruction or 'guided learning' per week although the student's parent(s) can claim child benefit for him/her during this period. For students under 19 in 'advanced education' (such as HND, teaching qualification, degree) full time is also defined as 12 hours' instruction, but there is no eligibility for child benefit. Full-time students aged 19 or over are also ineligible for JSA although JSA reg. 1(3) defines 'full time' as involving 16 hours' 'guided learning' per week.

Another important aspect of the ineligibility of a student for JSA relates to students who abandon or are dismissed from a course. The Court of Appeal decision in *O'Connor* v. *Chief Adjudication Office and Another* (Times Law Report 11 March 1999) indicates that, where a student intends to complete the course of study at some later date, he or she is still defined as a student even during periods when not attending, such as when he or she has failed examinations and is required to take a year (or some other period) out to re-sit. During that period, even if barred from attending classes or not being eligible to receive student finance, he or she is regarded as a student for benefit purposes. While the *O'Connor* case was expressly concerned with eligibility for income support (as it related to circumstances before JSA was introduced), it would appear to apply to other social security benefits, including JSA, for which students are ineligible. A more detailed discussion of this case is given in Chapter 5.

## Resident in Great Britain

Normally a claimant is required to be resident in Great Britain in order to be eligible for JSA although there is a number of limited exceptions, e.g. under JSA reg. 14, if a claimant goes abroad for a job interview or out of the country for up to 8 weeks to take his or her child for medical treatment he/she will remain eligible for JSA. A further important point to note is that, for income-based JSA, the *habitual residence test* (as set out in Chapter 6) also applies. This means that residence in Great Britain does not, of itself, guarantee entitlement to that benefit. It is important to read the section in Chapter 6 on the requirement of habitual residence.

As well as the common conditions of entitlement, there are other important features of JSA that it is necessary to understand.

## Voluntary unemployment

In order to be eligible for JSA, claimants must satisfy the requirement that they are not voluntarily unemployed. Before October 1996, the unemployment benefit and income support schemes contained sanctions whereby claimants deemed to be *voluntarily unemployed* in some way would be disqualified from benefit or receive a reduced rate of benefit. The JSA scheme retains these features as well as introducing new ones:

### Voluntarily leaving a job, compulsory training scheme or employment programme

If, under s.19(6)(c) JSA 1995, a claimant leaves a job *without just cause*, or, under s.19(5)(b), he/she voluntarily gives up a place on a compulsory training scheme or employment programme *without good cause*, he/she will be sanctioned. What constitutes 'good cause' is set out in JSA reg. 72 which stipulates that, when determining 'good cause', a number of factors into account must be taken into account, including:

–   any personal circumstances of the claimant that indicate that the job may cause him/her serious harm or physical or mental stress;
–   discrepancies between the job and the restrictions the claimant has been allowed to place on the type of job for which he/she is available;
–   when the claimant is responsible for the care of another member of the household;
–   the travelling time and whether the expenses incurred in doing the job would be an unreasonably high proportion of the claimant's income

'Just cause' is a test that has been developed by tribunal and court decisions under the former unemployment benefit scheme and involves balancing the interests of the claimant against those of all other contributors to the national insurance fund. In *Crewe* v. *Social Security Commissioner* [1982] 1 WLR 1209, the Court of Appeal stated that not only must the claimant show that he/she acted reasonably but that the circumstances of the case make it proper that the community support him/her. In that particular case, volunteering for early retirement was deemed probably not constituting just cause. Similarly, in *R(U) 14/52*, it was stated that if a claimant deems a job unsuitable, he/she is normally expected to find, or at least seriously search for, another job before giving the job up.

Under s.19(3) and JSA reg. 70, the period of sanction when a claimant has left a job, during which the claimant will be ineligible for JSA, can vary from one week to 26 weeks. If he/she has left a compulsory training scheme or employment programme, s.19(2) establishes that the sanction will be for two weeks in the first instance and four weeks for subsequent dismissals.

## Misconduct

If a claimant is dismissed from a job or a compulsory training scheme or employment programme then, under s.19 JSA 1995, this can constitute voluntary unemployment. What constitutes misconduct has been addressed, over the years, in a number of tribunal and commissioner decisions. In *R(U) 2/77*, R. J. A. Temple, a former Chief Commissioner, confirmed that misconduct can refer to behaviour outside employment but would, nevertheless, lead a reasonable employer to dismiss the employee. Thus, in *R(U) 7/57*, a lorry driver was deemed guilty of misconduct when he was banned from driving as a result of a driving offence committed outside working hours. In *R(U) 2/77*, R. J. A. Temple emphasised that the essential requirement in establishing misconduct was the 'blameworthiness' of the employee. He, thus, defined misconduct as:

> '...conduct which is causally but not necessarily directly connected with the employment...[but] can fairly be described as blameworthy, reprehensible and wrong.'

Examples of misconduct are acts of dishonesty, assaults on fellow employees and others, arson and continued absenteeism for no legitimate reason.

If a claimant is dismissed from a job, then the length of the disqualification from JSA (the 'sanction period') is governed by s.19(3) and JSA reg. 70 and will last between 1 to 26 weeks depending on the seriousness of the misconduct. If the dismissal is from a compulsory training scheme or employment programme s.19(2) establishes that it will be for two weeks in the first instance and four weeks for subsequent dismissals.

*Failure to apply for or take up a job or to take up a place on a compulsory training scheme or employment programme*

If a claimant fails to take up a job offered or fails to apply for a job (or take up a scheme or programme place), the Employment Service may conclude that the claimant is not really available for or actively seeking week and JSA will be withdrawn unless he can show that there was 'good cause'. Governed by s.19(6) JSA 1995 and JSA reg. 72, the definition of good cause is the same as for 'voluntarily leaving' as defined above as are the periods of sanction.

*Failure to carry out a jobseeker's direction*

In contrast to the three previous forms of voluntary disqualification, this is a new ground for sanctioning claimants, first introduced in October 1996. A jobseeker's direction is a written statement that can be issued at any time by an Employment Service officer to a claimant setting out specific activities that the claimant is required to take to assist him/her to obtain employment. Designed to improve a claimant's 'employability', such steps can include a direction to apply for a specific vacancy, attendance at a course to improve jobseeking skills or motivation or a requirement to improve appearance or behaviour in order to present an acceptable appearance to employers. Any such direction must be reasonable, though this is not defined in the legislation or regulations. The sanction period is, per s.19(2), two weeks disqualification in the first instance and four weeks for subsequent instances.

## The New Deal requirements

While the details of the New Deal are set out in Chapter 6, it is important to appreciate that failure to comply with its requirements can lead to claimants being disqualified from benefit. The scheme is currently compulsory for certain categories of claimant, such as 18–24 year olds who have been continuously claiming JSA for 26 weeks or more and long-term unemployed aged over 25 while certain other groups of claimants can opt for the New Deal at an earlier stage. Either way, for such claimants, once entering the New Deal, it is mandatory, so that those who refuse to take up an option by the end of the gateway period or who refuse or leave a subsidised job or other New Deal option without good cause or are dismissed for misconduct suffer a 'New Deal sanction'. Reflecting the sanction period for failure to carry out a jobseeker's direction, the sanction for claimants aged 18–24 years old is disqualification from receipt of benefit for two weeks in respect of the first breach, while subsequent breaches will earn a four-week sanction. For other claimants compulsorily on the New Deal programme, such as the long-term unemployed aged 25 or over, the normal JSA sanction of up to 26 weeks' denial of benefit applies if they refuse or leave a subsidised job without good cause or are dismissed for misconduct. During the sanction period, claimants will only be eligible for hardship payments if they are in a 'vulnerable group' (see the next section). It is, though, important to note that for some New Deal participants, e.g. lone parents, such sanctions do not apply (see pp. 132–3).

## Hardship payments

Another important change introduced by the Jobseeker's Act 1995 relates to benefit payment during the sanction period. Prior to October 1996, under the unemployment benefit and income support schemes, claimants who were voluntarily disqualified would lose entitlement to unemployment benefit but would have a right, if they satisfied the means test, to income support, albeit at a reduced rate. While the amount of income support received varied depending on the circumstances of claimants, the reduced rate was referred to as the '40% rule' because, in most cases, income support would be reduced by an amount equal to 40% of the personal allowance for a single person. From April to October 1996 this was £47.90 for claimants over 25, therefore the deduction would, in most cases, have been £19.16. Under JSA, however, there has been an important reduction in eligibility. There is no such *automatic* entitlement to JSA benefit. A discretionary *hardship payment* is paid only if a claimant can show that a member of his/her household would suffer hardship. Under JSA reg. 140(2), the Benefits Agency will only provide a hardship payment if it can be proved that the claimant or partner will suffer hardship if no payment is made. JSA reg. 140(2) requires the Benefits Agency, when deciding whether hardship exists, to consider the resources available to the household, whether a member of the claimant's family is so ill or disabled that they are eligible for a disability premium under income-based JSA and whether there is a risk that essential items such as food, clothes, heating and accommodation cannot be purchased and, if so, for how long. If refused, a claim for such a payment can be made every fortnight.

JSA reg. 142 stipulates that claimants cannot claim a hardship payment for the first two weeks of a sanction period unless, per JSA regs 140 and 141, they fall into one of a number of vulnerable groups such as whether there is a child, pregnant or disabled or chronically ill person in the family or if the claimant or partner has caring responsibilities. If a hardship payment is made, claimants will receive the applicable amount to which they are eligible under income-based JSA less 40% of the single person's allowance or less 20% if any member of the family is pregnant or seriously ill. The practical operation of hardship payments is explained as follows.

'When considering hardship an AO will have regard to the resources available to the claimant which may include how much food is in the freezer, the amount of any savings (even if below the IS capital allowances), the support the claimant can receive from another member of the household, the paper round earnings of children, etc. The AO has to consider whether these resources will cover essential items such as food, clothing, heating and accommodation. It is suggested that accommodation costs will only be considered if there is an immediate risk of eviction.' (Howard, 1996, p. 1071)

## Back to work bonus

A major criticism of the way benefits were provided for the unemployed prior to the introduction of JSA was that there was little incentive for claimants to undertake part-time work as a way of re-entering the labour market because, aside from a small amount of between £5 and £15 per week being disregarded, any earnings would be deducted from the amount of benefit received. The *back to work bonus* is an attempt to encourage claimants to undertake part-time work.

Introduced by s.26 JSA 1995, the back to work bonus is a tax-free lump sum of a maximum of £1,000 that a claimant of JSA or income support can earn through part-time work while claiming benefit. It is paid when the claimant ceases to be eligible for benefit, most notably if he/she returns to full-time work. Under regs 1(2), 7(1) and 7(6) of the Social Security (Back to Work Bonus) Regulations [SS(BTWB) Regs], a claimant must have been entitled to JSA or income support for a 'waiting period' of at least 91 consecutive days (13 weeks) to qualify for the bonus. After this 13-week waiting period, any money that a claimant or partner earns while working part time can be accumulated towards the bonus. However, of any income earned during a week, that which is disregarded for benefit purposes cannot be taken into account for the purposes of the bonus. For single claimants the first £5 of any weekly earnings is disregarded, for a claimant with a partner £10 is disregarded while for some categories of claimant, such as lone parents or where there is a disabled person in the family, £15 is disregarded. Any other earnings, which are set against benefit entitlement with a consequent reduction in the amount of weekly benefit equivalent to the amount in question, can contribute to the back to work bonus.

Thus, while claiming benefit, i.e. while working fewer than 16 hours or where a partner is working fewer than 24 hours, a claimant can accumulate a maximum of £2,000 of any earnings towards the back to work bonus. The bonus can then be obtained when the claimant satisfies the *work condition*. SS(BTWB) reg. 7(1) stipulates that this is satisfied when the claimant starts working for at least 16 hours a week or, if receiving income-based JSA or income support, the partner of a claimant commences working for at least 24 hours a week as, in either case, entitlement to benefit ends. Under reg. 8(1), the amount of bonus claimants can obtain is half the amount of earnings they have been credited with when engaged in part-time work while claiming benefit, the maximum amount therefore being £1,000 (i.e. half of £2,000). Any claim for a bonus must be made within 12 weeks of ceasing to be eligible for benefit.

## Contributory jobseeker's allowance

There are some important features in respect of eligibility that only apply to contributory JSA. Thus, as a contributory benefit, a claimant must satisfy the necessary *contribution conditions*. These are outlined in Chapter 3. Contributory JSA is paid for a maximum of 26 weeks, in contrast to its predecessor which, until April 1996, was paid for a maximum of 52 weeks. If a claimant is subject to a sanction period for voluntary disqualification or other reason, rather than delaying the 26-week period, it counts as part of the 26 weeks. Thus, any claimant who is subject to a maximum sanction period of 26 weeks loses all entitlement to contributory JSA.

Another important feature of contributory JSA concerns the reductions in the amount of weekly benefit received by claimants in contrast to its predecessor, unemployment benefit. The first reduction concerns the abolition of the partner's addition. Under unemployment benefit, claimants with a partner received an additional payment on top of the normal weekly rate. From April to October 1996 this was an addition of £29.75 per week to the weekly rate of £48.25. This has been abolished for contributory JSA, the standard weekly rate applying to both single claimants and those with partners.

The second reduction is that contributory JSA is paid at a lower rate to claimants under 25. This brings it into line with the operation of income support in recent years and means that the weekly rates for contributory JSA and the personal allowances for income-based JSA are the same. The rates are set out in the appendix. For contributory JSA, it is, however, important to note that weekly benefit is reduced, per s.4(1) JSA 1995 and JSA reg. 81(1), by the full amount of any occupational or personal pension a claimant receives in excess of £50 per week.

## Income-based jobseeker's allowance

Income-based JSA is paid to unemployed claimants who are 'available for, and actively seeking, work' and whose income and capital are such that they satisfy the means test. There are three categories of eligible claimants:

(a) Those who are not eligible for contributory JSA because they do not satisfy the contribution conditions.
(b) Claimants of contributory JSA whose lack of other resources may make them eligible for income-based JSA to top up contributory JSA.
(c) Claimants of contributory JSA who remain employed after 26 weeks. They lose entitlement to that benefit, becoming eligible for income-based JSA if they satisfy the means test.

The means test is the same as for income support. Income support is the benefit for which claimants who are not required to be 'available for, and actively seeking, work' are eligible and which was the benefit that income-based JSA claimants would have received prior to October 1996. There is, however, an important change in comparison with the pre-October 1996 set up. For income-based JSA a claimant's partner can work for up to 24 hours per week without ending the claimant's entitlement, although any earnings will affect the amount of benefit received. The details of the means test are set out in Chapter 6.

It is important to appreciate that income-based JSA is a 'passport' benefit whereby recipients of the benefit are automatically entitled to a number of other benefits, free prescriptions and legal aid. Such eligibility is the same as for recipients of income support (see p. 22 for details).

**Urgent cases payment**

Under JSA reg. 147 a claimant who, under the normal rules, is not eligible for income-based JSA may be able to obtain an urgent cases payment if he/she is a 'person from abroad' or if the claimant is treated as possessing income which is due but which has not yet been received.

## Conclusion

The Jobseeker's Act has possibly been the most important single reform to the British social security system since the 1945–51 Labour government largely implemented the Beveridge proposals. The reasons put forward for such a major change are set out as follows:

> 'The Act put into effect the stated principles of the White Paper which preceded it. The stated aims of the scheme are:
> – a common system of rules for the unemployed;
> – measures to help people back to work;
> – making a clear link between looking for work and receiving benefit;
> – better value for taxpayers, i.e. "targeting", which is DSS speak for cutbacks.' (Howard, 1996, p. 1070).

Measures such as the jobseeker's agreement, building on previous stipu-
lations such as the need to be 'actively seeking work' along with the
reduction in the period of eligibility for the contributory element of JSA
to 26 weeks might be deemed to be examples of 'helping people back to
work' and 'making a clear link between looking for work and receiving
benefit' by the advocates of the Act. An alternative interpretation of the
motive behind the changes introduced by the Act is that they were
designed both to further reduce public expenditure on social security and
to provide a social security system that does not distort the labour market
or, to put it another way, seeks to force participation in a low wage labour
market. Certainly, this latter objective is highlighted in the following
observation:

'Notwithstanding the new back to work bonus, there is little doubt that
the introduction of JSA signals an even harsher climate for unemployed claimants. Many will lose out financially; the labour market
conditions are expected to be applied even more harshly than at
present (with a less taut safety net); and rates of remuneration for
claimants who do not get work are likely to be driven down even
further.' (Thomas, 1996, p. 20)

The long-term consequences of moving to a deregulated low wage economy, along with the associated desire to reduce public expenditure on
social security, are outlined in the following comment on the Jobseeker's
Act 1995:

'Quite what the Jobseeker's Act is supposed to contribute towards
creating jobs is unclear. Yet many would argue that it is the lack of
secure jobs paying anything like a decent wage that is the problem, not
the innate reluctance of unemployed people to work. Although some
measures – such as the simplification of benefit rules and the introduction of the 'back-to-work bonus' – are welcome, the new benefit regime
promises to increase hardship for unemployed people. Together with
incapacity benefit, we appear to be witnessing a wholesale withdrawal
of state support for long-term unemployed people and the undermining of the contributory principle more generally.' (Barnes and Witcher,
1995, p. 16)

Despite these criticisms, the Labour government that came to power in
May 1997 did not seek to reform jobseeker's allowance. The government's
Welfare to Work strategy, initiated within weeks of assuming power, sees
the acquisition of a job as the major solution to the problems of many
benefit recipients. As such, its approach has been to establish the New

Deal strategy with the aim of incorporating a large number of employers into the New Deal. The jobs offered to benefit claimants under the New Deal have the obvious advantage, for its supporters, of introducing many to the rigours of the workplace but it also opens up the possibility that employers may retain some individuals when their New Deal period of employment comes to an end. Advocates of the New Deal thus argue that, as well as conditioning claimants to the demands of work, the strategy may generate more jobs which, with the implementation of a national minimum wage, means that the level of remuneration is adequate by imposing some form of regulation on the level of wages.

Such a view, however, is radically different to that of the critics of jobseeker's allowance referred to earlier who observe that, inter alia, the government has no plans to reduce the harshness of the labour market conditions imposed on recipients of JSA. In fact, the introduction of the New Deal has seen such conditions made even more severe with the addition of 'New Deal sanctions' which result in some claimants receiving no benefit at all if they opt out of the scheme. From this perspective, the current Labour government's approach to social security is seen as little different to that of its Conservative predecessors.

## Bibliography

Barnes, M. and Witcher, S. (1995) 'The new seekers', *Poverty*, 91.

Beveridge, W. (1942) *Social Insurance and Allied Services*, Cmnd 6404, HMSO.

Howard, H. (1996) 'Jobseeker's allowance'. *Solicitors Journal*, 8 November.

Ogus, A. I., Barendt, E. M. and Wikeley, N. J. (1995) *The Law of Social Security*, 4th Edition, Butterworths.

Thomas, D. (1996) 'Jobseeker's allowance', *Legal Action*, October, p. 20.

# 5 Income Support

## Context and Commentary

Income support is a non-contributory, means-tested benefit paid to claimants who are not in full-time work and who are not required to register for work. The role of income support in the British social security system was substantially reduced as a result of the introduction, in October 1996, of jobseeker's allowance. Prior to that date, income support was the principal means-tested benefit available to all claimants who were not in full-time work, both those who were required to register for work and to be available for, and actively seeking, work and those, such as lone parents, the disabled and pensioners, who were not required to satisfy such conditions. Since October 1996, income-based jobseeker's allowance has replaced income support in respect of all claimants who are required to register for work leaving income support as the means-tested benefit for claimants who do not work full time and are not required to seek work.

## Historical introduction

The proposals contained in the Beveridge Report and largely implemented by the 1945–51 Labour government saw a very limited role for a non-contributory, means-tested benefit to act as a safety net for what was envisaged would be a small number of people who would not be eligible for one of the comprehensive set of contributory (i.e. national insurance), non-means-tested benefits. However, as explained on pp. 45–6, national assistance, the safety net means-tested benefit introduced by the National Assistance Act 1948, quickly assumed a much more substantial role in the post-war social security system than Beveridge had envisaged. The main reason for this was that, in the post-war period, the level of insurance benefits never exceeded the minimum income guaranteed by national assistance (and its successors supplementary benefit, income support and income-based jobseeker's allowance). As a consequence, this means-tested benefit assumed the central role in social security, providing financial support to those ineligible for any national insurance benefit as well as topping up the income of national insurance benefit recipients if they had little or no other income. In other words, national insurance benefits were paid, by and large, at a rate lower than national assistance (and its successors), resulting in many claimants who lacked sources of income other than their national insurance benefit (such as unemployment benefit or state pension) being able to top that benefit up with national assistance.

The Labour Government of 1964–70 implemented reform under the Ministry of Social Security Act 1966 (later called the Supplementary Benefit Act 1966) replacing national assistance with supplementary benefit. The Act sought to reduce the amount of discretion that officials had. Thus it established a *right* of claimants to benefit. The Act's other main reform was to place the administration of the new scheme in the hands of the Ministry of Social Security, which later became part of the Department of Health and Social Security. The 1966 Act also set up the Supplementary Benefits Commission, a body independent of government, to monitor the operation of the supplementary benefits scheme, part of whose responsibility was the provision of Annual Reports suggesting possible reforms and improvements.

With the election of a Conservative Government in May 1979, major changes in social security took place reflecting its philosophy of reducing both the role of the state and public expenditure levels. This lead, inter alia, to the Fowler Review of the social security system in the mid-1980s, instigated by the then Secretary for Social Security, Norman Fowler. One consequence of this was the Social Security Act 1986. This Act replaced supplementary benefit with income support, tightening up eligibility and reducing entitlement, e.g. weekly rates for income support were reduced for claimants under 25 while the Social Security Act 1988 raised the basic age of entitlement for income support from 16 to 18. The last major reform of the social security system by the 1979–97 Conservative government was contained in the Jobseekers Act 1995. This lead to the jobseeker's allowance replacing unemployment benefit and income support in October 1996 as the social security benefit for the unemployed.

## The Legal Rules

Income support is the principal means-tested benefit available to claimants who are not in full-time work and are not required to be available for, and actively seeking, work. Eligible claimants are thus individuals such as single parents, the disabled and pensioners who are not required to be in the labour market in the sense of being required to look for a job. The main statutes in respect of income support are the Social Security Contributions and Benefits Act 1992 and the Social Security Administration Act 1992 though the detailed rules of entitlement are largely set out in the Income Support (General) Regulations, as amended, supplemented by a number of other sets of regulations.

## Conditions of entitlement

Under ss.124 and 134 of the Social Security Contributions and Benefits Act 1992 as amended by Schedule 2 of the Jobseekers Act 1995, the principal conditions of eligibility for income support are that a claimant:

(i)   is present and habitually resident in Great Britain; and
(ii)  aged 16 or over; and
(iii) is not in full-time education; and
(iv)  must not have income exceeding the 'applicable amount' nor more than the prescribed capital (i.e. satisfies the 'means test'); and
(v)   is not engaged in remunerative work and, if a member of a married or unmarried couple, the other member is not so engaged; and
(vi)  falls within one of the prescribed categories of people eligible for income support; and
(vii) is not entitled to jobseeker's allowance and, if a member of a married or unmarried couple, his/her partner is not entitled to income-based JSA.

### *Present and habitually resident in Great Britain*

A claimant of income support must normally be present in Great Britain although under, reg. 4 of the Income Support (General) Regulations, it is possible to receive income support while absent from Great Britain for a short period if entitlement to income support exists before leaving the country, the absence is not expected to be for more than a year and the claimant continues to satisfy the other conditions of entitlement. Under reg. 4(2)(c), income support can be paid for the first four weeks of such absence abroad if:

(i)   the claimant is in Northern Ireland; *or*
(ii)  the claimant and partner are both abroad and the partner qualifies for a disability premium, severe disability premium or one of the pensioner premiums; *or*
(iii) the claimant has been incapable of work during the 364 days before going abroad or for 196 days if terminally ill; *or*
(iv)  the claimant is incapable of work and is going abroad for the purpose of receiving treatment for the incapacity from an appropriately qualified person.

Under reg. 4(1) and (3), a claimant may be absent for up to eight weeks and continue to receive income support where the claimant is accompanying a child, who is part of the family, for the purposes of medical treatment.

A claimant must also be 'habitually resident' in what is known as the Common Travel Area, which constitutes the UK, the Channel Islands,

Eire and the Isle of Man. This controversial condition was introduced in 1994 and applies to JSA, housing benefit and council tax benefit as well as to income support. The test applies to both foreign and British nationals. The phrase 'habitually resident' has not been defined either statutorily or in the regulations although it is designed to require some form of intention to normally reside in the UK. A Social Security Commissioner's decision in *CS/1067/1995*, while stressing that a complete definition of habitual residence was not possible, set out a number of criteria to assist in reaching a decision in individual cases. This is examined in detail in Chapter 6. Some people, however, are automatically treated as satisfying the habitual residence test. Thus, under IS reg. 21(3), EC nationals with 'worker status' or the 'right to reside' under EC Directives are deemed to be 'habitually resident'.

## Age

Under s.124(1)(a) of the Social Security Contributions and Benefits Act 1992 as amended by Schedule 2 of the Jobseekers Act 1995, a claimant must be aged 16 or over in order to be eligible for income support. This contrasts with jobseeker's allowance, where claimants aged under 18 can only receive JSA in limited circumstances (see pp. 78/9). This distinction, however, reflects a major trend contained within the reforms of the 1979–97 Conservative government of reducing the eligibility of young people for social security benefit. For example, the Social Security Act 1988 terminated the eligibility for income support of 16 and 17 year olds unless they fell into certain categories, who were not required to be available for and actively seeking work, and this is now reflected in the differential treatment of 16 and 17 year olds in respect of JSA and income support. Eligibility for JSA is normally attained at the age of 18, this benefit requiring claimants to be available for and actively seeking work, whereas income support, where these two requirements do not exist, can be claimed from the age of 16. However, income support claimants aged 16 or 17 usually receive a lower rate of benefit than claimants aged 18 or over. The single person personal allowance rate for 16 and 17 year old is, per paras 1 and 2 of Schedule 2 of the IS regs (April 1999 rates), £30.95 in contrast to £40.70 for claimants aged 18 to 25 (claimants aged 25 or over receive £51.40).

Under paras 1 and 2 of Schedule 2 of the IS regs, a claimant aged 16 or 17 is eligible for a higher rate (£40.70) if he or she:

- qualifies for a disability premium; or
- is an orphan with no one acting as a parent; or
- is living away from parents or any person acting as a parent for one of a number of reasons, e.g. to avoid physical or sexual abuse; there

is a serious risk to physical or mental health; the claimant is estranged from his/her parents.

In respect of couples, a higher rate can be paid where one of the couple is aged 18 or over.

## Not in full-time education

Under regs 4ZA and 61, a full-time student cannot claim income support while studying, including during vacation periods. Regulation 61 defines student as any individual aged under 19 and on a full-time course of advanced education (advanced education being courses of study above A level) and individuals aged 19 or over on any full-time course of study.

As well as this, any person under 19 and still studying full time in non-advanced education (i.e. up to and including A levels) is in what is defined as 'relevant education' and is, under reg. 6, usually ineligible for income support. A major issue that arises here concerns how 'full time' is defined. For 'relevant education', it is defined, under s.142 of the Social Security Contributions and Benefits Act 1992, IS reg. 12 and reg. 5(2) of the Child Benefit Regulations as requiring 12 hours per week of instruction and supervised study. Full-time advanced education is defined under reg. 61 as requiring 16 hours of 'guided learning' per week.

Two decisions of the Court of Appeal, *Secretary of State* v. *Webber* ([1998] 1 WLR 625) and *O'Connor* v. *Chief Adjudication Officer and Another* (Times Law Report 11 March 1999), have important implications on how 'student' is defined. both decisions would appear to be relevant to similar regulations in respect of jobseeker's allowance, housing and council tax benefit. In the *Webber* case, Mr Webber was studying a modular undergraduate course at Oxford Brookes University. As a result of failing some exams, he changed from a full-time to a part-time mode of study and made an application for income support. This was rejected by the Benefits Agency on the grounds that he was a student, under reg. 61, despite his claim that he was an unemployed person and it was accepted that he was 'available for work' (in current circumstances, he would need to apply for income-based JSA not income support). The Court of Appeal, however, accepted that Mr Webber was not a student for the purposes of income support eligibility:

> '...the Court of Appeal held that a person who at the material time was pursuing a modular course part time was not a "student" for the purposes of reg. 61 of the IS Regs and was therefore not disentitled to benefit. The fact that he had started the course full time – and was therefore a "student" at that time – did not mean that he remained a "student" until the end of the course [and while t]he period of issue

pre-dated the amendments to reg. 61...two of the [three] judges indicated that they might have come to the same conclusion under the current provision.' (Robertson and Thomas, 1997)

As indicated, reg. 61 was amended following this decision. It now defines a student as '...a person...aged 19 or over but under pensionable age who is attending a full-time course of study at an educational establishment; and...(a) a person who has started on such a course shall be treated as attending it until the last day of the course or such earlier date as he abandons it or is dismissed from it...'. In *Connor*, the Court of Appeal was required to interpret this amended regulation and appear to have arrived at a decision that conflicts with that in the *Webber* case. Damian O'Connor had begun a full-time degree course at Sheffield University in October 1993, which is normally completed in three years. However, he failed some of the exams in the second year. The university agreed that he could take leave absence for the following year and re-take the examinations as an external student, and resume the course the following year. He was not entitled to attend lectures during his 'leave of absence' nor was he to use any of the university's facilities nor did he receive any form of student funding. For part of that year he combined his studies with a job, but in December 1995 he was unemployed and claimed income support. He satisfied the requirements that he was available for, and actively seeking, work – like Webber, he would now come under the scope of income-based JSA. In a majority decision, the Court of Appeal decided that O'Connor was not eligible for benefit as he was a student, within the scope of reg. 61, as he remained committed to finishing the course. Addressing the clear dissatisfaction of this regulation expressed by the judges in the *Webber* case, Lord Justice Auld stated:

'There was no uncertainty in the words or purposes of the regulation; they required that a person who had abandoned a full-time course should be treated as attending it until its last day subject to his earlier abandonment of or dismissal from it, and were thus intended to cover periods of non-attendance for whatever reason so long as the person remained committed to finish the course. The position was put beyond doubt by the amendment of the regulation. Its clear purpose was to underline the deemed continuity of full-time student status even when interrupted, for whatever reason, for as long as a complete academic year or more.'

However, in respect of both advanced and non-advanced education, some people deemed to be students may nevertheless be eligible for income support. For claimants under 19 and in non-advanced education (this being deemed 'relevant' education) regs 4ZA and 13(2) stipulate that individuals in the following categories can claim income support if:

- the claimant is responsible for a child; or
- the claimant is so severely disabled that he or she is unlikely to obtain a job in the next 12 months; or
- the claimant has to live away from parents or any person acting as a parent for one of a number of reasons, e.g. to avoid physical or sexual abuse; there is a serious risk to physical or mental health; estrangement from parents; or
- the claimant lives apart from his/her parents or any person acting as a parent and they are unable to support the claimant and they are either in prison or unable to enter the country because of immigration status or are chronically sick or are mentally or physically disabled.

Income support can also be claimed, under regs 4ZA and 61 and Schedule 1B, by a student who is aged under 19 and on a full-time course of advanced education or is aged 19 or over on any full-time course of study if he/she falls into one of the following categories:

- he/she is a single parent or is a foster parent of a child under 16;
- he/she is disabled and is thus either eligible for a disability premium or severe disability premium or has been incapable of work for 28 weeks or is in receipt of a disabled student's allowance due to deafness;
- he/she is a pensioner;
- he/she is a refugee learning English or a student from abroad who is temporarily out of funds (the last of these can only receive an urgent cases payment);
- during the summer vacation only, he/she is one of a couple, both of whom are full-time students and who are responsible for at least one child.

## *The claimant satisfies the 'means test'*

The means test for income support is identical (except for some very minor differences) to that for income-based JSA and it also forms the basis for determining eligibility for other income-based benefits such as housing benefit. While the details of how entitlement is calculated is explained in greater detail in Chapter 6, it may assist understanding if its basic characteristics are set out here.

There are *three steps* necessary to calculate the amount of weekly benefit for which a claimant is eligible. The *first step* is to determine the *applicable amount* for which the claimant is eligible. This consists of three elements. The first is the *personal allowance*. The weekly amount of the personal allowance will depend on the claimant's circumstances, e.g. whether single or with a partner; the claimant's age – under 18, 18–25, over 25; whether there are any children and their ages. The second element of the personal allowance consists of *premiums*. These are additional amounts which are available if the claimant or a member of his family fall into a certain category e.g. if a claimant has any children he/she should be eligible for a family premium, claimants over pension age receive one of the pensioner premiums while a disabled claimant receives a disability premium.

The third element in determining the amount of personal allowance is to establish if the claimant is liable for any *housing costs* that are covered by income support. The main aspect of housing costs covered by income support is *mortgage interest* paid by an owner occupier who has a mortgage. Rents are not covered by income support, but come within the scope of housing benefit. Thus, for owner occupiers, the applicable amount will cover an amount in respect of interest on a mortgage.

The *second step* is to determine a claimant's *weekly income*. The income of the claimant (and, where applicable, partner and other members of the family) is calculated. Most types of income are included e.g. earnings, most other benefit payments, bank interest. Some income is, however, disregarded (e.g. £5 per week earnings of a single claimant). The *third step* is to compare income with applicable amount. If the claimant's income exceeds the applicable amount the claimant is not eligible for benefit. If it is less than the applicable amount, the claimant will be paid an amount necessary to bring the income up to the applicable amount, i.e. the difference between income and applicable amount. However, even if claimants' income is below the applicable amount, they may not be eligible for income support or income-based JSA if they have disposable capital of £8,000 or more. Some capital, however, does not count as disposable capital and this includes the family home. However, any disposable capital between £3,000 and £8,000 is deemed to generate a weekly *tariff income* of £1 for each £250 or part thereof above £3,000. This will be added to the claimant's weekly income to determine his/her eligibility under the means test.

## Not engaged in remunerative work

A person is not eligible for income support if he/she, or any partner, is engaged in remunerative work. Under reg. 5 there is no entitlement to income support if the claimant works 16 hours or more a week or if any partner works 24 hours or more a week. Regulation 5 defines remunerative work as work 'for which payment is made or which is done in anticipation of payment'. Where a claimant or partner is working less than the hours set out above, eligibility for income support continues, though an amount equal to any weekly earnings received (less a small 'earnings disregard', e.g. £5 for a single claimant and £10 for a claimant with a partner) will be deducted from the amount of weekly benefit that a claimant receives. Another important point is that the different number of hours used to define full-time work for claimants (16 hours or more) and partner (24 hours or more) means that, for some married and unmarried couples where both partners are working part time, it may be crucial which one claims benefit. Any person working 16 hours plus is ineligible for income support but can work up to 24 hours if the partner is the claimant. This is also true in respect of claiming income-based JSA.

Under reg. 6, a claimant or partner who works more than 16 or 24 hours respectively is not regarded as in remunerative work, and thus eligibility for income support continues, if the person in question is physically or mentally disabled and any earnings are reduced to 75% or less than would be the case but for the disability. This also applies where the number of hours worked are 75% or less than would be worked but for such disability. Similarly, income support eligibility continues, even where the claimant or partner works above the stipulated maximum number of hours, where the claimant or partner is caring for someone who gets attendance allowance or the middle or higher rate of disability living allowance (DLA) or where the claimant or partner is working as a childminder at home. There are other such exceptions including, inter alia, those doing voluntary work and those engaged as local authority councillors.

## Prescribed categories of people eligible for income support

Under reg. 4ZA and Schedule 1B, the prescribed categories of people eligible to claim income support are those who, prior to 7 October 1996, were not required to register for work or to 'sign on', i.e. to sign a declaration every fortnight that the claimant was available for, and actively seeking, work in order to claim the benefit. The prescribed categories include:

- lone parents with a child under 16 or single people looking after a foster child under 16;
- persons who are temporarily looking after a child under 16;
- carers who receive invalid care or who care for someone in receipt of attendance allowance or the higher or middle rates of DLA
- claimants who are incapable of work due to illness or disability who either:
  (i) satisfy the *own occupation* or *all work* test for incapacity benefit; or
  (ii) are in receipt of statutory sick pay; or
  (iii) are treated as incapable of work because, e.g. they suffer from certain severe medical conditions or have an infectious disease or are blind.

Recipients of JSA can be treated as capable of work for up to two weeks if they are unable to work due to illness or disability, which means that they continue to receive JSA and do not have to apply for income support during that period:

- claimants aged 60 or over;
- people who are registered blind;
- pregnant women who are incapable of work or who are within the period of 11 weeks before the expected birth of the baby or seven weeks after the birth;
- some categories of students who are disabled or who are parents or, in certain prescribed circumstances, who are living apart from their parents.

*There is no eligibility for income support if a claimant is entitled to jobseeker's allowance or, if a member of a married or unmarried couple, the partner is entitled to income based JSA.*

If a claimant or partner is an unemployed person who is required to be available for and actively seeking work then, under ss.1–3 of the Jobseeker's Act 1995, eligibility is for jobseeker's allowance and not income support while s.3(1)(d) establishes that if one partner is claiming income-based JSA, the other partner cannot claim income-based JSA or income support for the same period.

## Other Features of Income Support

Other than the main conditions of entitlement, there are further important features of income support that are covered in Chapter 6. Most importantly there are the means-test arrangements including, under s.137 of the Social Security Contributions and Benefits Act 1992, the principle of aggregation. These are important features of income support as they are for other income related benefits, and an essential feature of the practical functioning of the principle of aggregation is the *Cohabitation Rule* which is also discussed in Chapter 6.

Another significant element of income support is that while most housing costs, such as rents, are covered by housing benefit, there is one important exception to this, namely mortgage payments. Where financial support is sought by an owner occupier to meet the cost of a mortgage (and a number of other minor housing costs), this is covered, not by housing benefit, but by income support and, since October 1996, income-based JSA. Within both income support and income-based JSA, provision can be made to meet mortgage interest payments, but not any part of a mortgage covering repayment of capital.

As part of a policy of reducing eligibility, and seeking to switch responsibility for ensuring that individuals can meet mortgage payments in the event of not having a job, new rules on the payment of mortgage interest to people on income support came into force on 2 October 1995. The rules are set out in the duly amended Schedule 3 of the Income Support (General) Regulations. Income support has always only covered the interest element of any mortgage payment and not any repayment of capital. Before October 1996, only 50% of the mortgage interest was covered during the first 16 weeks of receiving income support after that all mortgage interest payment was paid, and, since August 1993, there has been an upper limit on the amount of the mortgage covered by income support. For most claimants this is £100,000. The same provisions in respect of mortgages also apply to recipients of income-based JSA under the JSA Regulations.

Under para 4 of Schedule 3, income support is not available if a loan was taken out to buy a home when either the claimant or another member of the family unit was in receipt of income support or income-based JSA. This also applies where a claimant or member of the family unit is receiving income-based JSA (per para 4 of Schedule 2 of the JSA Regulations).

However, the key provisions of the current rules, in operation since October 1995, on the payment of mortgage interest to people on income suport are:

- those taking out a mortgage after 2 October 1995 receive no help for the first 39 weeks of any claim, then full payment from week 40;
- those who have taken out a mortgage before 2 October 1995 receive no help for the first eight weeks of any claim, then payment of 50% from week 9 and full payment from week 26;
- all payments are calculated using a standard rate of interest. This may be substantially less than the rate of interest actually paid by a claimant;
- special provision is made for persons aged 60 or over and for some other claimants;
- all mortgage interest is paid direct to the lender.

## Bibliography

Robertson, S. and Thomas, D. (1997) 'Recent developments in social security law', *Legal Action*, August.

# 6 General Provisions for Income-Related Benefits

## Introduction

For income-related (or means-tested) benefits, both the income and capital of the claimant, along with any income or capital of other members of his/her 'family', are used to determine whether the claimant's means fall below the prescribed level in order to be eligible for benefit. One important feature of the main income-related benefits of the British social security system, such as income-based jobseeker's allowance, income support (IS), housing benefit (HB), council tax benefit (CTB), working families tax credit (WFTC) and disabled person's tax credit (DPTC), is that the same standard means test, albeit with some variations, is used to establish eligibility for all of these benefits. Prior to 1988, this was not the case. One of the consequences of the major review of social security in the mid-1980s initiated by Norman Fowler, then Secretary of State for Social Security, was the call for restructuring of the various means-tested benefits. There were over 50 means-based benefits and associated forms of government assistance, which had evolved on a piecemeal basis, resulting in a wide variety of different and differing means tests. This created a highly complex patchwork of different means tests where eligibility varied considerably, which was both confusing and somewhat arbitrary to claimants. The Social Security Act 1986, which replaced supplementary benefit with income support, also established common rules of entitlement for the main means-tested benefits. These rules are now contained in the Social Security Contributions and Benefits Act 1992 and, as this is largely an enabling Act, in the specific sets of regulations that apply to each of the benefits. The Jobseekers Act 1995 extended these provisions to income-based jobseeker's allowance.

## The 'Family' and the Principle of Aggregation

### General features

Sections 123 and 124 of the Social Security Contributions and Benefits Act 1992 provide the general statutory basis that a person is entitled to an income-related benefit 'if he has no income or his income does not exceed the applicable amount' (s.124(1)(b)).

The same requirement is made, specifically in respect of means-based jobseeker's allowance, in s.3(1) of the Jobseekers Act 1995. Section 134(1) of the 1992 Act also declares that:

'No person shall be entitled to an income-related benefit if his capital or a prescribed part of it exceeds the prescribed amount.'

Section 13(1) of the 1995 Act contains the same requirement for means-based jobseeker's allowance.

These two statutory provisions establish the means test for a single claimant but, where the claimant is living with others, the *principle of aggregation* requires that, in certain situations, the income and capital of these other individuals are aggregated, or combined, with the claimant's in order to establish eligibility for the benefit. The essential feature of the principle of aggregation is that the 'family' is the unit of aggregation. This is established by the combination of s.134(2), which states that:

'...the entitlement of one member of a family to any one income-related benefit excludes entitlement to that benefit for any other member for the same period'

and s.136(1), which establishes that:

'Where a person claiming an income-related benefit is a member of a family, the income and capital of any member of that family shall, except in prescribed circumstances, be treated as the income and capital of that person.'

Section 13(2) of the 1995 Act contains the same requirement for income-based jobseeker's allowance.

Thus, it is only the income and capital of the members of the claimant's family that are aggregated with the claimant's for means-testing purposes. Any person living with the claimant who is deemed not to be part of the family is not subject to the principle of aggregation. It is, therefore, important to establish how 'family' is defined and this is set out in s.137(1) on the 1992 Act and s.35(1) of the 1995 Act to include:

(a) a married or unmarried couple;
(b) a married or unmarried couple and a member of the same household for whom one of them is or both are responsible and who is a child or a person of a prescribed description.

One important feature of this definition is that the income and capital of any children can be aggregated with that of the claimant's in order to establish eligibility although, as is set out later in the chapter, there are some important exceptions to this general rule. Section 137(1) (and s.35(1)) also mean that any other person, such as an adult son or daughter or a grandparent, who resides with a claimant of one of the means-tested benefits is not a member of his/her family and is, thus, ignored for means-testing purposes.

Another important feature of defining 'family' is that any partner or child should normally be a member of the same household as a claimant in order to be a member of his/her family. The term 'household', though, is not statutorily defined. It is treated as an issue of fact to be determined in each case. An obvious aspect of this is that the person in question resides with the claimant but the intention of the parties is an important factor, for example, whether, although living in the same dwelling, they consider themselves as separate 'households'.

One of the most controversial aspects of the principle of aggregation has been the so-called *cohabitation rule* whereby unmarried couples are treated in the same way as married couples. If a man and women are considered to be an 'unmarried couple' they are deemed to be a 'family unit' for means testing and their resources are aggregated together. Both the existence of this rule and the way it has been implemented are contentious issues. They are examined in the next section.

## Living together as husband and wife: the cohabitation rule

Where a couple live together, only one of them can claim an income-related benefit on behalf of both and any family, while any claim for benefit will be based on their resources being aggregated together to determine eligibility. Another important feature of this rule is, per s.124(1)(c) of the 1992 Act and, for JSA, s.13 of the 1995 Act, that if a claimant's partner is in remunerative work (which normally means that he/she works 24 hours or more per week) there can be no claim for income-based JSA or income support. These requirements operate in respect of both married and unmarried couples, on the basis that they should be treated equally with, for example, no advantage accruing from the fact that a couple are not married. For these purposes, both s.137 of the 1992 Act and s.35 of the 1995 Act define an unmarried couple as:

> '...a man and woman who are not married to each other but are living together as husband and wife...'

The rationale for the rule is that married and unmarried couples should be treated equally, which would not be the case if married couples came within the definition of family for income-related benefits while unmarried couples did not, thereby allowing, inter alia, claimants who had unmarried partners in remunerative work to continue to receive benefit whereas similar placed claimants with married partners did not. To allow this, claim supporters of the cohabitation rule, would lead to an inducement for people not to get married. In contrast, critics claim that, in many other important financial matters, unmarried couples are treated more harshly, e.g. in respect of tax and pension matters. Thus, to justify the cohabitation rule on grounds of treating married and unmarried couples equally, argue its critics, is a misnomer.

The operation of this rule is well established in the British social security system and can be traced back to the 1925 national insurance widow's scheme. The Ministry of Social Security Act 1966, which created the supplementary benefit scheme, embodied the rule in legislation. The difficulty has been, however, that neither that Act nor any of its successors, including the current Social Security Contributions and Benefits Act 1992 and the Jobseekers Act 1995, has statutorily defined it. What has evolved is a piecemeal development of criteria to assist in determining whether cohabitation exists. In fact, in 1977, the terms 'cohabiting' and 'the cohabitation rule' were replaced, by the then Department of Health and Social Security and the Supplementary Benefit Commission, with the phrase 'living together as husband and wife'. This is still the official phrase, although it often continues to be referred to as the cohabitation rule.

## The definition of cohabitation

The definition provided in s.137 of the 1992 Act and s.35 of the 1995 Act establishes two basic points:

(i) It refers to a man and woman who are not married to each other. It therefore precludes any lesbian or gay couple being treated as an unmarried couple for the purpose of eligibility for income-related benefits. In such situations, the principle of aggregation does not apply.
(ii) The section requires that a couple are '...living together as husband and wife...'. However, it provides no criteria to determine when an unmarried couple's relationship is similar to that of husband and wife. Instead, a number of such criteria have evolved.

A major source of such defining criteria was the Supplementary Benefits Commission which, from 1966 to 1980, as part of its reviewing role of the supplementary benefits scheme, published a number of reports, including one in 1976 on the Cohabitation Rule entitled *Living Together as Husband and Wife*, as well as regular editions of the *Supplementary Benefits Handbook*, which were designed to give guidance on the administration of the supplementary benefits scheme. From these non-legal sources emerged a set of six criteria which have been adopted both by the judiciary and commissioners. Being incorporated into judgements has thereby led to these criteria achieving legal status. Thus, in *Crake* v. *Supplementary Benefits Commission* [1982] 1 All ER 498, Mr Justice Woolf referred to the then existing version of these criteria as '...an admirable signpost; the approach cannot be faulted.' A commissioner's decision in *R(SB)/81* also approved them and they are now contained in the *Adjudication Officer's Guide*. The criteria are:

1. *Members of the same household.* It might appear obvious that, in order for an unmarried couple to be deemed to be living together as husband and wife, they should be members of the same household and this was confirmed in the case of *R(SB)17/81*. However, the difficulty arises, as mentioned above, in that there is no statutory definition of household, so a major issue is determining whether or not persons who reside in the same dwelling are members of the same household or not. In *CIS/671/92*, the commissioner stated that this is 'very much a question of fact' to be established in each case. However, even where a couple share a household (e.g. by sharing costs), this does not necessarily mean that they are living together as husband and wife. The reason why the household is shared must be explored. Thus where two people are living as lodger and landlady, and as a result, sharing the same household, they are not living together as husband and wife. In *Robson* v. *Secretary of State for Social Services* (1981) 3 FLR 282 , for example, a couple who were both disabled were deemed not to be cohabiting where they were members of the same household in order to provide mutual support for each other. Another important decision, *R(SB)8/85*, established that a person cannot be a member of more than one household at any point in time.

2. *Stability.* The stability and duration of a couple's cohabitation is deemed to be relevant in determining whether they are living together as husband and wife in that the longer the relationship is evidenced to have existed, the greater can be the assumption that it is similar to a married couple's relationship. The main difficulty with this criterion is that the absence of stability or duration is not necessarily evidence that the relationship is different. Thus the 1976 Supplementary Benefits Commission report *Living Together as Husband and Wife* rejected the idea that a couple should be allowed to live together for a number of months before benefit is withdrawn, in order to allow the relationship to blossom. The report's viewpoint is reflected in the current provisions, yet can be criticised on the grounds that it results in the Cohabitation Rule, rather than saving finances, possibly incurring greater expenditure by the Benefits Agency. The withdrawal of (or reduction in) the benefit of one or other of an alleged cohabiting couple at an early stage in their relationship may lead to the relationship breaking up under the

financial pressure, resulting in a return to the previous levels of benefit. In contrast, if a relationship is given the opportunity to flourish for a period without the threat of benefit withdrawal, this may result, particularly where one of the parties is employed, in substantial savings if the other, as a result, ceased to claim benefit.

3.   *Financial support.* On the face of it, whether the couple provide financial support for each other would appear to be the central issue. After all, the rationale for the rule, and the principle of aggregation in general, is that the couple are a single economic unit. If the two alleged cohabitees maintain separate financial affairs, is it appropriate, therefore, for them to come within the scope of the Cohabitation Rule? One argument against such an approach is that to rely too heavily on whether the two keep their financial resources separate provides an incentive for cohabiting couples to arrange their finances accordingly and continue to receive benefit when they are in fact 'living together as husband and wife' and, for example, one of them is in full-time work. The current position reflects this viewpoint, so that whether the two pool their finances is merely one of the criteria to take into account as a relevant factor to determine the true nature of the relationship. The practical difficulties of this approach, however, are exemplified in the following statement:

> 'The approach to financial support seems to make almost any arrangement point the same way, except a very clearly fixed commercial rate. If the man pays a lot, he is supporting the woman. If he pays very little, this shows that the relationship is more than a commercial one. This makes it very difficult for parties who are friends, or where the man pays what he can afford, where the proper conclusion may merely be that the two people share a household. (Mesher and Wood, 1996, p. 26)

4.   *Sexual relationship.* Whether the couple have a sexual relationship is another criterion that is taken into account to determine whether an unmarried couple's relationship is similar to that of a married couple although it is the one that has generated the most controversy. On the one hand, the existence of a sexual relationship is deemed to be evidence that the relationship is akin to that of a married couple whereas its absence is strong evidence that it is not. Thus Commissioner Rowland, in *CIS/087/1993*, stated that:

> 'It does seem to me that there must be strong alternative grounds for holding a relationship to be akin to be that of a husband and wife when there has never been a sexual relationship, because the absence of such a relationship in the past does suggest that the parties may be living together for reasons other than a particularly strong personal relationship.'

Thus in the case of *CSB/150/1985*, where a claimant and his fiancée lived in the same house but, as Mormons, did not, as a matter of principle, have a sexual relationship, Commissioner Rowland held that the absence of any sexual relationship meant that they could not be described as living together as husband and wife.

Opposition to this emphasis on the existence, or otherwise, of a sexual relationship is the view that such an approach has resulted in unacceptable methods of investigation to verify its existence. Over the years, criticism has been made of 'sex snooping' investigating officers who would claim a couple were cohabiting if they had spent three consecutive nights together or who would call at the residence of an alleged cohabitee and pressurise him/her into admitting that there was such a relationship or would seek to enter a female claimant's bedroom for evidence of male underwear or socks! This has led to changes in the way investigating offices operate, with the *Guidance* now stipulating that interviewing officers should not ask direct questions about sleeping arrangements, such information only being taken into account if it is volunteered. The difficulty with this approach is that claimants may not be aware of the significance of the issue and thus not realise the importance of providing evidence to rebut the claim.

Another criticism of the prominence placed on the existence of a sexual relationship is that its practical operation may lead to individual officers operating on the basis of their own moral perceptions, punishing what they might regard as 'undeserving' claimants who do not have a relationship with another that can be deemed to be 'living together as husband and wife' other than the fact that there is an occasional sexual liaison. How widespread this might be is, obviously, difficult to gauge.

5.   *Children*. It is clear that if there is a child (or children) of the union between the parties then this is an important criterion in establishing whether the relationship is similar to that of a husband and wife, while shared care of children, where for example one of the parties is not a parent, is also relevant.

6.   *Public acknowledgement*. When the couple present themselves publicly as a couple is another relevant criterion. Thus, in *R(G)1/79*, the fact that the woman had adopted the man's surname on the electoral register was decisive in determining cohabitation. Other issues in establishing public acknowledgement include whether the couple go on holidays together or visit friends and relatives together.

It is, however, important to emphasise how these six criteria are used to determine whether cohabitation exists. In *CSB/150/1985*, Commissioner Penny stressed that:

'...it is not appropriate to consider the criteria as a kind of score card from which the answer to the problem...could be read straight off.'

Furthermore, in *CIS/087/1985* Commissioner Rowland stated that:

> '...it is the parties' "general relationship" that is of paramount importance...'

What the commissioners appear to be arguing is that the criteria have to be used in a sensitive way to try and gauge whether, in the particular circumstances of each case, the couple's general relationship is akin to that of a husband and wife. Thus, it is not appropriate to apply the six criteria in a mechanistic way to every case, according each of them equal status. Furthermore, although Commissioner Rowland argued in *CIS/087/1993* that:

> 'It does seem to me that there must be strong alternative grounds for holding a relationship to be akin to be that of a husband and wife when there never has been a sexual relationship...'

he stressed in *CSB/087/1985* that neither the issue of a sexual relationship nor the nature of any financial relationship are necessarily decisive in every case:

> '...their sexual relationship and their financial relationship are only relevant for the light they throw upon the general relationship.'

The upshot of all this would appear to be that the 'general relationship' is a very elusive concept which accords substantial discretion to decision makers in the Benefits Agency. While this provides fertile ground for claimants to appeal, the reality is likely to be that many claimants do not appeal and are deprived of benefit in circumstances when they may well have been able to successfully challenge a claim of cohabitation.

## Trade Disputes Disqualification

### Introduction

As part of the requirement that claimants who are deemed to be *voluntarily unemployed* are disqualified from benefit or receive a reduced rate of benefit, the social security system provides a much reduced entitlement for benefit for claimants who are not working due to a trade dispute. Under s.14 of the Jobseekers Act 1995, a person is not entitled to either form of jobseeker's allowance for any week during which he/she is involved in a trade dispute, neither is he/she eligible for statutory sick pay. However, under ss.126 and 127 of the Social Security Contributions and Benefits

Act 1992 and para 20 of Sch 1B of the Income Support Regulations, a claimant may, in certain circumstances, be entitled to income support at a reduced rate.

## Context and commentary

The trade disputes disqualification is a well-established aspect of social security provision though one that has always been controversial. The usual justification for its existence is that it is an example of *state neutrality* in industrial disputes. Thus Gennard comments:

> 'The general practice...has been that the State attempts to stand aloof from considerations of merits and relative power in disputes by using the provisions of the Welfare State to penalise both sides. On the one side, the access of strikers and their families to public assistance is restricted. On the other, the employer is prevented from using public employment exchanges to recruit strike-breakers.' (Gennard, 1977)

As part of this approach, *R(U)27/56* and *R(U)5/77* illustrate that adjudication officers (AOs) must not examine whether strikers had 'just cause' to withdraw their labour. To allow AOs to make such decisions on the merits of the dispute would, it is argued, erode the state's neutrality which would involve the officers having to make subjective decisions on a claimant's eligibility for benefit and this, quite simply, is not their function. This argument that AOs' role should not make subjective decisions about the merits of the claimant's lack of employment does, however, sit uneasily with the fact that in deciding whether a claimant should be disqualified from benefit if deemed to have voluntarily left a job, an AO must decide, under s.19(6)(c) Jobseekers Act 1995, whether the claimant had *just cause*, and, under s.19(5)(b), where he/she voluntarily gives up a place on a compulsory training scheme or employment programme, the officer is required to examine whether he/she had *good cause*.

It can be further argued that the current provisions do not, in fact, equate to state neutrality. Depriving or substantially reducing entitlement to benefit of a striker or someone who has been 'locked out' by his employer is a far heavier sanction than to deny employers use of Jobcentres to recruit strike-breakers. There are many other methods of recruitment available.

Another important consideration concerns the amount of benefit to which a claimant is entitled. No entitlement to JSA means that a claimant must make a claim for means-tested income support. If he/she does not satisfy the means test, no benefit is available. However, where eligibility for income support is established, the amount that is paid is substantially reduced in comparison to general entitlement. The first feature of this is that any claim for income support (as was the case with its forerunner 'supplementary benefit') ignores the claimant in calculating entitlement. This means that single strikers are ineligible for benefit whereas strikers with dependants, such as a partner or children, are eligible to receive income support although the amount received is reduced to the extent that the striker's entitlement is ignored, i.e. the claimant is assumed not to exist when determining the amount of benefit. In 1980, however, the then recently elected Conservative government introduced a further reduction in benefit entitlement whereby it was to be assumed that all strikers would be in receipt of strike pay from a trade union whether or not this was actually received. This provision is currently contained in s.126(5)(b) of the Social Security Contributions and Benefits Act 1992 and para 34 of Sch 9 of the IS Regs, whereby a weekly figure of (in 1999–2000) £27.50 is further deducted from any amount of income support received. In the context of state neutrality, the obvious issue is that if the pre-1980 position of the state was neutral, how can the current set up also be neutral, with the additional deduction from benefits paid to a striker's family on the mere assumption that strike pay is paid irrespective of whether the claimant's union actually pays this strike money?

Increasingly, the myth of state neutrality is being replaced by a recognition that the constraints on strikers' benefit entitlement is, in fact, a policy of industrial or workplace discipline designed to discourage strikes. In fact, as long ago as 1974, the Conservative Political Centre published a document, *Financing Strikers*, which played an important role leading to the 1980 reform, that argued that people who paid taxes and national insurance contributions that financed benefits should not be required to financially support those who withdraw their labour in a trade dispute as this can encourage industrial stoppages. The state should not bear the financial costs of strikes, rather the strikers and/or their trade unions should do so. Whether one's view is to embrace or reject this view, it is clear that this is a radically different justification for the trade disputes disqualification than to claim that it reflects state neutrality.

## The legal rules

Section 14 of the Jobseekers Act 1995 establishes that a claimant is disqualified from receiving jobseeker's allowance if he/she is involved in a trade dispute. This provision replicates s.27 of the Social Security Contributions and Benefits Act 1992 which is itself an amended version of s.19 of the Social Security Act 1975. The main rule, as contained in s.14(1), sets out that a claimant is ineligible for JSA if:

(i)   there is a trade dispute; and
(ii)  it was at the claimant's place of work; and

(iii)  it resulted in a stoppage of work; and
(iv)  the claimant lost employment as a result of the stoppage.

Under *R(U)/17/52(T)*, the onus is on the adjudication officer to prove, on the balance of probabilities, that these four criteria exist. If they are proved, there are a number of ways to avoid the disqualification, although the onus then falls on the claimant to establish that any one of them applies. These 'escape routes' are:

(v)  the claimant, per s.14(1), is not 'directly interested' in the dispute in the sense that he/she is not affected by its outcome; or
(vi)  under s.14(3)(a), he/she finds bona fide employment elsewhere which is subsequently ended and the claimant then seeks benefit; or
(vii)  the claimant, under s.14(3)(b), is made redundant; or
(viii) per s.14(3)(c), the claimant resumes work with the employer and subsequently leaves for another reason.

It is necessary to examine each of these points in turn, commencing with the four aspects of the main rule:

(i) **Trade dispute**. This is the first thing to establish because, if a trade dispute is deemed not to exist, there can be no trade dispute disqualification and the other criteria, therefore, do not apply. Section 27(3)(b) of the Social Security Contributions and Benefits Act 1992 defines a trade dispute as:

> '...any dispute between employers and employees, or between employees and employers, which is connected with the employment or non-employment or the terms of employment or the conditions of employment of any persons, whether employees in the employment of the employers with whom the dispute arises, or not.'

This definition includes strikes, lockouts and demarcation disputes while there is no stipulation that the claimant needs to be actually participating in the dispute. The dispute must, however, refer to the employment or non-employment of persons or the terms or conditions of employment, and that has been interpreted, in *R(U)5/87*, to be wide enough to embrace any dispute that is connected with the manner in which employment is carried out, e.g. a dispute about safety procedures (*R(U)3/71* and *R(U)5/77*). However, as highlighted in *R(SSP)1/86*, in order to reflect the notion of neutrality, defining whether a trade dispute exists or not should not involve assessing the merits of the dispute by, for example, passing judgement on which of the parties in the dispute was correct.

(ii) **Place of employment**. This requires that the trade dispute must be at the claimant's place of employment. The onus is on the adjudication officer to establish what constitutes the place of employment which must be determined on the facts of each case e.g. in *R(U)4/58* a wide interpretation was adopted when the place of employment for a person loading ships was deemed to be the whole of the docks whereas, in *UD 5145/26*, a more restrictive interpretation was adopted when an engineering shop attached to a group of collieries but physically separated from them was deemed to be a separate place of employment from the collieries. This brings into focus s.14(5) which stipulates that:

> '...where separate branches of work which are commonly carried out as separate businesses in separate premises or at separate places of work are...carried on in separate departments on the same premises or at the same place, each of those departments shall...be deemed to be a...separate place...'

The onus of proof switches to the claimant to prove that there are separate branches of work so that there is no trade dispute in that particular branch where he/she is employed. This entails not only proving that there are separate branches of work where the claimant works and that these branches of work are carried out in 'separate departments' but also that it is common place throughout the industry in question or in similar businesses that they are carried out separately in separate departments or separate premises. Establishing common practice can create very difficult practical problems of evidence for a person to establish his/her claim. The case of *CU66/1986(T)* nevertheless illustrates the operation of this subsection. The claimant worked in the canteen of a Yorkshire colliery but was laid off because of the 1984–85 miners' strike. The commissioners accepted that she worked in a separate branch of work within the colliery and that a canteen can be regarded as a separate branch of work which is commonly carried out as a separate business in separate premises or at a separate place. The issue was whether the canteen was a 'separate department' within the colliery. Evidence was adduced that the canteen manageress was appointed by, and responsible to, the area catering management based elsewhere although applications for other canteen jobs went to the colliery's personnel manager and appointment was made by the manageress. Disciplinary matters were dealt with by the area catering management though the colliery manager would be kept informed. The profitability of the canteen was separate to that of the colliery. On the basis of these facts, the commissioners concluded that the canteen was a separate place of employment so that the canteen worker did not come within the scope of the trade disputes disqualification.

(iii) **Stoppage of work**. This requires a cessation of work by a substantial number of employees as result of an employment dispute, whereby work will not recommence until the dispute is settled:

'...a stoppage of work must be in the nature of a strike or lockout, that is to say it must be a move in a contest between an employer and his employees, the object of which is that employment shall be resumed on certain conditions. *(R(U)17/52(T))*'

The main difficulties centre around establishing when a stoppage commences and when it ends. Thus, in respect of commencement, it was stated in *R(U)1/87* that a stoppage of work constitutes '...a situation in which operations are being stopped or hindered otherwise than to a negligible extent'. As an illustration, a stoppage of work was deemed to exist in *R(U)7/58* when 38 out of 90 production workers withdrew their labour.

(iv) **Employment was lost as a result of the stoppage.** To be disqualified, it is not necessary that the claimant is participating in the trade dispute merely that he/she has lost employment as a result of the stoppage of work caused by the trade dispute. However, if a claimant lost employment for another reason there is no disqualification from benefit. In *Cartlidge* v. *Chief Adjudication Officer* [1986] 2 All ER 1, the Court of Appeal established, inter alia, that a claimant is deemed to have lost days of employment by reason of a stoppage of work only if this is the effective cause of his/her not working. Thus, if a there is an alternative cause, such as the employer's business closing due to factors unrelated to the trade dispute, the claimant should not be disqualified from benefit. However, commissioners' decisions have extended disqualification to include situations where they believe claimants have anticipated a stoppage and left employment to avoid disqualification – *R(U)30/55*.

If all four of these conditions exist, a claimant can still avoid the disqualification if he/she can satisfy one of the 'escape routes':

(v) **Not 'directly interested' in the dispute.** A claimant can avoid disqualification from benefit if he/she can prove that he/she is not directly interested in the outcome of the dispute that has caused the stoppage. 'Directly interested' is not statutorily defined but has been considered by the House of Lords in *Presho* v. *DHSS* [1984] 1 All ER 97. Lord Brandon explored a situation where workers, belonging to different unions, were employed by a common employer at the same place of work and the members of one union were engaged in a trade dispute. In this context, the issue was whether the members of the other unions were 'directly interested' in the trade dispute and Lord Brandon provided what is now the leading authority on this issue when he stated that the other workers are directly interested if two conditions prevail:

'The first condition is that, whatever may be the outcome of the trade dispute, it will be applied by the common employers not only to the group of workers belonging to the one union participating in the dispute, but also to the other groups of workers belonging to the other unions concerned. The second condition is that this application of the outcome of the dispute "across the board" ...should come automatically as a result of one or other of three things: first, a collective agreement which is legally binding; or, secondly, a collective agreement which is not legally binding; or, thirdly, established industrial custom at the place of work concerned.'

(vi) **Bona fide employment elsewhere**. If a claimant can show, under s.14(3)(a) that he/she obtained a job elsewhere by which he/she intended to permanently sever his/her employment relationship with the employer with whom there is a trade dispute and that job subsequently ended then he/she is not subject to the trade dispute disqualification.

(vii) **Redundancy**. If a claimant's employment is ended due to redundancy then, under s.14(3)(b), he/she is not subject to the disqualification.

(viii) **Resumption of work with the employer and subsequently leaves for another reason**. Section 14(3)(c) establishes that if a claimant is subject to the disqualification but then returns to work but subsequently ends employment for a reason unconnected to the dispute, he/she should not have the disqualification reimposed on him/her.

As well as this main provision of the trade disputes disqualification which covers situations where there is a stoppage of work, an additional disqualification, originally introduced by s.27(1)(b) of the Social Security Contributions and Benefits Act 1992 and now contained in s.14(2)(b) of the Jobseekers Act 1995, provides that disqualification also applies where a claimant withdraws his labour in furtherance of a trade dispute in circumstances where there is no stoppage and, in fact, even when the trade dispute does not apply to the claimant's own place of employment. In other words, the withdrawal of labour in furtherance of a trade dispute is enough for the disqualification to apply and it will continue for as long as the stoppage continues or as long as labour is withdrawn.

An important point concerning the disqualification concerns the period of time to which it applies. The first point to note is that a anyone disqualified or any partner is, under IS Reg 5(4), treated as in full-time work for the first seven days of any stoppage of work due to a trade dispute, and is therefore ineligible for benefit during that period. Secondly, under ss.14(1) and (2), the disqualification lasts for the duration of the period of the claimant's lack of employment due to the trade dispute. This contrasts with the general grounds for voluntary disqualification (see pp. 80–83) which last for a maximum of 26 weeks.

# General Rules Relating to the Means Test

## Context and commentary

The Social Security Contributions and Benefits Act 1992 sets out the main features for establishing financial eligibility for most means-tested benefits, with the Jobseeker's Act 1995 extending its provisions to income-based jobseeker's allowance. Common rules of entitlement to most means-tested benefits were established by the Social Security Act 1986 which came into operation in April 1988. The 1986 Act replaced supplementary benefit with income support as the main means-tested (or income-related benefit) within the British social security system. It was the culmination of the Fowler Reviews initiated in 1984, one of whose main objectives was the simplification of the main means-tested benefit, supplementary benefit, as well as to examine the potential for simplification of the general structure of means-tested benefits. The specific remit of one of the four review teams was to scrutinise the supplementary benefit scheme. This scrutiny was followed in June 1985 by a Green Paper and then a White Paper in December of the same year, the main proposals of which were then implemented in the 1986 Act. The supplementary benefit review team claimed that complexity was the main defect of the supplementary benefit scheme, examples of which were:

(i)   Over 500 pages of published regulations.
(ii)  In determining basic weekly rates of benefit, there were distinctions, such as the difference between 'householders' and 'non-householders' and between claimants on basic rate and long-term rate, which were often difficult to apply.
(iii) The existence of a substantial number of 'additional requirements' that individual claimants could, in certain circumstances, receive for items such as additional heating, dietary or laundry costs. The review team noted, for example, that over 90% of pensioner claimants received some form of weekly addition.
(iv)  The existence of a 'labyrinth' of rules to deal with the system of 'single payments' which claimants could receive for one-off needs that were deemed not to be covered under the weekly rates, e.g. if a claimant become pregnant she would be eligible for a single payment to meet the costs of purchasing a cot, baby bath, etc.

The Act implemented the general views contained in the Green and White Papers whereby the system of single payments was separated from that of weekly provision of benefit by the setting up of the Social Fund (see Chapter 13). Income support replaced supplementary benefit as the benefit designed to provide regular weekly income. One of the main changes was the replacement of the range of 'additional requirements' and various rates of benefits based on the individual circumstances of claimants with a simplified system of 'premiums' paid to different 'client groups'. Premiums are fixed-rate amounts paid in addition to standard weekly 'personal allowances' if a claimant falls into one of the client groups. Thus premiums are, for example, paid to claimants who have a family or are disabled or who have a disabled child or are lone parents or are pensioners. In other words, if a client falls into one of these groups he/she is eligible for a fixed-rate premium. The system of premiums is less individualised than supplementary benefit's additional requirements in that premiums tend to be paid at one single rate whereas there were often a number of different rates of additional requirements for each category which were paid depending on an individual's particular circumstances. This has led to criticism of the system of premiums:

> 'Instead of an attempt, through supplementary benefit additional requirements, to tailor the level of benefits to the individual needs and circumstances of the claimant and his family, higher amounts of benefit are now targeted on fairly broad categories of claimant. In such a structure benefit may be adequate for those with routine and pre-dictable needs...but it is almost impossible to make it adequate for those with unusually high needs.' (Mesher. 1989, p. 146)

Another important feature of the Fowler reviews and the subsequent Green and White Papers, was the perception that the general structure of means-tested benefits needed simplification. The 1985 White Paper, for example, argued that the piecemeal development of the various means-tested benefits had resulted in '...a system of bewildering complexity, with different benefit levels, different eligibility rules and different rules of assessment.' (para 1.27). The Social Security Act 1986, therefore, intro-duced a common means test for the then five main income-related bene-fits – income support, family credit, disability working allowance, housing benefit and council tax benefit. While there remain some differences in the operation of these benefits, the consequence of the 1986 Act and, subsequently, the Social Security Contributions and Benefits Act 1992, is that there are common provisions for assessing a claimant's needs and resources in respect of all these benefits as well as in respect of the principle of aggregation (see pp. 100–102). The Jobseekers Act 1995 extended these common provisions to income-based jobseeker's allow-ance, and, from October 1999, it applies to working families tax credit and disabled person's tax credit (the replacements for family credit and dis-ability working allowance, respectively). However, at the time of writing the regulations for these two tax credits are not available and are, there-fore, not quoted in the following section setting out the relevant legal rules. Nevertheless, the central point is that there is a standard means test in respect of these income-related social security benefits.

## The legal rules

The first step in establishing eligibility for one of the means-tested benefits is to determine the claimant's *applicable amount*. Section 135(1) of the Social Security Contributions and Benefits Act 1992 stipulates that:

> 'The applicable amount, in relation to any income-related benefit, shall be such amounts as may be prescribed in relation to that benefit.'

This enabling provision means that the detailed provisions are set out in the appropriate regulations for each benefit.

For income-based JSA and income support, the applicable amount constitutes the amount by which the claimant and any dependants are expected to live on each week. If a claimant's weekly income is less than this, the amount of weekly benefit received is the difference between the income and the claimant's applicable amount. In respect of housing benefit and council tax benefit, the applicable amount is used to calculate how much assistance a claimant requires with his/her rent or council tax. Calculating the applicable amount is very similar for all these four benefits, and varies depending on the particular circumstances of each claimant whereas, in respect of both working families tax credit and disabled person's tax credit, the applicable amount is a fixed sum. For working families tax credit it is £90 per week as is the case in respect of disabled person's tax credit for couples or lone parents. For other single claimants, the applicable amount for disabled person's tax credit is £70 (April 1999 rates).

## Calculating the applicable amount

For income-based JSA, income support, housing benefit and council tax benefit working out the applicable amount is very similar, though the benefits do vary in respect of some significant points. Generally, all four benefits calculate the applicable amount on the basis of *personal allowances* and *premiums* while, in respect of income-based JSA and income support only, the applicable amount also covers *housing costs*.

**Personal allowances** are weekly rates deemed to meet a claimant's basic living expenses and they vary according to the claimant's age and whether he/she is one of a couple or a single parent or a single person. There are also additional allowances for any dependent children. The 1999–2000 weekly rates, which operate for 12 months from April 1999, are set out in the appendix.

**Premiums** are additions to personal allowances which are designed to assist with extra expenses incurred as a result of the age, disability or family responsibilities of the claimant or one of his/her dependants. The weekly rates of the various premiums are also set out in the appendix. The regulations covering premiums are, for the respective benefits, contained in Sch 1 of the JSA Regs and the CTB Regs and Sch 2 of the HB Regs and the IS Regs. One of the most important features contained within each of these schedules is that, for all four benefits, some premiums are paid in addition to any other premium. These are family premium, severe disability premium, disabled child's premium and carer's premium. In contrast, in respect of other premiums, only one of them can be paid to a claimant at any point in time. These include family premium (lone parent), disability premium, pensioner premium, enhanced pensioner premium and higher pensioner premium. If a claimant qualifies for more than one of these latter premiums, only the highest one is received.

*Family premium*. If a member of the claimant's household for whom he/she is responsible is a child or young person then, under the relevant schedule, the claimant is entitled to a family premium in addition to any personal allowances. Only one premium is paid irrespective of the number of children in the household. However, the premium is paid even though no personal allowance may be available for the child, e.g. because the child has capital over £3,000.

Since 6 April 1998, as part of the controversial strategy of reducing lone parent entitlement to benefits in order to encourage single parents to return to work, the higher 'lone parent' rate of family premium has been phased out, although those in receipt of it on that date will continue to receive it.

*Disability premium*. Disability premium is paid to a claimant aged under 60 if, inter alia, either he/she or partner:

(i)   is registered as blind; or
(ii)  is receiving a qualifying benefit. These are attendance allowance, disability living allowance, disability working allowance or mobility supplement and (if the claimant but not the partner is receiving benefit) severe disablement allowance or long-term rate incapacity benefit. Eligibility for a disability premium continues even if the overlapping benefit rules (see pp. 133–134) means that the claimant no longer receives the qualifying benefit as a result of receiving the disability premium; or
(iii) has an invalid trike or a DSS grant towards the cost of maintaining a car; or
(iv)  has been incapable of work for a period of 364 days (or 196 days if certified terminally ill).

If a claimant has a partner, the couple rate is paid if one or other satisfies the qualifying conditions.

*Disabled child premium*. This applies where a child is either registered as blind or is in receipt of disability living allowance and the child does not have capital exceeding £3,000.

*Severe disability premium*. Under para 18 of Sch 1 of the JSA Regs and para 14 of Sch 1 of the CTB Regs and para 13 of Sch 2 of both the HB Regs and IS Regs, a claimant is eligible for a severe disability premium (SDP) if all the following conditions are met:

(i) he/she is in receipt of a qualifying benefit, which are attendance allowance and the medium or higher rate care component of disability living allowance. If a claimant has a partner, he/she must also be either receiving a qualifying benefit or be registered as blind; and

(ii) no non-dependant aged 18 or over, such as an adult son or daughter, resides with the claimant (and partner). Some people who reside with a claimant are not regarded as non-dependants. These include anyone who is registered blind or is him/herself in receipt of a qualifying benefit; and

(iii) no person receives invalid care allowance (ICA) for looking after the claimant or, where there is a couple, no one is receiving ICA for looking after both the claimant and partner. Eligibility still exists, however, if someone is in receipt of ICA for looking after one member of a couple.

The couple rate is paid when both partners receive a qualifying benefit and no person is in receipt of ICA for caring for either or both partners.

*Carer premium*. This is paid to a claimant who is caring for another person and not to the person being cared for. A person is eligible for this premium if he/she is receiving invalid care allowance (see pp. 158–161) for caring for another person(s). A double premium can be obtained for a couple where both partners are caring for others. However, it is necessary to examine the impact of receiving ICA on any benefit entitlement of the person(s) being cared. If both the carer and the person being cared for are in receipt of a means-tested benefit, such as income support, then it is important to appreciate the potentially serious impact of the carer's receipt of benefit on that of the person being cared for. Any claim for ICA by a carer in receipt of income support only increases by the amount of benefit received by the addition of the carer's premium. In the year from April 1999 this is £13.95 per week. The reason for this is that any amount of ICA received leads to the deduction of an equivalent amount from the weekly rate of income support received. However, as mentioned in point

(iii) above, if the carer receives ICA, the person being cared for is not eligible for severe disability premium. As this constitutes £39.95 per week, the loss of severe disability premium is, in the circumstances, far greater than any carer's premium received.

*Pensioner premium*. This is paid at two rates depending on the age of either the claimant or partner. If one or other has attained the age of 60–74, the pensioner premium is payable whereas, if one or other has attained the age of 75–79, the enhanced pensioner premium is payable. The amount for a couple is paid in respect of either rate if only one of the couple satisfies the relevant age condition.

*Higher pensioner premium*. This is paid if *either* the claimant or partner is over 80 *or* a claimant or partner over 60 would be eligible for a disability premium but for age *or* the claimant was in receipt of a disability premium as part of any income support or income-based JSA within 8 weeks of his/her 60th birthday and has remained continuously entitled to one of these benefit since then (excluding breaks in entitlement of less than 8 weeks).

**Housing costs**. This aspect of determining the applicable amount applies only in respect of income support and income-based JSA. Under Sch 3 of the IS Regs and Sch 2 of the JSA Regs, both benefits can include certain types of housing costs in the applicable amount if the claimant or someone in his/her family is liable for these costs. Housing costs that are covered include:

- mortgage interest payments;
- interest on any loans to pay for repairs or improvements;
- interest in respect of a hire purchase agreements;
- rent or ground rent;
- payments under a co-ownership scheme.

Housing costs incurred in respect of rent are covered by the housing benefit scheme.

In order to include housing costs in a claimant's applicable amount, he/she must be liable to pay the relevant housing costs. The decision in *CSB/213/1987* established that the claimant does not have to be 'legally liable' for such costs. So, for example, if the legally liable person is not paying the costs and, as a result, the claimant is paying them in order to continue to live in the home then, if this is deemed 'reasonable', they should be included in his/her 'housing costs' for benefit purposes. Further-more, housing costs are paid in respect of the home in which the claimant normally lives and para 3(1) of Sch 3 of the IS Regs and Sch 2 of the JSA

Regs establish that it usually cannot be paid in respect of two properties, though there are some exceptions to this, e.g. if the claimant has recently moved home.

In respect of any mortgage or loan, income support and income-based JSA covers only the interest element and not any part of a payment that relates to repayment of the capital amount or the cost of any associated insurance premium (para 10 of Sch 3 of the IS Regs and para 9 of Sch 2 of the JSA Regs). It is also important point to note the existence of a number of significant restrictions in determining the amount of housing costs for the purposes of establishing a claimant's applicable amount:

(i)   The amount of interest actually paid is calculated on a standard rate which may be substantially lower than the rate of interest actually paid by a claimant.

(ii)  Upper limits exist in respect of any mortgage or loan. The most important of these is that for any person who makes a claim after 10 April 1995, any applicable amount relates to a maximum of £100,000. Any claimant who, for example, has a larger mortgage will only have interest relating to £100,000 as part of his/her applicable amount.

(iii) In the first weeks of any claim, reduced payments are made. For any claimant who took out any loan or mortgage before 2 October 1995, paras 1(2) and 6 of the relevant schedule of both Sch 3 of the IS Regs and Sch 2 of the JSA Regs establish that a claimant receives nothing for the first 8 weeks of any claim, 50% of any interest for the next 18 weeks and then payment for the full amount of interest after 26 weeks of receiving benefit. For claimants who take out a loan or mortgage after 1 October 1995, no payment to cover housing costs is made for the first 39 weeks of a claim, with the full amount of interest covered after that. However, under para 9 of Sch 3 of the IS Regs and para 8 of Sch 2 of the JSA Regs, where the claimant or partner is over 60 or the claimant is claiming for payments as a Crown tenant or under a co-ownership scheme, full payment is paid from the beginning of any claim. Also certain claimants are exempt from the 39-week waiting period, being subject to the 26-week period instead. These include a single parent who is claiming benefit as a result of a former partner leaving or where the partner has died (para 8 of Sch 3 of the IS Regs and para 7 of Sch 2 of the JSA Regs).

(iv)  Where any non-dependant lives with a claimant, a deduction is made from any housing costs based on the assumption that the non-dependent makes a contribution to the housing costs. A non-dependant is a person, such as an adult son or daughter or any elderly relative, who is not defined as a member of the claimant's family as determined by the *principle of aggregation* (see ss.134.137 and 137 of the Social Security Contributions and Benefits Act 1992 and pp. 100–102). Such deductions are made on the basis of the following scale for 1999–2000, the amount of deduction depending on the financial circumstances of the non-dependant.

*Non-dependants in remunerative work whose gross weekly income is*

| | |
|---|---|
| £255 or more a week | £46.35 per week is deducted |
| £204 to £254.99 a week | £42.25 per week is deducted |
| £155 to £203.99 a week | £37.10 per week is deducted |
| £118 to £154.99 a week | £22.65 per week is deducted |
| £80 to £117.99 a week | £16.50 per week is deducted |
| Below £80 a week | £7.20 per week is deducted |

*Non-dependants in non-remunerative work (including those in receipt of benefits) regardless of income*: £7.20 per week is deducted

No deduction is made for any non-dependant aged 16–17, or aged 18–24 and on income support or anyone in receipt of a youth training allowance.

## Determining a claimant's income

The second step in establishing whether a claimant is eligible for a means-tested benefit is to ascertain his/her weekly income. The rules for working out income are, as for the applicable amount, very similar for all six main means-tested benefits – income support, income-based JSA, working families tax credit and disabled person's tax credit, housing benefit and council tax benefit. In respect of the first four of these benefits, any claimant whose weekly income is less than his/her applicable amount is, subject to the rules on capital, eligible to receive the difference between the two amounts, while for housing benefit and council tax benefit, the means test helps determine the amount of benefit. In fact, recipients of income support or income-based JSA have, by receiving either benefit, automatically established their eligibility for housing benefit or council tax benefit.

The main elements in determining income are:

(i)   aggregation of the income of members of the family unit;
(ii)  treatment of different sources of income, including the disregarding of income.

### *Aggregation of the income of members of the family unit*

The general rule for these means tested benefits is that all of the income of the family (as defined in s.137(1) of the Social Security Contributions and Benefits Act 1992, see pp. 100–102) is aggregated together and regarded as the claimant's income. This means that any partner's income is added to that of the claimant (see JSA Reg 88 and IS Reg 23). However, there are, in respect of children and young persons, a number of exceptions to this general rule under JSA Regs 83 and 106, IS Regs 44 and 47, HB Reg 36 and CTB Reg 27. Whereas any maintenance paid in respect of a child constitutes the claimant's income, any *earnings* of a child while still at school do not usually count. Other forms of income of a child do count as the claimant's income up to the amount of any personal allowance or disabled child premium that can be claimed for the child. However, if the child has capital of more than £3,000, the claimant receives no benefit for him/her (other than any family or lone parent premiums) but any income of the child is disregarded in determining the claimant's income.

## Different sources of income and the disregarding of income

There is a variety of sources of income such as earnings, social security benefits, maintenance and income from capital. While the general principle is that all the income of a family unit is aggregated together to establish eligibility, the fact is that the different sources of income are treated differently with, e.g. a variety of different amounts that can be disregarded in establishing a claimant's income for benefit purposes. 'Disregarding' involves ignoring part of a claimant's income when calculating how much income he/she has to set against his/her applicable income, the consequence of which is that the amount of benefit received is unaffected by this 'disregarded' amount of income, e.g. a single claimant, with no dependants, is entitled to a £5 'earnings disregard'. This means that he/she can earn up to £5 per week and the amount of benefit received remains unaffected. Any amount earned above that figure is part of his/her income and reduces any weekly benefit by the amount above £5 that is earned, e.g. a single person earning £20 per week would have any weekly benefit received reduced by £15.

(a) *Earnings*. Under the relevant regulation for each benefit (e.g. IS Reg 35), earnings are 'any remuneration derived from...employment'. For social security purposes, earnings are calculated as net earnings, i.e. after income tax, Class 1 national insurance contributions and 50% of any payment in respect of an occupational or personal pension scheme. They include any bonus or commission, holiday pay, any compensation for unfair dismissal or for sex or race discrimination and, except for income support and income-based JSA, any sick pay. Some payments are disregarded in defining earnings, such as expenses 'wholly, exclusively and necessarily' incurred (e.g. travelling expenses) while payments in kind (e.g. petrol) are usually ignored. Some payments in relation to employment are, however, regarded, not as earnings, but as another source of income. This is important as it usually means less of that income is disregarded than in respect of earnings, leaving claimants receiving less benefit. Thus any occupational pension and maternity or sick pay are regarded as 'other income' and taken in full as income (i.e. none of it is disregarded in calculating a claimant's income). An advance of earnings or a loan is, in most cases, treated as income from capital.

*Earnings disregarded*. Some parts of a claimant's earnings are disregarded. However, the disregarding of earnings and other sources of income involves substantial variation between the different benefits. In respect of disregard of any earnings, whereas disabled person's tax credit and working families tax credit, like their predecessors disability working alliance and family credit, have no earnings disregarded (except for certain child care costs), the other benefits provide a number of different amounts to be disregarded. The highest disregard is in respect of housing benefit and council tax benefit, where a lone parent who is not in receipt of income support or income-based JSA can have £25 of any weekly earnings disregarded in calculating entitlement to either benefit. In respect of both income-based JSA and income support (and therefore also housing benefit and council tax benefit) a £15 disregard in respect of any weekly earnings of a claimant or partner applies if the claimant falls into one of a number of categories. These include the claimant or partner qualifying for a carer's premium or (in respect of IS and JSA) for a disability premium or (for HB and CTB) where either qualifies for a severe disability premium. There is also a number of situations where this disregard applies where the claimant or partner is over 60.

Other than in such situations, the basic disregard applies whereby a single claimant has a £5 disregard on any earnings received and a couple have a £10 disregard of the combined earnings of both. Details of the earnings disregards are contained in paras 6–12 of Sch 6 of the JSA Regs, paras 4–9 of Sch 8 of the IS Regs and paras 3–8 of Sch 3 of both the HB Regs and CTB Regs.

(b) *Social security benefits*. Most social security benefits are taken fully into account in calculating a claimant's income. These include contribution-based JSA, retirement pension, widow's pension, invalid care allowance, incapacity benefit and severe disablement allowance. However, there are some social security benefits that are ignored completely when calculating a claimant's entitlement to an income-related benefit. These include housing benefit, council tax benefit, attendance allowance, disability living allowance, disability working allowance, constant attendance allowance, social fund payments and child benefit (for working families tax credit and disabled person's tax credit, but not for income support and income-based JSA where it is taken fully into account). Some benefits are taken into account with a £10 disregard. These include war disablement pension and war widow's pension. Details on benefits as income are contained in Schs 7 and 8 of the JSA Regs, Schs 9 and 10 of the IS Regs, Schs 4 and 5 of both the HB Regs and CTB Regs (no regulations exist for WFTC and DPTC at the time of writing).

(c) *Maintenance payments*. Child support maintenance payments and any other maintenance payments from a former partner, whether in respect of the claimant or for any child(ren), are regarded as income. In calculating entitlement to income-based JSA and income support, there is no disregard in respect of such payments whereas, for working families tax credit and disabled person's tax credit, housing benefit and council tax benefit, £15 of any weekly maintenance payment is disregarded.

(d) *Other income*. Most other forms of income are taken into account, less any income tax, and, in some situations, national insurance contributions. All such income has to be converted into a weekly amount and, as for maintenance payments, rules exist where such income is provided in a lump sum. Another important source of income is discussed in the next section. This is capital under £8,000, which can be deemed to generate a 'tariff income'.

## Determining a claimant's capital

As well as establishing a claimant's income, it is also necessary to determine what capital he/she has. The main reason for this is that, if a claimant has capital in excess of the prescribed limit, he/she is ineligible for benefit whatever his/her level of income is. Thus, in respect of income-based JSA, income support and working families tax credit, a claimant who has over £8,000 of capital is ineligible for benefit (per JSA Reg 107, IS Reg 45 and FC Reg 28) while, for disabled person's tax credit, housing benefit and council tax benefit, ineligibility for benefit exists if a claimant has over £16,000 of disposable capital (HB Reg 37, CTB Reg 28). Furthermore, even if the claimant's capital falls below the prescribed limit, it can affect the amount of weekly benefit received. For all of these benefits, any capital held between £3,000 and the prescribed limit is treated as generating a weekly income which is then set against the 'applicable amount', leading to a reduction in the amount of benefit received (per JSA Reg 116, IS Reg 53, HB Reg 45 and CTB Reg 37). Known as the *tariff income*, it as assumed that each £250 (or part thereof) generates an income of £1 per week. Thus capital of £5,000 has a tariff income of £8 per week (£1 for each of the eight £250s above £3,000) while £5,001 of capital results in a tariff income of £9 per week (the £1 of capital in excess of £5,000 constituting a part of the next £250, leading to the additional £1 of tariff income). For claimants permanently living in residential care or nursing homes, the higher £16,000 prescribed limit also applies to income-based JSA and income support with the tariff income starting at £10,000. There is, however, a number of important issues in terms of what counts as capital.

The first point to note is that, while the principle of aggregation applies in respect of capital held by any partner, the capital of any child is not aggregated to that of the claimant (per JSA Reg 109, IS Reg 47, HB Reg 39 and CTB Reg 30). However, if a child has capital in excess of £3,000, he/she is ignored in determining the amount of benefit payable other than in respect of receiving any family premium.

While 'capital' is neither defined statutorily nor in the regulations, it relates to lump sum or one-off payments (as opposed to regular payments) and includes property and savings such as money in bank and building society accounts, stocks and shares, unit trusts and premium bonds. Certain types of property and land are, however, disregarded, most notably the home that the claimant lives in (per JSA Regs Sch 8 para 1, IS Regs Sch 10 para 1, HB Regs Sch 5 para 1 and CTB Regs Sch 5 para 1). There are other types of capital that are also disregarded including personal possessions such as jewellery, car and furniture as well as the value of any fund in respect of a personal pension scheme, while the surrender value of any life assurance or endowment policy is also disregarded. Under JSA Reg 111(a), IS Reg 49(a), HB Reg 41(a) and CTB Reg 32(a), the general rule is that capital is valued at its market value though, for some items, the surrender value (which is likely to be less than the market value) can apply.

One important aspect in defining capital is that a claimant can be deemed to have capital which, in fact, he/she does not have. Known as *notional capital*, this arises most often in situations where it is considered that a claimant has deliberately disposed of capital in order to be eligible for benefit or to increase the amount of benefit. (per JSA Reg 113, IS Reg 51, HB Reg 43 and CTB Reg 34). To come within the scope of this, two points must be established. First, there is the requirement that the claimant has deprived him/herself of the actual capital. Examples of this include purchasing an item of furniture or household item or going on an expensive holiday. However, it also has to be established that the purpose in divesting the capital is to enhance benefit entitlement. One of the difficulties with this point is that there is, usually, unlikely to be direct evidence to establish the purpose of the claimant in reducing his/her amount of capital. This has generated a number of commissioners' decisions. Thus, in *R(SB)40/85*, the commissioner stated that the obtaining of benefit must be a 'significant operative purpose' in the claimant ridding him/herself of the capital and, if the obtaining of benefit was a foreseeable consequence of the transaction, then, in the absence of other evidence, it could be concluded that this was the claimant's purpose. However, in *CIS 124/1990*, it was held that it must be established that the person actually knew of the capital limit rule, otherwise the necessary deliberate intention to obtain benefit is not present.

## Habitual Residence

### Context and commentary

Introduced in 1994, the *habitual residence test* stipulates that a person is not normally eligible to claim income support, income-based JSA, housing benefit or council tax benefit unless he/she is 'habitually resident' in what is known as the Common Travel Area, which constitutes the UK, the Channel Islands, Eire and the Isle of Man. Although primarily aimed at ending foreign nationals' entitlement to UK benefits, the habitual residence test also applies to British nationals.

This additional condition in determining eligibility for these benefits was contentiously introduced by the then Conservative Government in 1994, as is explained below:

> 'Part of the Government's justification for this significant and controversial change in the conditions of entitlement for income support [and the other benefits] was its concern about the potential growth of "benefit tourism", particularly with the expansion of the EEA. No evidence, however, was produced to indicate that this is a widespread problem. Although the intended target of the new rule is EEA nationals, others, for example U.K. citizens, particularly those from ethnic minorities, with family ties in other countries who have spent time living and working in those countries, or U.K. nationals returning after working abroad for a long period, may experience difficulties in satisfying the test. The Social Security Advisory Committee's recommendation (Cm. 2609/1994) that an habitual residence condition should not be imposed without research being undertaken to quantify the perceived problem and the potential effects of the proposed test was not accepted.' (Mesher and Wood, 1996 p. 120)

The EEA is the European Economic Area which was set up in 1992. It consists of the member states of the European Community as well as Iceland, Liechtenstein and Norway.

## The legal rules

Under JSA Reg 85, IS Reg 21(3), HB Reg 7A(4)(e) and CTB Reg 7A(4)(e), a claimant is not eligible to claim income support, income-based JSA, housing benefit or council tax benefit unless he/she is 'habitually resident' in the Common Travel Area unless:

(i)   The claimant is an EEA national who is classified as a 'worker' or has the right to reside in the United Kingdom under specified EC legislation; or
(ii)  The claimant is a refugee or has been granted 'exceptional leave to remain' in the United Kingdom; or
(iii) The claimant left Montserrat after 1 November 1995 because of the volcanic eruption on the island.

The basic rule is that if the claimant is not deemed to be habitually resident in any part of the Common Travel Area of the UK, the Channel Islands, Eire or the Isle of Man he/she is defined as a 'person from abroad' and will not be entitled to any of the aforementioned benefits.

'Habitually resident' has not been defined either statutorily nor in the regulations, but refers to the place where an individual normally lives. This does not require continual presence in a country and it is possible to be habitually resident in more than one country. In establishing 'habitual residence' in a country, a person is required to be making a 'genuine home for the time being' in that country, though again there is no statutory or regulatory guide on this. However, two Social Security Commissioner's decisions, *CIS/1067/1995* and *CIS/2326/1995*, have provided guidance. In *CIS/1067/1995*, the claimant was a British national who had been born in Burma, living there all her life until coming to the UK in June 1992, while her husband and children remained in Burma. She obtained work in July 1992 until made redundant in May 1994 when she claimed income support until returning to Burma in July as she believed her husband to be terminally ill. She returned to the UK in August and reclaimed income support but was refused on the ground that she was not habitually resident in the UK. The commissioner allowed her appeal on the grounds that she had clearly become habitually resident in this country by July 1994, not withstanding her temporary absence for a month. The commissioner argued that a complete definition of habitual residence was not possible as the facts of each case had to be considered, nevertheless the following criteria were, inter alia, set out to assist in providing a definition:

(i) The adjudicating authorities must be satisfied that a claimant is *not* habitually resident rather than being positively satisfied that he/she is habitually resident, though any tribunal should seek to resolve this rather than regard it as a burden of proof on one or other of the parties.

(ii) Habitual residence is a criterion that is independent of any legal right of abode. However, habitual residence necessitates that a person is resident in the country in question and residence requires that a person must be seen to be making a home in the country in question.

(iii) Whether a person who is resident can be regarded as 'habitually resident' is a question of fact to be determined by the circumstances of each case, although the length, continuity and general nature of a claimant's actual residence is more important than intention as to the future. An *appreciable period of time* is necessary to enable a claimant to become habitually resident. What counts as an 'appreciable period of time' must depend on the facts of each case. However, 'it must be the kind of period which demonstrates according to the good sense and judgement of the tribunal a settled and viable pattern of living...as a resident, of the kind which would lead in normal parlance to the person being described as a habitual resident in this country.'

In *CIS 2326/1995*, the commissioner emphasised that, in determining an 'appreciable length of time', no minimum period is necessary to establish habitual residence and to give illustrative examples, such as 3 to 6 months, is inadvisable as these may be read as the minimum or normal periods necessary to satisfy this requirement. The commissioner also stated that, in determining a viable pattern of living, there was no condition that this required establishing viability without recourse to public funds, i.e. without receiving social security benefits. In *Nessa* v. *Chief Adjudication Officer* (*The Times* 11 February 1998), the Court of Appeal gave judicial approval to the requirement that habitual residence required a claimant to be in the British Isles for an 'appreciable amount of time'. However, in *Swaddling* v. *Adjudication Officer* (*The Times* 4 March 1999) the European Court of Justice concluded in respect of a British national who claimed income support on returning to the UK, having worked mainly in France between 1980 and 1995, that the length of time he had stayed in the UK was irrelevant in determining whether he was habitually resident here. As an employed person returning to his state of origin after working in another EC member state, Mr Swaddling had made it clear at the time of applying for income support that he intended to remain in the UK, where his close relatives lived, although, if the opportunity arose, he may seek to obtain work in another member state. The European Court of Justice determined that, in such circumstances, he could not be refused income support on the basis that he had not yet resided in the UK for long enough.

Under reg. 4(1) and (3), a claimant may be absent from the UK for up to 8 weeks and continue to receive income support where the claimant is accompanying a child, who is part of his/her family, for the purposes of medical treatment.

## The 'New Deal' and Entitlement to Benefit

### Introduction

The 'New Deal' is the central feature of the 1997 Labour government's *Welfare to Work* strategy which is based on the approach that the answer to the poverty and other problems that many benefit claimants suffer is to obtain work and thus cease to claim benefit. Funded by a windfall levy on the profits of privatised utility companies, the New Deal involves the Employment Service and Benefits Agency providing proactive support to claimants so that they can move from receiving benefits to obtaining work. The first group of claimants that came within the scope of the New Deal were claimants under 25, and it has now been extended to older claimants who have been unemployed for more than 6 months and to partners of unemployed people as well as to lone parents and the disabled. The issues surrounding the New Deal are examined in greater detail in Chapter 14.

A major consequence of the New Deal is that claimants of benefits such as jobseeker's allowance (both contributory and income-based), income support, housing benefit, council tax benefit and incapacity benefit can be required to participate in the New Deal scheme and, as a result, can be *sanctioned*, by being disqualified from receiving benefit for a period of time, if they refuse to do so or leave the scheme without just cause.

The New Deal has not required the passage of new primary legislation. Under delegated powers granted by the Social Security Contributions and Benefits Act 1992 and Sch 1 of the Jobseekers Act 1995, the Secretaries of State for Employment and for Social Security have introduced regulations and orders amending the grounds upon which the various benefits can be claimed to include certain requirements to participate in the New Deal. These regulations and orders include the Social Security Amendment (New Deal) Regulations 1997, the New Deal (Miscellaneous Provisions) Order 1998, the New Deal (Miscellaneous Provisions)(Amendment) Order 1998 and the Social Security Amendment (New Deal) Regulations 1998. These amend the Jobseeker's Allowance Regulations 1996, the Income Support (General) Regulations 1987, the Housing Benefit (General) Regulations 1987, the Council Tax Benefit (General) Regulations 1992, as well as regulations relevant to other benefits affected by the New Deal.

An examination of the reasons for the introduction of the New Deal is undertaken on pp. 283–290.

## New Deal: main features

There are four main New Deal programmes covering the following groups of benefit claimants:

- claimants aged 18–24 who have been unemployed for at least 6 months:
- claimants aged 25 or over who have been unemployed for at least 2 years;
- lone parents whose youngest child is at least 5 years old; and
- disabled and long-term sick claimants.

However, in the Budget in March 1998, two further New Deal programmes were announced:

- A New Deal programme for partners of JSA claimants to find work. Starting in 1999/2000 it is initially aimed at partners who are aged 25 or over.
- A New Deal programme for communities where funds are provided for *pathfinder projects* designed to tackle social and economic problems in deprived areas.

Deal commences with the *Gateway* period. This lasts for a
~~m~~ of four months when the claimant receives counselling, advice
~~dance~~ from a New Deal *personal advisor* from the Employment
~~~~ ~~e~~ to assist him/her in searching for a job. The New Deal personal
advisor's role includes drawing up a *New Deal Action Plan* which sets out
'realistic and achievable job goals' and the steps by which to realise these
goals. Any restrictions on a claimant's availability for work is also recorded
along with any additional needs. The New Deal includes an initial interview with the personal adviser along with other interviews throughout the
Gateway period as deemed necessary. The initial objective of this period
is to provide a range of services to assist the jobseeker in obtaining work.
To this end, advice and guidance to assist the jobseeker in motivation and
confidence building may be necessary as well as measures to improve skills
in searching for and obtaining a job. While the Employment Service has
overall responsibility for the New Deal, some aspects, such as delivering
training and providing *mentors*, who provide support and 'job-focused'
assistance, may be provided by other organisations, including private ones.
The provision of such services is made on a local basis and therefore
arrangements vary from locality to locality. Any non Employment Service
organisations providing such services are known as *partners* or *providers*.

While the initial objective of the Gateway period is for a claimant to
obtain an 'unsubsidised job' if, at the end of the Gateway period of four
months, a claimant has not been able to obtain work then different
alternatives arise depending on which category of claimant is involved.
For 18–24 year olds, a claimant must chose one of *four options*:

(i) A 'subsidised' job with an employer for up to 26 weeks which includes
the equivalent of at least one day a week in education or training to
an approved level; or

(ii) Full-time education for up to 52 weeks for claimants without National
Vocational Qualification (NVQ) level 2 or equivalent qualification
(or its Scottish equivalent); or

(iii) A job with the Environment Task Force or in the 'voluntary sector'
for a maximum of 26 weeks which includes the equivalent of at least
one day a week in education or training towards an approved qualification; or

(iv) The self-employment option. If a claimant has a business idea that is
likely to lead to a sustainable business, he/she can try out self-employment for up to 26 weeks whilst receiving support and guidance under
the New Deal, including an Employment Service allowance.

No 'fifth option' of remaining on benefit is available so that any claimant
refusing to take up one of the four options 'without good cause' can be
sanctioned by being denied benefit for a certain period.

For claimants in the other New Deal groups, the options available differ.

Thus, for long-term unemployed participants aged 25 or over, at the end of the gateway period, there are two options:

(i)   A 'subsidised' job with an employer for up to 26 weeks where the employer subsidy is higher than for 18–24 year old at £75 per week; or
(ii)  Full-time education or training for up to 52 weeks.

Claimants from the other groups who participate in the New Deal are not subject to the same compulsory options under threat of losing benefit except that partners of claimants who are themselves aged between 18 and 24 are subject to the same requirements as other 18–24-year-old participants.

During the Gateway period, those claimants previously required to do so must continue to attend the Jobcentre once a fortnight to 'sign on' (or do so by post where allowed to). This involves signing a declaration that he/she remains unemployed and is available for and actively seeking work. However, when on a New Deal option, a claimant ceases to be required to be available for and actively seeking work as he/she is either in remunerative work or in receipt of an allowance. This is outlined in the next section.

## Amount received during the New Deal

Claimants continue to receive benefit during the Gateway period unless the conditions of entitlement are not satisfied, e.g. when a claimant obtains an unsubsidised job. However, when a claimant is on one of the options, the payment received varies depending on the option. During the *employment option*, a claimant becomes an employee and thus receives a wage from the employer which must, at the least, be equivalent to the amount of weekly subsidy paid to the employer. In 1999–2000, the subsidy for 18–24 year olds amounted to £60 for each person on full-time employment and £40 per week for those on part-time employment, which is defined as more than 24 hours but fewer than 30 hours per week. Employers could also obtain up to £750 towards the cost of any training that has been arranged.

Individuals on the *full-time education and training option* receive an Employment Service allowance equivalent to the amount of benefit received before commencing the option and can also receive reimbursement for 'necessary' travel costs and for child care and other costs. Claimants on the *Environment Task Force* or *voluntary sector options* receive *either* an allowance plus a grant of, in 1999–2000, £400 paid in weekly instalments of £15.38 over six months or a wage by the provider. Reimbursement of travel costs in excess of £4 per week should also be met by the provider, while assistance with childcare costs is also available. The wage offered by a provider should at least be the equivalent of 'average benefit' plus the grant and, where this is offered, an individual can choose to receive either the wage or the allowance. Where an allowance is chosen, the individual continues to be eligible for passport benefits such as free prescriptions and free school meals. The Employment Service can advise on whether a wage or allowance is of most benefit to individuals though a recipient of income-based JSA in receipt of any premium or having mortgage interest paid as part of his/her benefit is likely to be better off receiving an allowance.

## Entry onto the New Deal

The element of compulsion to participate on the New Deal differs between the various groups of claimant covered by the scheme. There are currently five main groups:

- claimants aged 18–24 who have been unemployed for at least 6 months:
- claimants aged 25 or over who have been unemployed for at least 2 years;
- partners of JSA claimants; and
- lone parents whose youngest child is at least 5 years old; and
- disabled or long-term sick claimants.

Claimants from the first two groups of benefit are required to enter the programme relevant to them. So, for example, in respect of the first group, reg. 75(1)(a)(ii) and (b)(ii) of the Jobseeker's Allowance Regulations 1996 require that a benefit claimant aged between 18 and 24 inclusive, who has been claiming jobseeker's allowance continuously for six months, must take part in the New Deal. Some claimants can choose to enter the New Deal earlier than required, e.g. an 18–24 year old before having claimed JSA for six months. The Employment Service seeks, in particular, to encourage 18–24-year-old individuals from *special needs groups* to enter the New Deal earlier than required as they are recognised as having particular problems finding work. Such special needs groups include individuals with disabilities and those needing assistance with basic skills such as reading, writing and numeracy. People who enter any New Deal programme early, i.e. before they are required to, cannot opt out at a later stage. As with those compulsorily required to enter the New Deal, they may be sanctioned if they leave the programme without good cause.

## Sanctions

Of those groups of claimants for which the New Deal is compulsory, if an individual fails to take up any activity or any option in the New Deal, he/she can lose entitlement to benefit. Existing sanctions in respect of voluntary unemployment for those benefits where claimants are required to be available for and actively seeking work apply. So, for example, a claimant who refuses, without good cause, to attend an interview with an

Employment Service New Deal personal adviser when formally notified to do so is subject to withdrawal of benefit for up to 26 weeks as is a claimant who, during the Gateway period, fails, without good cause, to apply for a job notified to him/her or failed or refused, without good cause, to start a New Deal option.

For claimants or claimants' partners aged 18–24 on the New Deal, there are also *New Deal sanctions* which apply in respect of the New Deal *options*. A person is subject to a New Deal sanction if:

- he/she loses a place on a New Deal option through *misconduct*; or
- he/she *fails to apply for or accept* a place, *without good cause*, on a New Deal option that has been notified to him/her; or
- he/she *fails to attend* a place on a New Deal option *without good cause*; or
- he/she *gives up a place* on a New Deal option *without good cause*.

The sanction period is usually two weeks for the first New Deal sanction imposed and four weeks if a claimant has had any previous New Deal sanction imposed in the preceding 12 months. During the sanction period, a claimant receives no contribution-based JSA (or equivalent non-means-tested benefit) as well as not earning any national insurance credits. If a claimant's resources means that he/she may be entitled to income-based JSA (or income support), he/she is only eligible, during any New Deal sanction period, to receive *hardship payments* and these are only paid to those who come within a vulnerable group. The definition of vulnerable groups is covered by regs 140–2 of the JSA Regulations 1996. The operation of hardship payments generally as well as the definition of vulnerable groups is explained earlier in this chapter. However, one important consequence of the definition employed is that single claimants in good health with no children receive no benefit payment during any sanction period.

For a New Deal participant from the long-term unemployed aged over 25 group, a refusal to take up the offer of an unsubsidised employment without good cause makes him/her liable, not to a two- or four-week sanction, but the usual JSA sanction of up to 26 weeks as does leaving such a job voluntarily without good cause or losing it through misconduct. Furthermore, while there is no sanction for not taking up the education sanction for this group, if a participant does undertake a full-time course whilst on JSA, the normal 26-week sanction can apply if he/she leaves the course early or for poor attendance or poor progress.

## Overlapping Benefits

A general principle of the British social security system is that the double provision of benefit should not take place where there is an overlap of two or more benefits. Such overlap can take place where more than one benefit covers the same contingency. In practical terms, this most obviously arises where a claimant is in receipt of both a means-tested (or income-related) benefit and a non-means-tested benefit e.g. where a claimant receives both retirement pension and income support or where someone receives both child benefit and income-based JSA. The overlapping benefits principle is, in fact, dealt with in respect of income-related benefit in that most other benefits constitute 'income' which is then set against a claimant's 'applicable amount'. This means that the weekly amount of the income-related benefit is reduced by the amount of the other benefit(s) received (less any 'disregards') Governed by the Social Security (Overlapping Benefits) Regulations 1979, one consequence of this is that child benefit is deducted from all income-related benefits (other than family credit). This leads to the somewhat absurd result that all people with responsibility for children receive financial support from the state for that purpose, other than those in greatest need of it, namely those who are forced to rely on means-tested benefits.

The basic rule on overlapping benefits is set out in reg. 4(5) of the above regulations and governs, inter alia, situations where a claimant receives both non-contributory and contributory benefits. In such situations, any non-contributory benefit is deducted from a contributory benefit though, in all cases, a claimant is entitled to receive the higher or highest of the benefits to which he/she is entitled.

## Bibliography

Gennard, I. (1977) *Financing Strikers*.

Mesher, J. (1989) *CPAG's Income Support, the Social Fund and Family Credit: The Legislation*, Sweet and Maxwell.

Mesher, J. and Wood P. (1996) *Income Related Benefits: The Legislation*, Sweet and Maxwell.

# 7 Benefits for the Sick and Disabled

## Context and Commentary

There are a large number of benefits available within the British social security system in respect of claimants who are disabled or sick. They produce a patchwork of benefit entitlement that has led Ogus, Barendt and Wikeley to comment that:

> 'The system of benefits for sick and disabled people was described in 1978 as 'a ragbag of provisions based on differing, sometimes conflicting and anachronistic principles'....[T]his description remains valid today, despite (or, more accurately, owing to) the changes to disability benefits since then.' (Ogus, Barendt, Wikeley, 1995, quoting Simkins and Tickner, 1978, p. 17)

The practical consequences of this 'ragbag of provisions' for disabled individuals is spelled out by Judith Paterson in the 1998 edition of the *Disability Rights Handbook*:

> 'Disability inevitably leads to extra costs. It is far more difficult for a disabled person to manage on the same income as someone of the same age who is not disabled. Yet the average disabled person has a much lower income than the average non-disabled person. And, despite the range of benefits and other help available to people with disabilities, not all people manage to work their way through the jungle and claim their full legal entitlements. The weekly loss can be substantial. Even among people who have claimed all they are entitled to there are still anomalies. People who are severely disabled can be entitled to different amounts of non-means-tested income. How old you were when you became disabled; how you became disabled; the effects of your disability; how long you have lived in the UK; and whether you worked and paid the right National Insurance contributions at the right time: all can make a difference to the total amount you may be entitled to.' (Paterson, 1998, p. 7)

Furthermore, while the 'sick and disabled' are often presented as a single group in terms of the provision of social security benefits, it is important to appreciate that there are important differences between categories within this group. There are, in particular, two distinguishing features. First, many disabled and long-term sick have been unable, due to their disability or sickness, to work at any stage of their life. This means, inter alia, that no entitlement to contributory benefits has been generated. Secondly, many individuals who suffer sickness or disability suffer only a short interruption in their ability to work, returning in a matter of weeks or months. Their need for social security benefit, therefore, is for short periods while for others who suffer long-term sickness or chronic injury, their need for social security provision is of much greater duration. Clearly,the nature and financing of benefits for those whose long-term employment is briefly disrupted by short-term illness or injury is likely to be radically different to that for the benefits of chronically sick or disabled individuals who have not been able to work at any time during their life.

Recent reform proposals in respect of social security provision for the disabled are examined on pp. 282–283, 300.

## The Legal Rules

In recognising the previous comments, it is important to appreciate the variety of benefits available to the sick and disabled. Perhaps the best way to comprehend the current provision of benefits is to recall the categorisation of benefits made in Chapter 2. Non-means-tested benefits are designed either as a direct replacement for earnings or as a recognition that certain people have specific needs that generate extra costs because, for example, they are disabled. Earnings replacement benefits include statutory sick pay, incapacity benefit, severe disablement allowance and invalid care allowance. Benefits that recognise the additional costs generated by disability or injury include disability living allowance and attendance allowance. Usually, a claimant is eligible for only one earnings replacement benefit but can receive any number of the other benefits depending on his/her particular needs. All these benefits can, in principle, be topped up by a means-tested benefit such as income support or, exceptionally, income-based jobseeker's allowance. Earnings replacement benefits are examined in section one of this chapter with those benefits available to the disabled because of their needs for additional costs are outlined in the second section.

## Earnings Replacement Benefits for the Sick and Disabled

### Introduction

Most employees who are absent from work because of sickness receive *statutory sick pay* from their employers for the first 28 weeks absence. At the end of that period, most claimants are eligible for non-means-tested *incapacity benefit*, if enough national insurance contributions have been paid or credited, or for *severe disablement allowance*, a non-contributory benefit paid at a lower rate than incapacity benefit. Claimants may also be eligible for means-tested benefits such as *income support* and, in some cases, *income-based JSA*. Those who are not eligible for statutory sick pay, such as the self-employed, can receive incapacity benefit from the beginning of their absence from work if they have satisfied the contribution conditions. Incapacity benefit was introduced on 13 April 1995 as a replacement for sickness benefit and invalidity benefit as a result of the implementation of the Social Security (Incapacity for Work) Act 1994 whereas statutory sick pay has been in operation since 1983 as a result of the Social Security and Housing Benefits Act 1982 though the most important statute now governing statutory sick pay is the consolidating Social Security Contributions and Benefits Act 1992.

Many disabled people, as mentioned earlier, are not, however, eligible for contributory benefits, such as incapacity benefit, as they have been unable to work and, as a result, have not been able to build up the necessary contributions record. As a consequence, the main function of the non-contributory *severe disablement allowance* is to provide benefit for severely disabled people whose disability has prevented them working and thereby becoming entitled to contributory incapacity benefit. *Invalid care allowance* is the last earnings replacement benefit discussed in this chapter. It is paid to those who are caring full time for a disabled person and who, therefore, are not working.

## Statutory sick pay

Statutory sick pay (SSP) is a non-contributory, non-means-tested benefit that is paid to both full-time and part-time employees who are absent from work for up to 28 weeks (196 days) due to sickness. Since 1994, it is administered and paid for by employers. It is a flat-rate benefit with no additions for dependants. The current rate of benefit is set out in the appendix. It is paid for any period of four or more days absence from work due to sickness. Many employees may also be eligible, under their contract of employment, for an additional occupational sick pay payment. Statutory sick pay is, however, a statutory minimum which employers must pay to all eligible employees. A claimant whose SSP (and any other income) is below his/her income support 'applicable amount' may also be able to claim that benefit though those claimants who worked for 16 hours or more per week are likely to be ineligible for income support.

The detailed legal rules in respect of statutory sick pay are found in a number of sets of regulations, the most important of which are the Statutory Sick Pay (General) Regulations 1992, No. 894 (SSP Regs).

## General conditions of entitlement

The following are the general conditions of entitlement for statutory sick pay:

(i)    The claimant must be an employee, aged between 16 and 65.
(ii)   The claimant must be 'incapable of work'.
(iii)  A 'period of incapacity' must exist.
(iv)   There must be a 'period of entitlement'.
(v)    SSP is payable for 'qualifying days' only.
(vi)   A claimant's earnings are equal to, or more than, the 'lower earnings level'.

*(i) The claimant must be an employee.* Under s.151(1) of the Social Security Contributions and Benefits Act 1992, SSP covers those who are employed earners for social security purposes and thus pay Class 1 contributions. Under s.151(2) an employee's rights to receive SSP cannot be taken away, even if he/she has signed a document to that effect. There are, however, some employees who are not eligible for SSP. These include:

(a)    Employees over 65, per Sch 1, para 2 and SSP reg. 16, unless the 'period of entitlement' commenced before the 65th birthday and continues after that date.
(b)    Individuals employed for a period of less than three months. However, the facts of each case will determine this, so that if an employee has worked continuously for more than three months, he/she will be eligible for SSP even if the contract of employment is expressed differently. Thus, in *Brown* v. *Chief Adjudication Officer* (The Times 16 October 1996), the Court of Appeal ruled that an employee who had worked continuously for nine months on a renewable daily contract before she fell ill was entitled to statutory sick pay from her employer.
(c)    Any employee whose gross weekly earnings (that is before any tax or national insurance contributions are deducted) are less than the national insurance lower earnings limit which, for the year from April 1999, is £66 – s.163(2) and SSP reg. 19. If a claimant, as a consequence, does not qualify for SSP he/she may be eligible for incapacity benefit and/or income support.
(d)    Pregnant women who are entitled to statutory maternity pay cannot get SSP during the 'maternity pay period' or the 'maternity allowance period'.
(e)    Employees working outside the European Economic Area.

*(ii) The claimant must be 'incapable of work'.* With the introduction of incapacity benefit in April 1995, new tests to determine incapacity to work were introduced for that benefit along with a number of other benefits including SSP. For most claimants of SSP, the so-called 'own occupation' test is used to determine incapacity to work. In other words, for each day of receiving SSP, a claimant must be:

'...incapable by reason of some specific disease or bodily or mental disablement of doing work which he could reasonably be expected to do in the course of the occupation in which he was so engaged.'
(s.171B(2) Social Security Contributions and Benefits Act 1992)

This is, in essence, the same test that prevailed before April 1995 and applies for 28 weeks thereby covering SSP. Under reg. 4 of the Social Security (Incapacity for Work)(General) Regulations, the 'own occupation' test applies if a claimant has done paid work in one occupation for at least 16 hours or more a week for more than eight weeks in a period of 21 weeks prior to seeking benefit. However, for those claimants deemed not to have a regular occupation, the more stringent 'all work' test will apply (this is discussed in the section on 'incapacity benefit').

*(iii) A 'period of incapacity' must exist.* This means, per s.152(2) of the Social Security Contributions and Benefits Act 1992, that a claimant must be incapable of work for a period of at least four consecutive days, the first three days constituting 'waiting days' for which benefit is not paid. Under s.152, any day of the week (including Sundays) counts towards this even if they are not days on which the claimant would normally work. Any two periods separated by not more than eight weeks are, under s.152(3), treated as a single period. Thus a claimant is not caught by the three 'waiting days' requirement for the second period, meaning that SSP can be paid for all days of this latter period of incapacity.

*(iv) There must be a 'period of entitlement'.* Any day in a 'period of incapacity' must, under s.153 and Sch 11, be shown to fall within a 'period of entitlement'. The most important aspect of this is that, as the employer's liability extends only to paying SSP for a total of 28 weeks' incapacity of work, if a claimant's 'period of incapacity' is outside 28 weeks, it is not in the 'period of entitlement'. The period of entitlement can also come to an end in a number of other ways, before the 28 weeks is completed (per s.153(2) and SSP reg. 3(3)), as set out below:

(1) For claimants on fixed-term contracts, the 'period of entitlement' for SSP ends on the day on which the contract ends.
(2) After three years from the first date of receiving SSP for any employer who has been claiming SSP intermittently and, as a result of linking 'periods of incapacity', is still in a single period of incapacity yet 28 weeks of SSP entitlement have not been exhausted. If three years have elapsed the period of entitlement elapses even if the full 28 weeks of SSP have not been claimed.
(3) When, on grounds of pregnancy, SSP is superseded by statutory maternity pay or maternity allowance.

(4)   The day when the claimant ceases to be in a country within the European Economic Area.

If the period of entitlement ends, an employee is unable to claim SSP until he/she has returned to work for eight weeks.

*(v) SSP is payable for 'qualifying days' only*. The final requirement is that, under s.154, SSP is only paid for those days within a 'period of incapacity' that constitute 'qualifying days'. These are normally the days that a claimant would have been required to work under the terms of his/her contract of employment if he/she was not sick. Thus, an employee working a five-day week would be paid SSP for absence on those five days but, if not absent for work for a whole week, each of these days would entitle him/her to a fifth of the weekly rate. In contrast, a claimant who works four days a week would be paid SSP for absence on the four days, but each day's absence would entitle him/her to a quarter of the weekly rate. In other words, although any days of the week that a claimant does not normally work can constitute part of the four or more consecutive days necessary to establish a 'period of incapacity', SSP will only actually be paid for those 'qualifying days' that he/she normally works. Difficulties can arise, however, in determining 'qualifying days' where a claimant's working pattern varies from week to week.

*(vi) The claimant's earnings are equal to or more than the 'lower earnings level'*. Statutory sick pay is not available to employees whose 'normal weekly earnings' are less than the lower earnings level (LEL). This is the level of earnings below which national insurance contributions are not paid. Under s.163(2) of the Social Security Contributions and Benefits Act 1992 and regs 17 and 19 of the Statutory Sick Pay (General) Regulations 1992, 'normal weekly earnings' are a claimant's gross earnings (before tax and national insurance contributions are deducted) averaged over the last eight weeks before the last normal pay day. In 1999 the lower earnings level was £66 per week. However, over the next two years, as part of the Labour government's reforms, it is set to rise substantially in respect of making national insurance contributions. At the time of writing, the impact of this on entitlement to social security benefits, including statutory sick pay, is unclear. The well-established criticism of statutory sick pay that it fails to cover many part-time employees whose weekly pay is below the lower earnings level is likely to be exacerbated if entitlement to the benefit continues to be based on the lower earnings level for national insurance contributions.

The final point to note about SSP is that it is taxable and, if a claimant receives other earnings and/or occupational sick pay during the same period, under s.4(1) of the Social Security Contributions and Benefits Act 1992, national insurance contributions are deducted.

# Incapacity benefit

## *Context and commentary*

Introduced in April 1995, incapacity benefit is available to people unable to work because of illness or disability. It replaced sickness benefit and invalidity benefit. Of these predecessors, sickness benefit had played a minor role in social security provision following the introduction of statutory sick pay in 1986. It was a contributory, non-means-tested benefit payable for the first 28 weeks of absence from work due to sickness. It covered individuals who were not eligible for SSP, such as the self-employed and those employees not able to receive SSP because, e.g. their contract of employment was less than three months or they were of pensionable age. Invalidity benefit, available after 28 weeks, was also a contributory, non-means-tested benefit. Invalidity benefit, in fact, was a general term used to describe invalidity pension and invalidity allowance. The pension was a flat-rate benefit which had additional payments for any dependants a claimant had. Invalidity allowance was payable on top of any invalidity pension for those claimants whose incapacity commenced at least five years before pensionable age. It was graded according to age, meaning that the younger a claimant's incapacity commenced the higher the rate of invalidity allowance. From 1975 until April 1991, there was also an earnings-related pension but this was abolished '...as part of the [then Conservative] government's strategy of concentrating assistance on the most vulnerable disabled people' (Ogus, Barendt and Wikeley, 1995, pp. 165–6).

Invalidity benefit came under further scrutiny when, in '...pursuing its relentless quest to find savings in the social security budget...' (Ogus, Barendt and Wikeley, 1995, p. 167), the Department of Social Security produced a report entitled *The growth of social security* (HMSO, 1993) which stated that:

> 'Expenditure on Invalidity Benefit has doubled in real terms since 1982/83 and, even assuming unemployment falls by a quarter, is projected to increase by 50 per cent between 1992/3 and 1999/2000. The majority of the increase in Invalidity Benefit expenditure during the 1980s was due to an increased caseload, although a significant proportion of this increase was due to people over pension age who received a corresponding reduction in their pension...The number of Invalidity Benefit recipients has increased from 600,000 in 1978/79 to almost 1.5 million in 1992/93 at a time when the nation's health has improved. There was no readily identifiable correlation in the 1980s between the level of unemployment and either the flow to Invalidity Benefit or the likelihood that individuals would stay on the benefit. Even during the period of rapid economic growth in the late 80s, inflows to Invalidity

Benefit remained steady and people tended to receive the benefit for longer periods. Projected expenditure is therefore based largely on the assumption of the continuation of existing trends.' (paras 4.5 and 4.6)

While this report did not expressly identify the reasons for this increase in the numbers claiming invalidity benefit, '...[t]he implication was that at best the existing test for incapacity for work was being incorrectly applied, and at worst the system was encouraging absenteeism and fraud.' (Ogus, Barendt and Wikeley, 1995, p. 168). Much of the blame was directed at what the government saw as over-sympathetic doctors being too readily prepared to confirm that claimants were incapable of work. This was particularly claimed to be a problem in areas of industrial decline, such as South Wales, where claimants who were on unemployment benefit for 52 weeks following the loss of employment faced the prospect of loss of entitlement to benefit at the end of that period, as only means-tested benefit would be available, for which their means rendered many ineligible. In such situations, it was alleged that doctors were increasingly prepared to verify claimants as incapable of work, thus making them eligible for invalidity benefit. There was evidence, however, that pointed to the increase in the number of claimants being largely attributable to other reasons:

> 'Independent research has shown that more than half of this increase is attributable to three demographic factors: People over pensionable age drawing invalidity benefit, rather than the retirement pension, for tax reasons; the increased participation of women in the labour market; and a gradual increase in the number of disabled people in the relevant age groups.' (Ogus, Barendt and Wikeley, 1995, p. 168).

Whatever the reasons for the increased number of claimants, the Conservative government proceeded to reform this area of social security. Following the passing of the Social Security (Incapacity for Work) Act 1994, incapacity benefit replaced sickness benefit and invalidity benefit in April 1995. More stringent tests, particularly the new 'all work' test, to determine incapacity to work were introduced, which apply not only to the new incapacity benefit but to all benefits where this is a requirement, including premiums for income-related benefits. Medical examinations for the 'all work' test are undertaken by doctors from the Benefit Agency Medical Service (BAMS) rather than by general practitioners. The government's 'relentless quest to find savings in the social security budget' was predicted to be likely to be satisfied by this reform in that the new benefit was seen to have the following consequences:

> 'Of the estimated 1.8 million people receiving invalidity benefit at the time of its abolition, up to 240,000 are likely to be capable of working.

70,000 new claimants each year who would have qualified under the old rules will probably no longer do so. The government expects the measures to save £1.8 billion within 2 years'. (Barnes, 1995, p. 16)

The hoped-for savings did not, however, take place. The trend throughout the 1980s and 1990s of the number of claimants increasing did peak in 1995 and 1996, when the number of claimants of invalidity and sickness benefit/incapacity benefit in both years was 2,406,000, with the figure dropping to 2,373,000 in 1997 and even lower the following year. However, levels of expenditure did not match this. In 1994–5, expenditure on invalidity and sickness benefit was £7,705,000 rising to £7,906,000 in the transition year 1995–6. In 1996–7, expenditure did fall to £7,767,000 but by the following year had increased to £7,800,000 (all figures except the final one are taken from the *Social Security Statistics 1998*, HMSO pp. 158–9; the final figure is taken from *New Ambitions for our Country: A New Contract For Welfare*, Cm3805, HMSO, 1998, p. 54). In exploring possible reforms to incapacity benefit, the incoming Labour government in 1997 highlighted these increasing costs of the scheme and, while critical of its predecessor, supported the view that many in receipt of incapacity benefit should not be receiving it:

> 'From a relatively minor part of the benefit system 20 years ago, IB [incapacity benefit] has grown to a cost of £7.8 billion – almost one-tenth of the social security budget. Today 1.75 million people receive it – three times as many as in 1979. Over this period IB has proved a simple, but costly escape route to keep the employment numbers down. In some cases IB has taken on the characteristics of a more generous form of unemployment benefit. That was never the intention. It is an insurance benefit for those incapable of working.' (HMSO, 1998b, p. 54)

The new government were committed to reforming incapacity benefit in line with the central theme of its social security reform programme of 'welfare to work'. Thus, in the March 1998 Green Paper *New Ambitions for our Country: A New Contract For Welfare* (HMSO, 1998b), Frank Field (then Minister of State in the Department of Social Security) argued that the 'all work' test, upon which a claimant's incapacity to work (and thus entitlement to incapacity benefit is determined) acted as an obstacle to incapacity benefit recipients returning to work. This test, explained in detail in the next section, measures a person's ability to undertake certain tasks to establish whether he/she is incapable of work. It was criticised in the *Green Paper* as follows:

> 'A key problem with IB is the All Work Test. It writes off as unfit for work people who might, with some assistance, be able to return to

work, perhaps in a new occupation. It is an all or nothing test, in the sense that it assesses people as either fit for work or unfit for any work. Thus many people who would be capable of some work with the right help and rehabilitation are instead spending their working lives on benefit. We want a new approach to IB which focuses on what disabled people can do, not on what they cannot. While we will keep the current assessment system for existing claimants, we are examining the scope for a more effective test for future claimants which assesses the scale of their employability, recognising that capacity for work is a continuum. People with some capacity to work would then be given the opportunity of the assistance they need to help them to return to work.' (HMSO, 1998, p. 54)

In July 1998, however, Harriet Harman was replaced as Secretary of State for Social Security by Alistair Darling while Frank Field resigned as Minister of State with responsibility for social security reform, following the Prime Minister's refusal to appoint him as Harriet Harman's replacement at the head of the department. Criticism within government circles of the inadequacy of the Green Paper in March as a blueprint for reform leaked out, following Frank Field's acrimonious departure (see, e.g. *The Guardian*, 28 July 1998; *The Observer*, 2 August 1998; *The Independent*, 3 August 1998; *The Times* 3 August 1998). However, Alistair Darling's first step was to announce reform proposals in respect of incapacity benefit, which included reducing the level of benefit. These were announced in *The Times* as follows:

'Incapacity benefit...is Mr Darling's first target as he prepares a package of measures to kick-start the Government welfare reform programme...One option being considered is to lower the level of incapacity benefit to the less generous basic unemployment benefit, the jobseeker's allowance. This could result in new claimants getting £5 to £15 less than the current benefit a week...Mr Darling's key priority is incapacity benefit, which now goes to 1.8 million people. Ministers believe many jobless are encouraged to obtain sick notes from their doctors so they can obtain the higher incapacity benefit. There is then little incentive to make oneself available for work because there is a risk of failing to get a job, or losing one after several months and then going on to the lower jobseeker's allowance. Once someone is on incapacity benefit there is no review and it can be paid for up to 52 weeks after retirement...Peter Lilley, the previous Tory Social Security Secretary, made several attempts to reduce the benefit, including extending the period for the lower rate to 52 weeks and introducing tougher medical examinations [e.g. the 'all work' test]...But Mr Darling, hotfoot from his previous post as Chief Secretary to the Treasury, is determined to do better. The front-runner is introducing a lower rate for incapacity benefit for new claimants...An-other idea expected to go ahead is introducing new medical examina-tions to test whether claimants would be capable of light office work. The existing medical exam [the 'all work' test] was designed to test whether claimants could do manual labour. This involved getting people to walk a certain distance, to climb stairs and to lift certain objects such as a sack of potatoes. Mr Lilley made the examinations harder in physical terms and insisted on an independent medical examiner, rather than just a GP's report, for those going on the higher long-term rate...Ministers now argue that many people who are not severely disabled are capable of working with computers, telecommu-nications and other types of desk or office work.' (*The Times* 21 August 1998)

In November 1998, the Welfare Reform and Pensions Bill introduced a number of reforms to incapacity benefit. The first of these was the renaming of the 'All Work Test' as a 'Personal Capability Assessment'. Reflecting a consultation paper published by the Department of Social Security earlier in the year – *A New Contract for Welfare: Support for Disabled People* (Cm 4103) – clause 50 and Sch. 8 of the Bill seek to alter the rationale of the test to focus on activities that a person is capable of doing and not merely addressing what an individual's disabilities prevent him/her from doing. It was presented as part of a strategy to encourage or facilitate disabled individuals to obtain work. The Bill also makes it clear that claimants have a responsibility to report improvements in their medical condition if it is likely to affect entitlement to benefit while it also provides for the test to be repeated at any time. Another important change is set out in clause 51, which tightens up the first of the two contribution conditions for incapacity benefit. The result is that individuals who have not paid national insurance contributions in the last two years will not be eligible for incapacity benefit unless they have been carrying out caring responsibilities and receiving invalid care allowance. Clause 52 provides that claimants of incapacity benefit who are also in receipt of personal or occupational scheme in excess of £50 per week will have the amount of incapacity benefit reduced by 50% of the excess income over £50 per week.

These reforms to incapacity benefit, due to take effect in 2001, were seen in the discussion paper, as eventually leading to 170,000 fewer claimants receiving incapacity benefit, producing savings of £70 million in 2001/02 rising to over £700 million in 2010. Not surprisingly the reforms, allied to the requirement, also contained in the Bill, that a 'Single Work-Focused Gateway' into a range of benefits, including incapacity benefit, would require benefit recipients to attend work-focused interviews with a per-sonal adviser, brought stringent criticisms. The Disability Benefits Con-sortium stated that:

'The Bill will result in cuts of £750 million to Incapacity Benefits and means that thousands of people who become disabled in future will lose out. This makes a mockery of the Government's promises not to "harm the genuinely disabled".' (Press Release 10 February 1999)

The Disability Alliance argued that the proposals were an attack on the living standards of thousands of disabled people and, in particular, saw the proposals in clauses 51 and 52 as a major shift in incapacity benefit being a social insurance benefit to becoming a means-tested one (*Briefing Paper 36: Disability Benefits Consultation Paper*, undated). These proposals, in fact, led to the biggest backbench revolt against the Labour governemnt since its election. In May 1999, during the Bill's parliamentary passage, 67 Labour MPs signed an amendment seeking to delete both requirements from the Bill, though the government's large parliamentary majority meant that they were still retained. The wider implications of the developments, in terms of the nature of the philosophy underpinning the government's social security reforms, are considered in Chapter 14.

Such reform proposals appear to reflect a consistency of approach to that of the previous government. Whereas the March 1998 Green Paper's proposal sought to reform the medical test to encourage more disabled people back to work, this reform has subsequently been harnessed to new proposals to cut the provision of benefit. It is in the context of such reforms looming on the horizon that the existing functioning of incapacity benefit and its legal rules need to understood.

## The legal rules

### Main features of incapacity benefit

Incapacity benefit is a contributory, non-means-tested benefit. Introduced by the Social Security (Incapacity for Work) Act 1994, the detailed rules governing this benefit are contained in the Social Security (Incapacity for Work)(General) Regulations 1995. Incapacity benefit (IB) is paid at three rates: short-term lower rate, short-term higher rate and long-term incapacity benefit. The current rates are set out in the appendix. Short-term IB is paid for the first 52 weeks with the lower rate (equivalent to the previous sickness benefit) paid for the first 28 weeks and the higher rate (equivalent to statutory sick pay) paid for the next 24 weeks. Thus, for those receiving SSP for the first 28 weeks, the amount of benefit when they transfer to IB remains the same. A higher short-term rate is paid to claimants over pensionable age (currently 65 for men and 60 for women) if the contribution conditions for a category A or category B retirement pension have been made before pensionable age. Incapacity benefit and retirement pension are mutually exclusive and only short-term IB is payable after this age is reached so those of pensionable age can only claim IB (instead of a retirement pension) for a maximum of 52 weeks. Depen dants' allowances are also higher for claimants over pensionable age. Long-term incapacity benefit is paid after 52 weeks (i.e. from the 365th day of incapacity) and continues for as long as the claimant remains incapable of work up to pensionable age. Long-term IB is not paid after pensionable age. Under s.30B(4) of the Social Security Contributions and Benefits Act 1992, a claimant who is terminally ill or is entitled to the highest rate of the care component of disability living allowance (see pp. 167–168) is entitled to long-term IB after 28 weeks of incapacity.

There is also a number of possible additions to these three general rates. Under s.80(2)(b) and (c) a claimant is entitled to an addition for each qualifying child. The claimant must be entitled or treated as entitled to child benefit for the child(ren) and either the child(ren) live(s) with him/her or the claimant contributes to the maintenance of the child(ren) at least to the level of each child dependant addition (see the appendix for the current rate). For claimants over pensionable age this is paid in respect of all three rates of IB, for other claimants it is only paid on the short-term higher rate and the long-term rate. In other words, pensioner claimants receive the addition from the outset of their claim whereas other claimants have to wait 28 weeks. Additions for adult dependants are also available under s.86A for claimants who are either residing with or contributing to the maintenance of a husband or wife who is 60 or over or are caring for a child or children. In other words, unless the adult dependant is over 60, no addition is paid for an adult dependant unless there is also entitlement for a child dependant addition. It is also important to note that any earnings that a partner has can affect these additions (but not the three general rates). One child dependant addition is lost if the partner earns a certain amount which, for the year from April 1999, is £145 per week and each additional £19 per week loses another such addition. In respect of adult dependant additions, no addition is paid if the partner has earnings in excess of the relevant addition (e.g. a claimant under pensionable age would lose any adult-dependant's addition, in the year 1999–2000, if the partner had earnings in excess of £31.15 per week).

Finally, there are further additions to the basic weekly rate of long-term incapacity benefit for those claimants who were under 45 when the current period of incapacity for work began or, if previously a recipient of statutory sick pay, at the beginning of the period of entitlement for that benefit. This age-related addition is paid at two rates depending on the claimant's age on the first day of incapacity The current rates are £13.15 per week for claimants aged under 35 on the first day of incapacity and £6.60 for those aged 35–44 on that day.

## General conditions of entitlement

The general conditions of entitlement for incapacity benefit are set out in s.30A of the Social Security Contributions and Benefits Act 1992 which was inserted into that Act by s.1 of the Social Security (Incapacity for Work) Act 1994. Eligibility for incapacity benefit exists if:

(i)    a claimant is 'incapable of work'; and
(ii)   the days when he/she is incapable of work are part of a 'period of incapacity for work'; and
(iii)  the claimant is not eligible for statutory sick pay; and
(iv)  he/she satisfies the national insurance contribution condition.

*(i) The claimant is 'incapable of work'.* There are two tests to determine whether a person is 'incapable of work'. The 'own occupation' test looks at the ability of a person to do his/her usual work while the 'all work' test looks at the ability of a person to undertake a range of activities such as walking, standing and sitting and, where appropriate, includes an assessment of mental health. Under s.171B (3) and (4) of the Social Security Contributions and Benefits Act 1992 the 'own occupation' test applies only for the first 28 weeks of any claim, including any claim for SSP or maternity allowance. For most claimants, therefore, this test applies during the period of receiving SSP. After 28 weeks, when this ends and they seek incapacity benefit, claimants become subject to the 'all work' test. However, if a claimant has worked less than eight weeks out of the last 21 (and for each week he/she must work at least 16 hours a week), reg. 4 of the Social Security (Incapacity for Work) (General) Regulations establishes that the 'all work' test will apply from the beginning of the any claim for benefit.

*The 'own occupation' test.* As mentioned in the section on statutory sick pay, a claimant must be:

> 'incapable by reason of some specific disease or bodily or mental disablement of doing work which he could reasonably be expected to do in the course of the occupation in which he was so engaged.' (s.171B(2) Social Security Contributions and Benefits Act 1992)

Medical evidence, usually a doctor's certificate, is normally accepted by an Adjudication Officer as evidence that a claimant is incapable of work, though a claimant can be asked to attend a medical examination by a Benefits Agency Medical Service (BAMS) doctor.

*The 'all work' test.* The 'all work' test is an allegedly 'objective' test whereby a person's ability to perform specified activities is measured in order to determine whether he/she is incapable of work. Any impairment in function due to disability or illness is measured and given a number of points and a claimant is deemed incapable of work if he/she accrues a sufficient total of points. The test is undertaken without reference to any occupation that a claimant previously had. However, a claimant is tested on a disability when using any artificial aid designed to assist with the disability. Thus, for the test on the ability to walk upstairs, any claimant with an artificial leg, would have his/her disability based on the ability to undertake the task *with* the artificial leg and not without it.

*Activities, descriptors and points*. The 'all work' test is defined in reg. 24 of the Social Security (Incapacity for Work) (General) Regulations 1995 as 'the extent of a person's capacity...to perform the activities in the Schedule'. The schedule in question, contained in these regulations, is divided into two parts. Part I covers physical disability and Part II relates to mental disability. Both of these set out a series of 'disabilities which may make a person incapable of work'. The physical activities are walking; walking up and downstairs; sitting in a chair; getting up from a chair; standing; bending and kneeling; manual dexterity; lifting and carrying; reaching; speech; hearing; seeing; continence; and, fits and blackouts. The mental disability list covers the ability to complete certain tasks; dealing with daily living; coping with pressure; and, the ability to interact with other people. For each of these activities there is a further list of 'descriptors'. These seek to determine the level of the disability in question, resulting in points being given to illustrate how incapacitated a claimant is in respect of that disability. For each physical activity, points range from 0 to 15 while mental disabilities range from 0 to 2 points. A claimant passes the 'all work' test if he/she reaches a prescribed number of points.

An example of a list of descriptors and points for a physical activity is that for walking:

**Walking on level ground with a walking stick or other aid if such aid is normally used**

| Descriptor | Points |
|---|---|
| Cannot walk at all | 15 |
| Cannot walk more than a few steps without stopping or severe discomfort | 15 |
| Cannot walk more than 50 metres without stopping or severe discomfort | 15 |
| Cannot walk more than 200 metres without stopping or severe discomfort | 7 |
| Cannot walk more than 400 metres without stopping or severe discomfort | 3 |
| Cannot walk more than 800 metres without stopping or severe discomfort | 0 |
| No walking problem | 0 |

An example of a list of descriptors and points for a mental activity is that for coping with pressure:

### Coping with pressure

| Descriptor | Points |
| --- | --- |
| Mental stress was a factor in making him stop work | 2 |
| Frequently feels scared or panicky for no obvious reason | 2 |
| Avoids carrying out routine activities because he is convinced they will prove too tiring or stressful | 1 |
| Is unable to cope with changes in daily routine | 1 |
| Frequently finds that there are so many things to do that he gives up because of fatigue, apathy or disinterest | 1 |
| Is scared or anxious that work would bring back or worsen his illness | 1 |

Under reg. 26, when calculating points for physical activities, only one descriptor can be counted against any activity. So, for example, the test of manual dexterity awards 15 points if a person cannot turn the pages of a book with either hand and 6 points if he/she cannot turn a sink tap or the control knobs on a cooker with one hand, but can with the other. If a claimant satisfies both tests, he/she would earn 15 points for manual dexterity. The points for the two descriptors are not added together. The higher scoring single descriptor is used. However, under reg. 26(4), descriptors can be added together for each mental activity. So, in the above list for coping with pressure, if mental stress led to the claimant stopping work (2 points) and he/she is also unable to cope with changes in daily routine (1 point), he/she would be awarded 3 points in terms of being unable to cope with pressure.

Under reg. 25(1), a claimant is treated as incapable of work if he/she has a total score of 15 points from the physical activities list or 10 points from the mental activities list or 15 points from both lists as long as at least 6 of these points come from the mental activities list. The treatment of the mental activities list is further complicated by reg. 26(1) which stipulates that a score of from 6 to 9 counts as 9 if it is necessary to add it to a score from the physical activities list in order to establish 'incapacity to work' but a score of less than 6 on the mental activities list is completely disregarded for the same purpose.

It is important to note that some people are exempt from the 'all work' test and are therefore eligible for incapacity benefit without satisfying the test. This is set out in reg. 10 and includes claimants who are:

(i)  receiving the highest rate of the care component of disability living allowance or constant attendance allowance;

(ii) terminally ill, and death can 'reasonably be expected within six months';
(iii) registered blind;
(iv) assessed as 80% disabled for disablement benefit, severe disablement allowance, industrial injuries disablement pension or war pension;
(v) suffering from tetraplegia, paraplexia, dementia or persistent vegetative state;
(vi) suffering from a serious learning disability or one of a number of serious medical conditions including severe and progressive neurological or muscle wasting disease, paralysis, severe mental illness, multiple effects of impairment of function of the brain or nervous system and the effects of severe and progressive immune deficiency.

Regulation 27 also provides that, in exceptional circumstances, a person is deemed incapable of work if a BAMS doctor is of the opinion that:

(i) he/she suffers from a previously undiagnosed potentially life-threatening condition; or
(ii) he/she suffers from some specific disease or bodily or mental disablement and there would be substantial risk to the mental or physical health of any person if the claimant was found to be capable of work; or
(iii) he/she suffers from a severe uncontrolled or uncontrollable disease; or
(iv) within three months of the medical examination by a BAMS doctor, he/she will have a major surgical operation or other major therapeutic procedure.

If a BAMS doctor is of the opinion that a claimant falls into one of these categories, the claimant must be deemed as incapable of work.

To determine the all work test, claimants are required to complete a questionnaire which is returned to the Benefits Agency along with a medical statement from the claimant's general practitioner. These are normally sent to a BAMS doctor for assessment. If the Adjudication Officer is unable to reach a decision in the claimant's favour, he/she will be offered a medical examination by a BAMS doctor.

Under regs 11–14, a claimant may be 'treated' as incapable of work even when he/she has failed the 'all work' test if he/she falls into one of the following categories:

(i) the claimant is an in-patient in hospital;
(ii) he/she is under medical observation as a carrier of an infectious disease or has been in contact with such a disease and a Medical Officer for Environmental Health has issued a certificate excluding him/her from work;
(iii) the claimant receives regular weekly peritoneal or haemodialysis for chronic renal failure; or weekly parenteral nutrition for gross impair-

ment of enteric function; or treatment by plasmapheresis, parenteral chemotherapy with cytotoxic drugs, anti-tumour agents or immuno-suppressive drugs or radiotherapy;

(iv)  the claimant is pregnant and, to avoid serious risk to her health or the health of the unborn child, she must not work;

(v)  the claimant is pregnant but not entitled to maternity allowance or statutory maternity pay. She is 'treated' as incapable of work from six weeks before the baby is due until two weeks after the birth.

Certain types of work will not prevent a claimant from being deemed incapable of work, so that it is possible to work and still receive incapacity benefit. Under regs 16 and 17, the following are some of the types of work that are allowed:

(i)  caring for a close relative;

(ii)  voluntary work of fewer than 16 hours per week. Payment cannot be received, other than expenses '...reasonably incurred...in connection with that work'.

(iii)  therapeutic work of fewer than 16 hours per week if it helps to '...improve, or to prevent or delay deterioration in, the disease or bodily or mental disablement which causes the incapacity for work.' Alternatively, a claimant can work more than 16 hours per week if it part of a treatment programme or done under medical supervision or as a patient in a hospital or other institution. In all instances the work must be undertaken on the advice of a doctor and entitlement to incapacity benefit ends if, in 1999–2000, more than £58 per week is earned.

A claimant can be disqualified from incapacity benefit for a maximum of six weeks if, under reg. 18, he/she falls into one of the following categories:

(i)  he/she becomes incapable of work through his/her own misconduct;

(ii)  he/she does not accept medical or other treatment recommended by a doctor or hospital which would make him/her capable of work. This applies unless 'good cause' for refusing the treatment can be shown;

(iii)  he/she acts in a way, without good cause, designed to slow down recovery;

(iv)  he/she is absent from home and fails, without good cause, to leave any information on where he/she can be contacted.

Apart from the short-term lower rate, under s.617 of the Income and Corporation Taxes Act 1988 incapacity benefit constitutes taxable income.

***(ii) Every day of benefit entitlement must be part of a 'period of incapacity for work'.*** Although entitlement for incapacity benefit is determined on a daily basis, a claimant can only receive the benefit if he/she is incapable of work for a minimum period of days. Similar to the requirements for statutory sick pay, s.30C(i)(b) of the Social Security Contributions and Benefits Act 1992 stipulates that the minimum period of incapacity for work in order to be eligible of incapacity benefit is four days, the first three days being waiting days for which benefit is not paid. Again as with SSP, two periods of incapacity separated by eight weeks or less constitute a single period so that the waiting-day period does not have to be served again. Known as the 'linking rule', this is set out in s.25A(i)(d).

*(iii) The claimant is not eligible for statutory sick pay.* Under para 1 of Sch 12 of the Social Security Contributions and Benefits Act 1992 a claimant who is eligible for SSP must claim that benefit and is ineligible for incapacity benefit. Eligibility for SSP is set out on pp. 137–140.

*(iv) The claimant must satisfy the national insurance contribution condition.* Any individual who has paid either Class 1 national insurance contributions, as an employee, or Class 2 contributions as a self-employed person, is eligible for incapacity benefit if two contribution conditions have been satisfied. These are explained in detail in Chapter 3 but can be summarised here. The first condition, under s.21 and paras 1 and 2 of Sch 3 of the Social Security Contributions and Benefits Act 1992, is that a claimant must have actually *paid*, in one contribution year, an 'earnings factor' equivalent to at least 25 times that year's 'lower earnings level', e.g. in the year 1999–2000, the lower earnings level is £66 so the earnings factor for that year is 25 x £66 = £1,650 whereas in the previous year (1999–1999) the lower earnings level was £64 so the earnings factor for that year was 25 x £64 = £1,600. A claimant must, therefore, have paid the requisite contribution on an amount of income equivalent to the earnings factor. However, as outlined on p. 140, the lower earnings level increases substantially in the period 1998–2000. If it remains the basis for eligibility for incapacity benefit, this will substantially reduce the number of people entitled to benefit. The second contribution condition, also under s.21 and paras 1 and 2 of Sch 3, stipulates that in each of the last two completed contribution years (which end on 6 April every year) the claimant has *paid or been credited with* an earnings factor 50 times the lower earnings limit. Contributions are paid when a person is working but, if not working, his/her contribution record can, in some circumstances, be credited with a contribution even though no contribution is actually paid. For this condition, credits and paid contributions can be combined. However, as discussed on pp. 145–146, the Welfare Reform Bill is set to require claimants to have paid at least some contributions within the two-year period before claiming incapacity benefit. This means they will have to have been working at some time during this period.

The earnings that the partner of a claimant of incapacity benefit has does not affect the basic rate of benefit but can affect additions for children and adult dependants. In the year 1999–2000 any such net earnings of £145 or more per week will result in the loss of one addition for a dependant child and each extra £19 leads to a further loss of a child dependant addition. In respect of adult dependant additions, a claimant of short-term incapacity benefit loses this once the partner earns more than £31.15 per week (or £38.40 if the claimant is over pension age). Recipients of long-term incapacity benefit lose the addition if the partner earns more than £51.40 per week if the claimant and partner live together whereas if the claimant maintains an adult not living with him/her, the adult dependant addition is lost if the partner earns over £31.15 (or £38.40 if the claimant is over pension age) per week.

The final point to note is that, while incapacity benefit cannot be claimed with either form of jobseeker's allowance, as these require any claimant to be capable of work, a claimant of incapacity benefit may also, depending on his/her circumstances, be eligible for income support.

## Severe disablement allowance

### Context and commentary

Severe disablement allowance (SDA) is a tax-free, non-means-tested benefit. It is normally paid to claimants of working age who have been incapable of work for at least 28 consecutive weeks because of disablement or illness but are ineligible for incapacity benefit because they have not paid enough national insurance contributions. Introduced in November 1984, its predecessor was non-contributory invalidity pension (NCIP) which had been introduced by the then Labour government in 1975. The reason for such a benefit highlights the limits of national (or social) insurance as the basis for a comprehensive system of social security benefits:

> 'Social insurance cannot provide a comprehensive system of income maintenance for disabled people for the obvious reason that the congenitally disabled and others outside the labour market for considerable periods will have an inadequate contribution record.' (Ogus, Barendt and Wikeley, 1995, p. 170)

Non-contributory invalidity pension and its successor, severe disablement allowance, were introduced in order to fill this gap. However, the current Labour government has announced reforms to severe disablement allowance in the November 1998 Welfare Reform and Pensions Bill. The October consultation paper *A New Contract for Disabled People* (Cm 4103, DSS) identified two problems with severe disablement allowance:

(i)   As it is paid at a relatively low rate, around 70% of recipients have their entitlement to SDA topped up with income support which, in effect means, they receive no benefit from SDA as it is regarded as income which reduces the amount of income support received.

(ii) In contrast, it claimed that two-thirds of new awards for SDA are made to individuals over the age of 20 who already have adequate resources.

As a result, severe disablement allowance is to be abolished and replaced by an entitlement for individuals aged between 16 and 19 years old to receive incapacity benefit without needing to satisfy the contributions conditions. Clause 54 and Part IV of Schedule 10 of the Bill provide for the abolition of severe disablement allowance and clause 53 establishes entitlement to incapacity benefit. The main consequence of these changes is that individuals aged 20 or over who do not satisfy the contribution conditions for incapacity benefit will lose entitlement to benefit:

> 'The Government estimates that about 16,000 people who would previously have been able to claim Severe Disablement Allowance will be affected although about 70% of those will qualify for Income Support. For the 30% whose other income means they do not qualify for Income Support, the average loss will be £50 per week.' ('Welfare Reform and Pensions Bill', *House of Commons Research Paper 99/19*, p. 76)

One clear outcome of this reform is that whereas at present, for claimants whose disability emerges after the age of 20, entitlement to benefit is not based on making the necessary national insurance contributions nor is it based on a means test, one of other of these requirements will be necessary in the future. The result is that there is to be a greater emphasis on means testing as the method to establish entitlement to benefit. This reflects a general theme in the government's social security reform strategy that is discussed in Chapter 14.

## The legal rules

### General conditions of entitlement

The general conditions of entitlement for severe disablement allowance are set out in ss. 68 and 69 of the Social Security Contributions and Benefits Act 1992. To be entitled to SDA, a claimant must:

(i)   be aged at least 16 and under 65 when first claiming SDA; and
(ii)  satisfy the residence conditions; and
(iii) have been incapable of work for at least 196 days and still be incapable of work; and
(iv)  *either* have been incapable of work when young *or* be severely disabled *or* have previously been eligible for non-contributory invalidity pension (NCIP). These are known as the 'qualifying routes' for SDA.

*(i) Aged at least 16 and under 65.* Under s.68(4), SDA is not paid to claimants under 16, although the 196-day qualifying period of incapacity for work (see point (iii) below) can commence before the 16th birthday, thus allowing entitlement to SDA immediately a claimant becomes 16. However, under reg. 7 of the Social Security (Severe Disablement Allowance) Regulations 1984, claimants in full-time education must be aged 19 or over in order to be eligible. Regulation 7 defines 'full-time education' as courses with classes and periods of supervised study of at least 21 hours per week. Regulation 8(1)(b), however, stipulates that, in the case of those who have additional classes because of their disability:

> '...in calculating the number of hours a week during which [the claimant] attends that course no account shall be taken of any instruction or tuition which is not suitable for persons of the same age and sex who do not suffer from a physical or mental disability.'

Under s.68(4)(d) and regs 4 and 5, individuals over 65 are not normally eligible for SDA. Only those who would have been eligible for it immediately before reaching their 65th birthday are so eligible. Under reg. 5, if this is the case, SDA is payable until the claimant's death irrespective of whether the claimant's level of disability decreases or he/she ceases to be incapable of work.

*(ii) Residence.* Under regs 3(1)(a) and (3), most claimants, at the start of any claim, must be *ordinarily resident* and *present* in Great Britain and also have been *present* for at least 26 weeks in the past year. Like other non-means-tested benefits the more restrictive 'habitual residence' rule that operates for means-tested benefits does not apply. However, as with other non-contributory benefits, there are important immigration conditions that can affect entitlement. As with disability living allowance, attendance allowance, invalid care allowance and child benefit, the general rule is that any claimant is ineligible for severe disablement allowance if his/her immigration status is 'subject to any limitation or condition'.

*(iii) Incapable of work.* Under s.68 all claimants must satisfy the condition that they are incapable of work and have been so for 196 consecutive days (i.e. 28 weeks) prior to the day of claim. Determining incapacity for work is the same as for incapacity benefit. Thus the two tests to determine incapacity introduced with the implementation of incapacity benefit in April 1995 now also apply to SDA. These are the 'own occupation' test and the 'all work' test. The two tests are explained in detail on pp. 148–152.

*(iv) The 'qualifying routes'.* Severe disablement allowance is paid if the claimant is both incapable of work *and* one of the 'qualifying routes' is satisfied. These routes are:

(a)   *The claimant was under 20 when incapacity commenced*. Under s.68(1) and (2), eligibility for SDA can be established if a period of 196 consecutive days of incapacity to work began on or before a claimant's 20th birthday. SDA is paid on the completion of this period. However, under reg. 7(3), a claimant can return to work for a period of up to 182 days (26 weeks) and can requalify via this 'route' after serving a further 'waiting period' of 196 consecutive days of incapacity.

(b)   *The claimant is severely disabled*. A claimant of any age between the qualifying ages satisfies the second 'route' of entitlement if, for a period of 196 consecutive days, he/she has been 'disabled'. Under s.68(6) 'disabled' is defined as:

'...the loss of of physical or mental faculty such that the extent of the resulting disablement...is not less than 80 per cent.'

Many claimants automatically satisfy this 'disablement test' or, to use another phrase, are 'passported to the 80% test' if they already receive the higher rate care component of the disability living allowance or have an invalid car or tricycle or a DSS private car allowance or have already satisfied the test under the industrial injuries scheme or for a war pension. Any person who is registered blind or has had a vaccine damage payment is also 'passported'. In April 1997 five other ways that claimants could be passported to the 80% disablement test were withdrawn. This included those receiving attendance allowance and those receiving the middle rate care component or the mobility component of the disability living allowance. Those not passported must satisfy the 80% test which is carried out by one or more Adjudicating Medical Practitioners (AMP) to whom the case has been referred by the Disability Benefits Centre. There is a right of appeal from the decision of an AMP to the Social Security Appeal Tribunal. Determining what constitutes 80% disablement is difficult to establish. The *Disability Rights Handbook* comments:

'No one is completely sure what 80% disablement means in practice – apart from the fact that the assessment of 80% disablement must follow the same general principles of assessment which apply for industrial injuries disablement benefit. So the best advice [for those who are unsure whether they are eligible] is to claim SDA and find out.' (22nd edition, 1997, pp. 94 and 96)

In this context a list of different conditions and their prescribed degree of disablement are set out in the Social Security Regulations where, for example, the loss of four fingers of one hand constitutes 50% disablement while the loss of a foot is deemed to be a 30% disability. This leads Ogus, Barendt and Wikeley (1995) to comment that:

'Suffice it here to observe that the level of disablement required is severe and would not, for example, cover the loss of a hand for which the prescribed degree of disablement is only 60 per cent.' (pp. 172–3)

(c) *Previous entitlement to non-contributory invalidity pension*. As previously mentioned, SDA replaced non-contributory invalidity pension (NCIP) in 1984. NCIP had different conditions of entitlement and, under reg. 20, anyone entitled to NCIP continues to be eligible for SDA as long as the present claim falls within the same period of incapacity for work. If, however, a claimant were to return to work and end the previous period of incapacity, he/she would not be able to rely on previous eligibility for NCIP and would have to satisfy one of the other qualifying routes.

**Rate of benefit** Schedule 4 of the Social Security Contributions and Benefits Act 1992 sets out the framework of the weekly benefit rates for SDA. The current rates are set out in the appendix.

## Invalid care allowance

Originally introduced in 1975 by the Social Security Benefit Act 1995, invalid care allowance (ICA) is a non-means-tested, non-contributory benefit that is paid to claimants under the age of 65 who spend 35 hours or more a week caring for a severely disabled person. Under s.617 of the Income and Corporation Taxes Act 1988, ICA is taxable except for the additional amounts for child dependants. Claimants of ICA are, however, credited with a Class 1 national insurance contribution. It is an earnings replacement benefit designed to give some financial support to those who are caring full time for severely disabled people. There is a strong economic argument for the state doing this, as Ogus, Barendt and Wikeley explain:

'Quite apart from the social justice of compensating such persons, the granting of state financial support also makes economic sense. In many cases, the care supplied voluntarily by the individual involves a substantial saving on public facilities which would otherwise have been necessary.' (Ogus, Barendt and Wikeley, 1995, p. 208).

### General conditions of entitlement

The general conditions of entitlement for invalid care allowance are set out in s.70 of the Social Security Contributions and Benefits Act 1992. To be entitled to ICA, a claimant must:

(i)   be aged at least 16 and under 65; and

(ii)  meet the residence condition; and
(iii)  be caring for at least 35 hours a week for a severely disabled person; and
(iv)  not be 'gainfully employed'; and
(v)  not be in full-time education.

***(i) Aged at least 16 and under 65.*** Under s.70, ICA cannot be paid to claimants under 16. Those over 65 are also normally ineligible for ICA. As a result of the House of Lords' decision in *Thomas* v. *Chief Adjudication Officer* (ECJ Case C-328/91), following guidance from the European Court of Justice, the previous arrangement whereby women could normally claim ICA up to the age of 60 whereas men could claim up to the age of 65 was declared to be in breach of European Union law. Thus, since October 1994, as a result of amending s.70(5) and reg. 10 of the Social Security (Invalid Care Allowance) Regulations 1976, both men and women can claim ICA up to the age of 65. A claimant can only receive ICA after reaching 65 if he/she was entitled to it immediately before reaching that age. Under reg.11, such a claimant can continue to receive ICA after the age of 65 even if ceasing to care for a disabled person or can even have started full-time work.

***(ii) Residence.*** Under reg. 9(1) most claimants, at the start of any claim, must be *ordinarily resident* and *present* in Great Britain and also have been *present* for at least 26 weeks in the past year. Also, as outlined in the residence section for severe disablement allowance, a person's entitlement to benefit can be affected by his/her residence status (see p. 156).

***(iii) Caring for at least 35 hours a week for a severely disabled person.*** Section 70(1) requires that, to be eligible for ICA, a person must be caring for '...a severely disabled person' who is defined in s.70(2) as a person in receipt of the higher or middle rates of the care component of disability living allowance or attendance allowance, while reg. 3 extends the definition of disabled person to anyone receiving constant attendance allowance in respect of industrial or war disablement. Section 70(1) stipulates that a recipient of ICA must be 'regularly and substantially engaged in caring' for the severely disabled person. This is defined, in reg. 4(1), as requiring that, in any week, a claimant must engage in caring for 35 hours or more. It is not, however, possible to 'average' hours over a number of weeks. For each week, a claimant must be caring for a disabled person for at least 35 hours. Under reg. 4(1A), it is not possible to claim ICA for caring for two or more people for a total of 35 hours. In order to be eligible, a minimum of 35 hours caring for one person is required. Also, under s.70(7), if two or more people are cared for by a single person, each for at least 35 hours, only one award of ICA can be claimed. Similarly, if two people each spend

35 hours or more a week caring for the same person, only one can receive ICA.

Under reg. 4(2), once a claimant has established entitlement to ICA, breaks in caring, due to such things as the disabled person spending time in hospital or the need for a carer to take a holiday, do not affect entitlement. Under this regulation, four weeks' holiday are allowed in any six-month period along with a further eight weeks where a claimant is unable to care for the disabled person because the latter is in hospital before the claimant's entitlement to ICA is affected.

*(iv) Not be 'gainfully employed'*. Under reg. 8, a person is not eligible for ICA if he/she is 'gainfully employed'. This is determined by an earnings rule which, since 1994, stipulates that a person is deemed to be gainfully employed if he/she earns £50 or more per week (including any earnings from the person being looked after), net of any deductions for tax, national insurance contributions and half of any contribution towards an occupational or personal pension. Earnings for any weeks that the claimant is on holiday or not actually caring for the disabled person are, however, ignored.

*(v) Full-time education*. Under reg. 5, anyone in full-time education is not eligible for ICA. This is defined as attending a course where there are 21 hours or more of classes and supervised study. As the *Welfare Benefits Handbook* comments:

> 'The effect of this rule is that some people who might conventionally be regarded as "full time students", such as many undergraduates and postgraduates, are not disqualified from receiving the allowance.' (George et al., vol. 1, p. 82)

As well as these conditions of entitlement, claimants should, under reg. 9, satisfy certain rules in respect of immigration status. A claimant should not have any restriction on his/her right to reside in the UK unless he/she or a member of the family is a national of a European Economic Area country or a national of Algeria, Morocco, Tunisia or Slovenia or has refugee status or exceptional leave to remain in the country.

**Rates of benefit**. The benefit rates for invalid care allowance are set out in the appendix.

Under s.617 of the Income and Corporation Taxes Act 1988, ICA is taxable except for the weekly additions for any child(ren). Also no deduction for any child benefit is made. However, if a claimant's partner earns more than £23.90 per week, any adult dependant allowance for him/her is lost and, if he/she earns £145 per week, one child-dependant addition will also not be paid while each further £19 per week loses a further child dependant addition.

Claimants of ICA may also be eligible for a number of means-tested benefits such as income support, income-based JSA, housing benefit and council tax benefit and, if so, although the invalid care allowance will be deducted from any eligibility for these other benefits, a carer's premium of (currently) £13.35 per week is included in the calculations for the benefits. However, one effect of what is called the 'overlapping benefit rules' is that ICA cannot be paid to anyone receiving the same amount or more of severe disablement allowance, incapacity benefit, contribution-based JSA, retirement pension or widow's benefit.

# Other Benefits for the Disabled

## Introduction

Benefits in this section are paid, not as a substitute for reduced earning capacity as a result of sickness or disability, but as a recognition of the extra expenditure incurred as a result of disability. *Disability living allowance* is a benefit for people under the age of 66 who need assistance looking after themselves or have difficulty with walking and other mobility problems. It is a tax-free, non-means-tested, non-contributory benefit that is paid in recognition of the extra costs incurred as the result of being disabled. Thus it is paid in addition to any earnings or other income, including social security benefits, that a claimant may have. *Attendance allowance* is also a tax-free, non-means-tested, non-contributory benefit which is paid to claimants over 65 who are severely disabled, mentally or physically, and who therefore need help with personal care or require supervision. *Disablement benefit* is another tax-free, non-means-tested, non-contributory benefit paid to people who have suffered disability as a result of an accident at work or by an industrial disease.

## Disability living allowance

### Context and commentary

Introduced in April 1992, disability living allowance (DLA) was designed to extend the distribution of benefits to the disabled, in recognition of the limitations of attendance allowance and mobility allowance (two benefits introduced in the 1970s for severely disabled people) in failing to meet the needs of some groups of disabled people. DLA consists of a mobility component and a care component, both paid at more than one rate, the lowest rate of each component having been designed to extend benefit entitlement to those with lesser degrees of disability who were not eligible for its predecessors, attendance allowance or mobility allowance. In recent years, however, disability living allowance has been subject to extensive criticism. In March 1998, three reports on the benefit were published on the same day (12 March). These were a DSS in-house report (*A Study of Disability Allowance and Attendance Allowance Awards*, DSS In-house Report No. 41, March 1998); a Family Resources Survey (FRS) estimating disability living allowance and attendance allowance take-up (*First Findings of the Disability follow-up to the Family Resources Survey*, Research Summary No. 5, March 1998); and a report from the Disability Living Allowance Advisory Board (DLAAB), an independent body with statutory responsibility to advise the Secretary of State for Social Security on matters relating to disability living allowance and attendance allowance (*The Future of Disability Living Allowance and Attendance Allowance*, DLAAB, March 1998). The three reports all expressed concerns about the functioning of both disability living allowance and attendence allowance. In the foreword to this last report, for example, the DLAAB expressed '...serious misgivings about the way these Benefits are currently structured and administered.'

An important reservation centred around the cost to the Exchequer of disability living allowance and what were seen as unacceptable factors that had contributed to its increased cost. Since it was introduced, the number of persons receiving the benefit has almost doubled, from 1 million in 1992 to nearly 2 million in 1997/8, with the overall cost of the benefit correspondingly rising from £2.2 billion to £5 billion (the figures are taken from *Disability Living Allowance*, House of Common Select Committee on Social Security, July 1998, para 11). The DLAAB attributed a variety of causes to the much larger number of claimants than originally predicted. These include higher than predicted take-up, because of effective publicity and the help claimants received from welfare rights and disability organisations; 'a significant rate of incorrect payments...and a noticeable degree of over-statement of need'; the practical operation of the benefit by Benefits Agency staff who, the DLAAB claimed, had insufficient understanding of the disabling condition, failed to request adequate medical evidence and misinterpreted available medical evidence; and, a series of legal judgements that had broadened the original scope of the benefit. The DLAAB claimed that '[s]tatistical confirmation for many of these assertions' was provided by a Department of Social Security commissioned report of 1,200 DLA 'customers' [sic]:

> 'In this study the award in question was..."in conflict with the facts" in two thirds (63%) of cases. In this situation, it is the Board's view, that current administration of DLA and AA is seriously flawed.' (The

Future of Disability Living Allowance and Attendance Allowance, DLAAB, March 1998, para 2.2)

This picture of a profligate benefit paid in error to the majority of its recipients and whose costs are largely attributable to poor administration and to claimants overstating the extent of their disability was, however, challenged. First, a House of Commons Select Committee's report published in July 1998 included evidence that the claim that 63% of awards were 'in conflict with the facts' did not mean that nearly two-thirds of claimants had been incorrectly awarded the benefit. What it meant, in fact, was that '...there was insufficient evidence in 63 per cent of cases to make a judgement one way or the other, not that the awards themselves were necessarily incorrect in that proportion of cases' (*Disability Living Allowance*, House of Common Select Committee on Social Security, July 1998, para 14). Secondly, the larger than expected number of claimants could at least partly be attributable to factors such as the closing of long-stay hospitals and demographic changes (see Appendix 3 of the House of Common Select Committee Report) along with, as the DLAAB itself mentioned, '...a significant degree of avoidable physical and psychological disablement resulting from the lack of investment in local clinical and rehabilitation services leading to delayed or ineffectual management of treatable diseases' (DLAAB Report, para 2.2). Thirdly, the reality was that large numbers of eligible people, quite simply, were not claiming the benefit:

> 'Whilst the DLA is increasing in terms both of caseload and expenditure, the latest estimates indicate that take-up is low. The FRS estimates show that the take-up of the care component ranges from 30 to 50 per cent, and the take-up of the mobility component is estimated to be in the range of 50 to 70 per cent. A surprising figure is the estimate for DLA care for the age 55–64, which is only 20 to 40 per cent. Even for the highest severity categories...take-up is only 50 to 70 per cent (care) and 60 to 80 per cent (mobility).' (House of Common Select Committee Report, para 16)

Nevertheless, an important development that shaped official attitudes towards a belief that there was a substantial level of incorrect awards of DLA and that many of these were based on recipient fraud were the Benefit Reviews of the Conservative government in 1995 and 1996 which led to the *Benefits Integrity Project* (BIP). As part of that government's anti-fraud drive, the reviews set out to assess the correctness of disability living allowance awards. A small pilot study of 150 cases in 1995 was followed by the checking of 1,200 cases in 1996 (see Appendix 2 of *Disability Living Allowance*, report of the House of Common Select Committee on Social Security, July 1998). The Benefits Agency concluded that the 1996 study identified that there was an element of fraud in 16.7% of awards, concluding that annual losses from overpayments of DLA due to fraud amounted to £499 million. Critics, however, challenged these figures, stating that in most of the alleged cases of fraud in the study, fraud was not, in fact proved. Rather, the interviewing officer 'strongly expected that fraud existed' (Allirajah, 1997, p. 7). The Benefit Integrity Project was, nevertheless, announced in the November 1996 Budget as part of the 'Spend to Save' measures designed to reduce social security fraud. Commencing on 27 April 1997, four days before the General Election that saw the return of the Labour government, the Department of Social Security presented the project in terms of the need to collect up-to-date information about DLA recipients and their care and mobility needs. The project sought to gain information, via questionnaires and home visits, on 400,000 recipients of the higher rates of the care and mobility components of DLA over two years. The operation of the Benefit Integrity Project, however, soon led to trenchant criticism so that, within less than 12 months of its implementation, the House of Commons Select Committee on Social Security, in its March 1998 report, commented that:

> 'Although the description in the DSS memorandum [implementing the Project] implies that BIP is a straightforward administrative exercise to check entitlement details, the reality is that BIP has caused great distress to many vulnerable individuals. The Committee also has a number of very serious concerns about the implementation and operation of BIP.' (para 48)

The Committee noted that, by the end of March 1998, the project had led to 72,470 cases being examined, of which 5,331 had benefit withdrawn, 9,168 had resulted in benefit being reduced and 1,699 cases had benefit increased. This constituted an overall level of incorrect provision of benefit of 22.35% (the figures are taken from para 53 of the House of Commons Select Committee Report). However, as the Committee noted, controversy around the project had grown in intensity. A major criticism was that claimants were wrongly losing entitlement to DLA. Benefit could, and was, being withdrawn simply on the strength of one visit or the completion of a single form yet the use of such limited evidence was leading to many who were entitled to DLA having it incorrectly withdrawn or reduced. The Committee concluded that, as a consequence:

> '...some disabled people who have an overwhelmingly need of and right to DLA have lost the benefit. These cases, where vulnerable and needy people have been deprived of a benefit on which they depend for their

living and dignity, are the most disturbing and sometimes shocking aspect of BIP.' (para 62)

In fact while the Benefits Integrity Project lead to withdrawal or reduction of benefit, resulting in savings in the level of expenditure on DLA, the Department of Social Security (DSS), in its evidence to the House of Commons Committee, stated that there was no evidence of benefit fraud, leading the Committee to conclude that:

> 'Starting from one position that DLA had a serious problem with fraud, the DSS moved sharply in barely one year to the position that DLA has virtually no level of fraud whatsoever.' (para 59)

As well as basing many of the problems of the Benefits Integrity Project on the inconsistency between the original motivation to reduce fraud with that of the need to obtain objective information on the correctness of DLA, the Committee was also critical of the insensitivity in the way DLA recipients were dealt with. It based much of this on the limited amount of training of Benefits Agency staff allocated to the project. It concluded by stating that:

> 'The story of BIP has many unfortunate aspects. BIP has been responsible for introducing an element of fear and anxiety into the important debate on social security reform as it affects disabled people. In our view, there are proper grounds for reviewing social security provision, including that for disabled people. But conducting a rational and open debate has been severely jeopardised by the activities of BIP...It is now up to the Government to rebuild the trust of disabled people and make the case that those in genuine need of financial support have nothing to fear from social security reform. Any talk of change understandably can seem threatening to those who feel powerless and vulnerable. Reform of social security would always have been a delicate task. BIP has made the case for reform that much harder to make.' (para 72)

Despite the above comments, it is clear that reform of social security provision for the disabled is a contemporary issue. Although Alistair Darling's initial target for reform, following his appointment as Secretary of State for Social Security in July 1998, was incapacity benefit, disability living allowance was also identified as in need of reforms designed to reduce its cost:

> '...Mr Darling is determined to keep up momentum for welfare reform and has been looking at ways of curbing...the £5 billion bill for

disability living allowance…Although ministers have pledged that the benefit remains universal, they have not ruled out taxing it.' (*The Times* 21 August 1998)

This followed a major political row in the last months of 1997 when a letter was leaked to the press indicating that, as part of the DSS's *Comprehensive Spending Review*, the Department was considering means testing the benefit (i.e. not keeping it universal). Protests by disabled groups outside 10 Downing Street followed and David Blunkett, Secretary of State for Education and himself blind, sent a memorandum to Gordon Brown in the week before Christmas, duly leaked to the press, expressing his opposition to such ideas. The resulting furore lead to Harriet Harman promising that there would be consultation with disability organisations on any reform proposals. Frank Field's Green Paper in March 1998 stated that DLA, along with attendance allowance, would continue to be universal (see p. 55 of the Green Paper) although it indicated that there would be reforms to these benefits. One such reform, advocated by the Disability Living Allowance Advisory Board, involves the replacement of the existing tests to establish entitlement to DLA, which are based on 'severe disability' or the 'cooking test' and are discussed in detail in the next section, with a 'semi-objective' quantitative test that seeks to quantify the degree of disability in an objective way. Thus, the Board, in its March 1998 report, argued for an 'All Living Test' along the lines of the 'All Work Test' which is used to determine whether a claimant of incapacity benefit is incapable of work or not (*The Future of Disability Living Allowance and Attendance Allowance*, DLAAB, March 1998, para 4.3.1). This proposal brought the following response from Lorna Reith:

'The All Work Test for incapacity benefit has been widely discredited. It is a functionally based test: can you lift a saucepan, can you move up and down stairs, stand and sit, and it does not bear any relation to the world of work. If the DLA Advisory Board are saying "we will take this completely discredited model, the All Work Test, and we will call it an All Living Test and we will do something similar for DLA" then I am deeply, deeply pessimistic about it being of any use at all.' (quoted in para 33 of the House of Commons Select Committee Report).

The reforms that the government eventually proposed were contained in the October 1998 consultation paper *A New Contract for Welfare: Support for Disabled People* which also announced the demise of the Benefits Integrity Project. The consultation paper's reforms to DLA were subsequently included in the November Welfare Reform and Pensions Bill. These included, inter alia, extending eligibility for the higher rate of the mobility component of DLA to three and four year olds. Currently, a child must reach the age of five before being entitled to the mobility component but clause 56(3) reduces to the age of three entitlement to the higher (but not lower) rate. The *House of Commons Research Paper 99/19* 'Welfare Reform and Pensions Bill' highlighted the likely impact of this change:

> 'If the higher rate mobility component is extended to 3 and 4 year olds, it is estimated that 8,000 children will benefit. [However i]f the higher and lower rates were extended to all under 5 year olds it is estimated that 40,000 children might benefit.' (p. 81)

This brought the following response from the Disability Benefits Consortium:

> 'We welcome the proposal in the Government's Welfare Reform and Pensions Bill to extend the higher rate mobility component of disability living allowance (DLA) to children aged 3 and 4. However, we are disappointed that there is a cut-off age at 3 and that the lower rate mobility component is not being similarly extended. We believe that there should be no age limit on access to either the lower or higher rate mobility component.' (*Disability Benefits Consortium Briefing: Disabled Children under 5*, February 1999)

## The legal rules

Disability living allowance consists of two parts: a *care component* to provide help with personal care needs which is paid at three levels depending upon the amount of care required; and a *mobility component* to assist those with mobility difficulties which is paid at two levels. Both components require, as do invalid care allowance and attendance allowance, that the claimant is *ordinarily resident* and *present* in Great Britain and also has been *present* for at least 26 weeks in the past year – per reg. 2(1) of the Social Security (Disability Living Allowance) Regulations. Also the claimant should not be subject to certain immigration restrictions as spelled out in the residence section on severe disablement allowance (see p. 156).

## Disability living allowance – care component

### General conditions of entitlement

Under s.72(1) of the Social Security (Contributions and Benefits) Act 1992, the main conditions of entitlement, along with the aforementioned residence and immigration requirements, are as follows:

(a)   For the *lower rate*, s.72(1)(a) stipulates that the claimant:

'...is so severely disabled physically or mentally that –
(i) he requires in connection with his bodily functions attention from another person for a significant portion of the day (whether during a single period or a number of periods); or
(ii) he cannot prepare a cooked main meal for himself if he has the ingredients...'

The second of these two tests is known as the 'cooking test'.

A claimant who satisfies either of the following two conditions is eligible for the *middle rate* but fulfilment of both conditions is necessary for the *higher rate*.

(b)   The second or 'day' condition, as set out in s.72(1)(b), states that the claimant:

'...is so severely disabled physically or mentally that, by day, he requires from another person –
(i) frequent attention throughout the day in connection with his bodily functions; or
(ii) continual supervision throughout the day in order to avoid to himself or others.'

(c)   The third or 'night' condition, per s.72(1)(c), states that the claimant:

'...is so severely disabled physically or mentally that, at night –
(i) he requires from another person prolonged or repeated attention in connection with his bodily functions, or
(ii) in order to avoid substantial danger to himself or others he requires another to be awake for a prolonged period or at frequent intervals for the purpose of watching over him.'

In applying these conditions, the following issues need to be addressed:

*(i) What constitutes 'severely disabled'?*. For all three conditions, the first of two alternative tests requires that the claimant is severely disabled. In the case of *R(A) 2/92* 'severely disabled' was defined as excluding an individual who committed violent and irresponsible behaviour as a result of a personality disorder as he was deemed not to be suffering any physical or mental disability. In fact, all three conditions define severe disability by reference to 'attention in connection with bodily functions', this being the first alternative requirement under each of the conditions with the amount of attention required varying for each of the rates. For the lowest rate the attention must be for 'a significant portion of the day (whether during a

single period or a number of periods) e.g. about an hour a day to assist with such tasks as getting in or out of bed or in administering injections. For the day condition, Lord Denning MR, in *R.* v. *National Insurance Commissioners ex parte Secretary of State for Social Services* [1981] 2 All ER 738 (known as the *Packer* case), stipulated that the attention must be 'frequent', which means 'several times, not once or twice', while for the night condition it must be 'prolonged', that is lasting for 'some little time', or 'repeated', which means at least twice.

However, some difficulty has arisen over defining what constitutes 'bodily functions', leading to a number of cases being brought to the appellate courts. In the *Packer* case, Lord Denning defined 'bodily functions' to:

> 'include breathing, hearing, seeing, eating, drinking, walking, sleeping, getting in and out of bed, dressing, undressing, eliminating waste products, and the like, all of which an ordinary person, who is not suffering from any disability, does for himself. But they do not include cooking, shopping or any of the other things which a wife or daughter does as part of her domestic duties, or generally which one of the household normally does for the rest of the family.' ([1981] 2 All ER 738 at 741)

While the last sentence of Lord Denning's statement seems to exclude domestic activities as a form of 'attention in connection with bodily functions' which is eligible for the DLA care component nevertheless, in the House of Lords' decision in *Mallinson* v. *Secretary of State for Social Security* [1994] 2 All ER 295, '...cutting up food [and] lifting...[a] cup to the mouth...' were deemed to be tasks constituting such attention, as were reading, describing or giving verbal instructions to a blind person. However, the *Packer* case, in conjunction with the House of Lords' decision in *Woodling* v. *Secretary of State for Social Services* [1984] 1WLR 348 indicated that, generally, domestic help was not treated as 'attention in connection with bodily functions'. Lord Justice Dunn, in the *Packer* case, indicated that this requires 'a service of a close and intimate nature...[involving]...personal contact carried out in the presence of the disabled person' while Lord Bridge, in *Woodling*, said that such attention 'connotes a high degree of physical intimacy between the person giving the attention and the person receiving the attention'. A number of Commissioners' decisions subsequently addressed the issue (see e.g. *R(A)3/86*, *R(A)1/87* and *R(A)1/91*). The case of *R(A)3/86*, for example, indicated that the attention does not need to be medically required as long as it is 'reasonably required'. However, in May 1997, the House of Lords, in *Secretary of State* v. *Cockburn* [1997], appeared to extend the scope of 'attention in connection with bodily functions' beyond that outlined in the *Packer* and *Woodling* cases. The issue in this case concerned whether tasks required to meet the special laundry needs of a woman suffering from arthritis and incontinence constituted the necessary attention. Despite the majority rejecting the extension of any definition to include washing soiled sheets, nevertheless *obiter* statements by individual judges indicated that some domestic assistance can constitute such attention. The requirement that any tasks need to be undertaken in the presence of the disabled person was, for example, modified, Lord Clyde stating that this '...should not be understood to exclude any incidental activity which might occur outwith the presence of the [disabled person] during the course of what is otherwise an attention given to and in the presence of the [disabled person].' This approach to seems to define attention to include a sequence of tasks which, while largely carried out in the presence of the disabled person, necessitate other actions which do not have to take place in his/her presence. Thus, helping an incontinent person out of bed to remove soiled clothing and changing the bed lining involves tasks that are both in the presence of the disabled person and involve some degree of 'physical intimacy' or personal contact, but it also necessitates other tasks, such as rinsing out clothing and bedlinen and hanging it out to dry (though not washing it) that do not meet those requirements.

The *Cockburn* case, thus, appears to have extended the definition of attendance to include at least some domestic activities that do not include physical intimacy or personal contact with the disabled person nor need to take place in the presence of that person. Another important issue concerning the definition of 'attention in connection with bodily functions' relates to tasks that the disabled person can perform him/herself but which require some assistance in order to perform the task. This issue was examined by the House of Lords in *Secretary of State* v. *Halliday* [1997] (the judgement in this case being given jointly with that of the *Cockburn* case). In *Halliday*, the court recognised that the attendance of a hearing person in order to allow a profoundly deaf individual to communicate with others to enable her 'to carry out a reasonable level of social activity' came within the scope of requiring attention in connection with bodily functions.

The senior judiciary have been called upon, in the preceding cases, to define the scope of severe disability by reference to 'attention in connection with bodily functions'. An important consequence of these cases has, however, been to create a number of anomalies, as the following quote (which, while specifically commenting on the Court of Appeal decision in *Halliday* that was subsequently upheld by the House of Lords, highlights the general situation):

> '...it is hard to see how the distinction between domestic activities and other activities can survive *Halliday*. Why, for example, should guiding a blind person to a pub be included but guiding her/him to do food shopping be excluded? Is gardening to be characterised as a hobby

(and therefore a social activity) or as a domestic activity? In *Mallinson*, Lord Woolf said that reading correspondence to a blind person should be taken into account. However, dealing with some correspondence – e.g. bills – could properly be characterised as a domestic duty. It would be absurd if help with the more important sorts of correspondence had to be ignored while help with the less important could be included.'(*Welfare Rights Bulletin*, 1995, August, pp.15–16).

Even more recently, the House of Commons Select Committee on Social Security, in July 1998, commented that:

'The particular conditions of DLA have generated a considerable body of case law...The Social Security Advisory Committee has noted that over the years case law has extended the meaning of "bodily functions". The situation is far from satisfactory and eligibility may depend on whether the particular condition can be "squeezed in" under the existing rules, rather than any real intention on the part of the government to cater appropriately for certain disabilities as part of a deliberate policy. [For example] the *Mallinson* case affected the definition of "attention" to include the spoken word, and *Halliday* extended the help required for attention to include social activities. *Cockburn* allows some help with domestic tasks to be added to the aggregate of care needs.'(*Disability Living Allowance*, House of Common Select Committee on Social Security, July 1998, para 28)

*(ii) The cooking test*. It is possible, under s.72(1)(a), to claim the lower rate without satisfying the requirement that attendance is needed in connection with bodily functions if the claimant passes the alternative test, known as the 'cooking test' or 'main meal test'. This looks at whether or not a claimant's disabilities are such that he/she cannot prepare a cooked main meal. Only claimants who could reasonably be expected to prepare a cooked meal should be regarded as being able to do so, what is reasonable being determined by the circumstances of each case. The cooking test is designed to be a hypothetical or abstract test in that a claimant is not actually required to cook a meal, but to show that his/her disabilities mean that he/she is not able to perform the tasks to cook a meal. The decision in *CDLA/85/1994* confirmed that the meal upon which the test is based is a cooked main meal for one. A claimant is required, inter alia, to outline his/her ability to plan, prepare and cook such a meal including the ability to peel and chop vegetables, use taps and cooking utensils, use a cooker and use and manipulate other kitchen equipment. The cooking test cannot be used by claimants under the age of 16 to establish eligibility for the DLA care component. Nevertheless, a recent Department of Social Security report found that 85% of all lower rate care component awards were

based on this test rather than the 'attention with bodily functions' alternative. (*A Study of Disability Allowance and Attendance Allowance Awards*, DSS In-house Report No. 41, March 1998)

***(iii) Continual supervision to avoid substantial danger.*** The requirement to have continual supervision throughout the day in order to avoid substantial danger to the claimant or others is the alternative test to the requirement that attendance is needed in connection with bodily functions under the day condition as set out in s.72(1)(b. As a result of a Tribunal of Commissioners' decision in *R(A)1/83*, this is deemed to consist of four parts:

(a)   There is substantial danger to the claimant or others as a result of his/her medical condition, what constitutes 'substantial danger' being determined by the circumstances of each case.
(b)   The 'substantial danger' must not be too remote a possibility and, in weighing this up, the seriousness of the consequences needs to be taken into account.
(c)   Supervision by another party must be necessary in order to obtain a real reduction in the risk of harm.
(d)   The supervision must be continual.

***(iv) The need for another to be awake in order to avoid substantial danger.*** The alternative test to satisfy the night condition, under s.72(1)(c), is that in order to avoid substantial danger to the claimant or others, he/she requires another to be awake for a prolonged period or at frequent intervals for the purpose of watching over him/her. In practice, the Benefits Agency define 'prolonged' as more than 20 minutes and, in line with Lord Denning's statement in the *Packer* case (see p. 169), 'frequent intervals' as more than twice.

## Disability living allowance – mobility component

There are two rates of the mobility component of disability living allowance. The current rates are set out in the appendix.

### General conditions of entitlement

Under s.73 of the Social Security (Contributions and Benefits) Act 1992, the main conditions of entitlement for the mobility component of DLA, along with the previously mentioned residence and immigration requirements, are as follows:

(i)   The claimant is aged 5 or over but under 65 when the first claim is made; and

(ii) He/she is likely to be able, from time to time, to benefit from 'facilities for enhanced locomotion'; and

(iii) The claimant satisfies one of the 'disability conditions', as set in respect of the care component, for a qualifying period of at least the three months before the date of first payment and, unless terminally ill, be likely to satisfy that condition for at least six months from that date. To be eligible for the *higher rate* the claimant must, under s.73(1)(a), be '...suffering from physical disablement such that he is either unable to walk or virtually unable to walk'. Under s.73(1)(d), eligibility for the *lower rate* is established if the claimant '...is able to walk but is so severely disabled physically or mentally that, disregarding any ability he may have to use routes which are familiar to him, he cannot take advantage of that faculty out of doors without guidance or supervision from another person most of the time'.

*(i) Age*. Under s.73(1)(a) of the Social Security (Contributions and Benefits) Act 1992, the mobility component is not payable to children aged under 5 while s.73(4) stipulates that children aged between 5 and 16 inclusive must either require substantially more guidance or supervision than persons of their age in normal physical and mental health persons of their age in normal physical or mental health would not require such guidance or supervision. Clause 56(3) of the Welfare Reform and Pensions Bill will extend eligibility for the higher rate to 3 and 4 year olds. Reg. 3(1)(a) of the Social Security (Disability Living Allowance) Regulations stipulates that a claimant must claim mobility allowance *before* his/her 65th birthday.

*(ii) Benefit from enhanced facilities for locomotion*. If a claimant satisfies one of the conditions, it is unlikely that this condition will not be satisfied. It tends only to exclude people who are in a coma or whom it is unsafe to move.

*(iii) The disability conditions*.

*Unable to walk*. In order to be eligible for the *higher rate*, a claimant must be unable, or virtually unable, to walk. Under ss.73(1), (2) and (3) and reg. 12, the following are categories which satisfy this condition:

(a) Inability or virtual inability to walk due to the claimant suffering a physical disability. One consequence of this is that inability to walk due to a psychological reason, such as agoraphobia, does not qualify for higher rate mobility component.

(b) Persons who are both deaf and blind.

(c) Double amputees or persons born with no feet.

(d) Persons who have severe mental impairment. This condition is satisfied if the claimant is severely mentally impaired, displays severe behavioural problems and is so unpredictable that another person has to 'watch over' him/her whenever they are awake. If such a person qualifies for the higher rate of the care component of DLA, he/she is also eligible for the higher rate of mobility component.

Under reg. 12(4), a person's inability to walk is considered after taking into account any artificial aid that he/she habitually wears or which would be suitable and the test of inability is based on the capacity to walk 'out of doors'. In determining the ability or not to walk, reg. 12(1)(a) stipulates that the distance, speed, time and manner of someone's ability to walk outdoors are taken into account as well as the question of whether the claimant experiences 'severe discomfort', such as pain or breathlessness, in so doing.

To qualify for *lower rate* mobility component, a claimant, under s.73(1)(d), can be:

'...able to walk but is so severely disabled physically or mentally that, disregarding any ability he may have to use routes which are familiar to him, he cannot take advantage of that faculty out of doors without guidance or supervision from another person most of the time.'

Unlike the higher rate, therefore, this is available to those whose disability is due to mental as well as physical reasons and, as a consequence, its scope is much wider than the higher rate. Individuals who are physically capable of walking but lack independent mobility may be eligible as may be people with learning difficulties or behavioural problems who do not meet the strict conditions laid down for the higher rate of the mobility component. Those eligible for the lower rate also include blind and partially sighted people, as well as those who suffer from dementia, agoraphobia and panic attacks as long as supervision or guidance from another is necessary most of the time in order for the claimant to walk out of doors.

A further point in respect of both components of DLA is that they have an important role as passports to other benefits and other forms of help. Claimants receiving the lower rate of care component become, inter alia, automatically eligible, depending on individual circumstances, to either disability premium, higher pensioner premium or the disabled child premium of income support and income-based JSA. It also qualifies the claimant for disability working allowance. As well as these entitlements, middle rate claimants also automatically satisfy the disability test for disability working allowance and the invalid care allowance carer test, while any carer of someone receiving the middle rate who is him/herself claiming income support is exempt from signing on. Recipients of the higher rate, along with the aforementioned entitlements, are exempt from the 'all work' test and are automatically deemed to be 80% disabled in respect of severe disablement allowance. The lower rate of the mobility component brings entitlement for the disability premium, higher pensioner premium and the disabled child premium of income support and income-based JSA along with qualification for disability working allowance, while receipt of the higher rate satisfies the disability test for disability working allowance as well as entitling the claimant to exemption from road tax, a car parking 'orange badge' and access to the Motability scheme which provides for the opportunity to buy or lease cars on favourable terms.

A final aspect of both the care component and mobility component of DLA is that people living in certain types of accommodation are not eligible for either component. Under regs 8, 9 and 10 of the Social Security (Disability Living Allowance) Regulations, the care component is not paid to persons living in 'special accommodation' such as hospitals, hospices, local authority homes or hostels or other accommodation provided out of public or local authority funds. Mobility component is not paid to persons staying in hospitals but is unaffected by residence in the other types of accommodation.

## Attendance allowance

Attendance allowance is a benefit for people aged over 65 who are severely disabled, mentally or physically, and who therefore need help with personal care or require supervision but whose need for attendance by another person arose after reaching 65 and who are thus not eligible for disability living allowance. Like disability living allowance, it is a tax-free, non-means-tested, non-contributory benefit. It is paid at two rates. The lower rate, which is equivalent to the middle rate of DLA care component (in 1999–2000 £35.40 per week), and the higher rate, which is equivalent to the DLA care component higher rate (in 1999–2000 £52.95 per week). The lower rate is paid when the claimant is deemed to need attention or supervision either during the day or night while the higher rate is paid if this is required both day and night.

### General conditions of entitlement

As is the case for invalid care allowance and disability living allowance, a claimant of attendance allowance (AA) must, under reg. 2(1) of the Social Security (Attendance Allowance) Regulations, be *ordinarily resident* and *present* in Great Britain and have been *present* for at least 26 weeks in the past year (see p. 156). Also, again along with ICA and DLA, the claimant should not be subject to certain immigration restrictions set out in the residence section on severe disablement allowance (se p. 156). The other conditions of entitlement, as set out in s.64 of the Social Security (Contributions and Benefits) Act 1992, are:

(i)   The claimant satisfies one or both of the disability conditions.

(ii)  The claimant does not reside in certain types of accommodation.

*(i) The disability conditions*. Under s.64, there are two conditions that apply to claimants of attendance allowance other than those who are terminally all. The day condition is that the claimant is so severely disabled physically or mentally that he/she requires frequent attention throughout the day in connection with bodily functions or continual supervision throughout the day in order to avoid substantial danger to him/herself or others. The night condition is that the claimant is so severely disabled physically or mentally that he/she requires from another person prolonged or repeated attention in connection with bodily functions or, in order to avoid substantial danger to him/herself or others, the claimant requires another person to be awake for a prolonged period or at frequent intervals for the purpose of watching over him/her. If one of the conditions is satisfied, the claimant is eligible for the lower rate while both conditions have to be met to receive the higher rate. As may already be clear, these conditions, along with the two alternative ways that each can be met, are the same as the 'day' and 'night' conditions for disability living allowance. Therefore the explanation of them earlier in this chapter applies equally to attendance allowance as for disability living allowance (see p. 168).

*(ii) Residing in certain types of accommodation*. As with DLA, attendance allowance is not paid to people who live in certain types of accommodation. Under regs 6, 7 and 8 of the Social Security (Attendance Allowance) Regulations AA is not paid to persons living in 'special accommodation' such as hospitals, hospices, local authority homes or hostels or other accommodation provided out of public or local authority funds.

For claimants of attendance allowance, there is a *qualifying period* under s.65(i)(b) of six months whereby the claimant is required to show that he/she has met the conditions in respect of needing attendance or supervision for that period before benefit is paid. This applies in respect of both rates of benefit. For those who are terminally ill, however, there is no such qualifying period. Under s.66(2)(a), a claimant is terminally ill:

> 'at any time if at that time he suffers from a progressive disease and his death is expected in consequence of that disease and can reasonably be expected within six months.'

Furthermore any claimant who is deemed terminally ill is automatically eligible, under s.66(1), for the higher rate of AA and does not, therefore, have to further satisfy one of the disability conditions.

## Disablement benefit

Disablement benefit is a non-means-tested, non-contributory, non-taxable benefit that is paid to claimants who, under s.103(1) of the Social

Security Contributions and Benefits Act 1992, suffer disability due to a 'loss of faculty' as a result of an accident at work or due to an industrial disease. Section 94 states that disablement benefit is available if an '...employed earner suffers personal injury caused...by [an] accident arising out of and in the course of his employment' while ss.108–110 establish entitlement if a person suffers from a prescribed disease due to the nature of his/her employment.

## Personal injury caused by an accident at work

There are three elements to a claimant establishing entitlement to benefit under s.94. First, there is the need to establish a 'personal injury'. The second requirement is that this was caused by an accident which, thirdly, arose out of and in the course of employment.

*(i) A personal injury.* Defined by Lord Simon in *Jones* v. *Secretary of State for Social Services* [1972] AC 944 as a 'hurt to body or mind', this includes such obvious things as broken limbs but also covers strain and psychological injury such as nervous disorder or nervous shock.

*(ii) An accident.* This was defined by Lord Macnaghten in *Fenton* v. *J. Thorley and Co. Ltd* [1903] AC 443 as '...an unlooked-for mishap or an untoward event which is not expected or designed.' This includes deliberate acts by third parties such as assaults. A difficulty arises, however, in distinguishing between an 'accident' and a 'process', the latter not entitling a person to benefit, when a series of events, over a period of time, cause an injury. In *Roberts* v. *Dorothea Slate Quarries Co. Ltd* [1948] 2 All ER 201, the House of Lords stated that although an accident did not embrace the growth of incapacity by a continuous progress, nevertheless it did include '...an incident or series of incidents...which caused or contributed to the origin or progress of the disease.' This has resulted in what might best be called a 'grey area' in terms of trying to determine what constitutes an accident and what is deemed to be a process.

*(iii) Arising out of and in the course of employment.* Any injury caused by an accident must have arisen out of and in the course of employment. In another House of Lords decision, *Moore* v. *Manchester Liners Ltd* [1910] AC 498, Lord Loreburn stated that:

> 'An accident befalls a man "in the course of" his employment if it occurs while he is doing what a man so employed may reasonably do within a time during which he is employed, and at a place where he may reasonably be during that time to do that thing.'

Three factors are therefore used to determine what constitutes course of employment: place, time and activity. If a claimant is able to show that the accident occurred at the normal *place* of work during the normal *hours* of work he/she can establish a prima facie case. The *activity* at the time of the accident is important in extending the definition of 'course of employment' to cover hours or places that are not normally part of the claimant's employment pattern.

The point concerning hours or places not normally considered as employment has raised particular problems in respect of accidents while people travel to work. However, s.99 of the Social Security Contributions and Benefits Act 1992 establishes that a person is not in the course of employment during ordinary journeys to and from work unless travelling on transport operated by or on behalf of the employer.

The accident must also arise 'out of employment' which means that in some way the employment contributed to it. Accidents that happen at work, but are unrelated to the job do not establish entitlement. However, s.101 expressly states that an accident arising out of employment includes any accident, if it occurs in the course of employment, that was caused either (i) by another's misconduct, skylarking or negligence; or (ii) by the behaviour or presence of an animal (including a bird, fish or insect); or (iii) by the person being struck by any object or lightning; and that he/she did not directly or indirectly induce or contribute to the happening of the accident by his/her conduct outside the employment or by any act not incidental to the employment.

## Prescribed disease due to employment

An alternative ground of entitlement for disablement benefit to that of suffering personal injury as a result of an accident at work is that a claimant suffers from a prescribed disease arising out of and in the course of employment. The two basic conditions of entitlement for this are:

(i)   The claimant suffers from a disease which is 'prescribed', that is, it is a disease which is statutorily recognised, under ss.108(1) and 109(1), as having a link with the occupation in question; and
(ii)  The disease has been caused by the claimant's occupation.

*(i) Suffers from a 'prescribed disease'.* Part 1 of Schedule 1 of the Social Security (Industrial Injuries)(Prescribed Disease) Regulations 1985 outlines which diseases are prescribed against different occupations. Thus a claimant who suffers from a loss of faculty as a result of suffering from a disease must prove that he/she has worked in the relevant occupation. The list of diseases is long but includes such diseases as occupational deafness, occupational asthma and, for example, for those who have worked as underground miners, chronic bronchitis and emphysema. For most of the prescribed diseases, there is neither a minimum length of time required

for a claimant to have worked in the relevant occupation nor a set period from ceasing to work in the occupation during which the claim must be made. There are, however, important exceptions to this. Under regs 2(c) and 25 of the Social Security (Industrial Injuries)(Prescribed Disease) Regulations 1985, for example, a claimant for occupational deafness must have worked in a prescribed occupation for 10 years and made the claim within 5 years of ceasing that occupation.

*(ii) The disease has been caused by the claimant's occupation.* Under reg. 4(1), there is a presumption for most diseases that it was caused by the relevant occupation if the claimant has been treated as having the disease within one month of working in that occupation. Under regs 4(2)–(5), special conditions apply to diseases such as occupational deafness, pneumoconious and tuberculosis while for common diseases such as inflammation of the ear, nose and throat the connection between the disease and the occupation must be established on the 'balance of probabilities'.

## Loss of faculty and disablement

To be eligible for disablement benefit, a claimant must show that he/she suffers from a loss of physical or mental faculty as a result of the relevant accident or prescribed disease. This was defined by Lord Diplock in *Jones* v. *Secretary of State for Social Services* [1972] AC 944 as an '...impairment of the proper functioning of part of the body or mind'. Loss of faculty, therefore, is damage or injury to a part of a person's body or mind caused by an accident or disease. Disability is the inability to do something that has been caused by that damage while disablement is used to describe the total of all disabilities that a claimant might suffer. Therefore, it is necessary, in order to determine the amount of disablement benefit, to establish the extent of disablement resulting from a lack of faculty. This is undertaken on a percentage basis. Under s.103(1) and para 9(1) of Sch 7, disablement benefit is paid to claimants assessed as at least 14% disabled except in the cases of pneumoconiosis, byssinosis and diffuse mesothelioma where, under reg. 20(1), benefit is paid if disability is assessed at as little as1%. While, under Sch 3 of the Social Security (Industrial Injuries)(Prescribed Disease) Regulations 1985, the percentage accorded to some disabilities is laid down (e.g. amputation of one foot constitutes 30% disability), the decision on the percentage of disability accorded to a claimant is determined by Adjudicating Medical Authorities and, on appeal, by Social Security Appeal Tribunals.

The weekly rates of disablement benefit are set out in the appendix. It is important to note that, as disablement benefit is deemed to constitute compensation for the claimant's injury or disease, it is paid on top of any contributory benefit that he/she may be entitled to as well as in addition to any earnings. It is not taxable but constitutes income for the purposes of means-tested benefits such as income support, income-based JSA, housing benefit, council tax benefit and disability working allowance.

Under s.104, claimants who receive a 100% disablement benefit and require constant attendance as a result of their loss of faculty are eligible for *constant attendance allowance* which is paid at a number of rates (see appendix for current rates). The lower weekly rate is paid, under reg. 19(a), if the claimant is '...to a substantial extent dependent on (constant) attendance for the necessities of life and is likely to remain so dependent for a long period'. This can be increased to the intermediate rate if 'the extent of such attendance is greater by reason of the beneficiary's exceptionally severe disablement'. Under reg. 19(b), the higher rate is paid where a claimant is '...so exceptionally severely disabled as to be entirely, or almost entirely, dependent on (constant) attendance for the necessities of life, and is likely to remain so dependent for a prolonged period and the attendance so required is whole-time'. If attendance is part-time only, reg. 19(a) stipulates that the amount payable is 'such sum as may be reasonable in the circumstances'. This is usually the part-time rate (see the appendix for the current amount). A further *exceptionally severe disablement allowance* can be paid, under s.105, to any claimant if the need for the level of attendance is likely to be permanent. Claimants whose injury or disease commenced before 1 October 1990 may also be eligible for *reduced earnings allowance* or *retirement allowance*.

## Conclusion

This chapter has set out the main benefits available to claimants who are sick or disabled, although there are some benefits such as war disablement pension that have not been examined. It is difficult not to sympathise with the comments made at the beginning of this chapter that the British social security system has an unnecessarily complex patchwork of benefits where the weekly amount received by claimants of equal disability can vary depending on what can reasonably be argued to be irrelevant factors such as the age of a claimant when disability commenced and the reason for the disability. It is clear, however, that benefits for the disabled have been targeted by the government for reform. The reforms contained in the October 1998 consultation paper *A New Contract for Welfare: Support for Disabled People* (CM 4103) and the subsequent Welfare Reform and Pensions Bill, while extending the scope of entitlement in certain areas, e.g. some children below the age of five will be eligible for the mobility component of DLA, also signal an increasing reliance on means testing. The ending of entitlement to the non-means-tested, non-contributory severe disablement living allowance for those aged 21 to 64, for example, means that more people will only be eligible to means-tested benefits. The significance of such reforms is examined in Chapter 14.

## Bibliography

Allirajah, D. (1997) 'Disability Living Allowance 'Benefit Integrity Project', *Welfare Rights Bulletin*, August, p. 7.

Barnes, M. (1995) 'Incapacity benefit', *Legal Action*, May, p.16.

*Disability Rights Handbook* (1997), 22nd edition.

George, C. et al. (1999) *Welfare Benefits Handbook*, Child Poverty Action Group.

HMSO (1993) *The Growth of Social Security*, HMSO.

HMSO (1998a) *Social Security Statistics 1998*, HMSO.

HMSO (1998b) *New Ambitions for our Country: A New Contract For Welfare*, Cm3805, HMSO.

Ogus, A. I., Barendt, E. M. and Wikeley, N. J. (1995) *The Law of Social Security*, 4th Edition, Butterworths, quoting Simkins and Tickner (1978) *Whose Benefit?* p. 17

Paterson, J. (1998) *Disability Rights Handbook*, 23rd Edition, Disability Alliance Educational Research and Association, p. 7.

# 8 Pensions

## Context and Commentary

The provision of pensions for those in the later years of life, particularly when they cease to be economically active and retire from work, is at present an issue of some controversy. From the first decade of this century the state has provided a system of pensions for the elderly, and a state pension, based on contributions paid while working, was a central feature of the Beveridge Report and was implemented by the National Insurance Act 1946. As well as state provision of pensions, however, large numbers of people have also sought to secure financial resources in old age by paying into private pension schemes. These usually take one of two forms. An occupational pension scheme covers employees working for the same employer or in the same occupation while a personal pension is one created for a particular individual.

The post-war era has seen a number of changes largely as a result of the increasing numbers of people living longer which has created major funding problems for state pensions. This is explained as follows:

> 'Like all other advanced industrial societies, Britain is experiencing a growth in the proportion of the elderly partly as a result of declining birth rates and partly rising longevity. The proportion of the population aged 65 or over in Britain rose from 4.7% in 1901, to 10.9% in 1951, to 15.0% in 1981 and it is estimated that by 2001 it will be 15.1%...Moreover the proportion of the elderly who are over 75 years old has grown faster with the result that today one in three of the elderly are above that age...Because of this rise in the proportions of the elderly, fears have been expressed that governments will not be able to meet the costs of providing adequate pensions, health care, community care and other services.' (George and Howards, 1991, p. 33)

This problem, affecting how financial resources can be provided for the elderly, is set to increase in scope, and is referred to by the European Commission as the 'impending demographic time-bomb' (European Commission, 1995, p. 13) which is confronting all EC member countries. This report identified the problem:

'...of the increasing demands on systems of social protection which are certain to arise from the ageing of the population. In 1995, the population aged 65 or over (the present or planned official age of retirement in most Member States) amounted to some 23% of the population of working age (15 to 64) in the Union as a whole. In ten years' time in 2005, it will have risen to 26% on the latest projections...[However t]he major expansion in potential expenditure does not come until after 2005 when the post-war baby boom generation begins to retire. In 2015, the population aged 65 and over is likely to represent 30% of that of working age and in 2025, 35.5%. Whereas in 1995 there are 4–5 people of working age to support each person of retirement age, in 30 years' time there will be fewer than three.' (European Commission, 1995, p. 13)

At the present time, as discussed in Chapter 3, the largest share of social protection expenditure is already assigned to the elderly at, in 1992, 44.8% of total social protection expenditure across the European Community. In Great Britain, for example, 46% of all benefit expenditure in 1996–7 was accounted for by the elderly (HMSO, 1998, p. 141). The rate at which benefits are paid to elderly claimants in the British social security system placed the country eighth out of the 12 member countries for which figures were available in 1995 (Eurostat, 1995, p. 210).

However, in terms of dealing with this 'demographic time-bomb', individual member states have attempted to provide differing solutions and, in particular, have different attitudes to the amount of resources that the state should provide. Thus, while in real terms the amount of resources expended on benefits for the old aged has increased throughout the EU during the 1980s and 1990s, for example between 1980 and 1992 by 50.8%:

'In the individual countries, this [EU] trend was repeated in Italy, Belgium, Greece, the Netherlands and Luxembourg, while in Germany, Ireland and the United Kingdom, real expenditure on old age/survivors' benefits rose considerably more slowly...' (Eurostat, 1995).

British attempts at dealing with the costs of providing state pensions at an adequate level can be traced back at least to the 1950s. Following the passage of the National Insurance Act 1959 graduated state retirement pension, as an addition to the flat-rate state pension, was introduced in 1961. The graduated element was linked to earnings, the first time this had been done within the state scheme. Its scope was, however, limited although the Act is also important as it provided the first example of employers' occupational schemes being allowed to 'contract out' of the state graduated scheme if the occupational scheme guaranteed equivalent pension benefits. This was followed by the Labour government's National Insurance Act 1966 which introduced additional graduated national insurance contributions which, inter alia, earned entitlement to a graduated pension. In 1969, the same Labour government published a White Paper *National Superannuation and Social Insurance: Proposals for Earnings-Related Social Security* (Cmnd 3883) which proposed an earnings-related pension at 42.5% of the earnings of an average single male earner with lower paid employees receiving pensions at a higher percentage of their earnings. The Green Paper and subsequent Bill allowed individuals to contract out of the scheme in preference to a private or occupational pension but the government fell before the legislation could be enacted. The Conservative government of 1970–4 also attempted to reform pensions. Its strategy embraced a greater role for private and occupational schemes. However, despite the proposals being enacted in the Social Security Act 1973 the Conservative government lost the February 1974 General Election and the Act was never implemented. The incoming Labour government, in seeking to deal with the problem of funding state pensions that could be provided at an adequate level, instigated the Social Security Pensions Act 1975 which introduced the State Earnings-Related Pension Schemes (SERPS) as an addition to the existing flat-rate basic state pension. SERPS was to be paid by additional national insurance contributions. Any existing private occupational pension schemes that many employees paid into in lieu of SERPS were required, by and large, to provide the same standards as the state scheme. However, in the 1980s, the then Conservative government adopted a different approach. Its first major change to pensions was contained in s.1 of the Social Security Act 1980 whereby the annual increase in the flat-rate state pension would, henceforth, rise in line with prices rather than, as previously, with wages. The effect of this was to decrease the real value of state pensions. Then, in the Social Security Act 1986, the government sought to deal with the impact on public expenditure of the longevity of increasing numbers of people by encouraging individuals to opt out of SERPS by taking out private pensions. In contrast to the previous Labour government's 1975 Act, the 1986 legislation, reflecting the government's ideological commitment to reducing the role of the state, sought to increase the scope of private provision of pensions. An important feature of the Act and consequent difficulties are outlined below:

'The effect of the 1986 Act was to allow contracting out without any guarantee that the employee would get as good a pension as he or she would have received from the state scheme [i.e. SERPS]. Nevertheless...over 5 million individuals took out personal pensions under these arrangements in the five years following their implementation in 1988...However, it was not long after the commencement of the 1986 Act that concern began to be expressed about the capacity of many personal pension schemes to match the benefits provided by SERPS, in particular for lower paid and older earners...The long-term outcome of the growth of personal pensions is therefore unclear.' (Ogus, Barendt and Wikely, 1995, pp. 220–1)

These problems need to be placed into the wider context of increasing poverty amongst a large number of the elderly. The main social security benefits for the elderly provided by the state in Great Britain are the retirement pension and income support. In 1995–6 there were 9.6 million recipients of the retirement pension in comparison to 8.6 million in 1981–2 (HMSO, 1998, p. 150). Of these, 719,000 also claimed income support as well as a state pension while another 171,000 only received income support. Furthermore, in July 1998, 1 million recipients of the state pension, whose low income makes them eligible for income support, failed to claim the benefit. An important consequence of these figures is that around 2 million British pensioners have an income on or below the level of income support, having no, or a very small, private pension The 1980 decision not to maintain the real value of the pension, when the formal link to uprate it in line with average earnings was ended, has caused great hardship for those who rely on it as their main or sole source of income. Oppenheim and Harker have estimated (1996, p. 61) that if the 1980 decision to uprate in line with prices rather than wages had not taken place, the real value of the state pension in 1995 would have been £20.30 per week more for a single person and £33.05 for a couple. A major consequence of such a development was spelt out in September 1996 as follows:

'You can no longer rely on state pensions alone to see you through retirement comfortably. In the late 1970s, the basic old age pension was worth 20 per cent of average male earnings. But by the early 1990s this had dropped to 15 per cent, and experts believe it will be worth only 8 per cent by 2040.' *Which? Magazine*, September, 1996, p. 40)

Even when combined with an earnings-related SERPS additional pension, state provision is declining in value, with the combined value of the two state pensions steadily falling from 28% of average male earnings in 1985 to, according to the Government Actuary, 19% in 2050 (George and Howards, 1991, p. 35).

Such trends have resulted in two groups emerging within the pensioner population. The first, poorer group is reliant on the state pension which, because of its low level of payment, means that recipients are eligible to claim means-tested income support to top up their pension. The second, better-off group is in receipt of SERPS or private occupational pensions in addition to the state flat-rate pension:

> 'Broadly speaking, there are...two nations of elderly people. First, there are those who are dependent on income support...with no private or occupational pensions and with few or no savings. At the other end of the spectrum are those who have the generous bonuses of a life-time's secure and well-paid employment...[And while] women make up around two-thirds of the elderly population [t]hey are more likely than men to be poor pensioners because of their lower earnings, interrupted work patterns and greater life expectancy.' (Oppenheim and Harker, 1996, pp. 60-1)

Within each group, there are nevertheless, important variations. As high-lighted above, many of the poorest group, relying solely on state sources of income, do not receive all the state support for which they are eligible. In other words, there is a major take-up problem amongst pensioners particularly in respect of claiming means-tested benefits such as income support and housing benefit. Thus George and Howards opine that:

> 'The fact is...that many pensioners do not apply [for means-tested income support] either because they object to means tests, or because of pride or ignorance [of their eligibility for the benefit]. These facts have been known for decades now yet no government has attempted to find ways of overcoming these obstacles. In the present age of computer technology, it would not be beyond the administrative ability of governments to identify those pensioners who are entitled to...[the] benefit and to pay it to them automatically.' (George and Howards, 1991, p. 36)

However, in July 1998, Harriet Harman, in one of her last acts as Secretary of State for Social Security before her dismissal, announced a government initiative to address the problem of the low take-up of means-tested benefits by pensioners. As part of a £2.5 billion package of help for the elderly, and following pilot projects in nine areas, thousands of personal advisers were to be recruited by the Benefits Agency, whose job it is to visit pensioners to check that they are receiving all the benefits to which they are entitled.

Amongst the better-off group, most of whom are in receipt of private pensions, there are also difficulties. These centre round the advice that many receive from financial advisers concerning which private and occupational pensions are most appropriate to each individual's circumstances. *Which? Magazine*, for example, has claimed that:

> 'Many companies and advisers profess to offer pension advice, but our research shows that, in practice, the depth and quality of the service they provide differs widely.' (*Which? Magazine*, September, 1996, p. 42)

In fact, the same source argues that private pensions are not necessarily value for money products:

> 'Choosing a personal pension can be something of a lottery...Pension companies have generally failed to deliver decent, low-cost products. Quite simply, personal pensions in their current format don't meet consumers' needs in today's flexible job market. They aren't portable, and their complexity makes it difficult for consumers to make an informed choice. If people understood the charging structure of personal pensions and their general inflexibility, they wouldn't buy them.' (*Which? Magazine*, January, 1997, p. 48)

Concern about the quality of advice on, and the value of, private pensions has been heightened by the substantial increase in private pensions directly stimulated by the Social Security Act 1986 which, by 1993, had resulted in 5 million people opting out of SERPS in favour of a personal pension. This resulted in what has become known as the 'personal pensions mis-selling scandal'. With their launch in 1988, following the coming into force of the Social Security Act 1986, personal pensions were designed specifically for the self-employed and for those who did not have access to a company or occupational pension scheme. Thus, despite never being intended as a replacement for occupational pension schemes, insurance companies and other private pension providers actively sought and encouraged people to switch to a private pension plan from a SERPS accredited occupational (or company) scheme. In December 1993, the Securities and Investment Board (SIB), the chief regulator of financial services, was highly critical of the 5 million plans that had been sold by insurance companies, the main providers of personal pensions, to those who, as a consequence, had opted out of SERPS. The SIB claimed that most of these sales were based on poor advice and that employees would have been better off with their company pension scheme benefits. While many of the occupational and company pension scheme benefits are guaranteed, personal pensions offer no such guarantees, the retirement income being dependent on stock market returns. Most occupational pension schemes are 'earnings-related' or 'defined benefit' whereby the benefit or pension that an individual ultimately receives is 'defined' in that it is based on an individual's earnings, usually a percentage of his/her final year's salary when in employment. In contrast, personal pensions are usually 'money purchase' or 'defined contribution' schemes whereby the contributions are defined or fixed and are invested into a fund. How well or badly the investment performance of the fund is determines the rate at which the fund can be converted into a pension at the time of retirement. Most personal pensions are defined contribution schemes and, therefore, can fluctuate in terms of what pension rate is eventually provided. Criticism of insurance companies and other financial institutions was that, in advising clients to switch from occupational to personal pension schemes, such a consequence was either not made clear or that the potential investment success of proposed private pension plans was exaggerated. The financial press claimed that the motive behind this was the greed of insurance companies:

> 'Insurance companies raked off huge profits to cover their administration and investment management costs. They also paid substantial commissions to sales representatives and independent advisers – all of which came out of the victims' pension funds.' (Harrison, 1996)

As a consequence, the Securities and Investment Board launched a review in 1994 into this 'scandal' which resulted in those insurance companies and other financial institutions that had been found guilty of 'mis-selling' being required to compensate their victims. However, the second aspect of the scandal has been the lack of preparedness of such organisations to do so. Thus, while the total amount of compensation is estimated to be between £2–4 billion with over half a million cases involved, few victims have received any money. By February 1997, the Personal Investment Authority had identified 558,370 cases where individuals could have been sold the wrong personal pension, 478,809 being defined as priority cases. Of these only 10,389 people had been offered compensation, 6,810 having accepted. The total amount repaid at that date was a mere £61 million.

In November 1998, the Welfare Reform and Pensions Bill was published and it contained provisions to set up a new framework of pensions provided by the state, including the introduction of a new *stakeholder pension*. The Bill, however, only dealt with certain aspects of the reform of pensions, the main features of its pension reforms being set out in a Green Paper – *A New Contract for Welfare*, Cm 4179 – published in December 1998. The Green Paper identified that the central problem in existing pension provision was that many pensioners were facing poverty, recognising that a gap exists between those pensioners merely in receipt of the basic pension and those also in receipt of a private, occupational or

SERPS pension, though it also highlighted the limited value of SERPS pensions. The Green Paper also noted the 'demographic time-bomb' of an ageing population although it was not identified as a major problem. Rather, the main problem was seen to lie in the inadequacy of the existing pension regime, which was regarded as failing both those who cannot, and those who can, provide for themselves. Particular limitations identified were as follows:

- Existing arrangements fail to give financial security to those who cannot provide for themselves in retirement because either they have been outside the labour market, e.g. as carers or are disabled, or because their earnings were such that they could not afford to make contributions to private or occupational pension when working, or because their earnings were so low that they were not required to contribute to the state pension as the earnings were below the national insurance threshold. Also, for those paying into the earnings-related SERPS pension, it was seen as providing limited help for the lowest earners.
- A second problem was that existing pension provision was largely voluntary. Thus, other than the basic state pension, many people failed to provide more than the minimum into occupational, private or other pension schemes. This problem was seen as exacerbated by the scandal of the mis-selling of personal pensions.

The government's solution was based on the introduction of a mandatory second pension whereby SERPS is replaced by a State Second Pension. The Green Paper also committed the government to retaining the basic state pension and to continue to increase it at least in line with prices although, in the Budget of 9 March 1999, Gordon Brown committed the government to uprate pensions in line with increases in earnings, which is much more generous and was what prevailed until 1980 when the Conservative government adopted the more stringent policy of increasing benefits in line with the rise in prices. The Green Paper also announced a 'minimum income guarantee' for all pensioners of, from April 1999, £75 per week for single pensioners and £116.60 for couples. This is achieved via the combination of basic pension entitlement and income support. The State Second Pension is designed to ensure that individuals with a lifetime's work behind them obtain a pension above this 'minimum income guarantee'. This Second State Pension would, thus, provide a minimum flat-rate pension, in conjunction with the basic state pension, but individuals would have the opportunity to opt out of this second pension by taking out a 'stakeholder pension' which, for moderate and higher earners, would be more attractive.

It is in the context of these contemporary issues, and the likelihood of forthcoming radical reform, that the provision of state pensions and their legal framework needs to be considered.

## The Legal Rules

Pensions constitute, both in terms of number of recipients and total expenditure, the largest element of financial support provided by the British state social security system. In 1994–5, £27,884 million was spent on state pensions to over 10 million pensioners, this constituting 31.4% of the total social security budget.

The current provision of state pensions under the British social security system provides that a pensioner who has paid sufficient national insurance contributions is eligible for a 'basic' pension paid by the state. In addition, a claimant may be eligible for an earnings-related pension provided by the State Earnings Related Pension Scheme (SERPS). However, where an employee has chosen to 'contract out' of SERPS, either as a result of being a member of an employer's contracted-out occupational scheme or, as a result of the Social Security Act 1986, by taking out an 'appropriate' personal pension, this additional element of a state pension is not applicable. Furthermore, SERPS benefits do not apply to the self-employed. However, claimants who have paid national insurance contributions between 1961 and 1975, may be eligible to an additional 'graduated pension'.

The legal framework for state pensions is now largely contained in the Social Security Contributions and Benefits Act 1992 supplemented by a number of sets of regulations, the most important of which is the Social Security (Widow's Benefit and Retirement Pensions) Regulations 1979.

Other important features of state pensions include the fact that, under s.617 of the Income and Corporation Taxes Act 1988, state pensions, other than any additions due to a claimant or spouse being responsible for a child, are taxable. Secondly, since the Social Security Act 1989, a person does not have to retire from work in order to receive a state pension. A third important aspect of the state pension concerns the age at which it is payable. Currently, under s.122(1)of the Social Security Contributions and Benefits Act 1992, pensionable age is reached when a women reaches 60 and a man reaches 65. However, under s.126 and Sch 4 of the Pensions Act 1995, the pensionable age for women will be raised to 65. This reform was largely influenced by the ECJ's decision in *Barber* v. *Guardian Royal Exchange Assurance Group* (C-262/88, [1991] QB 344) which required that, under Article 119 of the Treaty of Rome, pensionable ages for men and women in occupational schemes should be equalised. While this did not require the same approach for state pensions, it nevertheless acted as a powerful stimulus towards implementing the same principle of equality into the state scheme. The age at which both genders should reach pensionable age was decided largely on the funding consequences, influenced by increasing human longevity, so that the female pensionable age was raised to 65 rather than either the male age being reduced to 60 or the establishment of a common retirement age somewhere between 60 and 65. There are interim arrangements for women aged between 40 and 45 on 6 April 1995 whereby pensionable age is increased on a sliding scale so that, depending on the exact date of birth, those born between 6 April 1950 and 5 April 1951 will entitled to a state pension some time in their 60th year, those born between 6 April 1951 and 5 April 1952 will be eligible in their 61st year. Claimants born between 6 April 1952 and 5 April 1953 will receive a pension in their 62nd year, those born between 6 April 1953 and 5 April 1954 in their 63rd year and those born between 6 April 1954 and 5 April 1955 in their 64th year. Equality between genders will be reached on 6 April 2020 when, from that date, both male and female claimants will reach pensionable age on their 65th birthday.

## Contributions record

Entitlement to pension (other than a Category D pension payable to pensioners over 80 years of age – see below) is based on meeting the two contribution conditions set out in para 5 of Sch 3 of the Social Security Contributions and Benefits Act 1992. These are:

(a) The claimant must have actually paid, in at least one year, contributions of the relevant class on earnings amounting to at least 52 times the lower earnings limit (or lower earnings level). The lower earnings limit for the year from April 1999 is £66 per week. Thus, this condition is satisfied during this year if the claimant paid contributions on an amount of earnings (known as the 'earnings factor') of £3,432 (52 x £66) while for 1998, the lower earnings limit is £64 per week so the earnings factor would need to be £3,328 (52 x £64); and

(b) Over the claimant's working life, he/she must have a contributions record showing a minimum number of 'qualifying years'. This requires that the claimant must have paid *or been credited with* contributions equivalent to the 'earnings factor' of each year for nine-tenths of his/her working life. This second condition is known as the 'continuing contributions condition'. A person's 'working life' commences with the tax year that a claimant reaches 16 and covers every tax year until the person dies or reaches pension age. The number of years of working life can be reduced if a claimant has a year or years of home responsibility e.g. if he/she was regularly engaged, for a minimum of 35 hours per week, 48 weeks a year in caring for a person who was disabled or in need of care per reg. 2 of the Social Security (Home Responsibilities) Regulations 1994. Each year of home responsibility is not part of a claimant's working life unless he/she earned at least 52 times the lower earnings factor in that year. Therefore, to determine whether a claimant satisfies the second condition, it is necessary, under para 5(5) of Sch 3 of the Social

Security Contributions and Benefits Act 1992, to calculate the number of years of his/her working life and thus the number of years for which the second condition applies. This is set out below:

| Length of working life | Required number of qualifying years |
|---|---|
| 1–10 years | Length of working life, minus 1 year |
| 11–20 years | Length of working life, minus 2 years |
| 21–30 years | Length of working life, minus 3 years |
| 31–40 years | Length of working life, minus 4 years |
| 41–50 years | Length of working life, minus 5 years |

As this regime was implemented in 1975, different arrangements prevail for years before 6 April 1975. These are outlined in the later section on graduated retirement pension.

Where, under the second condition, a claimant has insufficient contributions, the pension can be paid at a reduced rate provided that the claimant has at least one-quarter of the required number of qualifying years, the percentage of pension paid being calculated on a sliding scale based on the percentage of years satisfied. Also, under s.48 of the Social Security Contributions and Benefits Act 1992, if a claimant's own contribution record is insufficient, it may be possible to substitute it with the contribution of a deceased or former spouse. These are *Category B* pensions.

## Types of pension

The state pension consists of the *basic pension*, which can be topped up with increases for any dependants, and the *additional pension*, consisting of the SERPS earnings-related supplement and/or its predecessor *graduated retirement pension*.

### Basic pension

There are three main categories of 'basic' state pensions, all of which may be 'topped up' with earnings related and other additional components:

(i)   *Category A* pensions are payable based on the national insurance contribution of the recipient.
(ii)  *Category B* pensions are payable based on the national insurance contribution of the *spouse* of the recipient e.g. a married woman or widow, who had not engaged in employed work, can receive this type of pension based on her husband's contributions record.
(iii) *Category D* pensions are *non-contributory* pensions payable to pensioners over 80 years of age.

*Category C* pensions are now almost totally redundant. They were paid to people who were over pension age on 5 July 1948.

*(i) Category A pensions*: Under s.44(1) of the Social Security Contributions and Benefits Act 1992, a claimant is eligible for this pension if both contribution conditions are satisfied and the claimant is of pensionable age. The amount payable consists of an amount for the claimant plus an addition for any adult dependant and a further addition for any dependant child. The weekly rates are set out in the appendix. Section 85 along with reg.10 of the Social Security (Dependency) Regulations and reg. 9 of the Social Security (Overlapping Benefit) Regulations provides that a person in receipt of a Category A pension can also claim a dependant addition for a person who looks after any child(ren) for whom he/she is responsible and entitled to receive child benefit. An additional sum of 25 pence is payable to claimants aged 80 or over while category A pensioners are eligible, under ss.148, 149 and 150, for a Christmas bonus of £10 which is normally payable in the week with the first Monday in December.

*(ii) Category B pensions*. A Category B pension is paid, under s.49 of the Social Security Contributions and Benefits Act 1992, to a claimant who is a married woman claiming on her husband's contribution record or to a married man claiming on his wife's contribution record if she was born on or after 6 April 1950. Eligibility is based on the claimant being of pensionable age and that the spouse's contributions record meets the two contribution conditions. This pension is paid at the same rate as the dependant addition of the Category A pension, as set out in the appendix. For couples who are both receiving a state pension, there should be no financial impact as the Category A claimant cannot also receive the dependant addition. However, in other situations, for example where the couple no longer live together or there is no payment of a Category A pension, a Category B pension is an alternative or additional source of income to a Category A pension.

The death of the spouse on whose contribution record entitlement to Category B pension is based entitles the widow or widower to a Category B pension that is paid at the same weekly rate as a Category A pension. Category B pensioners are also eligible for the £10 Christmas bonus as well as a weekly age addition of 25 pence per week on reaching 80.

*(iii) Category D pensions*. Under s.78(3) of the Social Security Contributions and Benefits Act 1992 and reg. 10 of the Social Security (Widow's Benefits and Retirement Pensions) Regulations 1979, claimants aged 80 or over can claim a Category D pension which is non-contributory. Originally introduced by the National Insurance Act 1971, Category D pensions were designed (like Category C pensions) to cover claimants who were unable to claim the other forms of basic pension because they were unable to satisfy the contribution conditions. Category D pensions are paid at the

same weekly rate as Category B pensions, entitlement being based on lack of eligibility for a contributory pension (or for a reduced amount, whereby any Category D pension payment is the amount necessary to bring the total paid to the level of the contributory pension). There is also a residence condition under regs 9 and 10 which requires the claimant to have been resident in Great Britain for 10 years within a period of 20 years ending on the claimant's 80th birthday or later and is ordinarily resident in Great Britain on the 80th birthday or the day of claim if after that date. Category D pensioners also receive the age addition of 25 pence per week for all pensioners over 80 as well as the £10 Christmas bonus.

## Additional pension

As has been examined earlier in this chapter, the provision of an additional pension to 'top up' the basic state pension is an issue that, over the last 40 years or so, governments have sought to address. The original objective was to provide greater financial security to those who lacked any occupational pension, though the dubious selling activities of insurance companies and other pension providers in the aftermath of the Social Security Act 1986 saw many people incorrectly 'opting out' of the state SERPS scheme and occupational pension schemes for private pensions that could not provide the same guaranteed returns. Currently, the two most important sources of additional pension within the state pension scheme are *graduated retirement pension* and *state earnings related pension scheme (SERPS)*.

*(i) Graduated retirement pension.* Prior to the introduction of SERPS, an earlier attempt to top up basic pension had been implemented by the National Insurance Act 1959 as modified by the National Insurance Act 1965. Under this legislation, extra amounts of pension could be purchased by paying additional national insurance contributions on top of those paid in respect of the basic state pension. These were known as 'graduated contributions'. Under s.36 of the National Insurance Act 1965 (as kept in force by Sch 1 of the Social Security (Graduated Retirement Pensions) (No.2) Regulations 1978 and Art 7(1) of the Social Security Benefits Up-rating (No.2) Order 1991, every 'unit' of graduated contribution a claimant made now earns 8.67 pence additional weekly pension. Running from April 1961 to April 1975, a unit of graduated contribution cost £9 per man and £7.50 per woman. Many in receipt of a state pension are now receiving these additional graduated amounts, the exact amount received depending on the number of units a pensioner has purchased.

*(ii) State Earnings-Related Pension Scheme (SERPS).* Following the Pensions Act 1975, the graduated retirement pension was replaced by the

State Earnings-Related Pension Scheme. SERPS came into operation in April 1978. It provides for an earnings-related pension to be additionally paid to people receiving one of the basic state pensions, who have paid Class 1 contributions in excess of the amount of contribution for entitlement to the basic pension, although in certain situations some people may be able to receive a SERPS pension while not eligible for the basic state pension. Employees can 'opt out' of SERPS by taking out either an occupational pension scheme, which must be authorised by the Occupational Pension Board, or a personal pension scheme which has obtained, per s.7 of the Pension Schemes Act 1993, an 'appropriate scheme certificate' from the Board. The consequence of contracting out of SERPS is that both the employee and his/her employee only pay the minimum rate national insurance contributions so that no entitlement to any SERPS addition to the basic state pension is built up.

The amounts of the Class 1 national insurance contribution an employee and his employer make are thus based on whether the employee is in the SERPS scheme or not. Under ss.6 and 7 of the Social Security Contributions and Benefits Act 1992, class 1 contributions are paid by employed earners, known as primary contributors, and by their employers, known as secondary contributors. An employed earner is defined in s.2(1)(a) as:

'a person who is gainfully employed in Great Britain either under a contract of service, or in an office (including elective office) with emoluments chargeable to income tax under Schedule E.'

For employees in SERPS, as well as the contributions required for the basic pension, an additional amount towards SERPS entitlement is made. To determine the amount of contribution that is paid, reference must be made to the lower earnings and upper earnings limits. Changes in calculating the amount of both the employer's and the employee's contributions took place in April 1999. The contribution arrangements both before that date and after it are set out in the section on *class 1 contributions* in Chapter 2. For Category B pensions eligibility depends, under ss.50 and 51, on the spouse's contribution record, while widows and widowers may be entitled to a SERPS pension, in some circumstances, on a combination of his/her own and the spouse's contributions.

Having established how the SERPS additional pension is paid for, it is necessary to determine the amount of the SERPS addition that a pensioner is eligible for. This is determined by ss. 44 and 45 of the Social Security Contributions and Benefits Act 1992 and s.148 of the Social Security Administration Act 1992 allied to the Social Security (Revaluation of Earnings Factors) Orders and is based on calculating the claimant's 'surplus earnings'. For those who reach pension age before 6 April

2000, this is done by establishing the *total* amount of earnings on which a claimant has paid contributions in each relevant tax year since 1978–9. This is known as the 'earnings factor'. Other than for the year immediately prior to becoming a pensioner, each year's 'earnings factor' is 'revalued' by a percentage that reflects the increase in national average wages since the tax year concerned. The percentage revaluation therefore varies in respect of each year. Then, from each year's annual amount a deduction is made equivalent to 52 times the lower earnings limit in the last complete tax year before the one in which pension age is reached. For example, if a person reached pension age in December 1998, the deduction would be 52 times the lower earnings limit for the year ended 5 April 1998. As the lower earnings limit for that year was £62 per week the deduction would be £3,224. What is left is the surplus earnings for the year. When each year's surplus earnings are added together, the amount is divided by 80 to give the annual additional SERPS pension. This is divided by 52 to give the weekly amount.

For those who reach pension age on 6 April 2000 and after, s.128(1) of the Pensions Act 1995 (which lead to the insertion of s.44(5A) into the Social Security Contributions and Benefits Act 1992) changes the way of calculating the claimant's 'surplus earnings'. In calculating the earnings factor for each year, instead of using all the claimant's earnings up to the higher earnings limit, any amount below the lower earnings limit is ignored. So, for example, £62 per week in the tax year to 5 April 1998 is ignored and, in the previous year, it would be £61 per week. However, there is no deduction from the total amount of all the years' earnings factors in order to determine the surplus earnings. The consequence of such a change is likely to be that a smaller part of the claimant's earnings constitute 'surplus earnings' so that the amount of the SERPS pension will be reduced.

Another important change introduced by the Pensions Act 1995, leading to the insertion of s.45A into the Social Security Contributions and Benefits Act 1992, allows disability working allowance and family credit to be regarded as earnings for the purpose of calculating the earnings factor for each year. This applies to those who reach pensionable age on or after 6 April 1999 and relates to any year from the 1996–7 tax year.

## Pensions and overlapping benefits

Under the Social Security (Overlapping Benefits) Regulations, a recipient of a state pension who also receives another social security benefit is subject to rules in relation to overlapping benefits, the main purpose of which is that adjustments are made so that the claimant receives a total amount of benefit equivalent to the highest of the rates of benefit for which he/she is eligible. Where, for example, the other benefit is non-contributory, the amount of benefit is adjusted by deducting the amount of state pension received, with only the balance remaining paid to the claimant. Where the other benefit is contributory, then only the higher of the two benefits is paid.

## Deferring pension

A person is entitled to defer receiving both a Category A and Category B pension for up to five years. Under paras 1 and 2 of Sch 5 of the Social Security Contributions and Benefits Act 1992, each week of deferment results in the eventual pension received being increased by one-seventh of 1%. This increase applies to any graduated or SERPS element of a pension as well as the basic pension, but does not apply to any additions for dependants or age for which a claimant is eligible.

## Conclusion

With pensions and other benefits paid to the elderly currently constituting the largest part of social security expenditure, allied to the 'demographic time-bomb' of the elderly becoming an ever-increasing section of the population, the provision of financial resources for the elderly is an issue of great contemporary importance. This is true, not only of the Britain, but also of other countries, most obviously amongst the other member states of the European Community. There have been previous attempts to deal with this problem in Britain, all based on the recognition that the financial consequences of the increasing number of claimants of the basic state pension mean that it needs to be supplemented by an additional pension or source of income. The various solutions attempted reflect different political approaches. The introduction of SERPS by the Labour government of the mid-1970s placed an important role on the state in that, while it allowed for individuals to opt out of this state scheme, SERPS set the minimum standard for any private or occupational scheme. In contrast, the Conservative government of the mid-1980s, in line with its philosophical commitment to private provision and the reduction in the role of the state, more actively encouraged people to opt out into private schemes, without any requirement that these schemes would be as good as the state scheme. This resulted in the so-called 'pensions scandal' when insurance companies and other sellers of private pensions, in the stampede to sell these pensions, sold personal pensions to individuals that were inferior to their existing pension arrangements, usually as a member of an occupational private pension. Meanwhile, those pensioners who continue to rely on the state pension, particularly those not eligible for SERPS, have seen the value of their pension decline substantially as a percentage of average wages. The Labour government's proposals, announced in November 1998, for a second state pension to replace SERPS along with the stakeholder pension for those who opt out of the former is an attempt to deal with these problems.

## Bibliography

European Commission (1995) *Europe: Social Protection*.

Eurostat (1995) *Europe in Figures*, 4th Edition.

George, V. and Howards, I. (1991) *Poverty Amidst Affluence*, Edward Elgar.

Harrison, D. (1996) Three years of wasted effort, *Financial Times*, 16 November.

HMSO (1998) *Social Trends*.

Ogus, A. I., Barendt, E. M. and Wikeley, N. J. (1995) *The Law of Social Security*, 4th Edition, Butterworths.

Oppenheim, C. and Harker, L. (1996) *Poverty: the facts*, 3rd Edition, CPAG.

*Which? Magazine* (1996) Get the right pension advice, September, p. 40.

*Which? Magazine* (1997) Get the right pension advice, January, p. 48.

# 9 Working Families Tax Credit and Disabled Person's Tax Credit

## Introduction

October 1999 marks the replacement of family credit and disability working allowance with working families tax credit and disabled person's tax credit, respectively. At the time of writing (spring 1999), the Tax Credits Bill, which introduces the two tax credits, has been published but the regulations containing the details for both have not.

Family credit was introduced in 1988, replacing family income supplement, which had been in existence since 1971. It is a tax-free, non-contributory, means-tested benefit that is designed to supplement low wages. It is a weekly benefit paid to a lone parent or couple with children where the lone parent or one of the couple is working more than 16 hours per week. Disability working allowance, first introduced in April 1992, is also a tax-free, non-contributory, means-tested benefit and is aimed to top up the wages of low-paid workers with a disability who are working 16 hours or more per week.

The working families tax credit, administered by the Inland Revenue, has the same basic features as its predecessor, family credit, being a non-contributory, means-tested benefit for families with dependent children where one person works 16 hours or more a week but it is designed to be more generous. From April 2000, it will be paid via a claimant's pay packet although couples can arrange for the non-working partner to receive it. Disabled person's tax credit also has similar characteristics to disability working allowance, being a non-contributory, means-tested benefit for disabled individuals working 16 hours or more per week but it is also designed to be more generous than its predecessor.

The general aim of these reforms is to integrate the tax and social security systems more closely and, as a consequence, to deal with the problem of the poverty trap. This most obviously arises for some individuals in receipt of a low wage who are also receiving family credit or disability working allowance who, on receipt of an increase in wages, can have the amount of benefit reduced by 70 pence for every additional pound received as well as pay additional income tax and even lose entitlement to passported benefits such as free prescriptions. These consequences produced what Gordon Brown described as, '...the grotesque distortion where some low-paid employees have had to pay back more than £1 for every extra £1 they earn' (Budget Statement, 17 March 1998).

# Family Credit

## Context and commentary

With the demise of family credit on 5 October 1999, this section merely sets out family credit's main features rather than provide a detailed description. Payable to lone parents or couples with dependent children where someone is working full time and on a low wage, it is a tax-free, non-contributory, means-tested benefit where the amount of benefit paid is determined by the number and ages of children in, as well as the total income and capital of, the family. However, childcare costs of up to £60 per week can be deducted before calculating the amount of family credit. Claimants whose weekly income is less than the 'applicable amount' of £80.65 per week (from April 1999) receive the maximum family credit to which they are entitled. Claimants whose weekly income exceeds that amount have their family credit reduced by 70% of the difference between their income and the applicable amount.

Family credit was originally introduced by the Social Security Act 1986 though the main provisions of the benefit were consolidated into the Social Security Contributions and Benefits Act 1992. However, the detailed regulations are contained in the Family Credit (General) Regulations 1987. It acts as a passport benefit to receive free prescriptions, dental treatment, fares to hospital and vouchers for glasses but not for free school meals although claimants do qualify for social fund payments for maternity or funeral expenses and crisis loans. It is a benefit that is claimed every 26 weeks and, once awarded, lasts for that period even if the circumstances of the claimant change e.g. his/her income rises or falls.

Family credit replaced family income supplement (FIS), which had first been introduced in 1971. FIS had been introduced by the 1970–4 Conservative government as a top-up benefit for low wage earners to deal with the so-called 'unemployment trap' whereby families can be better off receiving social security payments if no one works rather than having someone working on low wages. There were, however, major 'poverty trap' problems with FIS, with marginal tax rates, produced by the combination of increased tax and national insurance payments along with the loss of benefits, of up to 120%. This meant that some claimants of FIS could lose £1.20 for a £1 increase in earnings (Marsh and McKay, 1993, p. 4). Some of the most extreme 'poverty trap' features of FIS were alleviated by family credit. Nevertheless, as the earlier extract from Gordon Brown's March 1998 Budget Statement indicates, problems of high marginal tax rates, caused by increased tax and national insurance deductions and the fact that family credit is withdrawn at a rate of 70 p in the pound (i.e. at a rate of 70%), remain.

The current scope of family credit is set out in the following statement:

> 'In May 1998, there were 767,000 families receiving Family Credit of which 377,000 were lone parent families. Take up by caseload is estimated at 72% of all families eligible and this is estimated to be 84% if measured by the level of expenditure.' (Jarvis, 1999, p. 9).

## The legal rules

### General conditions of entitlement

There are five general conditions of entitlement:

(i)   the claimant or partner normally works 16 hours or more per week; and
(ii)  the claimant or partner is responsible for at least one dependent child; and
(iii) the claimant must be present and reside in Great Britain; and
(iv)  the claimant's family unit must not have savings or capital over £8,000; and
(v)   the income of the family unit must be below the means test.

### (i) Full-time work

Under s.128(1)(b) of the Social Security Contributions and Benefits Act 1992 and reg. 4 of the Family Credit (General) Regulations 1987 (FC Regs), a claimant or any partner must be 'engaged and normally engaged in remunerative work' for not less than 16 hours a week or, if the number of hours varies each week, for 16 hours on average per week. Under reg. 4(5), a claimant must have worked at least 16 hours in the week of the claim or in one of the two preceding weeks. Under reg. 4(6), a claimant is treated as 'normally engaged' in that work if he/she is likely to continue in it for at least five weeks after the claim. Individuals working fewer than 16 hours per week are eligible to claim income support or income-based jobseeker's allowance.

### (ii) Responsible for at least one dependent child

Under s.128(1)(d), a claimant or partner must be responsible for at least one child who is member of the claimant's household. The claimant need not be the parent of the child. Child is defined as someone aged under 16 or under 19 if engaged in full-time non-advanced education.

### (iii) Present and reside in Great Britain

Under s.128(1), a claimant must be in Great Britain and reg. 3(1) states that this is satisfied if, on the date of the claim:

- the claimant is present and ordinarily resident in Great Britain; and
- the claimant's the right to reside is not subject to any limitation or condition; and
- any partner is ordinarily resident in the United Kingdom – this includes Northern Ireland as well as Great Britain; and
- at least part of the earnings of the claimant or any partner are derived from remunerative work in the United Kingdom; and
- the earnings of the claimant and any partner do not wholly derive from work outside the United Kingdom.

### (iv) No savings or capital over £8,000

Under reg. 28, there is no entitlement to family credit if the disposable capital of a claimant (and any partner) exceeds £8,000. Where the amount of capital exceeds £3,000, it is deemed, under reg. 36, to generate a tariff income of £1 per week for each £250 or part thereof above £3,000, which means the amount of weekly family credit is reduced accordingly. For further details on the impact of capital and savings on entitlement to family credit, see Chapter 6.

### (v) Income

A claimant's (and any partner's) income has to be established to determine whether it is low enough to be eligible for family credit. The details in determining a claimant's income to establish entitlement for family credit are set out in Chapter 6 and are based on the general rules for means-tested benefits operating in the British social security system.

### The amount of family credit received

Once a claimant's income has been established, it is necessary to establish the maximum family credit for which he/she is eligible. Under reg. 46, the maximum family credit consists of an adult credit and a credit for each child as well as an additional credit if the claimant or partner works 30 hours or more a week. The rates for each credit operating from April 1999 are:

|  | £ | p |
| --- | --- | --- |
| Adult credit (lone parent or couple) | 49 | 80 |
| 30 hours credit | 11 | 5 |
| Child aged up to 10 | 15 | 15 |
| Child from September following 11th birthday | 20 | 90 |
| Child from September following 16th birthday | 25 | 95 |

The next step is to compare a claimant's income with the applicable amount, which is the same for all claimants of, since April 1999, £80.65. If his/her income is less than the applicable amount, the claimant receives the maximum family credit to which he/she is entitled. If the income is greater than the applicable amount, the maximum family credit is reduced by 70% of the amount by which it exceeds the applicable amount.

# Disability Working Allowance

## Context and commentary

Disability working allowance (DWA) is a tax-free, non-contributory, means-tested benefit whose objective is to encourage individuals with disabilities to return to work by topping up low earnings. Many of its features are similar to family credit, although it is not a requirement for DWA that the claimant is responsible for any dependent child(ren). In fact, if a claimant is so responsible, DWA should be claimed, as it is more generous than family credit.

Disability working allowance was introduced in April 1992 by the Disability Living Allowance and Disability Working Allowance Act 1991 though its main provisions are now contained in the Social Security Contributions and Benefits Act 1992. However, the detailed regulations are contained in the Disability Working Allowance (General) Regulations 1991. DWA assists in qualifying for a disability premium in respect of income support, housing benefit and council tax benefit and acts as a passport benefit to receive free prescriptions, dental treatment, fares to hospital and vouchers for glasses. It does not establish eligibility for free school meals although claimants do qualify for social fund payments for maternity or funeral expenses and crisis loans. It is a benefit that is claimed every 26 weeks and, once awarded, lasts for that period even if the circumstances of the claimant change, e.g. his/her income rises or falls.

The main purpose in introducing DWA in 1992 was to encourage people with a disability to return to, or take up, work by providing benefit to supplement any low wages. It was predicted in the White Paper setting out the DWA proposals (DSS, 1990) that a total of 50,000 people would be eligible for the benefit, which would be largely self-financing as its costs would be offset by the savings from disabled people moving from out-of-work benefits. However, it would appear that DWA has largely failed to achieve its main purpose, as indicated in the following statement:

'Helping disabled people move into work is probably the key aim of DWA but the benefit has not been very successful in achieving it. Between the spring of 1992 and the autumn of 1995, only two per cent (30,000) of the 1.5 million working-age recipients of the main incapacity benefits...moved off these benefits and into full-time work. And virtually all of these made the transition from benefits to work without the help of DWA. Only 200 of those claiming DWA in October 1993 had been directly encouraged into work by the benefit. There are some signs that the incentive effect is increasing – in the first half of 1994, approximately 500 people took a job because of DWA. But this is still a very small figure – DWA has not been successful in encouraging many people into work...' (DSS, 1996, para 5.12)

This failure is further highlighted in that, despite the 1990 White Paper's claim that 50,000 people would be eligible, in 1998 fewer than 16,000 individuals were receiving DWA (see DSS, 1998).

## The legal rules

### General conditions of entitlement

There are seven general conditions of entitlement:

(i)    the claimant must normally work 'full time' i.e.16 hours or more per week; and
(ii)   the claimant be aged 16 or over; and
(iii)  the claimant must be present and reside in Great Britain; and
(iv)   the claimant must have '...a physical or mental disability which puts [the claimant] at a disadvantage in getting a job' (s.129(1)(b) of the Social Security Contributions and Benefits Act 1992); and
(v)    the claimant is in receipt, or has recently been receiving, a qualifying sickness or disability benefit; and
(vi)   the claimant's family unit must not have savings or capital over £16,000; and
(vii)  the income of the family unit must be below the means test.

### (i) Full-time work

The requirements are the same as for family credit. Under s.129(1)(a) of the Social Security Contributions and Benefits Act 1992 and reg. 6 of the Disability Working Allowance (General) Regulations 1991 (DWA Regs), a claimant must be 'engaged and normally engaged in remunerative work' for not less than 16 hours a week or, if the number of hours varies each week, for 16 hours on average per week. Under reg. 6(5), a claimant must have worked at least 16 hours in the week of the claim or in one of the two preceding weeks. Under reg. 6(6), a claimant is treated as 'normally engaged' in that work if he/she is likely to continue in it for at least five weeks after the claim.

### (ii) Aged 16 or over

Unlike family credit, DWA has, under s.129(1), a minimum age entitlement of 16 years of age.

### (iii) Present and reside in Great Britain

The rules again reflect the same requirement as for family credit. Under s.129(1), a claimant must be in Great Britain and reg. 5(1) states that this is satisfied if, on the date of the claim:

- the claimant is present and ordinarily resident in Great Britain; and
- the claimant's right to reside is not subject to any limitation or condition; and
- any partner is ordinarily resident in the United Kingdom – this includes Northern Ireland as well as Great Britain; and
- at least part of the earnings of the claimant or any partner are derived from remunerative work in the United Kingdom; and
- the earnings of the claimant and any partner do not wholly derive from work outside the United Kingdom.

### (iv) Disadvantage in getting a job

Under s.129(1)(b), a person is entitled to DWA if he/she has '…a physical or mental disability which puts him at a disadvantage in getting a job.' Part 1 of Schedule 1 of the Disability Working Allowance (General) Regulations 1991 sets out a list of 20 conditions that constitute a disability which puts a person at a disadvantage in getting a job. These include being registered as blind or partially sighted; when standing the claimant cannot balance without continually holding on to something; he/she can turn neither hand sideways through 180 degrees; he/she cannot walk 100 metres on level ground without stopping or suffering severe pain; and, due to mental illness, the claimant is often confused or forgetful.

In practice, the declaration made by a claimant in respect of a first application for DWA (which lasts for 26 weeks) that any illness or disability puts him/her at a disadvantage in getting a job is accepted. For any subsequent applications for DWA, a claimant can be 'passported' through this requirement if he/she meets the next general condition, namely that he/she is in receipt, or has recently been receiving, a qualifying sickness or disability benefit. If not receiving a 'qualifying benefit', the claimant must complete a self-assessment form indicating which of the condition(s) exist that constitute(s) a disability that is at a disadvantage in getting a job.

### (v) In receipt, or recently been receiving, a qualifying sickness or disability benefit

Under s.129(2) a claimant must establish that he/she is in receipt, or has recently been receiving, a qualifying sickness or disability benefit. This can be achieved in one of two ways. The first way exists if, for at least one day during the eight-week period before the initial claim for DWA, the claimant received one of the following benefits:

- higher rate short-term incapacity benefit;
- long-term incapacity benefit;
- severe disablement allowance;
- the disability or higher pensioner premium in respect of income support, income based JSA, housing benefit or council tax benefit;
- any equivalent Northern Ireland benefit.

The second way exists if, on the day of the initial claim for DWA, the claimant was in receipt of one of the following benefits:

- disability living allowance;
- attendance allowance;
- industrial injuries or war pensions constant attendance allowance;
- war pensions mobility supplement;
- an invalid trike from the DSS;
- any equivalent Northern Ireland benefit.

### (vi) No savings or capital over £16,000

Under reg. 31, there is no entitlement to disability working allowance if the disposable capital of a claimant (and any partner) exceeds £16,000. Where the amount of capital exceeds £3,000, it is deemed, under reg. 40, to generate a tariff income of £1 per week for each £250 or part thereof above £3,000, which means the amount of disability working allowance is reduced accordingly.

### (vii) Income

A claimant's (and any partner's) income has to be established to determine whether it is low enough to be eligible for disability working allowance. The details in determining a claimant's income to establish entitlement are set out on pp. 113–125 in Chapter 6 and are based on the general rules for means-tested benefits operating in the British social security system.

### The amount of disability working allowance received

Once a claimant's income has been established, it is necessary to establish the maximum disability working allowance for which he/she is eligible. Under reg. 51, the maximum allowance consists of an adult credit and a credit for each child as well as an additional credit if the claimant or partner works 30 hours or more a week. Unlike family credit there is a higher adult credit for couples and lone parents than for single claimants. The rates for each credit operating from April 1999 are:

|                                                 | £  | p  |
|-------------------------------------------------|----|----|
| Adult credit (single)                           | 51 | 80 |
| Adult credit (lone parent/couple)               | 81 | 05 |
| 30 hours credit                                 | 11 | 05 |
| Child aged up to 10                             | 15 | 15 |
| Child from September following 11th birthday    | 20 | 90 |
| Child from September following 16th birthday    | 25 | 95 |
| Disabled child's allowance                      | 21 | 90 |

The next step is to compare a claimant's income with the applicable amount, which is, since April 1999, £60.50 for single claimants or, where the claimant has a partner, £80.65. If his/her income is less than the applicable amount, the claimant receives the maximum allowance to which he/she is entitled. If the income is greater than the applicable amount, the maximum allowance is reduced by 70% of the amount by which it exceeds the applicable amount.

# Working Families Tax Credit and Disabled Person's Tax Credit

## Context and commentary

The Labour Party Manifesto for the General Election of 1 May 1997 stated that the incoming government would '...examine the interaction of the tax and benefits systems so that they can be streamlined and modernised...[in order to] promot[e] work, reduc[e] poverty and welfare dependency and strengthen... community and family life.' (p. 13)

Following the election of the Labour government, a taskforce, headed by Martin Taylor, then of Barclays Bank, was established by Gordon Brown to explore the relationship of the tax and benefits systems and make suggestions for reform. In the second of its reports (HM Treasury, 1998), the taskforce recommended the introduction of a system of tax credits to replace family credit. A tax credit is an amount that is set against a wage earner's liability for tax, thus reducing the quantity of tax deducted or, where the credit exceeds the liability for tax, is paid to the wage earner as a supplement to his/her wages. However, the current proposals are not, strictly speaking, tax credits. They are not tax allowances, used to determine the amount of tax paid, but are merely social security benefits paid via the pay packet and administered by the Inland Revenue.

In his Pre-Budget statement in November 1997, Gordon Brown announced that a system of tax credits for working families would be implemented as part of the government's 'welfare to work' strategy. This was followed by the March 1998 Budget, when he announced that working families tax credit and disabled person's tax credit would replace family credit and disability working allowance, respectively. Instead of the state paying benefit via the social security system, those eligible would receive cash in their pay packets, via the tax system. A number of arguments were put forward in favour of paying a supplement to low wage earners through the tax system rather than by payment of a social security benefit (see House of Commons, 1998, pp. 7 and 10):

- There would be less stigma in receiving a supplement to low wages as a tax credit rather than as a social security benefit.
- It would be more acceptable than social security benefits both to most claimants and to taxpayers generally.
- If it is seen as more acceptable to claimants and has less stigma, it should increase take-up.
- If paid via the wage packet, it would reinforce the distinction between the rewards of work and remaining on welfare.
- It could help to lower marginal tax rates and, thus, reduce 'poverty trap' problems.
- It could reinforce the impact of the national minimum wage by making work pay and thus increase incentives to work.

Criticisms have, however, been expressed about this approach, including the following:

- The 'purse to wallet' issue centres around who receives the payment. As a traditional social security benefit, family credit tends to be paid to the mother. If payment is via the pay packet, however, it is increasingly likely to result in the money going to male partners. Such transfer of payment from female to male partners is criticised in that, inter alia, it will mean that for many families less of the money will be spent on the children as well as altering the control of, and access to, financial resources amongst many couples, to the detriment of female partners.
- The poverty trap will continue to exist for some claimants, because high marginal tax rates, created by withdrawal of benefit combined to increased tax and national insurance contributions, are inevitable where a system of means-testing is used to determine entitlement to benefit.
- It is claimed that a system of tax credits paid through the pay packet puts an unfair administrative burden on employers.

## Main features

At the time of writing (spring 1999), the Tax Credits Bill is still going through its legislative passage while the detailed regulations for both working families tax credit and disabled person's tax credit have not been published. It is, thus, not possible to provide a detailed account of their legal framework. In its place, what follows is an account of the chief characteristics of the two new benefits.

The main features of working families tax credit (WFTC) and disabled person's tax credit (DPTC) are contained in the Tax Credits Bill 1998 though the details are set out in regulations. The Inland Revenue administers both forms of tax credit rather than, as previously, the Benefits Agency although, in fact, they both retain many of the features of their predecessors. Thus, in respect of WFTC, the *Welfare Rights Bulletin* (1998, p. 7) comments that:

> 'The easiest way to understand the WFTC is to look on it simply as a more generous form of FC [family credit]. Confusion can step in because of the connection with the tax system and the description of payments as "tax credits". The WFTC is not a tax allowance. It is like FC but calculated and paid by the Inland Revenue instead of the Benefits Agency.'

The most significant differences between working families tax credit and disabled person's tax credit compared to their predecessors are twofold. First, the 'applicable amount' or threshold, from where the amount of benefit starts to be withdrawn once a claimant reaches that level of income, has been increased by almost £10 per week. Secondly, the amount that is withdrawn (known as the 'taper') has been reduced from 70 p for every pound above the threshold to 55 p in each pound. The combination of these two changes makes WFTC and DPTC substantially more generous than family credit and disability working allowance. The reduction of the taper from 70p to 55p in the pound also means that marginal tax rates are lower, resulting in a reduction in the harshness of the 'poverty trap' problem.

The two new benefits operate from October 1999, with payment by employers through the pay packet commencing in April 2000. However, for WFTC, couples can elect for the payment to be received by the non-working partner. Where partners disagree, WFTC is paid to the one with primary responsibility for care of the child(ren).

Couples or lone parents will qualify for WFTC if they satisfy the following four conditions:

(i) there is one or more children living with them; and
(ii) the claimant or partner works at least 16 hours per week; and
(iii) they reside in the United Kingdom and are entitled to work here; and
(iv) they have savings of £8,000 or less.

The calculations to establish the amount of WFTC are the same as for family credit. The first step is to calculate the maximum WFTC to which a claimant is entitled, depending on his/her circumstances. This consists of four elements:

(a)   a basic tax credit of £49.80 (both for a couple and lone parent);
(b)   a 30-hour tax credit of £11.05 (where the claimant or partner works at least 30 hours per week);
(c)   a tax credit for each child.

The rate depends on the child's age:

|  | £ | p |
|---|---|---|
| Child aged up to 10 | 15 | 15 |
| Child from September following 11th birthday | 20 | 90 |
| Child from September following 16th birthday | 25 | 95 |

(d)   a child care tax credit of up to 70% of eligible childcare costs up to maximum costs of £100 per week for one child and £150 per week for two or more children

It is then necessary to establish the weekly income of the claimant and (where relevant) partner after having deducted any income tax and national insurance payments if the net income is less than the threshold or 'applicable amount' of £90 then the maximum WFTC is payable. If the net income is above £90, the maximum WFTC is reduced by 55 p for each £1 above that figure. As with family credit once WFTC is awarded, it is paid for 26 weeks and then another application has to be made.

Disabled person's tax credit is payable to individuals who have a disability which puts them at a disadvantage in getting a job and who satisfy the following conditions:

(i)    they work at least 16 hours a week; and
(ii)   they reside in the United Kingdom and are entitled to work here; and
(iii)  they receive one of the qualifying benefits for disability – these are the same benefits as in respect of determining eligibility for its predecessor, disability working allowance. One change, however, is that receipt of one of the following qualifying benefits up to 182 days prior to the date of application of DPTC establishes eligibility – higher rate short-term incapacity benefit, long-term incapacity benefit, severe disablement allowance and the disability or higher pensioner premium in respect of income support, income-based JSA, housing benefit or council tax benefit. This is more generous than in respect of DWA where the time limit was only 56 days;
(iv)   they have savings of £16,000 or less.

The calculations to establish the amount of DPTC are the same as for disability working allowance. The first step is to calculate the maximum DPTC to which a claimant is entitled, depending on his/her circumstances. This consists of four elements:

(a)   a basic tax credit of £51.90 for a single person and £81.05 for a couple;
(b)   a 30-hour tax credit of £11.05 (where the claimant works at least 30 hours per week);
(c)   a tax credit for each child.

The rate depends on the child's age:

|  | £ | p |
|---|---|---|
| Child aged up to 10 | 15 | 15 |
| Child from September following 11th birthday | 20 | 90 |
| Child from September following 16th birthday | 25 | 95 |

(d)   a child care tax credit of up to 70% of eligible childcare costs up to maximum costs of £100 per week for one child and £150 per week for two or more children

The claimant will receive the maximum DPTC if his/her net income (and that of any partner) is less than the threshold or 'applicable amount' of £70 per week for a single person or £90 for a couple or lone parent. If the net income exceeds the threshold, the maximum DPTC is reduced by 55 p for each £1 above that figure. As with in respect of disability working allowance, once DPTC is awarded, it is paid for 26 weeks and then another application has to be made.

## Conclusion

The Labour government's introduction of these two reforms constitutes part of its overall strategy towards reform of social security. The Pre-Budget Report produced by the Treasury in November 1998 stated that working families tax credit, in combination with the national minimum wage, would guarantee families with one member in full-time work a weekly wage of £190 (Cm 4076, para 4.41). The disabled person's tax credit is part of a series of reforms in respect of social security provision for disabled people. This includes extending the New Deal to disabled claimants and exploring possible reform of the all work test in respect of incapacity benefit. The Pre-Budget Report also argued that disabled person's tax credit:

'...will provide a guaranteed minimum income of at least £150 a week for a single disabled person who moves from benefits to full-time work earning the national minimum wage, and £220 for a couple with one earner and one child' (para 4.45)

However, these minimum levels of income will only be achieved if individuals claim the new credits. This raises the issue of take-up. The government's view is that the changes introduced will increase levels of take-up in comparison to family credit and disability living allowance. As mentioned earlier, family credit, e.g. had a take up level of 72% of those entitled to claim (or 84% by expenditure). The government claim that the move to providing this financial support via the tax system should enhance levels of take-up. Thus, in respect of working families tax credit, Martin Taylor's taskforce concluded that:

> 'As a tax credit rather than a welfare benefit, [WFTC] should reduce the stigma associated with claiming in-work support, and encourage higher take-up.' (HM Treasury, 1998, para 2.09)

Whether the levels of take-up will rise, and whether the government is prepared to channel resources into publicity campaigns to achieve this, are issues that will unfold. Equally difficult to predict is whether working families tax credit and disabled person's tax credit will provide the financial incentive to encourage large numbers of people to move from welfare to work.

## Bibliography

DSS (1990) *The Way Ahead: Benefits for Disabled People*, Cm. 917.

DSS (1996) *Disability, Benefits and Employment*, DSS Research Report No. 54.

DSS (1998) *Disability Working Allowance Statistics: Quarterly Enquiry*, July.

HM Treasury (1998) *The Modernisation of Britain's Tax and Benefit System Number Two – Work Incentives: A Report by Martin Taylor.*

House of Commons (1998) *Working Families Tax Credit and Family Credit*, Research Paper 98/46.

Jarvis, B. (1999) 'Tax Credits', House of Commons Research Paper 99/3.

Marsh and McKay (1993) *Families: Work and Benefits*.

'The working families tax credit', *Welfare Rights Bulletin*, April 1998.

# 10 Child Benefit

## Context and Commentary

Child benefit is a non-taxable, non-contributory, non-means-tested benefit, which is paid to people who are responsible for a child. It is sometimes presented as the most obvious example in the British social security system of a *universal* benefit, as eligibility is neither based on payment of any contributions nor on satisfying a means test while no recipient of child benefit has any of the benefit 'clawed back' via the tax system. Universal benefits are available to all in contrast with selective benefits, which are only paid to people who are deemed to be in need, for example their income falls below a means-test level. However, this distinction, as discussed in Chapter 2, is not necessarily accurate. It is equally selective to base eligibility for a benefit on grounds of having a child in the household (or, in fact, on any ground) as it is to base it on level of income. Thus it is more appropriate to regard child benefit as a *categorical* benefit, in that eligibility is based on falling into a category of people, namely those that are responsible for a child.

Child benefit is paid at a higher rate for the first eligible child than for other children. In April 1999, the weekly amount for the first child is £14.40 and for each subsequent child, it is £9.60. It has a take-up rate of almost 100%. In 1996, it was paid to 7 million families throughout Great Britain in respect of 12.7 million children, its annual costs being £6.7 billion (DSS, 1997, p. 254).

The use of child benefit to provide assistance to families with children has been justified on a number of grounds. Some of these are set out in the following quote:

'Child benefit is a family income support mechanism with multiple functions:
– It reduces poverty among families with children.
– It removes a possible disincentive to work which could arise if children in families on social security were treated much more favourably than children from low income working families, and therefore helps the labour market to function better.
– It acts as a form of tax relief, ensuring fairness in the taxation of those with and without children.
– It serves the general community interest in the well-being of children

by sharing with families the high cost of child-rearing...' (Brown, 1988, p. 4)

There are, however, criticisms of child benefit and these tend to reflect the general arguments against non-means-tested benefits that were examined in Chapter 2. The two main arguments are that child benefit is poorly targeted and that, as a consequence, it is costly. If, as mentioned in the quote above, a major purpose of child benefit is to relieve poverty then, its critics argue, it is an inefficient way of doing this, as most child benefit does not go to those that are in poverty. Three-quarters of child benefit, for example, currently goes to people whose income is above the income-based JSA/income support means-test level. As a consequence, the second criticism is that child benefit is unnecessarily costly because, as it is paid in respect of all children irrespective of parental income, resources are not channelled to the poor and thus miss the target. From this perspective, child benefit leads to a waste of valuable financial resources that could be better directed towards those who need such resources, for example by replacing it with some form of means-tested benefit. Supporters of child benefit, however, challenge such accusations by suggesting that child benefit is very cheap to administer, as there is no need for a large bureaucracy, which would be the case if it were a means-tested benefit. Furthermore, the fact that it is not a means-tested benefit, but is available to all claimants who fall into the category of bringing up children, means that it has almost a 100% take-up rate. As a result, its supporters argue, in one sense it targets benefit better than means-tested benefits, in that all eligible claimants in poverty receive the benefit. This is in contrast to means-tested benefits where there are notorious problems of take-up e.g. family credit has a take-up rate of 72%, resulting in 28% of claimants whose income is below the means test and who are therefore eligible for the benefit not receiving it. Also, child benefit avoids the major 'poverty trap' and disincentive problems of means-tested benefits.

## Historical introduction

Child benefit was introduced in 1977 as a result of the Child Benefit Act 1975, becoming fully implemented in 1980. Prior to child benefit, financial support by the state for individuals bringing up children was provided in two ways. The first of these was the provision of family allowances. The Family Allowance Act 1945 introduced family allowance, which was non-contributory and non-means-tested but, unlike child benefit, was taxable. Another important difference to its successor was that family allowance was not paid for the first child. Between 1948 and 1967 the rate of payment was only increased twice but, in 1968, the then Labour government raised the rate twice, although this was targeted at those whose income was so low that they did not pay income tax.

This brings us to the second way that state provided financial support, prior to child benefit, for those responsible for children. This was through the tax system. Allowances were provided in respect of income tax for those who were bringing up children. This meant that part of a person's income was ignored for income tax purposes, namely the amount of the allowance, so that less tax was paid and, as a consequence, more income was retained. From 1957, the amount of child income tax allowances varied according to the age of a child, which differed from family allowance. One of the difficulties with this form of state provision of finance, however, is that it does not benefit those who are not paying income tax, for example those who are not working. Another difficulty is that a tax allowance benefits higher earners paying higher rates of income tax more than those paying basic rate. A person paying 40% rate income tax, for example, retains twice as much money as another with the same tax allowance who only pays tax at 20%. A third issue concerning such use of the tax system is that the money tends to accrue to male wage earners (in terms of a higher wage than if the allowance did not exist) rather than being received by the mother of the child. This contrasted with family allowance, which was paid to the mother.

In May 1975, Barbara Castle, then Secretary of Social Services, introduced the Child Benefit Bill, which had all-party support, as an attempt to integrate family allowances and child income tax allowances. This led to the demise of the tax system as a way of state subsidy of assistance in rearing children, thereby addressing the first two difficulties set out in the previous paragraph. The third difficulty was also addressed as child benefit is paid to the mother. Important changes, in comparison to family allowance, were that child benefit would be paid for the first child and that the benefit would not be taxable. The new benefit included Child Benefit Increase, which was a higher rate benefit for single parents. In 1980, this was renamed One Parent Benefit. Section 5(5) of the Child Benefit Act 1975 introduced another important change whereby the Secretary of State was required to annually consider the need for uprating the benefit. This did not though provide a statutory duty to index the rate of child benefit in line with either inflation, prices or wages. Nevertheless, in parliamentary debate, Barbara Castle argued that this was an improvement on family allowance, which had only been sporadically increased since its introduction (see Hansard, 1975, col. 161). In 1986, however, the then Conservative government repealed this statutory duty in the Social Security Act 1986. This contrasted with earlier commitments in 1980 and 1983 that the value of child benefit would be maintained in line with inflation (see Cracknell, 1998, p. 9). Following the 1986 Act, the rate of child benefit was frozen for three years between 1988 and 1990 (though the rate of one parent benefit was raised during this period). The reasons for freezing the rate of child benefit were twofold. First it was part of the overall strategy of consecutive Conservative governments from 1979 to 1997 to seek to reduce public expenditure on social security. Secondly, it was part of another, and associated, strategy of 'targeting' resources on those that needed them. Based on the criticisms of child benefit discussed earlier, this involved, inter alia, placing greater priority on means-tested benefits. Thus, while child benefit was frozen, needs allowances for children under the housing benefit scheme were increased and family credit, another means-tested benefit, came into operation in April 1988. A change in policy, however, took place in April 1991 when a higher rate for the first eligible child was introduced by providing an extra £1 per week though the rate for other children remained frozen. This introduction of a higher rate of benefit for the first child differed dramatically from family allowance which, until its demise in 1977, was not paid at all for the first child. A further £1 increase for the first child, and smaller increases for other children, was provided for by the November 1991 Budget and 1992 saw the government commit itself to increase child benefit in line with inflation.

Since the return of a Labour government on 1 May 1997, child benefit has been the target of various proposals for reform. One of the government's first steps in reforming social security was to commit itself to implementing its predecessor's policy of abolishing the higher rate one parent benefit for single parents. This change was based on an amendment to s.145(4) of the Social Security Contributions and Benefits Act 1992 which was introduced by the Social Security Act 1998. Section 145(4) prevents a rate of child benefit once set from being reduced. However the amendment in the 1998 statute created an exception to this in respect of one parent benefit. This was consequently abolished for most new claimants from 6 July 1998 as a result of the Child Benefit and Social Security (Fixing and Adjustment of Rates)(Amendment) Regulations 1998. However, claimants receiving the benefit on that date continue to receive it. Other contemporary reform proposals are examined in the next section.

## Contemporary issues

### Child benefit rates

The trend throughout much of the period of Conservative administration between 1979 and 1997 of not increasing the rate of benefit in line with inflation, culminating in the freezing of the rate of child benefit between 1988 and 1990, saw the real value of the benefit fall dramatically. Thus, in July 1998, Cracknell commented:

'In real terms, the benefit is now below its real 1979 value for both first and second children. This is largely due to the freezing of Child Benefit between 1988 and 1990.' (Cracknell, 1998, p. 11)

Concern about this led to the rate for the first child being raised in April 1999 by £2.50 in addition to the usual increase to reflect inflation. Thus, the weekly first child rate rose, in total, from £11.45 to £14.40. This was originally announced by Gordon Brown in his Budget on 17 March 1998 when he also announced this reform would be paid for by reducing the rate of income tax relief for the married couples allowance by one-third. However, the child benefit rate for other children was only uprated, in April 1999, in line with inflation. As a consequence, while the real value of the first child rate, since April 1999, is 15% higher than the April 1979 rate, the rate for other children is below its 1979 counterpart (Cracknell, 1998, p.11).

## Child benefit for recipients of income-related benefits

Child benefit is not means tested, and thus is payable to all individuals who fall into the category of being responsible for a child. However, those who are in receipt of an income-related (i.e. means-tested) benefit such as income-based jobseeker's allowance, income support or working families tax credit have the benefit fully taken into account in assessing their entitlement to the income-related benefit. This means that the income-related benefit that an individual receives is reduced by the amount of child benefit he/she receives. In other words, those claiming an income-related benefit receive no value from child benefit. This current feature of child benefit is, perhaps, the strongest aspect of the claim that it is poorly targeted, as the one group that, in effect, does not receive it are those whose weekly income is so low that they are eligible for means-tested benefits. Despite claims that the family responsibilities of those claiming income-related benefits are expressly recognised in that there are additional children's rates while most also have a 'family premium' element that provides additional benefit where a claimant or partner is bringing up children, it does seem absurd that child benefit is denied to this most financially vulnerable of groups. One obvious reform, therefore, would be to make child benefit one of the types of income that are disregarded in calculating entitlement to means-tested benefits.

## Taxation of child benefit

Taxation of child benefit has been seen as one way of reducing its costs and targeting it more directly to those in most need. If it became taxable, this would mean that, while those paying no income tax would retain all the benefit, those paying the tax would lose part of it in the form of the additional taxation paid. In a progressive system of income tax, where there were a large number of different rates of tax, getting progressively higher as income rises, this would mean that the higher an individual's income the less child benefit he/she would retain. Thus a person on a high income where income tax, for example, might be paid at 50% would lose half of the benefit whereas a lower earner paying income tax at a 25% rate would lose only a quarter of the benefit. However, the current British income tax system is not very progressive. While higher rates are paid by some higher earners, the vast majority of income tax payers actually pay income tax at the same 'basic rate'. Furthermore, tax is deducted from those with quite low incomes because the amount of income disregarded in the form of tax allowances is small. One consequence of this low 'threshold' at which income tax is paid is that taxing the child benefit of basic rate taxpayers would mean taking child benefit from many low wage earners who are universally recognised as one group on which it should be targeted. The issues raised in this paragraph are set out by McDermott and Howard as follows:

> 'The income tax thresholds in this country are so low that [child benefit] would be taxed back from those who need it. Further the tax rates are so flat now that the majority of taxpayers would be paying the same rate of tax on their child benefit. The argument in favour of taxing child benefit would be stronger if the threshold was higher and the rates more progressive.' (McDermott and Howard, 1998, p. 2)

As a consequence of these points, the debate on taxation of child benefit has concentrated on those paying income tax on higher rates and not those paying basic rate tax. In 1994, for example, the Commission on Social Justice, set up by the then Labour Party leader John Smith and chaired by Sir Gordon Borrie, advocated taxing the child benefit of higher rate income tax payers thereby generating resources which could be used to increase the rate at which the benefit is paid (Commission for Social Justice, 1994, pp. 316–7). Similarly, in his March 1998 Budget, Gordon Brown suggested that this is a reform that the Labour government were examining:

> 'For those who want child benefit raised, the question undoubtedly arises whether it should be taxed for those at the top of the income scale.' (*Hansard*, 1998, col.1108)

One likely consequence of such a move would be the need for the income of both partners in a family unit to be added together to establish its total income for tax purposes. Otherwise, for example, those families where the male partner has a large income and the female partner has little or no direct income would retain a disproportionately large amount of the benefit, in comparison to other family units with the same total income. Consequently, taxation of child benefit would, therefore, require the abolition of the independent taxation of husbands and wives.

Many of the arguments for and against taxing the child benefit of higher rate income tax payers are set out in the following two quotes. The first quote sets out arguments that support such a change:

> 'Bringing up children is expensive. It reduces your ability to buy things that childless people have. Tough: we all have a duty to try to work and pay our way through life. For those of us who are – touch wood – healthy, educated and in good employment, I can't see why the state should hand us a weekly tip simply because we decide to repro-duce...Parenthood...is neither a public duty nor a special vir-tue...Most of us can manage and we should be left to do so; those who can't should be helped, to ensure that children are not brought up in poverty.
> Some critics say child benefit gives middle class women an inde-pendent income. But the need for a female subsidy is also outdated, and patronising. Others object on principle: taxing child benefit un-dermines universal provision...I have two responses. One: what uni-versal provision? And two: that there is a higher, overriding principle: the best tax and benefit system is one that is simple and fair. That means taking money from people who can most afford it, and giving it to people who need it most, with as little buggering about in between as possible. The more this is so, the more people in real need will be helped, and the more moral authority the system has.' (Marr, 1999, p. 20)

Arguments against taxing the child benefit of higher rate taxpayers are set out in the next quote:

> 'It seems too simple to argue with. What could be more reasonable than taxing the rich who receive child benefit and giving the proceeds to the poor? For all its superficial attractions the idea is wrong in principle, and would end up turning the clock back for women in all social classes.
> For a start, I don't see why helping poor children should be the responsibility of richer families with children and not of society as a whole. Why shouldn't the better-off who are childless also put their hands in their pocket and chip in? Children are badly off because of generalised inequality, and the proper response is for everybody to be

asked to pay, not to place the burden disproportionately on families, even if they have higher incomes.

And whatever your income, if you have children you are worse off than somebody else on the same wage without them: kids are expensive. Of course those who have children generally do so from choice but they are also a collective investment in our future. Child benefit may go only a small way towards closing the gap between those with and without children in every income group, but it established the principle that children matter to every one.

...[It is] paid to mothers directly...because of the rampant sexism in most men and women's financial dealings...Women getting child benefit is an important counterbalance. But more important still the independent taxation of husband and wife, another buttress to women's equality, will be challenged. To make sufficient money from a child benefit tax Gordon Brown will have to end independent taxation and tax total household income, including child benefit. And men will receive higher tax bills because of their partner's child benefit. In a lot of households the result will be pure poison, and the cause of women's financial independence will be set back years.

So I'm against. I'm for women's equality and for everyone contributing to relieving child poverty. And for the principle that children are important to every one equally. To abandon all that for a meagre £450 million is wrong.' (Hutton, 1999, p. 20)

# The Legal Rules

## General conditions of entitlement

The Social Security Contributions and Benefits Act 1992 sets out the main provisions of child benefit although the detailed regulations are contained in a number of sets or regulations. The most important of these are the Child Benefit (General) Regulations 1976 No. 965.

Section 141 of the Social Security Contributions and Benefits Act 1992 states that:

> 'A person who is responsible for one or more children in any week shall be entitled...to [child] benefit for that week in respect of the child or each of the children for whom he is responsible.'

There are five general conditions of entitlement for child benefit:

(i)   the claimant is responsible for a child; and
(ii)  the claimant has a priority over other potential claimants; and
(iii) the child is one for whom child benefit is payable; and

(iv) both the claimant and child satisfy the residence conditions; and
(v) the claimant is not subject to any immigration status restrictions.

## (i) The claimant is responsible for a child

Under s.143(1):

> '...a person shall be treated as responsible for a child in any week if
> (a) he has the child living with him in that week; or
> (b) he is contributing to the cost of providing for the child at a weekly
> rate which is not less than the weekly rate of child benefit payable in
> respect of the child for that week...'

Section 143(1)(a) provides the first way that a person may be regarded as responsible for a child, namely if the child is living with him/her. However, the Act does not provide a definition of what constitutes 'living with' although a number of commissioner's decisions have addressed the issue. In *R(F)2/79*, the commissioner stipulated that the phrase 'living with' should bear its ordinary and natural meaning, each case being determined on its own particular facts and circumstances. He also stated that a child 'living with' a claimant is not necessarily the same as 'residing together'. The latter requires a greater degree of permanence and continuity. Nevertheless, in *R(F)2/81*, where a daughter was deemed not to be living with her father when with him from 11.30 a.m. to 6.30 p.m. at weekends, the Commissioner stated that 'living with' required that the child '...must live in the same house as [the claimant] and also be carrying on there with him a settled course of daily living.'

The second way that a person may be deemed responsible for a child and, thus, eligible for child benefit arises under s.143(1)(b). Under this section, a person can receive child benefit, even where a child does not live with him/her, if he/she is contributing to the cost of providing for the child at a weekly rate which is not less than the weekly rate of child benefit payable in respect of the child for that week. Under the priority rules referred to in the next section, eligibility for child benefit on this ground only exists if the person with whom the child is living with does not make a claim for the benefit.

## (ii) Priority over other potential claimants

Under s.144(3) and Sch 10 of the Social Security Contributions and Benefits Act 1992, where there is more than one potential claimant of child benefit, a number of priority rules exist to determine who, in the event of any competing claims, should receive the benefit. Under Sch 10, priority is in the following descending order:

(a)  the person with whom the child lives (para 2);
(b)  'as between a husband and wife residing together the wife shall be entitled' (para 3);
(c)  the parent of the child (under s.147(3) this includes step-parent or adoptive parent);
(d)  'as between two persons residing together who are the parents of the child but not husband and wife, the mother shall be entitled' (para 4);
(e)  in any other case a person agreed by those entitled above or, failing agreement, as determined by a person selected by the Secretary of State (para 5).

### (iii) The child is one for whom child benefit is payable

Section 142(1) of the Social Security Contributions and Benefits Act 1992 states that:

> '...a person shall be treated as a child for any week in which
> (a) He is under the age of 16; or
> (b) He is under the age of 18 and not receiving full-time education and prescribed conditions are satisfied in relation to him; or
> (c) He is under the age of 19 and receiving full-time education either by attendance at a recognised educational establishment or, if the education is recognised by the Secretary of State, elsewhere.'

This section thus establishes that the normal age limit for which child benefit can be received for any child is up to (but not including) the age of 16 although, in certain circumstances, this upper age limit can rise to 18 or 19. Therefore, under s.142(1)(b), child benefit can be paid for a child over 16 but under 18, in what is called the 'child benefit extension period' if, under reg. 7D, he/she satisfies the following requirements that he/she is:

(a)  registered as available for work or youth training; and
(b)  not working 24 hours or more a week; and
(c)  not receiving income-based jobseeker's allowance or income support; and
(d)  not on a youth training scheme.

Child benefit can also be paid, under s.142 (1)(c), in respect of a child up to the age of 19 if he/she is attending a full-time course of non-advanced education. Under regs 1(2) and 7A, non-advanced education is defined as up to A level or NVQ level 3 (or Scottish equivalents). HND, NVQ level 4 and degree studies are all advanced education so that no eligibility for child benefit applies to anyone studying on such courses. In *R(F)1/93* it was determined that a course at a 'recognised educational establishment' is 'full time' for child benefit purposes if it has more than 12 hours per week of any combination of instruction, tuition, supervised study, exams, practical work (including experiments and projects). There appears to be no such similar definition for courses undertaken elsewhere, though para 55233 of the *Adjudication Officer's Guide* indicates that, in such cases, 'full time' should be given its natural and ordinary meaning.

There are also important categories of children for whom there is no eligibility for child benefit. These include the following:

(a) If the child is married (para 3 of Sch 9 of the Social Security Contributions and Benefits Act 1992) or if he/she is living with someone as husband and wife (reg. 9A); or
(b) The child has spent more than eight consecutive weeks in prison or custody (reg. 16); or
(c) The child has spent more than eight consecutive weeks in the care of the local authority (reg. 16); or
(d) The child receives severe disablement allowance, income support or income-based JSA in his/her own right (reg. 7c and d).

### (iv) Both the claimant and child satisfy the residence conditions

The residence conditions for child benefit are fairly complex because, inter alia, entitlement is based both on the residence of the recipient of the benefit and the child (and, in some circumstances, on the child's parent, if he/she is not the recipient of child benefit). Section 146 of the Social Security Contributions and Benefits Act 1992 sets out the general statutory framework but there is also a specific set of regulations covering residence conditions – the Child Benefit (Residence and Persons Abroad) Regulations 1976 No. 963. The general conditions of residence are:

(a) Under s.146(2)(a), the child must be in Great Britain; and
(b) Under s.146(3)(a), the claimant is in Great Britain and has been here for at least 182 days in the previous 52 weeks; and
(c) Under ss.146(2)(b) and (3)(b), a parent of the child or the child or the claimant must have been in Great Britain for at least 182 days in the previous 52 weeks.

There is a number of exceptions to each of these conditions. For example, if a recipient of child benefit goes abroad on a temporary absence, he/she can continue to receive child benefit, under reg. 4 of the Child Benefit (Residence and Persons Abroad) Regulations, for up to eight weeks while, under reg. 2(2), child benefit can be paid for a similar period if the child is abroad on a temporary absence.

### (v) The claimant is not subject to any immigration status restrictions

In general, any person who is subject to immigration control in that s/he requires leave to enter or remain in Great Britain is not eligible, under s.146 and reg. 14B of the Child Benefit (General) Regulations, for child benefit. There is, however, a number of exceptions to this general condition, allowing individuals who fall into any of the exempt categories to claim child benefit. They include:

(a)   any EEA national or family member of an EEA national;
(b)   a person who has indefinite leave to remain;
(c)   a person who has refugee status;
(d)   a person who is working in Great Britain who is a national of a country with which the European Community has an agreement concerning equal treatment in social security. This includes Algeria, Morocco, Slovenia and Tunisia.

As well as these five general conditions of eligibility, there is transitional protection for individuals in receipt of child benefit when restrictions on eligibility based on immigration status were introduced in October 1996.

### Rates of child benefit

Child benefit is paid at two weekly rates because, since April 1991, a higher rate is paid for the eldest eligible child. As mentioned earlier, April 1999 saw a substantial increase in the weekly rate for the eldest child but this was not reflected in a similar rise for other children. The rates for the year from April 1999 are £14.40 per week for the eldest eligible child and £9.60 per week for every other eligible child.

### Lone parent rate of child benefit

Until April 1997, one parent benefit was paid to single parents rather than child benefit and was paid at a higher rate. It was replaced by a higher rate of child benefit for lone parents until that was also abolished on 6 July 1998. However, some claimants continue to receive the higher rate which, in the year from April 1999, is £17.10 per week for the eldest child and £9.60 per week for each other child. The most obvious group that continues to receive the lone parent rate of child benefit are those claimants that were receiving it on 5 July 1998 and continue to be eligible for it.

## Conclusion

Child benefit is one of the most simple and cheap benefits to administer in the British social security system. This is largely due to eligibility being neither determined by a means test nor based on a contributions record. Furthermore, its take-up rate is almost 100% of its target constituency. Yet, despite these virtues, it is one of the most controversial of social security benefits. The Conservative governments of the 1979–97 period, particularly when Margaret Thatcher was prime minister, were, at best, ambivalent to the benefit and, at worst, openly hostile. Its lack of means testing as a basis of entitlement was contrary to the general thrust of the reforms of social security in that era which, inter alia, sought to target benefits to those deemed to be in need by, amongst other things, embracing means testing as the primary basis of benefit entitlement. This ambivalence/hostility accounted for a freeze on increasing the level of child benefit for three years from 1988 to 1990. That child benefit was not radically reformed by, for example, basing entitlement on a means test was largely due to concern about the political consequences of taking benefit away from a large number of the electorate.

The current Labour government has shown greater support for the benefit, with the substantial increase in the rate for the first child in April 1999 being the most obvious aspect of this. Nevertheless, Gordon Brown, amongst others, has signalled that the government is considering a form of 'means testing in reverse' by suggesting that taxing of child benefit is a proposal that may be introduced in the near future, whereby some of the value of the benefit is siphoned away from higher rate income tax payers.

## Bibliography

Brown, J. (1988) *Child Benefit: Investing in the Future* Child Poverty Action Group.

Commission for Social Justice (1994) *Social Justice: Strategies for National Renewal*, pp. 316-7.

Cracknell, R. (1998) *Child Benefit*, House of Commons Research Paper 98/79.

DSS (1997) *Social Security Statistics 1997*, Department of Social Security.

*Hansard* (1975) 'Select Committee Debate A', 26 April, col. 161.

*Hansard*, 17 March 1998, col. 1108.

Hutton, W. (999) 'Should we tax child benefit? No', *The Observer*, 7 March.

Marr, A. (1999) 'Should we tax child benefit? Yes', *The Observer*, 7 March.

McDermott, T. and Howard, M. (1998) *Child Benefit: Arguments For and Against Taxation*, Child Poverty Action Group.

# 11 Housing Benefit

## Context and Commentary

Housing benefit is a tax-free, means-tested, non-contributory benefit that is paid to claimants, whether or not in full-time work, on low income who pay rent, . Housing benefit is paid by local authorities, though it is a national scheme. Governed by the Social Security Contributions and Benefits Act 1992, its detailed provisions are contained in rules largely determined by Department of Social Security regulations.

## Historical Introduction

Prior to the Social Security and Housing Benefits Act 1982, which introduced the first system of housing benefits in 1983, assistance to help meet housing costs such as rent, rates and mortgage payments for those deemed to be in need (i.e. who fell below the relevant means test) was provided by two separate systems. The supplementary benefits scheme contained provisions to cover housing costs while local authorities also played a role via the rate rebate and rent rebate and rent allowance schemes. A major problem was the overlap between the two schemes so that, in some situations, a claimant had a choice of claiming under either to meet his/her housing costs. This created what became known as the *better-off problem*. The provisions of the schemes were not identical so that, if a claimant applied for support under the wrong scheme, less financial assistance could be received than would have been obtained under the alternative scheme i.e. he/she would have been better off under the alternative scheme. This problem, along with others, was highlighted by the Supplementary Benefits Commissions, who oversaw the operation of the supplementary benefits system, in a succession of Annual Reports from 1976 to 1979:

> 'The Commission took as its focus the "better-off" problem, described as confusion of, and actual loss to, some householders caused by the overlap. Because of the different means tests and allowances, it was difficult to estimate whether a person not in full-time work should claim supplementary benefits or rebates. The SBC proposed a single housing benefit to replace rent and rates rebates, rent allowances and the rent and mortgage interest element of supplementary benefit.' (Ogus and Barendt, 1995, p. 487)

The return of the Conservative government in 1979 saw an immediate examination of possible reforms, culminating in the introduction of the housing benefit scheme in 1983 to replace the local authority schemes along with the supplementary benefit schemes responsibility for housing costs. Consistent with the new government's approach towards controlling public expenditure, this new scheme operated on a 'nil cost basis' whereby no additional funding was forthcoming. The scheme was operated by local authorities, thereby having the added advantage to the government of administrative savings at central government level. However, when implemented, the scheme proved to be an administrative disaster, a review of its operation by the National Association of Citizens Advice Bureaux (NACAB) published in January 1984 identifying, inter alia, the following problems. First, there had been a failure by local authorities to recruit enough staff to administer the scheme:

> '...the picture which emerges from the majority of cases submitted by bureaux shows that inadequate staffing of local authority Housing Benefit offices has caused a considerable backlog of cases. Few local authorities fully anticipated the implications of the new scheme and they are now faced with unmanageable numbers of claimants seeking help with their housing costs.' (NACAB, 1984)

Secondly, NACAB identified the lack of training of staff to deal with the requirements of the new scheme, while a third problem was the widespread confusion and dissatisfaction in respect of the appeals system:

> 'Considerable bewilderment and uncertainty still surrounds the system set up for appeals by claimants under the Housing Benefit scheme...Moreover, NACAB is concerned that the principle of independence is undermined by the fact that an elected representative, who may not know or understand a great deal of the law relating to Housing Benefit, is asked to pass judgement on an employee of the same local authority.' (NACAB Report)

However, the main criticism was that many recipients of housing benefit were worse off financially than they were before its introduction.

## Structure of the housing benefit scheme 1983–88

The original aim of the changes that came into force in 1983 was to replace the existing systems with a single benefit for housing costs. Nevertheless, from the outset, it never achieved a single *unified* system. The housing costs of owner-occupiers, most notably mortgage payments, continued to be dealt with under the supplementary benefit scheme and its successors,

228 Social Security Law

income support and jobseeker's allowance. Housing benefit, therefore, was, and continues to be, a means-tested scheme for assisting *tenants* with their housing costs. The 1983 scheme sought to do this via three different types of housing benefit. *Certificated housing benefit* was paid to claimants also in receipt of supplementary benefit. *Standard housing benefit* was paid to claimants, such as those in low paid jobs, who were not in receipt of supplementary benefit. *Housing benefit supplement* was a 'top-up' benefit designed to assist those who lost out most following the replacement of the old schemes by housing benefit.

The 1983 reforms, however, soon become subject to further changes. In the Autumn Budget Statement in November 1983, the Chancellor of the Exchequer announced that the housing benefit scheme would be subject to a cut of £230 million, although a Conservative backbench MP revolt the following January saw the cut reduced to £185 million. This was followed in April 1984 by Norman Fowler, then Secretary of State for Social Services, announcing what he described as the 'most comprehensive review of the social security system for 40 years'. Included in this was a review of housing benefits, the findings of which were published the following year. These identified three main problems. First, the housing benefit scheme provided differing levels of financial support for households with similar needs and incomes. This was particularly noticeable when claimants in receipt of supplementary benefit were compared with those who were not, such as those in full-time employment but on low wages. Supplementary benefit recipients, by and large, tended to be treated more favourably and this was seen as substantially weakening any incentive for them to seek work. Secondly, the three different types of housing benefit meant that the scheme was unduly complicated. Thirdly, the review team argued that housing benefit was too widely available, resulting in the call for reducing eligibility.

As part of these wide scale 'Fowler reforms', government proposals for reform of housing benefit along the above lines were set out in both the White Paper in December 1985 and the subsequent Social Security Bill in January 1986, the latter becoming the Social Security Act 1986. The major change that took place was to tie in housing benefit with the new income support scheme introduced by that Act to replace supplementary benefits. The Act introduced a common basis of assessment for housing benefit and income support and abolished housing benefit supplement. This common assessment using the income support means test for all housing benefit claimants (irrespective of whether a claimant was in work – and hence ineligible for income support – or not) meant the end of the certificated/standard distinction.

While these changes represented a simplification of the structure of housing benefit, they were accompanied by a further reduction in the housing benefit budget, leading to reduced benefit rates. This led one pressure group to identify the consequences of these reforms as follows:

'These measures represent yet another chapter in the troubled history of housing benefit and the loss of something like a further £450 million from the housing benefit budget. The proposed changes are not all bad. Aspects of the new *structure* would indeed represent an improvement on the present arrangements. Much of the problem lies, not in the structure, but in the level of resources which will be fed into it: a quart of need cannot be met out of a pint point, however well crafted that vessel might be. The Government's pint-sized approach to housing benefit resources spoils a more rational structure by imposing deficient needs allowances, over-steep withdrawal rates and a harsh across-the-board cut in assistance with rates' (Social Security Consortium, 1986).

## Current developments

The current government is seeking to reform housing benefit. Its driving motivation is the belief that a substantial amount of fraud is perpetrated in respect of this benefit. Of an estimated total of £4 billion social security fraud per year, the March 1998 Green Paper stated that £1 billion is housing benefit fraud and it confirmed that:

'The Government is committed to tough action to stop social security fraud.' (Green Paper, 1998, p. 67)

To this extent the government, then in opposition, supported the rush through Parliament of the previous government's Social Security (Administration) Fraud Act 1997 which facilitated the exchange of information between the Department of Social Security and local authorities and other government departments. The Act also created powers whereby claimants suspected of fraud can be given the opportunity to pay back the amount in question plus a penalty of 30%, as an alternative to prosecution. Since being in power, the government has undertaken a review of housing benefit fraud in 1997 and 1998. This operated in collaboration with the series of reviews of fraud in social security run by the Department of Social Security since 1994. The *Benefit Fraud Inspectorate* was also established in November 1997 and a major part of its brief has involved working with a number of local authorities, focusing on their administration of housing benefit and council tax benefit. In his initial Annual Report (*Securing the System*, July 1998) the Director General of the Inspectorate, Ian Stewart, highlighted that the work with local authorities had resulted in the authorities being in a position to counter housing and council tax benefit fraud more effectively. Evidence of the scope of housing benefit fraud was provided in the second housing benefit accuracy review, whose main findings were published in July 1998 (the first review having taken place in 1995). Based on a sample of 4,700 cases across 96 local authorities, the review indicated that 19% of housing benefit claimants were receiving an incorrect amount of payment of housing benefit with a net cost to the taxpayer of £840 million per annum. While approximately £240 million of this was attributed to claimant error and £20 million to official error, fraud was deemed to cost around £590 million (the figures are taken from the *Second National Housing Benefit Review*, Government Statistical Service, July 1998). However, as the Review makes clear, evidence of fraud was not always obvious and the figures are therefore based on the perceptions of investigators on whether, where errors of payment took place, the claimant intended to defraud. As the Press Release accompanying the publication of the main results of the Review stated:

> '...where an investigator established that the wrong rate of HB was being paid, and there was not enough evidence to prove fraud, they [sic] had to judge whether the claimant had deliberately intended to receive more benefit that their [sic] entitlement. The judgments made will inevitably not be correct in all of the sample cases.' (*Press Release 98/222*, Department of Social Security)

Some of these figures, in fact, can be labelled as little more than 'guestimates' in that, while the cases where fraud could be proved resulted in a loss of £180 million, cases where there was deemed to be a 'strong suspicion of fraud'cost £430 million and those where there was a 'mild suspicion of fraud' were claimed to cost £80 million. The reliability of such statistics based on investigators, who are committed to dealing with an already preconceived 'problem' of fraud, being required to assess the intention of claimants to defraud where there is an error in the amount of housing benefit they receive, can surely be questioned. This evidence, nevertheless, fuelled the government's commitment to deal with housing benefit fraud and a further Green Paper was also published in July 1998. Entitled *Beating Fraud is Everyone's Business: securing the future* it was concerned with social security fraud in general, although it paid particular attention to housing benefit fraud. The Green Paper, relying on the evidence of internal DSS reviews such as the one outlined above, argued that the social security budget is 'under attack' from two types of fraud, namely:

> '...from a large number of individuals, finding ways to commit fraud among the plethora of detailed rules governing the benefits...and from

organised attempts at major fraud each involving enormous sums of public money'. (*Beating Fraud is Everyone's Business: securing the future*, para 2.2)

However, the concern about the accuracy of the figures on the extent of housing benefit fraud, can be extended to social security fraud in general, particularly in respect of individual fraud, in light of the following statement in the Green Paper:

'The system's complexity also means that we are vulnerable to mistakes leading to incorrect payments, even where there is no intention to defraud. For example, with 33 million changes of circumstances reported each year to the Benefits Agency alone, there is substantial scope for error. Claimants do not always fully understand when to report a change, what to report or whether a call to one agency notifies all others that might also be involved. The collection or assessment of millions of pieces of information over many years has also produced a system where the data is not always reliable...' (para 2.3)

Within such a context, any attempts to assess the 'intention to defraud' of individual claimants in situations where errors in payment are made is surely exceedingly difficult and open to substantial error. However, the Department's response was to suggest that while '[m]easuring the level of fraud in the system is difficult...even more in-depth investigation might potentially uncover more sophisticated fraud' (paras 2.4 and 2.9).

While this may be true, so might the opposite as might be the case that the current 'guestimates' on fraud are, in fact, of very little use in determining the scope of social security fraud in general and housing benefit fraud in particular. Such a view was expressed, in respect of the evidence provided in the first housing benefit accuracy review in 1995, by a House of Commons Select Committee report on housing benefit fraud published in May 1996, which expressed concern '...that there is not a more coherent consensus on the level and nature of Housing Benefit fraud' (*Welfare Rights Bulletin*, 1997, p. 6).

The Green Paper nevertheless argued that:

'There is clear evidence that very substantial sums are being paid incorrectly, both in genuine error but also because of fraud. The systems for delivering social security, and the environment in which they operate, do not produce the level of security necessary for a modern service. To change this, the Government is committed to a systematic, across the board assault on fraud and incorrectness' (paras 2.21 and 2.22).

To achieve this, it sets out, in para 3.6, four aims to provide the framework for change:

(i)   To develop an anti-fraud culture among staff and the public and to deter fraud.
(ii)  To design and operate policies and systems which minimise fraud.
(iii) To create an environment in which the work against fraud can flourish; and
(iv)  To develop a highly skilled anti-fraud profession.

If such a reform strategy is implemented, it is difficult not to sympathise with the following statement made in respect of the 1995 review of housing benefit fraud and the political consequences that followed:

> 'There are dangers that the culture in the benefit agencies will become more "anti-claimant" with stereotypes and prejudices reinforced by the emphasis on checks and onus of proof.' (*Welfare Rights Bulletin*, 1997, p. 6)

## The Legal Rules

### Current eligibility for housing benefit

The legal framework for housing benefit eligibility is primarily provided by the Social Security Contributions and Benefits Act 1992. This consolidating piece of legislation left largely unchanged the reforms to housing benefit introduced by the Social Security Act 1986. The detailed rules on housing benefit eligibility are, however, set out in a number of sets of regulations, the most important of which is the Housing Benefit (General) Regulations 1987 (HB regs). These have been amended quite substantially since 1992, recent important instances being the Housing Benefit (General) Amendment Regulations of 1995 and 1996.

Under the housing benefit scheme, tenants living in council or 'new town' accommodation are – per s.134(1(b) of the Security Contributions and Benefits Act 1992 – eligible for a *rent rebate*. Under HB regs 8(2) and 10(2) this includes people living in local authority or NHS group homes that do not provide 'board' arrangements and people who are 'shared owners', i.e. buying part of their accommodation and rent the rest from the council. Those *ineligible* for rent rebate include occupants of a local authority old people's home and those who are renting on a lease in excess of 21 years (HB reg. 8(2)). Tenants living in private accommodation, whether furnished or unfurnished are eligible for a *rent allowance* – s.134(1)(c) Security Contributions and Benefits Act 1992. This includes accommodation provided by a housing association and tenants who live in board and lodging accommodation or a hostel. Those *ineligible* for rent allowance include those who are renting on a lease in excess of 21 years (HB regs 2(1) and 10(2)(a) as well as the ground rent and mortgage payments of owner-occupiers.

An important element of housing benefit is that the weekly amount received can be substantially reduced where individuals, who are not deemed to be members of the claimant's family, reside with him/her. A significant aspect of this relates to 'non-dependants', where set deductions are made from a claimant's housing benefit on the assumption that a non-dependant is making a contribution to the claimant's housing costs, whether or not he/she actually is. A second important aspect of housing benefit concerns 'rent restrictions'. Where a claimant's rent is regarded as being too high or the accommodation is deemed to be too large for him/her and those living with him/her, the amount of housing benefit received will be less than the amount of rent actually paid.

## Main eligibility requirements

General eligibility for housing benefit is set out in s.130 of the Social Security Contributions and Benefits Act 1992. A claimant is eligible for housing benefit if the following conditions are satisfied:

(i)  the claimant or partner is liable to pay rent for accommodation; and
(ii)  the claimant normally occupies the accommodation as his or her home; and
(iii)  the claimant has capital or savings of less than £16,000; and
(iv)  the claimant is on a low income. The means test for income support benefit is used to determine the claimant's income. If his/her income is below the 'applicable amount' of income support relevant to the claimant's financial circumstances, he/she will receive 100% of his eligible rent, which is his *maximum housing benefit*. If the claimant's income is above his/her income support 'applicable amount', he/she may nevertheless still be eligible for housing benefit, though the amount of benefit will be reduced. The amount of housing benefit will be the maximum housing benefit less 65% of the amount by which the claimant's income exceeds his/her income support 'applicable amount'. This 65% sliding scale reduction is known as a *taper*; and
(v)  the claimant must satisfy the *habitual residence* test and not be ineligible on any other ground.

### (i) Liable to pay rent

Under reg. 6, the person legally liable to make payments of rent is eligible for housing benefit as is any other person deemed liable. While the term 'legally liable' clearly embraces the legal tenant, liability has been extended to others 'deemed liable' in order to cover, inter alia, situations where the tenant has left the accommodation, e.g. where the end of a relationship has seen the tenant leave the accommodation. In fact reg. 6 sets out the following situations where a person who is not legally liable can be deemed liable to make payments of rent and thus be eligible for housing benefit:

(a)   where the claimant is the partner of the legally liable person;
(b)   under reg. 6(1)(c)(i), where the legally liable person has left the accommodation, the local authority *must* treat the former partner as liable if he/she is required to pay rent in order to remain living in the dwelling.
(c)   under reg. 6(1)(c)(ii), where a claimant who is not the former spouse of the legally liable person is paying rent for accommodation, the local authority has a discretion to treat that person as so liable and thus eligible for housing benefit, if it considers it reasonable to do so.

### (ii) Occupation of a dwelling as a home

Section 130(1) Security Contributions and Benefits Act 1992 entitles a claimant to housing benefit '...in respect of a dwelling in Great Britain which he occupies as his home...' and HB reg. 5(1) develops this by stating that 'a person shall be treated as occupying as his home the dwelling *normally occupied* as his home...'. The main difficulty arises where a claimant is deemed to have more than one home. In such situations the general rule is that housing benefit is only payable in respect of the *main home*, although there is a number of important exceptions to this set out in reg. 5, thereby allowing a claimant to receive housing benefit for two homes. Such exceptions include the following:

(a)   If the claimant has left the previous home, and remains absent from it, *through fear of violence* in that home or from a former member of the family then, under regs 5(5)(a) and 7(A), the local authority can pay housing benefit for both homes for up to 52 weeks as long as it is 'reasonable that housing benefit should be paid in respect of both'.
(b)   Under reg. 5(5)(b) if the claimant or partner is a trainee or student and has unavoidably to live away from home so that the partners occupy two separate dwellings, then housing benefit can be paid for two homes if it is 'reasonable that housing benefit should be paid in respect of both dwellings'.
(c)   If the claimant's family is so large that the local authority have housed it in two separate dwellings, reg. 5(5)(c) provides that housing benefit can be paid for both dwellings.
(d)   Reg. 5(5)(d) provides that housing benefit can be paid to a claimant for two homes where he/she is moving home or transferring tenancies 'for a period not exceeding four weeks if his liability to make payments in respect of two dwellings is unavoidable'.

## (iii) The impact of capital on eligibility

Under reg. 37 there is no entitlement to housing benefit if the capital of a claimant (and partner, if any) exceeds an upper threshold of £16,000 (this being raised in 1990 from the original £6,000). Under reg. 45 any capital below this amount but above a lower threshold of £3,000 is deemed to give rise to a 'tariff income' of £1 per week for each complete £250 or part thereof, e.g. capital of £4,600 = £7 per week tariff income. (Since April 1996, the lower threshold for claimants permanently in residential care or similar accommodation was raised to £10,000.) This is then aggregated with assessable earnings and any other income when calculating a claimant's means test.

One of the main difficulties is that capital is not defined in either the regulations or statutorily, though the Department of Social Security's *Guidance Manual* states that it includes all categories of holding of a clear monetary value which can reasonably be considered to be available to the claimant. It includes cash, savings in bank, building society or similar accounts, shares, property, lump sums such as redundancy payments and National Savings Certificates and premium bonds.

There are *three* potential elements of capital: ordinary capital; income which is treated as capital; and notional capital. All of a claimant's capital that is not disregarded or treated as income is taken into account and is regarded as ordinary capital. Under reg. 41 capital is valued at its current market or surrender value though reg. 41(a) states that 'where there would be expenses attributable to sale' 10% of the value can be deducted from this capital amount.

Reg. 40 stipulates that certain forms of income are treated as capital. These include income tax refunds, any holiday pay received more than four weeks after the end of employment and any income derived from savings or investment (e.g. interest on a building society account). Notional capital refers to situations where a claimant is deemed to have capital which he/she does not, in fact, possess. Set out in regs 12 and 43, this covers such situations as a claimant being deemed to have deprived himself of assets in order to be eligible for benefit. The DSS's *Housing Benefit Guidance Manual* gives examples of the kinds of expenditure that can amount to deprivation, e.g. an expensive holiday, putting money in trust. However, the essential test under the regulations is not the kind of item that the money has been spent on but that the *intention* behind the expenditure was to make the claimant eligible for benefit. Other examples of notional capital include failure to apply for available assets and payment of capital to third parties (e.g. the electricity board or building society) used to purchase food, clothing, fuel or additional housing expenditure.

Some elements of capital are *disregarded* in assessing housing benefit. These include personal possessions such as jewellery, furniture and a car (unless they were deemed to have been purchased in order to be eligible for benefit – per Sch 5, para 11), the surrender value of any life insurance or endowment policy (Sch 5 para 16) and, perhaps most importantly, the home that a claimant normally lives in (Sch 5 para 1).

A major exception to the principle of aggregation in housing benefit (see pp. 101–102), as in all income-based benefits, is that, under reg. 39, the capital of dependent children or young persons who are members of the 'family unit' is *not* aggregated with that of the claimant though, if a child has more than £3,000 capital, the claimant does not receive a dependant's personal allowance for that child when calculating his/her 'applicable amount'.

### (iv) The claimant is on a low income

Since 1988, the income support means test has been used to determine eligibility on income grounds for housing benefit. In practical terms, this means that if a claimant is in receipt of income support or, since October 1996, income-based jobseeker's allowance, he/she is automatically entitled to housing benefit. For other claimants, the necessary calculations will need to be made. While this is set out in detail in Chapter 8, it may be helpful to set out the main features here. The first step is to establish the claimant's *applicable amount*. This is assessed in the same way as for income support, except for a few slight differences, and will vary according to the personal circumstances of the claimant and any other members of the family unit. It involves calculating all personal allowances and premiums for which there is eligibility. Set out in regs 13–15 and Sch 2, the one main difference to income support is that the *family premium–lone parent rate* is higher (in the year from April 1999 it is £22.05 per week in contrast to £15.75 for income support), although this is only available for lone parents who were in receipt of it in April 1998. It has been abolished for other lone parent claimants.

The next step is to determine the *weekly income* of the claimant. Essentially the same task as for income support, it includes establishing what income of other members of the family unit is regarded as the claimant's and what is not, and how much of any earnings, other benefits and maintenance payments are disregarded in determining the claimant's total weekly income. The main difference to income support and income-based JSA is that, for housing benefit, £15 per week of any maintenance from a former spouse is disregarded as being part of a claimant's income whereas, for the other two benefits, none of this is disregarded and also, under Sch 3, up to £25 per week of earnings can be disregarded in contrast to a maximum of £15 per week for the other two benefits.

The income of the claimant is then compared with the applicable amount to which he/she is entitled. If income is equal to or less than the applicable amount, the claimant is entitled to the *maximum housing benefit*. If income is more than the applicable amount then, under s.21(5) Social Security Contributions and Benefits Act 1992 and HB regs 61 and 62, the amount of housing benefit is the maximum housing benefit (otherwise known as the 'eligible rent') less 65% of the amount by which income exceeds the applicable amount. The effect of this *taper* is that for each £1 of excess income maximum benefit is reduced by 65p per week. The higher the income the greater the impact of the taper so that, at some point the taper exceeds the amount of housing benefit, so that none is paid. The minimum weekly amount of housing benefit payable is, per reg. 46, 50p.

### (v) Those who are ineligible for housing benefit – the habitual residence test and other criteria of eligibility

There are certain individuals who are not entitled to housing benefit. These include the following:

(a) **Students**. Under reg. 48(A)(1), full-time students, with some exceptions, are not eligible for housing benefit. Full-time student is not defined, other than reg. 46 stating that it includes someone on a sandwich course, i.e. a course that involves some work experience within it. While eligibility for a grant is not, officially, a determining factor, as student grants are normally only payable for full-time courses, in practice it is likely to be highly influential in local authorities deciding on eligibility for housing benefit. Under reg. 48(A)(2), those full-time students who are eligible for housing benefit include those receiving income support; those students under 19 and not following a course of higher education (i.e. HND and above); where both the claimant and partner are students and there are dependent children; and where the claimant has a disability and meets the conditions for either the severe disability or the disability premium of income support (even if he/she is not in receipt of income support).

(b) **Owner-occupiers**. Anyone who owns the accommodation or has a lease of more than 21 years is not, per reg. 2(1), eligible for housing benefit. Any assistance with the housing costs for individuals in these categories is covered by income support or income-based JSA

(c) **Close relatives**. Under reg. 7(1)(a), any person who pays rent to someone else living in the same dwelling and either that person is a close relative or it is deemed that it is not a commercial relationship is ineligible for housing benefit. Reg. 2(10) defines 'close relative' as a parent, parent-in-law, son, son-in-law, daughter, daughter-in-law, step-parent, step-son, step-daughter, brother, sister or the partner of any of these. In such situations the person to whom rent is paid may be eligible for housing benefit, depending on his/her circumstances.

(d) **Contrived tenancies**. Reg. 7(1)(b) covers situations where it is deemed that an arrangement to pay rent has been created in order to take advantage of the housing benefit scheme. In such situations there is no eligibility for housing benefit.

(e) ***Persons from abroad***. There are two categories of persons from abroad who are ineligible for housing benefit (and council tax benefit) namely those who do not satisfy the *immigration status* test and those who fail the *habitual residence* test.

*Those who fail the immigration status test*. A person fails the immigration status test, and is thus deemed to be a person from abroad and not eligible for housing benefit, if, under reg. 7A, he/she does *not* fall into one of the following categories:

(a) He/she is an asylum seeker who applied for asylum on arrival in the United Kingdom or, in very limited circumstances, within three months of arrival (reg. 7A(5)).
(b) He/she is a sponsored immigrant.
(c) He/she is in receipt of income-based JSA or income support.

Persons in these categories are eligible for housing benefit. Others from abroad are not including any individual who has limited leave to enter or remain in the United Kingdom or is subject to the requirement that he/she will not have recourse to public funds.

*Those deemed not to be habitually resident*. Under reg. 7A, no one is entitled to housing benefit under the normal rules unless *habitually resident* in what is known as the Common Travel Area, which constitutes the UK, the Channel Islands, Eire and the Isle of Man unless:

(a) the claimant is an EEA national who is classified as a worker or has the right to reside in the United Kingdom under specified EC legislation; or
(b) the claimant is a refugee or has been granted exceptional leave to remain in the United Kingdom; or
(c) the claimant left Montserrat after 1 November 1995 because of the volcanic eruption on the island.

Though primarily aimed at curtailing the entitlement of foreign nationals to UK social security benefits, the 'habitual residence' test also applies to British nationals. The basic rule is that if the claimant is not deemed to be habitually resident in the Common Travel Area he/she is defined as a person from abroad and is not entitled to housing benefit (or council tax benefit, income support or income-related JSA).

While not defined either statutorily or in the regulations, habitual residence refers to the place where an individual normally lives. In establishing habitual residence in the United Kingdom, two Social Security Commissioners' decisions, *CIS/1067/1995* and *CIS/2326/1995* have set out a number of relevant criteria, and the test has also been judicially examined in the cases of *Nessa* v. *CAO* and *Swaddling* v. *AO*. These are examined in detail on pp. 126–128.

While the main conditions of entitlement have been set out, a number of other important features of the housing benefit scheme need to be appreciated and consequently are explained in the rest of the chapter.

## Claiming for People Living Together

Section 134(2) of the Social Security Contributions and Benefits Act 1992 provides that, except in prescribed circumstances, the entitlement of one member of a family to any income-related benefit excludes entitlement to that benefit for any other member for the same period. The consequences of this are explained as follows.

### Partner

Section 137(1) defines family as including 'a married or unmarried couple'. This means that, where a couple live together, then only one of them can claim on behalf of both and any family. Section 137 defines an unmarried couple as 'a man and woman who are not married to each other but are living together as husband and wife...'. The treatment of unmarried couples in the same way as married couples is not without controversy. It is discussed in detail on pp. 100–107 but for a discussion on its practical operation in the sphere of housing benefits see Loveland (1989).

This definition of unmarried couple means that gay couples are not treated as a couple for housing benefit purposes but are treated in the same way as single persons jointly occupying accommodation. This is discussed below.

### Children and young persons

The definition of 'family' in s.137(1) of the Social Security Contributions and Benefits Act 1992 provides that any child (under 16) or any young person (aged 16 to 18 and in receipt of full-time non-advanced education) who is a member of the same household as a claimant is treated as part of the family provided that the claimant or the claimant's partner, if also a member of the household, is *responsible* for the child or young person. HB reg. 14(1) defines 'responsible' as requiring that the child is *normally living* with the claimant. Reg. 14(2) elaborates on 'normally living' as follows:

> 'Where a child or young person spends equal amounts of time in different households, or where there is a question as to which household he is living in, the child or young person shall be treated for the purposes of paragraph (1) as normally living with –
> (a) the person who is receiving child benefit has been made in respect of him, the person who made that claim, or
> (b) if there is no such person –

(i) where only one claim for child benefit has been made in respect of him, the person who made that claim, or
(ii) in other case the person who has the primary responsibility for him.'

# Other persons

There may be other people living in the same accommodation as the claimant who are not treated as members of the claimant's family for whom he/she cannot claim but whose presence may nevertheless affect the amount of housing benefit the claimant receives. Usually a deduction is made from a claimant's housing benefit where someone living with him/her is not part of the family. It is important to determine into which of the following categories such a person might fall as this has an impact on the size of deduction made. The actual amount of any rent paid by a tenant, subtenant or boarder to a claimant is usually taken into account in assessing his/her income (less an allowance for expenses) when calculating the claimant's eligibility for housing benefit. In contrast, there are fixed deductions made in respect of non-dependants irrespective of the amount actually given to the claimant.

## *Tenants*

Paragraph 20 of Sch 3 of the Housing Benefit Guidance Regulations provides that a tenant or subtenant is someone who pays the claimant for the right to occupy part of his/her accommodation separately from the claimant, but is not a member of the claimant's family, a non-dependant, a joint occupier or a boarder. A subtenant pays rent to a tenant whereas a tenant pays rent to an owner-occupier. Where payment includes something for meals then the person will be regarded as a boarder. Tenants and subtenants make independent claims for housing benefit. However, if the local authority believes the tenancy or subtenancy is contrived, the tenant or subtenant is treated as a non-dependant, leading to a reduction in the amount of the claimant's housing benefit.

## *Boarders*

Under Sch 4 para 42 of the HB regulations, a boarder is someone who is liable to pay an accommodation charge which covers payment for at least some cooked or prepared meals which are prepared and consumed in that accommodation or associated premises. Boarders, like tenants and subtenants, are treated separately from the landlord for housing benefit. However reg. 7(1)(a) provides that if the boarder is a close relative of the landlord, or the local authority thinks the arrangement is not, in reality, a commercial one, he/she will not be eligible for housing benefit in his/her own right but will be treated as a non-dependant of the landlord.

## Non-dependants

There are set deductions from housing benefit if non-dependants live with a claimant as it is assumed that a non-dependant contributes towards the cost of accommodation irrespective of whether this actually is the case. A non-dependant is someone, such as an adult son or daughter or a grand-parent, who normally resides with the claimant in his/her household and who is not treated as a tenant, subtenant, boarder, etc. but who is not a member of the claimant's family as defined by s.137(1) Social Security Contributions and Benefits Act 1992. Non-dependant is defined in reg. 3, the definition being essentially negative in that it includes anyone that resides with a claimant who does not fall into some other category such as those mentioned in the previous sentence. Thus reg. 3(1) states that non-dependant means any person, except someone to whom para (2) applies, who normally resides with a claimant. Paragraph (2) then estab-lishes that the following categories of person living with a claimant are *not* regarded as non-dependants – any family member; any child or young person living with the claimant but for whom the claimant or spouse are not responsible (and hence is not part of the family); any tenant or subtenant: any joint tenant (i.e. any person who jointly occupies the accommodation and shares liability for payments in respect of occupation; any person who lives with the claimant in order to care for him/her or a partner of his/her and who is engaged by a charitable or voluntary body other than a public or local authority) which makes a charge to the claimant or his partner for the services provided by that person.

The amount of weekly deduction made primarily depends on the size of the weekly income of the non-dependant. There are, in fact, a number of standard deductions from housing benefit depending on the gross weekly income of the non-dependant. For 1999/2000 these range from £7.20 per week when the weekly income is less than £80 to £46.35 if it is £255 or over. The full rate of deductions is set out in the appendix. It is important to note that a non-dependant deduction is made before any taper is calculated.

## Single persons jointly occupying accommodation

Where single people share accommodation they may be regarded as joint tenants and thus separate units for housing benefit purposes. This will allow, for example, one of the joint tenants to make a claim for housing benefit which would not be subject to any non-dependant deductions. Reg. 10(5), thus, provides that each joint tenant is eligible for housing benefit for his/her share of the rent with the local authority having the power to decide what is fair to attribute to each joint tenant on the basis of the number of rooms each occupies as well as the terms of any agreement between the parties. In some situations, disputes may arise as to whether such a joint tenant arrangement does in fact exist or whether one party is a tenant and the other(s) are non-dependants. This is important as generally a joint tenant arrangement will result in the receipt of a greater amount of housing benefit.

# Rent Restrictions

## Commentary

A very important issue in respect of housing benefit is that if a claimant's rent is deemed to be too high or the accommodation to be too large for the needs of the claimant and those living with him/her then the amount of rent upon which any housing benefit is calculated will be less than the actual rent paid. This means that the amount of housing benefit paid is less than the claimant's actual rent. A highly complex set of regulations has been created in order to assess when rent is deemed to be unreasonably high or when accommodation is deemed to be unreasonably large for the needs of the claimant and those living with him/her.

The reasons for the emergence of such complex rules reflect a dilemma in the 1979–97 Conservative government's philosophy towards housing. On the one hand, it sought to deregulate the market in rented accommodation, by dismantling much of the 'fair rent' controls implemented by earlier governments, on the grounds that such controls kept rents at an artificially low level. The marketplace was seen as the correct mechanism to determine rent levels. On the other hand, the commitment to control public expenditure, as outlined at the beginning of this chapter, meant a disinclination to pay housing benefit at what are deemed to be unreasonably high levels. How to harmonise these two policies created problems for the housing benefit scheme. This was exacerbated by the level of fraud in the housing benefit scheme where landlords, in particular, have sought to benefit from 'contrived tenancies' whereby inflated rents are charged to housing benefit claimants in order to receive large housing benefit payments, which are paid directly to landlords. This issue was examined in *R.* v. *Manchester CC ex parte Baragrove Properties Ltd* [1991] HLR 337; LGR 953.

The emergence of the rules to deal with perceived high rent also highlights the tension in the relationship between central and local government. While housing benefit is administered by local authorities, much of the money for the scheme is paid directly by central government to local authorities. In the 1980s this led to the problem of the 'rent stop' whereby local authorities used the amount of money received from central government to determine what was an unreasonably high rent. The operation of such policy at that time was explained in December 1988 as follows:

'[Local authorities] are...refus[ing] to pay housing benefit on rents which are in excess of the subsidy thresholds laid down by the DSS for their areas.

Each [local authority] has such a threshold, and payments of housing benefit based on rents below the threshold receive a subsidy [from central government] of 97% of the benefit paid. For payment above the subsidy threshold level, however, the subsidy is dramatically reduced to 25% with the result that the local authority moves from a position in which it pays only a tiny fraction of the benefit to a position where it is responsible for the bulk of the payment beyond the threshold level.

In such circumstances, the temptation for councils to set their rent-stops at the threshold level is obvious and, in many cases, irresistible.'
(Poynter, 1988, p. 6)

The operation of this policy led to a number of cases of judicial review e.g. *Macleod* v. *Banff and Buchan District* [1988] SCLR 165, *R.* v. *Brent ex parte Connery* [1990] Legal Action 22, *R.* v. *Sefton ex parte Cunningham* [1991] HLR 534, *Malcolm* v. *Tweedale* [1991] August 6 Court of Session and *R.* v. *East Devon ex parte Gibson* [1991] September 29 QBD. These established, inter alia, that the use of the subsidy threshold as a *carte blanche* ceiling to establish what constitutes an unreasonably high rent or unreasonably large accommodation was unlawful as it failed to take into account the individual circumstances of each claimant. These cases were also concerned with determining whether, as a consequence of imposing a rent restriction, it is reasonable to expect a claimant to move. This centred on the availability of 'suitable alternative accommodation' and the cases confirmed that a local authority needs evidence that, in general, such accommodation exists in the locality though there is no duty to identify individual properties. For a detailed discussion of these cases see East (1992).

The housing benefit regulations changed a number of times as a result of these cases. Most notably, in order to avoid the problems of using the rent stop to determine the reasonableness of rent levels, the Conservative government sought to use the services of rent officers to help establish what constitute 'reasonable' rent levels for housing benefit purposes. The use of rent officers was also introduced to counter an alternative problem for central government whereby some local authorities, sympathetic to the difficulties confronting claimants, had been interpreting this 'reasonable rent restriction' more generously so that they paid housing benefit at levels above which the government wished.

## The legal rules

The changes in housing benefit have meant that different arrangements prevail depending upon when the tenancy was originally created. As a consequence, two different schemes operate depending upon whether the claimant is an 'exempt' or 'non-exempt' claimant.

## Exempt claimants

A claimant is 'exempt' if he/she was entitled to housing benefit on 1 January 1996. This exempt status can be passed on to the partner of such a claimant if the claimant subsequently dies, leaves the dwelling or is detained in custody following conviction if the claimant had continued to be in receipt of housing benefit until that date. As long as the partner was occupying the dwelling on that same date, exempt status can be so transferred and remains as long as entitlement to, and receipt of, housing benefit has been continuous from 1 January 1996 (disregarding breaks of less than four weeks).

Under reg. 11(2) (of the version of the regulations prior to amendments introduced on 2 January 1996), restrictions on the amount of housing benefit for exempt tenants can only be made if, compared with 'suitable alternative accommodation', the rent is deemed to be 'unreasonably high' or the accommodation is 'unreasonably large' or a rent increase is 'unreasonable'. In determining what is unreasonable in all the above categories, regs 11(2) and 12(1) stipulate that local authorities must make comparison (as regards rent, size of accommodation or rent increase) with suitable alternative accommodation within their area or elsewhere. These regulations stipulate that, in deciding this matter, a local authority *may* take into account a rent officer's determination about whether the rent and size of accommodation is reasonable, although it is not mandatory to do so.

Regs 11 and 12 set out three groups who are protected against the operation of these 'unreasonable rent' restrictions. Under regs 11(4) and (5), claimants who could afford the rent for the accommodation when their tenancy began, and no claim has been made for housing benefit within the last 52 weeks, will not have the rent restricted (and hence housing benefit reduced) for the first 13 weeks of the claim. This is designed to provide time for the claimant to move to more suitable accommodation. Secondly, under regs 11(3), 12(2) and (3), where an occupant of the claimant's home has died, no rent restriction is allowable for 12 months. Under regs 11(3) and (6)(b) the third protected group are claimants where any of those occupying the accommodation is a child or young person, is aged 60 or more or any such occupant is incapable of work for social security purposes. For this third protected group, there is no time limit after which a rent restriction can apply so that the local authority must not reduce the amount of housing benefit unless suitable alternative accommodation is available and it is reasonable to expect the claimant to move. To determine whether it is reasonable to expect the claimant to move reg. 6(b) stipulates that both the impact of the move on the claimant's prospects of retaining employment and the educational effect on any change of school of any child or young person must be taken into account. The cases of *R. v. Sefton ex parte Cunningham* [1991] HLR 534 and *R. v. East Devon Council ex parte Gibson* [1993] HLR 487 CA indicate that, in determining this, a local authority must have sufficient evidence that an active housing market exists in respect of the accommodation in question, particularly if the claimant falls into one of the protected groups.

Only *after* it has been established that the rent is unreasonably high or the accommodation unreasonably large by comparison with suitable alternative accommodation, and that protected group status does not apply, can local authorities then consider the issue of the amount by which the rent should be reduced (and hence the amount of housing benefit payable). *R. v. Brent LBC ex parte Connery* [1989] HLR 40 QBD established that, in deciding this, a local authority can take its own financial situation into account, which includes the housing benefit subsidy threshold . In other words the subsidy threshold should not be taken into account in establishing whether the rent is unreasonably high but, once that is established, it can be taken into account to determine what the level of 'reasonable rent' will be.

## Non-exempt claimants

As part of its attempt both to reduce public expenditure on the housing benefit scheme and to limit the discretion of local authorities, particularly those sympathetic to what they saw as the plight of housing benefit recipients, the then government introduced changes on 1 January 1996 in respect of determining the maximum eligible rent for housing benefit purposes. This has resulted in a bewilderingly complicated scheme for 'non-exempt' claimants. At its heart is the removal of a local authority's discretion to ignore what a rent officer has determined to be the correct rent befitting any claimant's accommodation rent. Under the new arrangements, a rent officer's determinations *must* be used by local authorities in contrast to the old scheme for exempt claimants where a local authority is not required to follow the rent officer's decision. Another major change is the removal of the safeguard given to 'vulnerable' claimants in the protected groups so that, for example, a local authority is not required to have evidence that suitable alternative accommodation is, in fact, available in order impose a rent restriction on a protected claimant.

Under reg. 12A(2)(b) and Sch 1A of the Housing Benefit Regulations, as amended from 2 January 1996, all housing benefit claims and after that date must be referred by local authorities to a rent officer, who is required to make a number of determinations after the local authority has determined the *reckonable rent*. This constitutes the actual rent paid, including some service charges that are not covered by housing benefit (such as charges for fuel, meals and water charges). The Rent Officer Service is then required to assess the rent to determine whether or not it is unreasonably high. This is done as follows:

(a) If the reckonable rent is deemed *not* to be unreasonably high, the reckonable rent is used to establish the *eligible rent* for housing benefit calculations.

(b) If the rent officer decides the reckonable rent is unreasonably high, he is required to establish a *maximum rent* for the accommodation. The first step in establishing this is to determine the *appropriate rent*. This is the lowest of the following (all of which the rent officer is required to determine):
   − A *significantly high rent* (SHR) determination : the rent officer determines whether the rent paid is 'significantly higher than the rent which the landlord might reasonably have been expected to obtain' having regard to the level of rent of similar tenancies in the locality.
   − A *size-related rent* (SRR) determination : the rent officer is also required to determine whether the accommodation exceeds the established size criteria for the claimant and those living with him/her. These include the stipulation that one bedroom should be available for each of the following – a (married or unmarried) couple; a single person aged 16 or over; two children of the same gender under 16; two children of either gender under 10; and a child under 16. The accommodation should also have 'one room suitable for living' for up to three occupiers, two such rooms for four to six occupiers and three in the case of seven or more occupiers. If the accommodation exceeds these criteria, the rent officer provides an SRR.
   − An *exceptionally high rent* (EHR) determination: if the rent officer, having undertaken either of the above determinations, believes either of those figures or the actual rent for the dwelling is still 'exceptionally high' he is required to decide what is the highest rent for an assured tenancy in the same locality in respect of accommodation with the same size criteria and which is in a reasonable state of repair.

The *appropriate rent* is the lowest of these figures and is, inter alia, designed to ensure that the rent used to calculate housing benefit for particular accommodation is reasonable within the context of the market rent for that particular type of accommodation. However, in order to determine the *maximum rent*, it is also necessary to determine the *local reference rent* (LRR) and this is designed to ensure that market rent levels for *all* types of rented accommodation are used in order that a ceiling is set for accommodation at the higher end of the market. Except in the case of hostels or residential care homes or nursing homes, the rent officer is required to determine whether the SHR, SRR or EHR in respect of the rent of particular accommodation is greater than the 'local reference rent'. The 'local reference rent' constitutes a figure halfway between the lowest rent which is not 'an exceptionally low rent' and the highest rent which is not 'an exceptionally high rent' for accommodation that matches the size criteria for the claimant of an assured tenancy in a reasonable state of repair. Clearly designed to let local housing market conditions act as a constraint on the payment of housing benefit in respect of accommodation when all of the other determinations are higher, the local authority (on receipt of the various determinations from a rent officer) is required to set the *maximum rent* in order to calculate housing benefit by comparing the 'local reference rent' with the 'appropriate rent'. Where the 'appropriate rent' is below the LRR this constitutes the 'maximum rent'. However, if the 'appropriate rent' is above the LRR, the 'maximum rent' is half of the amount by which it exceeds the LRR and, in order to set a maximum limit, the appropriate rent for any accommodation cannot be greater than twice the LRR.

In comparison to the pre January 1996 scheme for exempt claimants, protection for 'vulnerable groups' has been substantially reduced. Under reg. 11(7)-(12) there are only two groups whose eligible rent for housing benefit purpose should not be reduced to the 'maximum rent' level:

- As long as housing benefit was not received in the previous 52 weeks, any claimant and/or occupiers who could afford the rent when the tenancy commenced will not have the maximum rent applied for the first 13 weeks of receiving housing benefit.
- If a member of the claimant's household has died, no lower maximum rent will operate for 12 months following the death.

There is no similar protection for the other 'vulnerable groups' under the exempt scheme. For those groups and others, local authorities do, however, have a discretion under reg. 61(3) when determining the level of housing benefit to use a rental figure higher than the 'maximum rent' (but not higher than the rent actually paid by a claimant) if it appears that, by applying the 'maximum rent' level to determine housing benefit, the claimant or any member of the family would suffer *exceptional hardship*. This is not defined in the relevant guidance (circular HB/CTB A23/95) though it does state that its ordinary, everyday meaning should be provided and that 'as an illustration, the *Shorter Oxford English Dictionary* defines exceptional as "forming an exception, unusual" and hardship as "severe suffering; extreme privation".' Allied to this restrictive definition is that local authority funds for exercising this discretion are capped so that, in practice, few authorities appear to have made any such awards.

*Further restrictions for single claimants under 25*

As part of another of the then government's strategy of reducing benefits for claimants under 25, further restrictions were introduced on 7 October 1996. Single claimants aged 16–24 who live in private rented accommodation (but not housing association or local authority housing) now have housing benefit payments restricted to a single-room rent. With some exceptions, such as lone parents, a rent officer must calculate a *single room rent*. As with the 'local reference rent' (LRR), this involves using the market for accommodation without security of tenure to limit the levels at which housing benefit is paid, meaning that some claimants will receive housing benefit payments much lower than the actual rent paid. The 'single room rent' is calculated by determining the mid-point between the highest and lowest market rents for an assured tenancy in the locality where the tenant has exclusive use of one room; *and* does not have the use of any other room suitable for living in; *and* shares the use of a toilet; *and* shares or has no use of a kitchen; *and* the rent does not include any payment for board and attendance. The 'single room rent' forms the *maximum rent* for housing benefit purposes. Unlike the use of the local reference rent for over 25s, the claimant does *not* receive 50% of the difference between the single room rent and any higher determination. The same discretion for increases in payment on grounds of 'severe hardship' does, however, exist.

## Conclusion

It is difficult to deny that the arrangements created to impose rent restrictions in respect of the housing benefit scheme constitute an extremely complicated web of regulations that has been devised largely for central government to control the level of housing benefit expenditure. This has been achieved by using a deregulated market in rented housing that provides no security of tenure to clients (in that *assured* tenancies are used as the basis of rent officers' determinations) in order to determine acceptable rent levels to calculate housing benefit. As a consequence housing benefit payments are made to some claimants below the levels of rent that they are actually paying.

The current government's main concern in respect of housing benefit is to deal with the perceived high level of fraud. While fraud may exist in the scheme, there is a danger that, in dealing with it, much of which is by organised gangs and often 'landlord based' with many housing benefit payments paid directly to landlords (see Audit Commission, 1996), an over-rigorous strategy may impose undue scrutiny and financial hardship on many innocent tenants who are receiving incorrect amounts of housing benefit as a result of misunderstanding the complex regulations of entitlement rather than from an intention to defraud. It is again difficult to deny that a major consequence of this strategy is to financially penalise some of the most vulnerable members of society.

## Bibliography

Audit Commission (1996) *Protecting the Public Purse: Ensuring Probity In Local Government*, November.

East, R. (1992) Housing benefit and 'unreasonable rent', *Legal Action*, October, p. 18.

Green Paper (1998) *New Ambitions for Our Country: A New Contract for Welfare*, Cm 3805.

Loveland, I. (1989) The micro-politics of welfare rights: the interpretation of the cohabitation rule in the housing benefit scheme, *Journal of Social Welfare Law*, 22.

Ogus, A. I., Barendt, E. M. and Wikeley, N. J. (1995) *The Law of Social Security*, 4th Edition, Butterworths.

Poynter, R. (1988) Rent-stops and subsidy thresholds *Welfare Rights Bulletin*, December, p. 6.

Social Security Consortium (1986) *Of Little Benefit: A Critical Guide to the Social Security Act 1986*.

*Welfare Rights Bulletin* (1997), 136, February.

# 12 Council Tax Benefit

## Context and Commentary

Council tax is a non-taxable, non-contributory, means-tested benefit designed to provide assistance to people on low incomes who are required to pay council tax. It is administered by local authorities but operates according to Department of Social Security regulations, the most important of which are the Council Tax Benefit (General) Regulations 1992.

Council tax was introduced on 1 April 1993 as the replacement for community charge as the mechanism for local authorities to raise revenue from those living within their boundaries in order to help pay for the services provided by them. Community charge, more commonly known as the poll tax, had itself replaced the rates system in Scotland on 1 April 1989 and in England and Wales on 1 April 1990. The poll tax, introduced by the then Secretary of State for the Environment, Nicholas Ridley, and championed by Margaret Thatcher, was possibly the most controversial reform introduced under her leadership and directly resulted in her demise as Prime Minister in November 1990. The essence of the poll tax was that it was a flat-rate tax so that everyone was required to pay the same amount irrespective of how rich or poor they were. Community charge benefit (otherwise known as poll tax rebate) existed to provide support for those whose means fell below the prescribed level. However, the maximum amount of community charge benefit was 80% of the community charge for which a person was liable. In other words, every individual liable for community charge was required to pay at least 20% of the community charge no matter how low his/her income was. It was the flat-rate nature of the tax and the requirement that all, no matter how low their income, would be required to pay 20% that were the two features of the community charge/poll tax regime that generated the greatest hostility with many individuals refusing to pay the charge, resulting in some being imprisoned. Following Margaret Thatcher's replacement as Prime Minister by John Major in November 1990, Michael Heseltine returned to the Cabinet as Secretary of State for the Environment and, on 21 March 1991, he announced to the House of Commons that poll tax/community charge would be replaced by the council tax.

The essence of the council tax is that, as was the case with the rates system, liability is based on the value of the property within which people reside. Properties are placed into eight valuation bands and the amount of council tax for which a person is liable is determined by which band that person's property is placed in. The higher the value of the property, the more council tax is paid. However, under s.10 of the Local Government Finance Act 1992, which implemented the council tax, the amount of council tax for which a person is liable also takes account of the number of persons over the age of 18 that reside in the property. So, for example, if only one person resides in a dwelling, there is a 25% reduction in the amount of council tax payable. Council tax benefit provides assistance for those on low income to meet the costs of the council tax. Unlike community charge, it can cover 100% of a person's council tax. It uses the income support/income-based JSA means test to determine eligibility but, like housing benefit, for those whose income is above this means test, a 'taper system' is used to provide financial support to meet council tax payments.

# The Legal Rules

There are two types of council tax benefit. Most recipients are likely to obtain main council tax benefit. The second type of council tax benefit is second adult rebate (otherwise known as alternative maximum council tax benefit). Second adult rebate is available when there is more than one adult residing with the claimant in a dwelling who is neither liable for council tax nor pays any rent to the claimant and who is in receipt of income support, income-based JSA or on a low income. In many such situations, the claimant may be eligible for both types of council tax benefit and will receive whichever provides the larger weekly amount.

## Main council tax benefit

A person is eligible for main council tax benefit if the following conditions are satisfied:

(i)   he/she is liable to pay council tax; and
(ii)  savings and other disposable capital do not exceed £16,000; and
(iii) he/she is in receipt of income-based jobseeker's allowance, income support or on a low income.

### (i) Liable to pay council tax

Council tax applies only to domestic, not commercial properties. These are termed in the legislation and regulations as dwellings. Council tax is usually payable by someone, aged 18 years or over, who resides in the dwelling. Where more than one such person is resident in a dwelling, s.6 establishes a *liability hierarchy* to determine who is liable for council tax. This sets out the following six categories in rank order, the liable person being the person who falls into the highest category:

(a)   the resident owner;
(b)   a leaseholder;
(c)   a statutory, statutory assured or secure tenant;
(d)   a subtenant;
(e)   a licensee;
(f)   any other resident (including any squatter).

Under s.6(1)(f), where there is no one residing in a dwelling, the owner of the property is liable to pay council tax. Also, *joint liability* for payment of council tax applies in situations where more than one resident falls into the highest category and such liability also extends to any partner of such liable persons. The definition of partner for council tax is the same as for income based benefits, per s.137 of the Social Security Contributions and Benefits Act 1992, and covers any married or unmarried heterosexual couple who are living together (see pp. 100–107). Where joint liability exists and one or more of those jointly liable claims council tax benefit, reg. 51(3) provides that the local authority calculates the claimant's share by dividing the total amount of council tax liability by the number of liable persons.

In most circumstances, council tax benefit is available in respect of a claimant's normal home, this being defined as the 'sole or main residence'. Where there is a dispute as to what constitutes a claimant's main home, a local authority should take account of factors such as how much time the claimant spends at the different addresses, where he/she works and where any children attend school as well as the security of tenure at the different addresses. There may also be some situations where a couple may be liable for council tax on more than one dwelling, e.g. where one of them works away from the normal home and is required to live away from that residence. In such situations, DSS guidance (*HB/CCB(92)34*) allows for council tax benefit to be claimed for more than one dwelling.

### (ii) Capital does not exceed £16,000

As is the case with housing benefit, any disposable capital that a claimant has up to £3,000 does not affect entitlement to main council tax benefit while any such capital above that figure up to £16,000 is deemed to generate a *tariff income* on the basis that each £250 or part thereof generates a weekly income of £1 per week. This is deducted from the amount of council tax benefit that a claimant receives. Any disposable capital in excess of £16,000 will render a claimant ineligible for main council tax benefit. The details on what constitutes disposable capital, how the principle of aggregation applies to the capital of different members of a claimant's family and other relevant issues are discussed in more detail on pp. 123–125 and pp. 134–236. As is outlined later, there are such no rules concerning capital applying to the second adult rebate.

*(iii) The claimant receives income-based JSA, income support or is on a low income*

If a claimant is in receipt of either of these two benefits then he/she satisfies the means test for eligibility for council tax benefit.

## Determining the Amount of Council Tax Benefit

The amount of council tax benefit that is received is based on two issues:

(a) The first step is to establish the claimant's weekly council tax liability. Under reg. 51(1), this is done by dividing the annual charge by the number of days in the financial year (365 or 366) and multiplying that figure by 7. Where there is any joint liability, the claimant's and any partner's share is also calculated by dividing the total amount of council tax liability by the number of persons jointly liable. From April 1998, council tax benefit is paid only up to a property value of £120,000. For those who live in accommodation of a higher value, council tax benefit is calculated only on this figure.

(b) It is then necessary to identify whether or not there are 'non-dependants' living with the claimant. Under reg. 3, a non-dependant is a person who lives in the claimant's household on a non-commercial basis who is not the claimant's partner or a dependent child. Typical examples of a non-dependant are where an adult son or daughter resides with a parent and where a homosexual couple live together. Non-dependants are not liable to pay council tax but, under regs 51 and 52, are assumed to make a contribution towards the claimant's council tax liability, whether or not this actually takes place. As a result, where there are any non-dependants, deductions are made to the amount of council tax benefit that a claimant receives. The amount of the deduction depends on the financial circumstances of the non-dependant in the following way:

| *Financial position of the non-dependant* | *Weekly deduction* |
|---|---|
| Aged 18 or over, in full-time work with a gross weekly income of: | |
| Up to £117.99 | £2.15 |
| £118–£203.99 | £4.30 |
| £204–£254.99 | £5.40 |
| £255 or more | £6.50 |

These figures are for the year commencing April 1999.

A deduction is made for each non-dependant with only a single deduction applying in respect of a non-dependant couple although, under reg. 52(4), the income of both partners is combined to establish gross income. However, there are certain situations where no non-dependant deduction should be made. These include, per reg. 52(6), where the claimant or partner is blind or receives attendance allowance, constant attendance allowance or the care component of disability living allowance. Further, there are certain categories of people who are not regarded as non-dependant and thus no deduction should be made to the claimant's council tax benefit. These include, under regs 52(6)–(8), anyone temporarily residing in the household whose normal home is elsewhere, any full-time student even during the vacation and if working, anyone under 18, anyone aged 18 for whom child benefit is being received and, per Sch 1(2) of the Local Government Finance Act 1992, anyone who is mentally impaired.

It is also necessary to establish whether the claimant's income is above or below the income support/income-based JSA level. If below, the amount he/she receives is as set out here. If it is above, the deductions are made under the 'taper system' as described earlier.

For claimants who are not receiving either income-based jobseeker's allowance or income support, it is necessary to establish whether their financial circumstances render them eligible for benefit. This involves applying the general means test which applies to income support, income-based jobseeker's allowance and housing benefit as well as council tax benefit. This is explained in detail on pp. 115–123. Briefly, it requires working out the claimant's *applicable amount*. This is the maximum weekly amount of income support or income-based jobseeker's allowance to which the claimant, in his/her financial circumstances, might be entitled. This is based firstly on establishing any weekly *personal allowances*. The total amount of a claimant's personal allowances varies depending on such factors as whether the claimant is single or has a partner and whether there are any dependant children. In addition, a claimant may be eligible for *premiums*. These are additional weekly amounts if the claimant, or a member of his/her family unit, falls into one of a number of categories. These include a lone parent premium, a disability premium, a disabled child premium and a number of pensioner premiums. On the basis of personal allowances and premiums, a claimant's applicable amount is calculated. The next step is to establish his/her *weekly income*. This includes earnings, any benefit payments, interest from savings, etc. though some sources of income are disregarded. If the claimant's weekly income is less than his/her applicable amount then he/she is in the same position as those receiving income support or income-based jobseeker's allowance.

Eligibility for council tax benefit is not, however, lost if the claimant's income is greater than his/her applicable amount, that is if he/she has any *excess income*. In such cases, it is then necessary to calculate the amount by which the income exceeds applicable amount. Any council tax benefit that a claimant receives is reduced by a figure of 20% of the amount by which income exceeds the applicable amount. Thus if a claimant had a weekly council tax liability of £8 and his/her weekly income exceeded the applicable amount by £25, it is necessary to calculate 20% of £25 (i.e. £5) and deduct that amount from council tax liability, leaving the claimant with a council tax benefit of £3 per week (£8 – £5). This 20% deduction, like the similar 65% deduction for housing benefit, is known as a *taper* because, as the amount of income in excess of the applicable amount increases, the amount of council tax benefit decreases or 'tapers away'. Thus, in the above example, if the claimant's income increased to £35 more than the applicable amount, then the council tax benefit would be £1 per week, i.e. £8 – £7 (£7 = 20% of £35). If the claimant's income rose to £40 more than the applicable amount, he/she would lose entitlement to any council tax benefit as 20% of £40 is £8 which, when deducted from council tax liability of £8, results in zero.

## (iv) People excluded from receiving main council tax benefit

There are two important categories of people who are excluded from receiving main council tax benefit. These are full-time students, though there are some exceptions to this, and 'persons from abroad'.

(a) **Students.** Most full-time students are not eligible to receive council tax benefit, the definition of student, and what constitutes 'full-time', being the same as for housing benefit (see p.????). Again, as is the case with housing benefits, there are some exceptions so, under reg. 40(3), a full-time student is eligible for council tax benefit if he/she falls into one of a number of categories, which include:

- a recipient of income support or income-based JSA;
- a pensioner who satisfies the condition for one of the pensioner premiums;
- where the claimant and partner are both full-time students and have at least one dependent child;
- where the claimant has been incapable of work for 28 weeks;
- where the claimant is a lone parent who satisfies the condition for the lone parent rate of a family premium.

(b) **Persons from abroad.** There are two categories of 'persons from abroad' who are ineligible for council tax benefit (and housing benefit). These are people who do not satisfy the *immigration status* test and those who fail the *habitual residence* test. These are discussed in some detail in Chapter 11.

## Second adult rebate

Second adult rebate (or alternative maximum council tax benefit) can be claimed when a person has other residents living in his/her home who do not pay rent or share council tax liability but are in receipt of income support or income-based JSA or on a low income. In many such situations the presence of such a person (known as a second adult) denies a claimant from being a single resident and thereby claiming a 25% reduction in council tax liability, yet the second adult's income is so low that he/she may be unable to contribute towards this additional expenditure. Second adult rebate is partly aimed at addressing this problem. In situations where a claimant is eligible for both main council tax benefit and second adult rebate, he/she can only receive whichever is the highest. As a general rule, anyone who receives more than one-third of their council tax liability from main council tax benefit is likely to receive more from that than from second adult rebate. However, eligibility for second adult rebate can arise where a person is ineligible for main council tax benefit. This is because, per reg. 54 and Schs 2 and 5, a claimant's income and capital are ignored when determining entitlement for second adult rebate, eligibility being determined on the basis of the income of the second adult(s). Thus second adult rebate can be claimed where the claimant has disposable capital of more than £16,000 or has an income higher than would entitle him/her to main council tax benefit.

Under s.131 of the Social Security Contributions and Benefits Act 1992, a person is eligible for second adult rebate if the following conditions are satisfied:

(i)   the claimant is liable to pay council tax; and
(ii)  there are one or more 'second adults' residing in the dwelling; and
(iii) the second adult(s) is(are) in receipt of income support or income-based JSA or has(have) a low income.

## (i) Liable to pay council tax

The same general requirements on liability apply for second adult rebate as for main council tax benefit (see pp. 251–252). Under reg. 55, however, a person cannot claim second adult rebate if, with some exceptions, there is another person (including a partner) who is jointly liable for council tax. Where there is joint liability, second adult rebate can only be claimed if at least all but one of those jointly liable is 'disregarded'. Such disregarded persons include any full-time students in further and higher education, anyone who is 'severely mentally impaired', carers, and people in prison or other forms of detention.

## (ii) One or more 'second adults' resides in the dwelling

Under s.131(6) of the Social Security Contributions and Benefits Act 1992 and reg. 55 and Sch 2, a 'second adult' is someone who resides with a person liable for council tax on a non-commercial basis. In other words, he/she is defined as a non-dependant. A second adult must be aged 18 or over but anyone defined as a 'disregarded person' is not considered to be a second adult. Disregarded persons are defined as in the previous section and include full-time students, those 'severely mentally impaired' and most carers.

## (iii) A second adult is receiving income support or income-based JSA or has a low income

If all the second adults residing in the dwelling are on the above benefits, the claimant receives, under reg. 54 and para 1 of Sch 2, the maximum discount of 25% of the claimant's weekly eligible council tax. Where any of the second adults is not receiving these benefits, the gross income of all second adults must be aggregated together. Gross income includes earnings, actual income from capital (but not tariff income) and any non-earned income such as social security benefits. Some benefits, however, are disregarded. These include attendance allowance and disability living allowance. If the total gross income exceeds (April 1999 rates) £155 per week no eligibility for second adult rebate exists. If it is between £154.99 and £118, the discount is 7.5% and if it is below £118, the discount is 15%.

# 13 The Social Fund

## Context and Commentary

The Social Fund was introduced into the British social security system by the Social Security Act 1986. It provides payments to claimants of income support and income-based jobseeker's allowance to meet 'one-off' needs that are deemed to be 'over and above' the regular costs of day-to-day living and therefore are not covered by weekly benefits. It consists of two different elements. The **regulated Social Fund**, first introduced in April 1987, provides grants to cover additional fuel costs during cold weather as well as grants to cover maternity and funeral expenses. The **discretionary Social Fund**, which came into operation in April 1988, provides loans, known as *budgeting loans* and *crisis loans*, as well as *community care grants* to claimants. Budgeting loans are paid to claimants who can show that they need help to meet important intermittent expenses such as the purchase of essential furniture or household equipment or for fuel reconnection charges. Crisis loans are available to people, whether or not in receipt of income support or income-based JSA, who need help to meet expenses in an emergency or disaster. As loans, both of these are normally repaid by deductions from the weekly benefit received by recipients. Community care grants are paid to people leaving institutional care to assist them to lead independent lives in the community. An important difference between the regulated and discretionary Social Funds is that grants made under the regulated Social Fund are mandatory in the sense that a claimant is automatically entitled to the grant if he/she satisfies the eligibility criteria. In contrast, under the discretionary Social Fund, as its name suggests, the community care grants and loans are awarded on a discretionary basis by Social Fund officers according to Directions and Guidance issued by the Secretary of State. Social Fund officers will be renamed 'appropriate officers' when the relevant provisions of the Social Security Act 1998 are implemented. A claimant who satisfies the criteria for receiving a payment, can therefore, be refused it if, for example, there is deemed to be no money available to provide it or it is felt that he/she is unlikely to be able to repay any loan.

The substantial discretion exercised by Social Fund officers in respect of the discretionary Social Fund, along with the use of repayable loans, are two of the most controversial features of the Social Fund.

## Historical introduction

The use of single payments to meet one-off urgent needs is a well-established feature of the British social security system. Since the 1930s, there has been some provision for making one-off payments to claimants who ask for more than their basic benefit to meet 'exceptional needs'. Under the Ministry of Social Security Act 1966 (later renamed the Supplementary Benefits Act 1966), this took the form of grants known as *exceptional needs payments* until the Conservative government, which was elected in 1979, introduced reforms in 1980. The regime of exceptional needs payments between 1966 and 1980 had two important features. The system was highly discretionary, with staff in local benefit offices having substantial discretion. It was also 'demand-led', in other words, the demand for payments determined the amount of money that the system of 'one-off' payments required. For the Conservative government elected in 1979, with a central tenet of its philosophy being to control public expenditure levels, this was seen as a problem that needed to be addressed. The 1980 reforms to supplementary benefit, including the replacement of exceptional needs payments with *single payments*, were an attempt both to end discretion and to reduce levels of expenditure. This was achieved by narrowing the grounds of entitlement although the system still remained 'demand-led':

> 'Changes to supplementary benefit introduced in 1980 attempted to stem the increasing demand for these [one-off] payments. Previously, particularly at appeal tribunals, claimants had been able to benefit from the wide discretion and flexibility allowed by the Supplementary Benefits Act. The new system, based on entitlement specified in regulations, which came into force in 1980, gave them clearer rights; but the single payments regulations cut the items allowed and limited, by law, the circumstances under which claimants qualified.' (Cohen and Tarpey, 1988, p. 2).

Despite the aspirations of such reforms, public expenditure on single payments started to increase. After a brief fall in claims in 1980 following the above changes, expenditure rose quite substantially in respect of single payments so that such payments cost over £300 million in 1985, compared with around £140 million in 1983.

This led, in 1985, to the then Secretary of State for Social Security, Norman Fowler, examining the possibility of further reform, leading to the idea of a Social Fund to replace single payments. One feature of the Social Fund was a return to a more discretionary approach, with substantial discretion being vested in Social Fund officers, in particular when deciding whether to grant a budgeting or crisis loan. This was deemed necessary in order to impose strict budgetary control on the amount of money available to the Fund because, aside from further tightening eligibility, the major change introduced with the creation of the Social Fund was to implement 'supply side economics' into the provision of payments to meet emergencies and exceptional needs. This contrasted with the traditional 'demand-led' provision of social security benefits whereby, for example, any increase in the number of claimants dictates the supply of public monies necessary to pay for those benefits. The introduction of the Social Fund marks a change to this in that a set amount of money is set aside and, once that amount is exhausted, no more monies are available. In other words, the provision of money for the Social Fund is 'supply-led', rather than 'demand-led', in that once the supply of money is exhausted no further claims for payments can be met. Thus, the Social Fund marks a radical shift in approach towards providing social security in that it:

> '...places resource allocation decisions right at the centre of a policy area which has hitherto primarily been demand-led.' (Walker and Lawton, 1989)

## The contemporary operation of the social fund

The way the Social Fund operates in practice is explained as follows:

> 'Each office has a budget allocated to it, initially based in large measure on previous experience of demand for single payments...But, because the total budget is cash limited, each office must manage within its share of the total. Whenever there is pressure on the local budget, those whose applications are considered of lesser importance may be refused help. At other times of the year or in another area, the same application may have been accepted.' (Social Security Advisory Committee, 1992, p. 4)

This strategy clearly requires a system of substantial discretion as decisions have to be made in the context of how much money is available in the local office's budget. A system that gave legal entitlement to payments to all claimants who satisfied certain set criteria would lack the flexibility to accommodate the issue of the availability or not of resources. Thus, the government sets the total budget for the discretionary Social Fund each year, with individual Benefits Agency district offices being allocated a fixed sum. It is the responsibility of each district Social Fund manager to monitor and plan expenditure on a monthly basis which involves constantly monitoring how much money has been allocated during the month and thus often requires reassessing how an office deals with claims as available resources decrease. However, while the implementation of the Social Fund, with strict budgetary control as a central feature, satisfied the then government's desire to keep a tight control on public expenditure, it has its costs. As the Social Security Advisory Committee pointed out, '...in practice [it] has produced inequality of provision and availability...' (p. 4) in that identical claims can be treated differently by different Benefit Agency offices, so that one claim might be successful at one office while another – identical – claim refused at another. In fact, the same office may, at different times, treat identical claims differently depending on whether or not money is available in the budget at the time a claim is made:

> 'This helps to explain why the term "lottery" has been applied by some critics to the Fund.' (Social Security Advisory Committee, 1992, p. 4)

However, following its election in May 1997, the incoming Labour government undertook a review of the Social Fund leading to a new budgeting loan scheme being introduced on 5 April 1999. This sought to reduce the 'lottery' element so that most claimants in receipt of income support or means-based JSA for at least six months are likely to be awarded a loan on their first application. The new scheme provides a set of 'objective criteria', such as length of time on benefit and size of family unit, which are weighted to establish the priority of an application relative to others.

Two other major criticisms of the Social Fund relate first to the previously mentioned use of loans rather than, as in the past, having all payments in the form of grants and secondly to the denial of an independent appeal system. In respect of the first of these, any recipient of income support or income-based JSA who receives a budgeting loan or crisis loan is required to pay it back. Under s.140 of the Social Security Contributions and Benefits Act 1992, one of the circumstances which Social Fund officers are required to take into account, when exercising their discretion on whether or not to make a payment from the fund, is whether a loan is likely to be repaid. While there are no statutory guidelines, the *Social Fund Decision and Review Guide* provides non-legally binding guidance. This states that loans should normally be repaid within a maximum period of 78 weeks (para 4003) or exceptionally 104 weeks (para 4004) at a maximum rate of 15% of the weekly amount of income support or income-based JSA (excluding housing costs) received by a claimant (para 4013). One major consequence of this, particularly for a claimant already in receipt of a previous loan, is that a request for a loan could be denied on the basis that he/she cannot afford to repay the loan. To put it another way, a claimant can be denied a Social Fund loan because he/she is deemed to be too poor to repay it! This is, surely, a case of a social security system 'gone mad'. The overriding objective of any social security system is to provide financial assistance to those who need it. It surely fails this objective if it denies it to the people who are identified as being most in need.

Turning to the issue of appeals, under the regulated Social Fund there is a right of appeal to an independent Social Security Appeal Tribunal against any decision of a Benefit Agency adjudication officer with a further appeal to social security commissioners, whose decisions are binding on both tribunals and adjudication officers. In contrast, a major criticism of the discretionary social fund is that such decisions are not subject to an independent appeal mechanism only to a right of review. The first step is an internal review by the Benefits Agency office that made the initial decision. If a claimant is dissatisfied with this first level of review, a further review by a Social Fund Inspector can be requested. Social Fund Inspectors are based in Birmingham and a review to an inspector is invariably conducted on the basis of written information, claimants having no right to an oral hearing. Critics claim that this system of review lacks the independence of a fully fledged appeal system such as prevails in the rest of the social security system as well as, inter alia, in the court system:

'This is not a fully independent review in institutional terms in that the inspectors are appointed and their training directed by the Social Fund Commissioner, herself an appointee of the Secretary of State. Moreover, the inspectors, like the [social fund] officers are subject to the [merely administrative] guidance and directions issued by the Secretary of State.' (Ogus, Barendt and Wikeley, 1995, p. 685)

As such, the system of review has been criticised as breaching the notion of due process, a central tenet of which is the provision of a mechanism to challenge the decision of adjudicatory bodies before a tribunal independent of the disputing parties. In fact, the government's original intention was not even to have the second tier of review by Social Fund Inspectors but it was forced to concede this during the legislative passage of the Social Security Act 1986, as explained below:

'The original Social Fund proposals attracted almost universal criticism from outside Parliament, and much within. There was sufficient disquiet to persuade the Government to introduce at report stage in the Commons the concept of the Social Fund Inspector as a second tier review. The House of Lords was not [however] convinced of the independence of the Social Fund Inspector. Three eminent law lords, Scarman (Ind), Wigoder (Lib) and Elwyn-Jones (Lab), supported by Baroness Faithfull (Con), successfully moved an amendment calling for the right of appeal to a tribunal. This was won in the Lords Committee by 131 votes to 115...By the time of the report back to the Commons on Lords amendments, the government had been forced into rethinking their approach. It was at this point that the [idea of] the Social Fund Commissioner [was] announced. Because of the strict guillotine imposed by the Government, only some 45 minutes was allowed for debate on this crucial subject. The Government inevitably won the vote. The Bill was sent back to the Lords the following day. The lords who originally moved the successful amendment some three weeks earlier defended the right of appeal, but unsuccessfully.' (Social Security Consortium, 1986, p. 15)

# The Legal Rules

## The regulated social fund

First introduced in April 1987, the regulated social fund provides grants to cover maternity and funeral expenses as well as for additional fuel costs during cold weather. Adjudication officers have a much reduced amount of discretion in comparison to the discretionary social fund in that if a claimant satisfies the conditions of eligibility, he/she is legally entitled to a payment from the regulated social fund.

### Maternity expenses payments

A maximum payment of £100 is available to eligible claimants to meet the maternity expenses of each new born or adopted baby.

### Conditions of entitlement

Under reg. 5 of the Social Fund Funeral and Maternity Expenses (General) Regulations, a claimant is entitled to a maternity expenses payment if:

(i)  the claimant (or partner) has been awarded income-based JSA, income support, working families tax credit or disabled person's tax credit; and
(ii)  the claimant (or a member of the claimant's family) is expecting a child within 11 weeks of the date of making a claim or has recently given birth or has adopted a child who is not older than 12 months or is having a child by a surrogate mother.

Regulation 9 imposes a third condition:

(iii) the claimant's capital cannot exceed the capital limit.

## (i) Awarded a qualifying benefit

Claimants of one of the four above-mentioned means-tested benefits are eligible for maternity expenses payments. This includes those claimants who, as a result of a sanction under the voluntary disqualification rules, are only in receipt of a JSA hardship payment. Also, under reg. 6, if a claimant or partner is involved in a trade dispute and either is in receipt of income-based JSA or income support, he/she will be eligible for a maternity expenses payment if the dispute has been going on for at least six weeks at the date of claim. Recipients of working families tax credit or disabled person's tax credit are eligible for a maternity expenses payment if the claim for either benefit was made before the beginning of the trade dispute.

## (ii) Pregnant or arrival of baby

A claim for a maternity expenses payment can be made for a member of the family other than the claimant or partner and, for this purpose, 'family' includes young persons above 16 years of age. Under reg. 19 and para 8 of Sch 4, a claim can be made at any time between the 29th week of pregnancy until three months after the day of birth. Where a baby is adopted, a claim must be made within three months of the date of the adoption order.

## (iii) Capital limit

Under reg. 5(2), the maternity expenses payment is £100 for each child. However, only claimants whose capital (as calculated in the same way as for income-based JSA and income support) is £500 or less (or £1,000 if the claimant or partner is 60 or over) receive the full amount. Under reg. 9(1), the £100 is reduced by any amount by which the claimant's capital exceeds £500 (or £1,000 as the case maybe).

## Funeral expenses payments

A grant for funeral expenses can be made from the regulated social fund if the following conditions are satisfied.

## Conditions of entitlement

Under reg. 7, eligibility for a funeral expenses payment is based on the following conditions:

(i)  the claimant has been awarded a qualifying benefit; and
(ii) the claimant (or partner) accepts responsibility for paying the costs of the funeral *and* the Benefits Agency accepts him/her as the responsible person; and

(iii) the funeral takes place in the United Kingdom; and
(iv) the deceased was ordinarily resident in the United Kingdom at the time of death.

### (i) Awarded a qualifying benefit

Under reg. 7(1)(a), the 'qualifying benefits' include not only those for maternity expenses payments (income-based JSA, income support, working families tax credit and disabled person's tax credit) but also housing benefit and council tax benefit. The inclusion of the last two benefits substantially extends the scope of eligibility for funeral expenses payments.

### (ii) Responsibility for the costs of a funeral

Under reg. 7(1)(e), a claimant is deemed to be a responsible person and thus eligible for a funeral expenses payment in the following circumstances:

(a) he/she is the partner of the deceased;
(b) he/she is an immediate family member (i.e. parent, son or daughter) *or* a close relative of the deceased *or* a close friend of the deceased and it is reasonable for the claimant to accept responsibility for those costs. However, in determining what is reasonable, the existence of other people who could meet the costs, particularly those who are not eligible for a funeral expenses payment, will be explored. Thus, there is no entitlement for a claimant if the deceased had a partner at the time of death or where there is an immediate member of the family, not in receipt of qualifying benefit, who was not estranged from the deceased at the time of death. Similarly a claimant will be deemed not to be the 'responsible person' for funeral expenses if, under reg. 7(7), there is an immediate family member or a close relative who was in closer contact with the deceased than the claimant *or* was in equally close contact and did not receive a qualifying benefit or have capital of more than £500 (£1,000 if aged 60 or over).

### (iii) Funeral in United Kingdom

Under reg. 7(1)(b), the funeral, whether burial or cremation, must take place in the United Kingdom in order to be eligible for a funeral payment from the Social Fund.

### (iv) Deceased was ordinarily resident in the United Kingdom at the time of death

Under reg. 7(1)(c), a funeral payment is only available if the deceased was ordinarily resident in the United Kingdom at the time of death. This means that he/she 'normally lives' in the United Kingdom which denotes residence with 'some degree of continuity' (per *R(P)1/78*) and, in *Shah* v. *Barnet* LBC [1983] 2 AC 309, the House of Lords defined 'ordinarily resident' as meaning, '...that the person must be habitually and normally resident here, apart from temporary occasional absences of long or short duration.'

### Amount payable and the impact of the claimant's capital

Under reg. 7A, funeral expenses covered by a funeral payment comprise paying for a burial (including buying a burial plot) or the cost of a cremation along with payment for any documentation necessary to obtain access to the deceased's assets as well as transport costs for any part of a necessary journey in excess of 50 miles. Additional funeral expenses of up to £600 can also be claimed. However, under reg. 8, deductions from any award of a funeral payment are made in the following circumstances:

(a)   Any capital that the claimant (or partner) has in excess of £500 (£1,000 if either the claimant or partner is over 60) is deducted, under reg. 9(1), from any award.
(b)   The value of any assets of the deceased that are available to the claimant without probate or letters of administration – per *R(IS)14/91*.
(c)   Any contribution from a charity or relative to meet funeral expenses.
(d)   Any payment to the claimant on the death of the deceased from an insurance company, occupational pension scheme, burial club or similar source.
(d)   A war pensioner's funeral grant.

Under reg. 19 and para 9 of Sch 4 of the Social Security (Claims and Payments) Regulations, a claim for a funeral payment must be made within three months of the funeral.

### Cold weather payments

The third type of payment under the regulated Social Fund is a cold weather payment. This is paid at a rate of £8.50 per week.

### Conditions of entitlement

Under regs 1A and 2 of the Social Fund Cold Weather Payments Regulations, a claimant is eligible for a cold weather payment if he/she satisfies the following conditions:

(i)   a 'period of cold weather' has been forecasted or recorded for the area in which the claimant's home is situated; and

(ii) he/she has been awarded income-based JSA or income support for at least one day during that period; and

(iii) the income-based JSA or income support includes a pensioner, higher pensioner, disability, severe disability or disabled child premium or the family includes a child aged under 5.

Of these conditions, only the first requires greater elaboration:

### (i) A 'period of cold weather'

Under reg. 1(2) this is defined as a period of seven consecutive days during which the average mean daily temperature is forecast or recorded as equal to or below 0 degrees Celsius. Under Sch 1, the country is divided up into 70 areas, based on postcode, each covered by a weather station where temperatures are forecast and recorded.

Cold weather payments are automatically paid by the Benefits Agency, a claimant does not therefore have to apply for the payments. Furthermore, as long as a claimant is in receipt of a qualifying premium from income-based JSA or income support, there are no other financial critieria to meet. Most notably, any capital the claimant might have does not affect eligibility.

The final point to note in respect of the regulated social fund is that, unlike the discretionary social fund, there is a system of independent appeals to the Social Security Appeal Tribunal and then to the Social Security Commissioners.

## The discretionary social fund

As outlined at the beginning of this chapter, the discretionary social fund provides *community care grants*, *budgeting loans* and *crisis loans*. Whereas the community care grant is non-repayable, the two loans require a recipient to repay the money received, usually via a deduction from any weekly benefit received.

### Community care grants

The non-repayable community care grant (CCG) is intended to help recipients of income support or income-based JSA who are experiencing certain difficulties. Most obviously, CCGs are designed to assist those claimants who are leaving institutional or residential care to assist in re-establishing themselves in the community so that they can live as independent lives as possible. Other examples when CCGs can be paid include where a claimant or member of his/her family are experiencing 'exceptional pressures' such as mental stress or depression or where there is a breakdown of a relationship or where a disaster such as a flood has damaged a claimant's home.

## Conditions of entitlement

The following conditions must be satisfied in order for a community care grant to be paid:

(i)   a claimant is in receipt of a qualifying benefit, namely income support or income-based JSA; and
(ii)  the claimant's capital is below the prescribed limit; and
(iii) the claimant or partner is not involved in a trade dispute; and
(iv)  the payment is not for an item that is expressly excluded; and
(v)   the payment is required for one or more of the recognised purposes for which a CCG can be granted.

### (i) A claimant is in receipt of a qualifying benefit

Under Social Fund Direction 25, a claimant must be in receipt of either income support or income-based JSA or, under Direction 25(2)(b), is due to leave institutional care within six weeks and is likely to receive one of the benefits once leaving. Under para 7002 of the *Social Fund Guidance*, a claimant is eligible for a CCG if he/she is receiving a hardship payment of JSA.

### (ii) Capital

Under Social Fund Direction 27, the amount of any CCG awarded is reduced by the amount of disposable capital, as calculated according to the qualifying benefit the claimant receives, that a claimant possesses in excess of £500 (or £1,000 if the claimant or partner is 60 or over).

### (iii) Trade dispute

Under s.24 of the Jobseeker's Act 1995, a person is involved in a trade dispute if he/she is not working due to a stoppage of work at his/her place of work due to a trade dispute or he/she withdraws his/her labour in furtherance of any trade dispute. This is examined in greater detail on pp. 107–113. If a claimant or partner is involved in a trade dispute he/she is not eligible for a CCG other than, under Direction 26, for travelling expenses to visit a person who is ill.

### (iv) Excluded items

Payment for a number of items is excluded in respect of all three elements of the discretionary social fund. Under Directions 12, 23 and 29, this general list of exclusions includes:

- a need occurring outside the United Kingdom;
- a number of educational needs such as school uniform, school meals and travelling expenses to school;
- expenses, such as fees and fines, in respect of court proceedings;
- debts, such as income tax liabilities and national insurance arrears, owed to government departments;
- most housing costs.

As well as these generally excluded items, there are a number of items that are also excluded only in respect of CCG. These include, under Directions 28 and 29:

- costs in respect of the installation of, and charges for, a telephone;
- fuel and standing charges;
- daily living expenses;
- items worth less than £30.

### (v) Payment is for a recognised purpose

Under Direction 4, a CCG can be awarded if community care can be seen to be promoted in one of the following ways:

(a) helping a member of the claimant's family or another person for whom he/she is caring to become re-established into the community after leaving institutional or residential care;

(b) helping a member of the claimant's family or another person for whom he/she is caring to remain in the community rather than entering institutional or residential care;

(c) assisting the claimant or partner to care for a prisoner or young offender on temporary release;

(d) helping the claimant or a family member with travelling expenses within the UK, for example, to visit someone who is ill or to attend a relative's funeral or to deal with a domestic crisis;

(e) easing 'exceptional pressures' on the claimant and his/her family. The phrase 'exceptional pressures', however, is not defined either statutorily or in any guidance, although the guidance outlines some examples of the circumstances when it may be appropriate for Social Fund Officers to award a CCG. These include where there has been a breakdown in a relationship, particularly if due to domestic violence, or where items have to be repaired or replaced because of behavioural problems within the family or where high washing costs, clothing or footwear is needed for a disabled child or when meter reconnection or installation charges exist for families with a disabled child or child under five. These, and other examples set out in the guidance, are not, however, exhaustive merely illustrative of what can constitute the basis for 'exceptional pressures'.

### Priorities and the Social Fund guidance

A claimant can seek a CCG for any item or service not expressly excluded. To assist them in the exercise of their discretion in prioritising and deciding upon claims, Social Fund Officers are issued with guidance, such as the *Social Fund Guide* (which includes the Social Fund Directions). While para 2147 of the *Guide* states that '...the overriding concern in determining priority is the assessment of individual need' and it would thus be unlawful to refuse a payment solely on the grounds that a Benefits Agency district office had exceeded its monthly budget, nevertheless s.140(1)(e) of the Social Security Contributions and Benefits Act 1992 stipulates that Social Fund Officers must have regard to the budget when deciding on whether to make a grant and on the amount to be awarded. The purpose of the Guide is thus to help prioritise claims within this budgetary context and, to this end, outlines three categories of priority:

- **High priority** should normally be given if a grant will have a significant and substantial impact in resolving or improving the circumstances of the claimant and be very important in meeting one or more of the purposes outlined in Direction 4.
- **Medium priority** should normally be given if a grant will have a significant and substantial impact in resolving or improving the circumstances of the claimant but is less important in fulfilling one or more of the Direction 4 purposes.
- **Low priority** should normally be given if the need is indirectly linked to the claimant's circumstances or will be of minor importance in fulfilling one or more of the Direction 4 purposes.

Although the *Guide* is not legally binding, the following comment gives some insight into the reality of the way that Social Fund Officers (SFOs) operate:

> 'The SF Guide ... stresses that social fund officers (SFOs) must take into account the circumstances of each individual case and exercise their discretion accordingly, sensitively and in a non-judgmental way. They are also advised to avoid a rigid interpretation of the guidance and the absence of guidance relating to a particular situation does not mean that a payment should be refused. In spite of this, SFOs tend to use the SF Guide as a rule book, even though the guidance is not legally binding.' (George et al, 1998, vol. 1, p. 650)

## Budgeting loans

These are designed to assist individuals who have been receiving income support or income-based JSA for 26 weeks or more to cover, per Direction 2, '...important intermittent expenses...for which it may be difficult to budget' out of the weekly benefit the claimant receives. While there is no legal entitlement to budgeting loans, s.140(A) of the Social Security Contributions and Benefits Act 1992 requires that social fund officers make their decisions on applications for a loan on the basis of legally binding criteria, rather than by exercising their discretion. This is examined on pp. 272–273. The use of such legally binding criteria was introduced in April 1999. Prior to that date, discretion was exercised by social fund officers on the same basis as for community care grants. Another very important aspect of both budgeting and crisis loans is that a claimant cannot be awarded an amount greater than it is deemed he/she can afford to repay.

## Conditions of entitlement

The following conditions must be satisfied in order for a budgeting loan to be paid:

(i)    the claimant must be in receipt of income support or income-based JSA when an application for a loan is considered by an SFO; and
(ii)   the claimant or partner has been in receipt of income support or income-based JSA for 26 weeks; and
(iii)  the claimant's capital is below the prescribed limit; and
(iv)   the claimant or partner is not involved in a trade dispute; and
(v)    the loan is not for an excluded item; and
(vi)   the loan is designed to meet important intermittent expenses for which it is difficult to budget out of weekly benefit; and
(vii)  the amount awarded is not more than the claimant can afford to repay.

### (i) Receiving income support or income-based JSA

Under Direction 8(1)(a), a claimant is eligible for a budgeting loan only if, on the day that an SFO makes the decision, he/she is in receipt of either income support or income-based JSA. Direction 8(3) and stipulates that a claimant is not treated as in receipt of JSA during the three-day waiting period at the beginning of a claim. However, JSA Regs 46 and 48 establish that claimant is entitled to receive benefit in the first three days if he/she was previously entitled to income support, incapacity benefit or invalid care allowance within 12 weeks of becoming entitled to income-based JSA or where the claimant is under 19 and entitled to a severe hardship payment or the present jobseeking period is linked to an earlier jobseeking period.

### (ii) Claimant or partner receiving benefit for 26 weeks

The claimant or partner must, per Direction 8(1)(a), have been in receipt of either of the qualifying benefits throughout the 26 weeks before the date on which the decision on the application for a loan is made. Under Direction 8(2), a break of up to 14 days during this period, when benefit was not paid, does not render a claimant ineligible for a loan application.

## (iii) Capital

As in the case of CCGs, the amount of any budgeting loan awarded is reduced, under Social Fund Direction 27, by the amount of disposable capital that a claimant possesses, as calculated according to the qualifying benefit he/she is in receipt of, in excess of £500 (or £1,000 if the claimant or partner is 60 or over).

## (iv) Trade dispute

Direction 8(1)(b) states that a claimant is not eligible for a budgeting loan if he/she or partner is involved in a trade dispute.

## (v) Excluded items

As set out in respect of CCGs, there is a number of items for which a grant or loan is excluded, under Directions 12, 23 and 29, in respect of all three elements of the discretionary social fund (see pp. 268–269 for a list of these items). However, as well as these generally excluded items, there are a number of other items that are excluded only in respect of budgeting loans. Under Direction 12, no budgeting loan can be made to meet the cost of mains fuel consumption (but not coal, liquid gas or paraffin) and any associated standing charges, while Direction 10 establishes that no such loan can be made where the item(s) in question is(are) worth less than £30 while the maximum amount is £1,000 less any amount of a previous social fund loan that remains unpaid.

## (vi) Important intermittent expenses

The purpose of a budgeting loan is to meet important intermittent expenses for which it may be difficult to budget out of weekly benefit received. In determining the priority of any application for a budgeting loan, social fund officers, since 5 April 1999, have to make a decision on the basis of a number of factual criteria which help to determine the 'weighting' of, and therefore the priority to be attached to, the application. A new edition of the *Social Fund Guide*, introduced on that date, sets out the basis for determining this weighting, based on **initial criteria** and **wider criteria**:

- *Initial criteria* involve establishing two factual aspects of the claimant – the length of time that he/she or partner has been in receipt of income support or income-based JSA and the number of people within his/her family unit. These are set out in Directions 50 and 52 of the *Social Fund Guide*. The weighting for length of time varies from 1 for the minimum period of six months to 1.5 for the maximum period of three years. There is a pro rata weighting for each complete month between these two periods. For example, 21 months is exactly halfway between the minimum period of six months and the three-year maximum and therefore receices a weighting of 1.25. In respect of size of family unit, the larger it is the greater the weighting. A single claimant receives a weighting of 1, any partner receives an additional 1/3 weighting, while the first child gives a further 2/3 weighting and all other children provide a total of a 1/3 weighting. These weightings are calculated by computer and apply nationally. They establish the relative priority of a claim and the maximum amount that can be offered.

- *Wider criteria* apply only if a claimant is not awarded a budgeting loan on the initial criteria and do not apply if the initial criteria result in a claimant being awarded a smaller loan than was applied for. As determined by Directions 51 and 52, these wider criteria are aimed at providing additional weighting to a claim. The first of these involves taking into account the length of time the claimant or partner has been in receipt of working families tax credit, housing benefit or council tax benefit. If the period is longer than receipt of income suport or income-based JSA, the benefit that provides the longest period, up to a maximum of three years, can be used to increase the weighting of a claimant's budgeting loan application. The second of these 'wider criteria' involves giving weighting to any non-dependants (i.e. not members of the claimant's family unit) who are members of the claimant's household if they are receiving income support or income-based JSA. These are given the same weighting as family members. Also, if the claimant or partner is pregnant, the number of expected children are included in the family for weighting purposes.

The operation of these two sets of criteria helps to determine the weighting attached to each application for a budgeting loan and therefore the relative priority of claims as well as the maximum amount that can be offered. They do not, however, determine the actual amount, if any, that a claimant will receive. This is also dependent on other factors set out below.

### (vii) Amount is not more than can be repaid

Under Direction 5, any award of a budgeting loan must include a determination by the SFO that the loan is capable of being repaid by the claimant. The *Social Fund Decision and Review Guide* states that loans should normally be recovered by making deductions from a claimant's weekly benefit over a maximum of 78 weeks (para 4003) or, exceptionally, 104 weeks (para 4004). There are three rates of payment suggested (paras 4013–16) – 15% of a claimant's 'applicable amount' if there are no 'continuing commitments' i.e. others debts, 10% if the 'continuing commitments' are up to £7.71 per week and 5% if there are higher 'continuing commitments'.

## Amount of budgeting loans

The exact amount of budgeting loan that a claimant receives is determined by a number of factors, only some of which have been previously set out. The maximum amount of a budgeting loan is £1,000 and the minimum is £30. A claimant, though, cannot receive a larger loan than he/she applied for, even if his/her weighting provides for it. In fact a claimant will not necessarily receive the amount claimed. As well as using the initial and wider criteria to determine the priority of an application, two other factors are used to establish the exact amount that will be awarded to an applicant for a budgeting loan.

- ***The availability of resources*** Although the changes announced in April 1999 sought to introduce factual criteria to establish eligibility for a budgeting loan, thereby providing a degree of objectivity into the process, the amount received is still also determined by the amount of resources within the budgeting loan of the local Benefits Agency office. Every district Social Fund manager has a yearly budget which is regularly monitored. A maximum budgeting loan is determined for each level of weighting. This varies throughout the year, depending on the demands on the budget and will also differ between districts. This is explained as follows:

  'Personal circumstances (length of time on benefit and size of family unit) are weighted to give each application a priority relative to other applications. However, although the position in the priority stakes is fixed according to objective criteria, the local budget will dictate the cash value of the maximum size of BLs [budgeting loans] available to any claimant at any time. If there has been a high level of demand on the loans budget then the amount payable to all applicants in that area will be less, and then the cash value of each person's maximum limit will be reduced.' (*1999 Welfare Rights Bulletin*, p. 6)

- ***Existing budgeting loans*** A claimant's weighting determines the maximum amount of **all** budgeting loans that he/she can receive. If he/she is still repaying a previous loan, this can substantially reduce the amount awarded for any new claim. In order to prevent claimants 'topping up' any previous budgeting loan to his/her maximum level by claiming a further loan up to that level, any new loan (whatever amount is sought) will be reduced by double the existing loan debt. Thus, for example, where a claimant has £200 of a previous loan still to pay, any new loan will be reduced by £400. If the amount sought is less than this, no loan will be made available.

## Crisis loans

Under Direction 3 of the *Social Fund Guide*, a crisis loan can be paid to meet a claimant's expenses:

'in an emergency, or as consequence of a disaster, provided that the provision of such assistance is the only means by which serious damage or serious risk to the health or safety of that person, or to a member of his family, can be prevented.'

## Conditions of entitlement

The following conditions must be satisfied in order for a crisis loan to be paid:

(i) a claimant must be over 16 and not be an 'excluded person'; and
(ii) the claimant does *not* have to be in receipt of income support or income-based JSA; and
(iii) he/she lacks sufficient resources to meet the short-term needs of him/herself and, where appropriate, family; and
(iv) the loan must be for expenses to deal with the consequences of an emergency or a disaster to prevent serious damage to health or safety; and
(v) the loan must not be for an excluded item; and
(vi) the loan must not exceed an amount which the claimant is likely to be able to repay.

## (i) Claimant is over 16 and not an 'excluded person'

Under Direction 14, a claimant must be aged 16 or over while Directions 15, 16 and 17 outline those claimants who are not eligible for a crisis loan. These include, per Direction 15, hospital in-patients, prisoners and those lawfully detained, members of religious orders who are fully maintained by the order and people in full-time non-advanced (i.e. up to, and including, A levels) education. There are also some groups who are only able to obtain a crisis loans in very limited circumstances. Thus, students in advanced education can, under Direction 16(a), only receive expenses arising out of a 'disaster' but not an 'emergency' unless they are students, such as single parents or disabled, who are in receipt of income support or income-based JSA. Direction 16(b) limits 'persons from abroad' who are not eligible for either income support or income-based JSA (and this now includes nearly all asylum seekers) to obtaining a crisis loan only for expenses arising out of a 'disaster' and not an 'emergency' (see below on how these are defined). Direction 17 stipulates that where a claimant or partner is involved in a trade dispute (see pp. 107–113), he/she is entitled to a crisis loan only in respect of expenses arising out of a 'disaster' or for the costs of items required for cooking or space heating. Paragraphs (b), (c) and (d) of Direction 17 also limits the entitlement of claimants who have been disallowed income-based JSA for being in breach of one of the 'labour market conditions' (i.e. not being available for, or actively seeking, work or not having a current jobseeker's agreement) or where benefit has not been granted or has been stopped because the claimant has been sanctioned (e.g. because he/she is deemed to be voluntarily unemployed or has failed to carry out a reasonable jobseeker's direction). For such claimants, paras 3500 and 3502 of the *Social Fund Guide* state that, during the first 14 days following benefit being disallowed or stopped, a claimant can only receive a crisis loan for expenses, including living expenses, arising from a disaster or to obtain items for cooking or space heating.

### (ii) Receipt of income support or income-based JSA not required

Unlike budgeting loans, crisis loans are, in principle, available to people who are not in receipt of either income support or income-based JSA.

### (iii) Insufficient resources to meet short-term needs

Direction 14 states that a claimant must be 'without sufficient resources to meet the immediate short-term needs of himself or his family.' In practice, substantial discretion exists in the hands of Social Fund Officers in determining whether a claimant lacks the resources to meet the short-term needs of him/herself and any family, and assessing what resources a claimant has is an issue of some controversy. Para 5051 of the *SF Guide* requires that all resources available to the claimant should be taken into account although paras 5053–105 set out certain types of resources that should be disregarded such as any other Social Fund payment and the value of the claimant's home. One area of controversy, however, concerns the fact that while para 5107 states that Social Fund Officers should refer claimants to employers, relatives or close friends to seek assistance only 'if there is reason to believe their help will be forthcoming' pressure may be placed on claimants to obtain resources from charities, friends and others before being considered for a crisis loan.

### (iv) Expenses to deal with the consequences of an emergency or a disaster to prevent serious damage to health or safety

Neither 'emergency' nor 'disaster' is defined either statutorily or in the *directions* nor is 'serious damage to health or safety'. The non-legally binding *Social Fund Guide* does, however, indicate examples of a disaster as including a fire or flood resulting in significant loss or destruction whereas examples of emergencies include loss of money, being stranded away from home without any means of support, fuel reconnection charges or being unable to live on normal income because of misfortune. What constitutes 'serious damage to health and safety' is determined on the circumstances of each claim, though lack of money to obtain food or shelter might be an obvious example of such a threat.

## (v) *The loan is not for an excluded item*

As well as the items that are excluded for all three parts of the discretionary social fund (see pp. 268–269) , there are some additional items for which, under Direction 23, a crisis loan is not available. These include installation, rental and call charges for a telephone; garaging, parking, purchase and running costs of a motor vehicle; and television or radio, TV licence, aerial or TV rental.

## (vi) *Amount is not more than can be repaid*

As in the case of budgeting loans, any award of a crisis loan must, under Direction 5, include a determination by the SFO that the loan is capable of being repaid by the claimant. The non-legally binding *Social Fund Decision and Review Guide* states that, for those recipients of a crisis loan who are in receipt of income support or income-based JSA (these being the vast majority), loans should normally be recovered by making deductions from a claimant's weekly benefit over a maximum of 78 weeks (para 4003) or, exceptionally, 104 weeks (para 4004). There are three rates of payment suggested (paras 4013–16) – 15% of a claimant's 'applicable amount' if there are no 'continuing commitments', i.e. other debts, 10% if the 'continuing commitments' are up to £7.71 per week and 5% if there are higher 'continuing commitments'.

## Review and the Discretionary Social Fund

There is no right of appeal to an independent body, such as the Social Security Tribunal, against decisions of Social Fund Officers in respect of the discretionary Social Fund. There is, in its place, a system of review, consisting of two stages. The first stage is an internal review carried out by the Benefits Agency office where the original decision was made. A request for such a review must be made in writing within 28 days of the date of the decision unless there are 'special reasons' for a later request. There is, however, no review against any decision about the rate of repayment of a budgeting or crisis loan. If a claimant is dissatisfied with the outcome of this first stage, a further review can be requested, which must be initiated by a written request made within 28 days of receiving the decision of the first review. The second review is carried out by a Social Fund Inspector who is based at the Independent Review Service in Birmingham.

## Bibliography

Cohen, R. and Tarpey, M. (1988) *Single payments: The Disappearing Safety Net*, Child Poverty Action Group.

George, C. et al. (1999) *Welfare Benefits Handbook*, Child Poverty Action Group.

Social Security Advisory Committee (1992) *The Social Fund: A New Structure.*

Social Security Consortium (1986) *Of Little Benefit: A Critical Guide to the Social Security Act 1986.*

Walker and Lawton (1989) 67 *Public Administration* 295.

*Welfare Rights Bulletin* (1999) Budgeting loans: more light on the new rules, June.

# 14 Reform – Past and Present

## The Past: An Assessment of the Reforms of the Conservative Governments 1979–97

Throughout the 1950s, 60s and 70s there was a basic consensus between the major British political parties that saw them largely embrace, albeit with some differences of opinion, the central tenets of Beveridge's ideas modified by the fact that, when in power, both the Labour and Conservative parties had allowed means-tested benefits to assume a far greater importance in the provision of social security than was envisaged by Sir William Beveridge. However, the four sucessive Conservative governments of 1979 to 1997 brought a fundamental change in approach. Rejecting Beveridge's idea that the state should provide financial assistance 'from the cradle to the grave' to those deemed to be in need, reforms were directed towards reducing the role of the state in providing financial support to those in need. This manifested itself in a number of ways. Most obviously, from 1980 benefits were uprated in line with prices rather than with wages, the consequence of which was that benefit levels fell sharply in comparison to the standard of living enjoyed by those not having to resort to state support, e.g. between 1978 and 1987 a married couple's normal entitlement to supplementary benefit fell from 61% of personal disposable income per capita to 53%. Secondly, increased conditions were imposed on eligibility for entitlement to benefits. Thus, as an example, in 1989 the requirement to be 'actively seeking work' was added to that of being 'available for work' for those claiming unemployment benefit while, when jobseeker's allowance replaced unemployment benefit in 1996, a further requirement of needing to agree a 'jobseeker's agreement' was also imposed.

A third strategy was to reduce entitlement to benefit by defining need more narrowly. An example of this is incapacity benefit, which was introduced in 1995 to replace invalidity and sickness benefit. Incapacity benefit requires that, for most claimants, eligibility after 28 weeks is dependent upon the 'all work test'. This test was introduced for the very purpose of narrowing entitlement in comparison to invalidity benefit. Fourthly, there was the approach of passing the financial burden from the state to the individual claimant. This was achieved in two obvious ways. The first was to encourage more individuals to take out private, rather than state, provision. Manifesting itself in a number of spheres, e.g. private medical insurance, the most spectacular example was the 'encouragement' for people to opt out of SERPS and take out private pensions, which resulted in the, as yet unresolved, 'pensions scandal' of the early 1990s. The other way to pass the burden to the individual is the infamous use of loans in respect of the Social Fund. This has produced situations whereby most claimants, in order to pay back the loan, have deductions made from weekly means-tested benefits while other claimants can be denied a loan if it is deemed that they are too poor to be able to repay the loan. The rationale for this approach, and a stinging rebuke of its consequences, are set out in the following quote:

'...[T]he underlying justification for an innovation which, as soon became apparent, was causing real distress to hard-pressed families who were either denied help or gained it in exchange for a cut in their Income Support, was that there did indeed exist a section of the population separated from the rest of society by the strategies it adopted to manage its resources. There was positive gain in making the outcome of applications conditional on the funds held by the local [Social Fund] office that month, and in making the fortunate recipients incur further debts. They needed, it was argued, to learn what those independent of state assistance already knew, that it was an uncertain world, and that money had to be husbanded from week to week. So complete a failure to understand the experience of poverty served only to confirm its existence.' (Vincent, 1991, p. 204).

These were merely some of the strands of the Conservative government's approach to social security. Others included channelling more resources towards dealing with fraud while concentrating less on tackling the problem of low take-up of benefits even though, e.g., by the end of the Conservative period of office there were around 1 million pensioners eligible for income support who were not claiming it, losing an average of £16 per week.

However, despite these strategies, the social security budget continued to increase throughout the Conservatives' tenure of office. In 1993, the Department of Social Security published *The Growth of Social Security* which provided detailed statistics which clearly outlined this trend. Since 1978/79 social security expenditure had risen by an average annual rate in real terms (i.e. excluding the influence of inflation) of 3.7% and was predicted to grow by an annual rate of 3.3% to the end of the century. In 1992/93 social security expenditure, at £15.9 billion in 1978/9, stood at £74.1 billion and it rose to over £92 billion by the last year of Conservative government (1996/97). The reasons put forward by the DSS in this publication for such a development were demographic (e.g. an increasing number of elderly persons as people lived longer); economic (in particular the level of unemployment); government policy; and, social factors such as the change in family structures including the increasing number of families headed by a single parent. This nevertheless raises the question as to why, despite the large number of reforms that were directly aimed at rolling back the role of the state and, thus, reducing public expenditure in the sphere of social security, did such government policy fail to achieve its espoused objectives? One argument is that, despite the underlying philosophy and the accompanying rhetoric, the Thatcher and Major administrations never undertook reforms that radically altered the social security system because there was, amongst Tory supporters, clear support for the existing welfare state. This support was part of a consensus in favour of retaining the essential features of, not only a national health service and universal provision of education, but also the basic tenets of the existing social security system. Thus, as a consequence, David Vincent argues that:

> 'The radical reformer in Mrs Thatcher had to give way to the pragmatic politician. The frontiers of the state could be rolled back only an inch at a time. Despite her secure parliamentary majorities, she lacked the constituency for wholesale dismantling of the system she had inherited. Instead the Conservatives' room for manoeuvre was confined to exploiting...two assumptions inherent in the post-war settlement, that beyond the adjustments required to establish a national minimum the pursuit of economic equality was not a necessary objective of the state, and that in granting public assistance it remained possible to distinguish between the deserving and the undeserving poor.. In the first instance it was possible to embark on a deliberate policy of widening differentials...[While] tax cuts were weighted heavily towards the better off,...from 1980 benefits were no longer uprated in line with earnings, but only with prices...At the same time the long-standing lack of public sympathy for the able-bodied poor became a more potent force as they came to dominate the work of the supplementary benefit system. If the basic cost of supporting the poor could not be reduced, it was possible to undermine their status and dignity. The severity of the recession during the first Thatcher Administration meant that for the first time since 1948, unemployed families overtook pensioners as recipients of means-tested relief. With the number of single-parent families also continuing to grow, the field was left open for an intensification of the official campaign against those who could be held responsible for their own plight.' (Vincent, 1991, pp. 202–3)

It is possible to see this incremental approach operating throughout the 18 years of the Conservative administration in respect of the host of changes referred to earlier.

Another reason forwarded to help explain the failure to reduce levels of public expenditure in the sphere of social security was that the underlying objectives were not always compatible. The fervent commitment to rolling back the frontiers of the state did not, for example, always lead to saving of public monies. Thus, in talking of the governments headed by Margaret Thatcher, Michael Hill comments:

> '[A major] reason why social security was high on the Thatcherite agenda can be found in the ideology of the New Right. The Thatcher government was not merely concerned to cut back the role of the state because of its cost, it also was...committed to reducing the role of the state in the lives of individuals, strengthening the operation of free markets, and stimulating self-reliance on the part of citizens. One way in which the concern to cut public expenditure and the concern to reduce the role of the state were brought together by the Thatcher Government was in the desire to replace public provisions by private provisions. The manifestations of this in social security policy were the delegation of responsibility for initial assistance to employees who became sick or pregnant to employers and the encouragement of private pension schemes. *However, both of these developments had to be underwritten by extensive amounts of public money.*' (my emphasis) (Hill, 1990, p. 55)

## The Present: The Reforms of the 1997 Labour Government

### Introduction

The return of the Labour government on 1 May 1997 appeared to herald a change in approach although the Labour Party's vision of social security was, on being elected, a little uncertain. Despite the fact that in 1992, the then Labour leader, John Smith, had established the Social Justice Commission to examine social security and in 1994, under the chairmanship of Lord Borrie, it had produced a radical, comprehensive blueprint, the proposals were not embraced by the then Shadow Cabinet under Tony Blair's leadership. The main reason for this was the then Shadow Chancellor Gordon Brown's fears of the potential cost of such reforms. In its place, the 1997 Labour Party manifesto contained very few detailed proposals on social security aside from promising to retain universal child benefit and not to means test the basic state pension.

Following Harriet Harman's appointment as Secretary of State for Social Security with Frank Field as her Minister of State, the first year of the Labour government saw it seeking to establish the framework of its

approach to the provision of social security. A central problem that was
perceived to exist was the dilemma of a growing level of social security
expenditure – in 1997–98 the figure had reached £95 billion – whereas the
scale of poverty had increased. This state of affairs was largely attributed
to the policies of the previous Conservative government. The central
theme of Labour's ideas for dealing with this dilemma was the idea of
'welfare to work' whereby the main solution to poverty was seen as getting
benefit claimants into employment and thus off social security:

> 'Labour appears to believe that "welfare to work" definitively answers
> the question of poverty...Gordon Brown claimed [less than 2 weeks
> after the general election]...that he wished to be judged on his success
> in helping to reshape the welfare state, confirming his interest in
> "developing a welfare state built around the work ethic".' (Witcher,
> 1997, p. 9)

In January 1998, Tony Blair set out the ideas behind the government's
approach to reforming social security in more detail. In a speech in
Dudley, in the West Midlands, and in an article in *The Times*, he outlined
the reasons for change and the principles underlying reform proposals. Of
the existing social security system, he argued that:

> 'Over the last 18 years we have become two nations – one trapped on
> benefits, the other paying for them. One nation in growing poverty,
> shut out from society's mainstream, the other watching social security
> spending rise and rise, until it costs more than health, education and
> law and order and employment put together.' (*The Independent*, 1998.
> p. 10)

He thus argued that changes would be made to the social security system
in line with the following principles:

> 'First those in genuine need will always be helped by a Labour Gov-
> ernment...Second, anyone of working age who can work should work.
> Work, for those that can work, is in our view the best form of welfare.
> It provides financial independence, a network of contacts, and dignity.
> So those who have in the past been excluded from job opportunities,
> such as lone parents or the disabled, many of whom can work and want
> to work, will be given the chance to do so. Third, we believe in the
> responsibility of individuals to help provide for themselves where they
> can do so. And we will build on these principles. Our welfare state will
> root out fraud, wherever it is found. It will be based on a partnership
> between public and private sectors. It will be about providing services

not just cash. That is behind the New Deal welfare to work programme,
the biggest ever attack on long term and youth unemployment...It is
the key building block to our welfare reform plans for this Parliament.'
(*The Times*, 1998, p. 18)

One of the main reasons for the Prime Minister setting out this blueprint
for reform at the beginning of 1998 was that some of the reforms that had
been implemented by the government in 1997 had created a political
storm. The first of these was the decision to continue with the cuts in
benefit to lone parents originally introduced by the Conservative Budget
in November 1996. Operating from April 1998, the lone-parent rate of the
family premium (giving an additional amount to lone-parent families as
compared to two-parent families) was abolished for means-tested benefits
such as income support, income-based JSA, housing benefit and council
tax benefit while the lone parent rate for child benefit (previously known
as one-parent benefit) was also abolished. The decision to embrace this
policy was ostensibly justified by the new Labour government on the
grounds that it would encourage lone parents to move 'from welfare to
work' in that it would both increase the attractiveness of seeking a job
rather than relying on benefits and realise £300 million to increase childcare facilities (seen as an essential development if more lone parents are
to return to work). Critics argued that reducing lone parents' entitlement
to benefit was not the way to encourage them into work At best, it smacked
of the previous government's approach, having little to do with any notion
of social justice, while it also ran counter to Tony Blair's claim that those
in genuine need would always be assisted. At worse, some benefit claimants would lose money by returning to work, most notably because they
would be reassessed for housing benefit and the amount to which they
would be entitled would, in 1998, have been reduced by up to £9.35 per
week due to there ceasing to be an additional lone parent premium under
housing benefit:

> 'This is hardly consistent with the government's claim to be helping
> lone parents move from welfare into work.' (MacDermott, Garnham
> and Holtermann, 1998, p. 20)

The other controversy that arose in 1997 in respect of the Labour government's views on social security reform related to benefits for the disabled.
'Off the record' leaks had generated press speculation culminating in a
leaked letter in December 1997 that indicated that, as part of the DSS's
*Comprehensive Spending Review*, the Department was considering a large
reduction in expenditure on disability benefits. The letter suggested that
such savings were necessary to release resources to finance reforms in the

spheres of health and education. Policies to achieve such savings were suggested to include means testing or taxing benefits for the disabled such as disability living allowance and attendance allowance. This led to protests by disabled groups in Downing Street in December and to David Blunkett, Secretary of State for Education and himself blind, sending a memorandum to Gordon Brown in the week before Christmas, duly leaked to the press, expressing his opposition to such ideas. The resulting turmoil is confirmed in the following statement:

> 'Media speculation, cabinet rifts, letters to MPs from anxious disabled constituents, a delegation to Harriet Harman, Secretary of State for Social Security, led by Lord (Jack) Ashley representing the powerful All-party Disablement Group finally resulted in an announcement by the Prime Minister that he personally would be taking the lead on the Welfare Reform initiative. Harriet Harman was forced to promise that there would be consultation with disability organisations on any reform proposals. Aware of the depth of concern amongst Labour Party members as well as the public at large, Tony Blair announced a series of Reforming Welfare Roadshows. These would tour the country and provide a platform for senior ministers to explain the Government's plans and reassure party members.' (Keith, 1998, p. 4)

The speech at Dudley on 15 January 1998 was the first of these roadshows, which were designed to obtain public support for the government's reform proposals based on the principles set out by the Prime Minister. Some of these proposals had, in fact, already been set in motion while others were announced in the spring of 1998 with the Budget of 17 March followed nine days later by the presentation to Parliament of the Green Paper *New Ambitions for our Country: a New Contract for Welfare* by Frank Field, Minister of State for Social Security with responsibility for welfare reform. The specific policies introduced by the Labour government are set out in the next section.

## Social security proposals

### Welfare to work and the New Deal

Welfare to work has already been identified as the main principle underlying the government's approach to social security. The so-called *New Deal* is the main initiative towards helping unemployed people find work and is funded by a one-off 'windfall levy' on the profits of privatised companies in public utility industries such as electricity, gas, water and telecommunications. In the first budget of the new government in July 1997, Gordon Brown as Chancellor of the Exchequer announced the New Deal as a radical reform in the way that the Employment Service and Benefits Agency provide support to people to move from receiving benefits to obtaining employment. Initially aimed at claimants under 25, Gordon Brown's second Budget in March 1998 announced that it would extend to older claimants who have been unemployed for more than six months and to partners of unemployed people and subsequently the New Deal has been extended to lone parents and the disabled. The New Deal for 18–24 year olds was fully implemented in April 1998 although from January 1998 it had already been piloted in 12 so-called 'Pathfinder' areas which included Cambridge, Tayside, Swansea, the Wirral and Lambeth. In October 1998, a similar piloting of the scheme was implemented for disabled claimants.

***The New Deal for 18-24 year olds***. The essence of the New Deal for this group, which is run by the Employment Service, is that it seeks to provide a proactive strategy to assist those claiming benefits, particularly those who have been doing so for a substantial period, to obtain employment. Its first element is the *Gateway* period. This lasts for a maximum of four months where a claimant is assigned a New Deal personal adviser whose role is to counsel, advise and guide the claimant towards returning to work. This period consists of a number of features. In the first instance, there is an initial phase of 'intensive help' to find a job and advice and guidance is provided throughout Gateway to identify action that is needed to assist the claimant to find work such as job search skills, training, independent careers advice and guidance and motivation and confidence building. The essence of this support is that it is directed towards the claimant obtaining *unsubsidised* employment, that is to obtain a job that does not require any New Deal subsidy.

The first interview is the initial Gateway step when the claimant and New Deal personal adviser (or disability employment adviser for disabled people) meet to, inter alia, explore the claimant's situation and to begin to draw up a *New Deal Action Plan* for the claimant which sets out realistic and achievable 'job goals' and the steps needed to achieve them. This meeting also explores the claimant's needs and whether he/she has had any problems in seeking a job along with the adviser providing job search advice. Subsequent interviews review progress, examine whether the claimant's Action Plan needs altering and explores possible unsubsidised jobs, particularly where the claimant is deemed to be 'job ready'. It also considers whether the claimant needs to be referred to any 'Gateway activities' whereby, e.g. the claimant can be referred to careers advice or to programmes to improve motivation, confidence or job search skills. Some of these activities, including some of the advisory function may, depending upon local delivery arrangements, be contracted out to private or voluntary bodies, known as 'partner' (or 'provider') organisations, to be performed by them rather than by the Employment Service. A minority of claimants are also allocated 'volunteer mentors', mostly provided by a partner organisation, to provide friendly and supportive 'job-focused' assistance.

Those claimants who are unsuccessful in obtaining unsubsidised work are required to consider one of four options at the end of the Gateway period. These are:

(a) Full-time education or training. This is aimed at claimants who do not have the equivalent of level 2 National (or Scottish) Vocational Qualifications; or

(b) A subsidised job with an employer which includes the equivalent of at least one day a week in education or training. The employee receives a subsidy for a maximum of 26 weeks of £60 per week for each New Deal employee working 30 hours or more a week and £40 for each employee working fewer hours as well as training costs up to £750; or

(c) As part of the employment option, the opportunity exists for self-employment, whereby help can be obtained in setting up a business. This has been available since 1 June 1998. Help is available during the Gateway period and for a further 26 weeks. Known as the self-employment route, this constitutes a special version of the employment option and has three stages. During the first two stages the claimant continues to claim JSA and must, therefore be *available for work*. Stage 1 involves exploring whether a sustainable business is likely to result from the claimant's business idea and involves the claimant being referred to a provider with expertise in helping people into self-employment. Stage 2 involves a short course or one-to-one counselling to give the claimant more advice about setting up and running a business. Stage 3 normally takes place after the Gateway period. The claimant enters the New Deal option, thus ceasing to claim JSA, and has the opportunity to undertake self-employment for 26 weeks while still receiving support and guidance from the Employment Service and an appointed provider. The allowance received is equal to JSA plus £15.38 per week, totalling £400 over the 26 week period; or

(d) Work with a voluntary organisation or the Environmental Taskforce. Both of these last for a maximum of 26 weeks and also require the equivalent of at least one day a week in education.

The express aim of the New Deal options is that the self-employment option gives assistance in setting up a business while the other options are designed to improve the employability of claimants through high quality work placements. These should provide realistic work appropriate to the participants' needs which makes good use of their talents and delivers benefits to local communities as well as giving training or education for participants towards them obtaining an approved qualification.

Any 18–24 year old who enters the New Deal is liable to a sanction if he/she refuses 'without good cause' to attend a relevant interview or fails to take up or leaves a New Deal option or if he/she is dismissed from a New Deal option for misconduct. In the first instance, the sanction is a loss of benefit for two weeks with the period extended to four weeks for subsequent refusals although, for disabled claimants and those with dependants, there is a 40% deduction of benefit rather than loss of the total benefit.

***The New Deal for the long-term unemployed*** In June 1998, the New Deal programme was extended to this second group of claimants. A claimant is eligible to join the New Deal if he/she is 25 or over and has been claiming JSA or signing on for national insurance credits for a continuous period of two years or more, although some claimants can enter the programme earlier. Funded by £450 million from the windfall tax, the New Deal for this group differs substantially to that for those under 25, There is, for example, no Gateway period where claimants can access advice and guidance from independent 'provider' organisations. In its place, there is an advisory process involving a series of compulsory interviews with an Employment Service personal advisor, who can refer claimants to specific assistance to improve their job prospects. During this period, which can last up to six months, a claimant continues to receive JSA. It is intended to result in a claimant obtaining employment or entering onto a government training programme. As such, this New Deal group of claimants are entitled to participate in such existing schemes as *JobClub*, *Programme Centres* and *Work Trial* which are designed to help benefit claimants to return to work. The New Deal also provides for two new opportunities. The first is a subsidised job. Employers are paid a higher subsidy than for 18–24 year olds of £75 per week for a maximum of 26 weeks while there is, also, no condition that the job provides a training or education element. The second new option is full-time education or training for up to 52 weeks, during which the claimant continues to receive JSA. This involves a relaxing of the normal JSA conditions for a claimant to be available for, and actively seeking, work.

There continues to be a compulsory element to the New Deal for this group of claimants in that failure to attend any interview in the advisory process can lead to a sanction as can refusing to apply for or accept a New Deal job or leave without good cause. The sanction, however, is the usual JSA sanction of losing benefit for up to 26 weeks. There is no specific New Deal sanction, as there is for those under 25, of a two- or four-week loss of benefit.

***The New Deal for lone parents.*** Funded by £90 million over four years, the New Deal for parents, which started in eight pilot areas in July 1997, operates nationally, since April 1998, to cover all new lone parent claimants of benefit, most of whom will be recipients of income support, not JSA. The purpose of the scheme is to provide a programme of advice and guidance for those lone parent benefit recipients who are seeking to obtain work. For this group of claimants, the New Deal does not, at the time of writing, have an element of compulsion. Entitlement to benefit, therefore, is not affected if a lone parent does not wish to participate. For those who do, however, the first step is an initial interview with a personal adviser in which, inter alia, the individual circumstances of the claimant are ascertained, including preference for the amount of hours to be worked and previous work history. The interview should result in an agreed 'action plan' between the claimant and personal adviser on how the claimant can obtain work. The second step is that the personal adviser keeps in regular touch, at least once every fortnight, the primary objective being to help the claimant become 'job ready' which could include encouraging the claimant to participate in Employment Service schemes such as *JobClub*, *Programme Centres*, *Work Trials* or training programmes to acquire more employability skills. The third aspect of the New Deal for lone parents is the payment of expenses. In order that lone parents should not be worse off as a consequence of participating in the New Deal, the Employment Service can reimburse lone parents for certain expenses in respect engaging in 'approved activities' such as attending courses or going to a job interview or interview with a personal adviser. Expenses that can be reimbursed include travel expenses, childcare costs and training and education course fees.

**The New Deal for the disabled and long-term sick.** The aim is to assist individuals to obtain work largely by providing training. It is targeted at claimants receiving incapacity benefit, severe disablement allowance and the disability premium in income support. As well as providing personal advisors to help disabled and long-term sick individuals overcome the barriers to work, it includes 'innovative schemes' to examine the most effective ways of such individuals obtaining work.

## The New Deal as workfare

The most controversial aspect of the New Deal is the element of compulsion. For example, 18–24 year olds are subject to New Deal sanctions which can lead to the loss of benefit for four weeks. Claimants from the other groups who participate in the New Deal are not subject to the same compulsory options under threat of losing benefit except that partners of claimants who are themselves aged between 18 and 24 are subject to the same requirements as other 18–24-year-old participants.

The imposition of these benefit sanctions for some participating groups of claimants has led to criticism that the New Deal is merely a *workfare* scheme. Workfare requires claimants of benefit to undertake some form of work as a condition of obtaining benefit. It is well established in the USA where, for example, some recipients of benefit under the *Aid to Families with Dependent Children* (AFDC) are compelled to work. The justification for workfare is essentially fourfold:

(a)   If someone is seeking to obtain resources from the state, it is entitled to impose a condition of work as a means of deterrence. A claimant must realise that he/she cannot expect 'something for nothing' and that he/she will be better off seeking a job, albeit a lowly paid one. This is, in essence, the 20th-century version of the 'less eligibility' principle that formed the basis of the workhouse regime introduced by the Poor Law Amendment Act 1834, as discussed in chapter 1.

(b)   The second argument is that claimants will be able to offset much of the state's costs in providing benefit if they are required to work, most obviously by providing cheap labour for the state to use as it thinks fit. It will also save public monies if its effect is to force people back to work, thereby reducing the number of benefit claimants.

(c)   Workfare is a way helping unemployed people re-establish themselves in the labour market and it requires a compulsory 'work condition' for entitlement to benefit in order to force claimants to help themselves in this way:

'Most unemployed young people are anxious to work but their confidence and self-esteem has been so eroded by the experience of unemployment that they will not volunteer for work experience or training. Benefit sanctions may be hard in some cases, but it is reasonable to compel young people to take steps which are in their long-term interests. The best known advocate of...[this] approach is the American political scientist Lawrence Mead whose work has been enormously influential in the US. Mead argues that voluntary schemes fail because they assume that even those who have been out of work for long periods are nevertheless competent individuals who can be relied upon to act rationally in the pursuit of their self-interest. This, Mead claims, is not the case. In fact they are often "dutiful but depressed", and do not respond to incentives in the same manner as everyone else.' (Deacon, 1997, p. 8)

(d)   A slightly different argument to the last one is that which recognises that the state has a duty to provide assistance to the unemployed, e.g. in the form of advice or training, to facilitate a return to employment but, as a consequence, a claimant has a reciprocal duty to make the most of this assistance and, if he/she refuses to do so, should lose entitlement to benefit:

'The state should ensure that the individual has a set of real opportunities for work or training. And the individual should use these opportunities (or forgo benefits).' (Layard and Philpott, 1990, p. 6)

Workfare, particularly as its operates in the USA, has been subject to criticism based largely on the grounds that it is both expensive and fails to act as a springboard to employment. In fact, it is, in reality, merely a way of punishing benefit recipients. The main arguments against workfare are:

(a) The approach of Mead, in particular, assumes that an individual's unemployment is a consequence of his/her own inadequacy and the purpose of workfare is to, in part at least, punish the individual for his/her shortcomings. Thus, the real motive of those like Mead who blame the unemployed for their lack of work is not to use workfare as a mechanism to proactively assist them in returning to work but as a form of discipline. This manifests itself in two ways. First is the view that the perceived indolence or moral turpitude of the unemployed is behaviour that cannot be tolerated and thus warrants punishment. Secondly, workfare makes receipt of benefit so unpleasant that it disciplines people to accept the alternative of a job at any cost. It therefore acts as a policing element of a low wage economy.

(b) If unemployment is due, not to the behaviour or attitude of the unemployed, but to other factors then workfare is:

'...futile because by focusing upon the behaviour of the unemployed themselves, it is doing nothing to remedy the real causes of unemployment.' (Deacon, 1997, p. 10

(c) Workfare is expensive. Rather than providing cheap labour, the costs of running workfare programmes is a drain on the public purse.

While the various arguments for and against workfare have been articulated, the central issue is not really whether New Labour's New Deal warrants being called a form of workfare but, more significantly, whether the motivation is punishment or a genuine attempt to assist the unemployed to obtain 'real' employment. As Louie Burghes observes in his comments in respect of workfare in the USA:

'The orthodox concept of workfare has proved of little value. All it does is to place obligations on recipients – without providing a way out of poverty. Good quality voluntary work programmes, offering education and skills training as well as job-hunting, may genuinely help some recipients off welfare...And, in the end, their success depends on the availability of secure, well-paid employment...' (Burges, 1987, p. 11)

On the basis of such observations, it is possible to argue that the New Deal has more positive aspirations than mere punishment. It does seem to be geared towards the Employment Service genuinely assisting the unemployed in obtaining work. The mood of optimism is captured in the following quote from an article in *The Guardian* on the eve of the implementation of the New Deal:

> 'Out there on the ground, battalions of new-deal managers in job centres everywhere are...rearing to go, brimming with conviction that it will work. It is rare to find such straightforward optimism from a long depressed and derided branch of the civil service. Even the manager in Knowsley, Merseyside, one of the worst unemployment blackspots, waxed lyrical. His young people just did not get fair access to the available jobs. No, they would not be going through the revolving door of yet another scheme. He will not give up on anyone and he was determined, absolutely determined, they will get work. Local employers are helpful, more work is coming in, new jobs created. This was what the employment service has always wanted, the chance to work intensively with each client. His new personal advisers couldn't wait to begin. It was the same story when I talked to managers in Lambeth, Cornwall and Newcastle. Those who have been running pathfinder projects for the past three months are, if anything, even more enthusiastic. "We're changing people's lives and employers are responding magnificently". "The word on the street is so good, we're being inundated with young people coming of their own accord". "We're raising young people's expectations, encouraging them to go for better jobs that they believed they could do"...Listening to the tales from the front, it's impossible not to believe new deal will do immense good.' (Toynbee, 1998, p. 14)

Whether this optimism is misplaced or not, only time will tell.

### 'New Ambitions for our Country: A New Contract For Welfare' Green Paper March 1998

On 27 March 1998, Frank Field, the minister entrusted with the task of exploring welfare reform, presented a Green Paper to Parliament setting out the government's views on how the social security system should be changed. It was short on detailed policies, setting out instead the guiding principles for proposed reforms. The reasons for this were spelt out by the Prime Minister in a foreword to the Green Paper:

> 'This Green Paper marks the beginning of a debate, not its conclusion. We want it to be debated up and down the country, re-worked and refined, before we publish our proposals on the detail of the individual components of reform. But the principles guiding reform and our vision of the future of the welfare state are clear. We want to rebuild the system around work and security. Work for those who can; security for those who cannot.' (p. iii, Cm 3805)

The Green Paper identified three key problems with the then existing system. First there had been an increase in inequality and social exclusion leading to a substantial number of families and communities being cut off from mainstream society. These included the poorest pensioners as well as increasing numbers of 'workless households' which had led to some areas that 'bear...the brunt of long-term dependency and worklessness [and where] educational standards falter, crime rises and disillusionment sets in.'(Green Paper, p. 11). Secondly, people faced a series of barriers to paid work which resulted in them being trapped on benefit rather than helped off. When some people, for example, obtained a job and moved off benefits, the marginal rate of tax created by the combination of withdrawal of benefit and the payment of income tax and national insurance contributions was such that only a small amount of each extra pound earned ends up in extra income. 740,000 people, for example, were subject to a marginal rate of 70% while 130,000 had a marginal rate of 90%, meaning that less than 10p is actually gained for every extra £1 earned. Also, in households with two working adults, where one loses a job, the family could be worse off if the other carries on working than if he/she did not. Disabled people were seen as facing particular difficulties including problems created by the use of the 'all work test' to determine eligibility for incapacity benefit:

> '[This]...can have perverse effects. It is an "all or nothing" test: people who pass are not expected to look for any kind of work, even of a different nature to their old job. As a result, some people who would be able to work again...can end up spending the rest of their working life on benefit.' (Green Paper, p. 12).

The third key problem was identified as fraud. This was estimated as costing £4 billion annually and was seen both as taking money away from genuine claimants as well as undermining public support for the social security system.

The Green Paper argued that, in dealing with these and other issues, there were three choices of approach for the welfare state. The first was to argue that the welfare state is unaffordable and needs to be scaled back merely to provide a residual safety net, with most individuals being responsible for their own 'social security' needs via the private sector. The second approach argued for the continuation of the existing social security system but with the level of benefits being much more generous.

> 'The Government rejects both approaches. The first leaves the welfare state to disintegrate, fails to address poverty and leaves those on middle incomes more insecure. The second leads to rising bills and

people trapped in poverty. We propose a third way. A modern form of welfare that believes in empowerment not dependency. We believe that work is the best route out of poverty for those who can work. We believe in ensuring dignity and security for those who are unable to work because of disability or because of caring responsibilities, as well as for those who have retired. This system is about combining public and private provision in a new partnership for the new age.' (Green Paper, p. 19)

In order to develop such an approach the Green Paper set out eight 'key principles' for the future welfare state:

1.  *The new welfare state should help and encourage people of working age to work where they are capable of doing so*. This central theme of the government's approach, already manifested in the New Deal programme, was also to be fostered in other ways including the working families tax credit, introduced in the previous week's Budget by the Chancellor of the Exchequer. This aimed to reduce the marginal tax rate for those who were working and had children, decreasing the number of families facing marginal rates of over 70% by two-thirds. This principle was also to be achieved by the already announced national minimum wage as well as by proposed changes to the national insurance system.
2.  *The public and private sectors should work in partnership to ensure that, wherever possible, people are insured against foreseeable risks and make provision for their retirement*. The Green Paper argued that many people had already benefited from a private-public partnership in the sphere of pensions where three-quarters of workers have private or occupational pensions supplementing the state pension. This private provision is encouraged by the state giving tax relief on contributions. It was recognised, however, that many people cannot join good occupational pension schemes and thus do not benefit from improved provision for retirement while many people had been victims of the pension mis-selling scandal in the 1980s when private pension organisations had encouraged many to replace their SERPS or occupational pension with a personal pension. A new 'stakeholder' pension was therefore proposed as a supplement to the flat-rate basic state pension. However, the details were left to another Green Paper in the autumn of 1998. This Green Paper also proposed pilot exercises to address the issue of one million pensioners failing to take up income support to which they are entitled, losing on average £16 per week, as well as seeking to encourage savings through Individual Savings Accounts (ISAs). It also recognised that private-public partnerships highlight the need for regulation of financial services whereby the government provides an effective and reliable regulatory environment.

3.   *The new welfare state should provide public services of high quality to the whole community, as well as cash benefits.* The Green Paper argued that the welfare state was not only about the payment of social security benefits, but also about the provision of a range of services such as education, health, job assistance, social services and housing. A new emphasis should be placed on the standards, quality and efficiency of these services and, where appropriate, barriers between public and private provision should be removed. In respect of housing, it identified that the housing benefit scheme has disadvantages. Not only can landlords exploit the scheme by setting rents at the maximum housing benefit payable, it suffers from high marginal tax rates in the form of the taper of 65% while the marginal rate is even higher for low paid recipients of housing benefit who also receive family credit and council tax benefit. Housing benefit was also seen as a major area of benefit fraud with a annual figure of £1 billion fraud identified.

4.   *Those who are disabled should get the support they need to lead a fulfilling life with dignity.* Based on the claim that '[e]nsuring the wider social participation of disabled people is a key goal for the Government' (p. 52), this principle was reflected in two themes; providing assistance for those disabled people who want to, to obtain work; and ensuring dignity and independence for those who are unable to work. As well as advocating a Disability Rights Task Force and a Disability Rights Commission, and accompanying legislation, to guarantee civil rights and equal opportunities for disabled people, the Green Paper proposed changes to the provision of social security for disabled people in order to assist them to obtain work. It was therefore proposed to extend the New Deal to cover disabled claimants and this was, in fact, implemented in October 1998. The Green Paper also advocated dismantling what it saw as barriers to work for the disabled. Thus the unemployment trap, whereby disabled people can end up less well off when they return to work because of loss of benefits, was to be tackled by the replacement of disability working alliance with the disabled person's tax credit in October 1999. Also changes to the limits on the amount of work that disabled people could do without losing benefit were proposed. As a consequence, it was proposed to modify the rule that a maximum of 16 hours per week of voluntary or therapeutic work was allowed before entitlement to benefit was lost. The Green Paper was also critical of the 'all work test' for incapacity benefit (IB) in that:

'It writes off as unfit for work, people who might, with some assistance, be able to return to work, perhaps in a new occupation. It is an all or nothing test, in the sense that it assesses people as either fit for work or unfit for any work. Thus many people who would be capable of some work with the right help and rehabilitation are instead spending their working lives on benefit. We want a new approach to

IB which focuses on what disabled people can do, not on what they cannot. While we will keep the current assessment system for existing claimants, we are examining the scope for a more effective test for future claimants which assesses the scale of their employability, recognising that capacity for work is a continuum. People with some capacity to work would then be given the opportunity of the assistance they need to help them return to work.' (p.54)

Significantly, it was argued that such reforms of incapacity benefit would reduce levels of public expenditure on the benefit although, as a result of the opposition of disabled groups in December 1997 to earlier proposals, the Green Paper rejected means testing disability living allowance and attendance allowance.

5. *The system should support families and children, as well as tackling child poverty*. Arguing that, despite changing significantly in recent decades, the family remained 'the building block of society' (p. 57), the Green Paper claimed that there was nevertheless a 'huge problem of child poverty' with 3 million children living in workless households. It proposed a number of reforms including measures to deal with the high rate of teenage pregnancies in the United Kingdom. In respect of social security reforms, it rejected the case for one-parent families having additional support in comparison to two-parent families but supported the notion of child benefit remaining a universal (i.e. non-means-tested) benefit. The twin problems of the unemployment and poverty traps for families with children were to be met by the new working families tax credit which was announced in the Budget to replace family credit:

'For those bearing the extra costs of children – and receiving higher out-of-work benefits as a result – the gap between benefit levels and pay levels is often narrow. Indeed, some parents might make their families worse off by working. The Working Families Tax Credit...will offer more generous support to working families, reducing the numbers facing high marginal tax rates and improving work incentives.' (p. 58)

6. *Specific action is needed to tackle social exclusion and help those in poverty*. Social exclusion was identified as existing in communities where multiple disadvantages, such as high levels of unemployment, poor skills, low income, poor quality housing, high levels of crime and bad health existed. This was deemed to require a new cross-departmental approach with long-term policy objectives. In the first instance, the Green Paper endorsed the already established *Social Exclusion Unit* to help co-ordinate such an approach.

7. *Openness and honesty should be encouraged and the gateways to benefit should be clear and enforceable*. Under this principle, the Green Paper

spelled out a rigorous approach to fraud. Claiming that existing social security fraud was highly complex, it argued that existing methods of dealing with fraud 'lack coherence and vision' (p. 67). While endorsing the increased powers contained in the Social Security Administration (Fraud) Act 1997 as well as the extended responsibilities of the *Benefit Fraud Inspectorate*, it argued that the most effective approach towards fraud was to prevent its commission '...by designing more secure and accurate benefit systems' (p. 67). This could, for example, be achieved by co-ordinating computerised information between local authorities and the Department of Social Security so that discrepancies – both deliberate and accidental – are identified before claims for housing benefit are processed by local authorities.

8. *A flexible, modern, efficient, easy to use system of social security should be created.* The Green Paper stated that:

'Customers and staff tell us that they want changes to the way social security services are delivered. They are fed up with duplication, inefficiency, red tape and unnecessary complexity. Customers and taxpayers want improved services; they do not want money wasted on artificial barriers and inefficient processes. The Government is responding to that demand for change and listening to ideas and suggestions. We are determined to build an **Active Modern Service** to meet the needs and expectations of customers.' (p. 71)

This was to be achieved, inter alia, by personal advisers (already in place under the New Deal) to advise claimants and help them to return to work. Simplifying benefit claim forms and streamlining decision making were also advocated along with utilising the advantages of information technology more extensively than was then the case.

Responses to the Green Paper were mixed, even contradictory. The *Welfare Rights Bulletin*, reflecting the views of the pressure group Child Poverty Action Group, observed:

'It is difficult to know quite what to make of the long awaited Green Paper on welfare reform. Despite one commentator describing it as "the most important development in welfare in decades" it is markedly short on detail with a strong emphasis on principles and "success measures". Although the first draft was apparently ready last autumn, it was not presented to Parliament by Frank Field...until 26 March. The Government claims its agenda for reform is not "cuts-driven" but, despite some positive measures, concern about new benefit rules remains. Part of the problem is that it is not the DSS but the Treasury that is leading on welfare reform. The Chancellor, Gordon Brown, has been setting the agenda for change – even if that includes means testing, which Frank Field has in the past described as a "cancer" in the welfare system. Maybe the Government is keeping its powder dry until the spending review is complete. Like the proverbial iceberg, it is what you do not see in the Green Paper which could prove the greatest danger.' (143 *Welfare Rights Bulletin*, April 1998, p. 5)

A more enthusiastic response came from Will Hutton:

'After all the rhetoric about rethinking welfare from first founda-tions,...[the] Green Paper on the welfare state represented a return to political reality. The Government wants no more disabled protest-ers chaining themselves to the railings of Downing Street; nor will there be Prime Ministerial intervention warning of the need for eve-ryone to steel themselves for change even if he cannot say what the changes will be. Instead there is to be a carefully managed process of welfare state reorganisation in which there will be as few losers as possible. There is a genuine commitment to opening up the arguments, not least because of the political consequences of not doing so. Nor is the prime concern any longer about saving money, although the pressure remains to make changes self-financing. Both Gordon Brown and Tony Blair have come to recognise that the first round of welfare reform may initially involve extra billions, even if they expect savings in the years ahead. If the case can be proven, says Brown in private discussions, then the money will be found – which, as a Chancellor with one of the strongest fiscal positions in modern times, is a commitment he can deliver.' (Hutton, 1998)

A more sceptical assessment was, however, given in an editorial in *The Independent*:

'[Frank Field's] statement in the Commons showed all the signs of being put through the Treasury wringer. It sounded as if it had once had specifics in it, which had all been taken out. Its timing, nine days after the Budget, said it all... [And] important questions for the welfare state remain...What was missing...in the green paper was a statement of how the Government sees the path of welfare spending as a share of national income, and a clear description of the kinds of people who should gain and lose.' (*The Independent*, 27 March 1998)

## Subsequent developments

In the summer of 1998 government policy seemed to take a major change in direction when, in the first ministerial shuffle of the government on 27

July, Harriet Harman was dismissed as Secretary of State for Social Security and Frank Field resigned as her number 2 after the Prime Minister had refused to appoint him as Secretary of State. Instead, Alistair Darling, previously Chief Secretary to the Treasury, was appointed as Harman's replacement, with Stephen Timms as his deputy. In the aftermath of these changes, it emerged that there had been great friction between the previous two social security ministers:

> 'The low mutual esteem and high mutual suspicion between Ms Harman, Social Security Secretary, and Mr Field, Minister for Welfare Reform, has undoubtedly hobbled the Government's attempts to get to grips with reform of the £100 billion welfare budget.' (*The Guardian*, 28 July 1998)

It also became clear that there had been Treasury opposition to his proposals when, in a personal statement to the House of Commons on 30 July, Field indicated that the Chancellor of the Exchequer had been the major opponent of his reform proposals. In fact the relationship between Frank Field, who had originally been appointed by Tony Blair to 'think the unthinkable' in respect of welfare reform, and the Government became very strained following his resignation. Alistair Campbell, the Prime Minister's Press Secretary, is reported to have said that Field's proposals 'never took the form of policy capable of being implemented by a government' while Gordon Brown said his proposals would have cost the taxpayer billions. The press also reported that one senior minister had described Field as 'a joke' while another said the he was 'wrapped up in his own ego' and that his Green Paper proposals were 'paltry, an embarrassment and unpublishable' (see *The Times* and *The Independent* 3 August 1998 where the above comments are reported).

In light of his earlier comments concerning the Green Paper, Will Hutton's observations of these developments are illuminating:

> 'The loss of both a Secretary of State and Minister for Welfare Reform, appointed in tandem 15 months ago to make policy in an area to which the Government attaches such singular importance, highlights a profound confusion at the heart of Government policy...The dilemma is this. The Government is undecided whether it is a liberal conservative administration, governing within the New Right traditions set by Thatcher and Major but around more decent values, or whether it is trying to reinvent and modernise social democracy. Because it wants to be both, it cannot set out a body of coherent principles on which welfare reform should proceed. It was this confusion that lay behind the arguments and policy stasis [i.e. stoppage] that precipitated Harman's sacking and Field's resignation. Field, it turned out, was no

radical conservative in New Labour clothes. When it came down to detail, he was a social-democratic moderniser whose schemes for a new Beveridgean social insurance settlement were judged too dear. He never got far enough for the detailed costings the lack of which he is now castigated; the argument was lost at the first hurdle. With his resignation, we know that Blair wants to keep the ambiguities alive until he plumps for one philosophy or the other, with his own preferred inclination apparently to lean to the Right' (*The Observer*, 2 August, 1998)

The social-democratic model, which Hutton argued is favoured by Frank Field, is based on universal, not means-tested benefits, which is largely funded by social insurance and is allied to some degree of government management of the economy that is aimed towards maintaining appropriate levels of employment. The social security system thus promotes social solidarity by providing a system of financial support for every person who may be confronted by hazards, such as lack of work or being in poorly paid work, which are the consequence of the inevitable instability and inequity of a market economy. In contrast, the New Right neo-conservative model places heavy reliance on means-tested benefits, paid out of general taxation rather than by social insurance contributions. The state's provision of social security should provide a minimal level of 'safety net' support, leaving it to individuals to take their chance in the labour market in terms of whether work can be obtained and how well paid that work might be. This approach also promotes individual responsibility by leaving it up to individuals to be responsible for providing more than the state's basic minimum in the event that unemployment, illness, old age or other reason might affect their ability to work. Most obviously this would be achieved by individuals taking out private insurance, private medical health and private pensions. At the centre of this approach is the view that the state's responsibility for the provision of social security rests largely, for want of a better phrase as the right dislikes using it, with assisting the poor. State resources should thus be 'targeted' on the poor and this necessitates a central role for means testing. One of the main justifications for this approach is the claim that it keeps taxes down, as the level of revenue required to finance state provision of social security would be substantially less than is the case in the social democratic model.

Hints as to which of these approaches might be adopted by the new regime at the Department of Social Security were given by the fact that the new Secretary of State for Social Security, Alistair Darling, was previously Gordon Brown's deputy at the Treasury, during the period when the Treasury were opposed to Field's 'social-democratic model' ideas for reform because of their cost. In the autumn of 1998, Darling appeared to be moving towards the neo-conservative model. Thus, in a speech to the IPPR in September, he articulated the government's general 'welfare to work' approach by stating that:

> 'Our objective is to help people prepare for and get work as well as making work pay...By cutting the bills of economic failure we can devote more resources to our priorities.' (quoted in 101 *Poverty*, Autumn 1998, p. 1)

In another speech, to the Fabian Society the following month, he give a clear indication of what, in fact, the government's priorities were. He stated that the aim was to extend the requirement that all benefit claimants, including lone parents and the long-term sick and disabled, would be required to look for work in order to be eligible for benefit. As part of this, a new work test would be introduced for incapacity benefit claimants designed to establish whether they could do light work such as clerical or computer work. Darling also stated that he was considering means-testing widow's benefit, although this would be extended to men as well as women. Claiming that the existing social security system led to unnecessary dependence on benefits whereby people were worse off than they need be and should, therefore, be encouraged to take up work and thereby be better off, he argued that any reform of social security should focus on giving more to the most needy (these details of the speech were reported in *The Times* 20 October 1998). On the face of it, these proposals reflect a rejection of the social democratic blueprint proposed by Frank Field in his Green Paper only six or seven months earlier and, on 29 October, Alistair Darling announced to the House of Commons his proposals for reform which were subsequently contained in the Welfare Reform and Pensions Bill published the following month. This Bill included the following reforms:

- Setting up a new framework of pensions provided by the state, including the introduction of a new *stakeholder pension*. The Bill only dealt with certain aspects of the reform of pensions, the main features of its proposed reforms being set out in a Green Paper – *A New Contract for Welfare*, Cm 4179 – in December 1998.
- Replacing the existing bereavement benefits currently available only to widows with benefits paid to both widows and widowers. Thus widowed mother's allowance paid to widows with dependent children is to be replaced by widowed parent's allowance, widow's pension (previously paid to widows without dependent children) is abolished and bereavement allowance is introduced and the lump sum £1,000 widow's payment is to be replaced by a bereavement payment of £2,000. These changes were proposed as a direct consequence of a legal challenge in the European Court of Human Rights by Kevin

Willis, supported by Child Poverty Action Group, over the lack of equal availability of the existing benefits to widows and widowers.

- Introducing a single work-focused gateway to benefit. The March Green Paper had advocated that a single, unified gateway to benefit be established where benefit claimants can receive advice and assistance from personal advisers to identify benefit needs as well as to explore their potential for obtaining work. In October 1998, a consultation paper, *A New Contract for Welfare: the gateway to work* (Cm 4102), advocated such an approach but added an element of compulsion whereby most benefit claimants would be required to attend 'work-focused interviews'. This was an existing condition for receipt of benefit only in respect of jobseeker's allowance but clause 47 of the Bill sought to extend the requirement to attend such an interview to claimants of income support, housing benefit, council tax benefit, incapacity benefit, severe disablement benefit, invalid care allowance, widow's benefit and the new bereavement benefits, with sanctions being imposed if a claimant failed to attend such an interview. This proposal generated a great deal of opposition, with *The Times* describing it as a '...move...which brings the British system closer to the American Workfare scheme...' (29 October 1998).

- Reforming incapacity benefit by replacing the 'all work test' with a 'personal capability assessment' as well as tightening up the contribution conditions in order to receive the benefit. The Bill also provides for a recipient of incapacity benefit to have the amount of benefit received reduced if he/she is in receipt of an occupational or personal pension of more than £50 per week. This last proposal led to criticism that it was introducing a form of means testing to incapacity benefit, while the general impact of these reforms is to eventually save £700 million per annum and reduce the number of recipients by 170,000.

- Abolishing severe disablement allowance and replacing it with an entitlement to incapacity benefit for 16–19 year olds only.

- Ending 'life awards' for disability living allowance and attendance allowance and extending to three and four year olds the higher rate mobility component of disability living allowance.

This was quickly followed by the Tax Credits Bill published on 10 December 1998. This Bill introduced working families tax credits and disabled person's tax credits which were to replace family credit and disability living allowance, respectively. The two replaced benefits were means-tested benefits available to working people on low wages, the former being available to those who have dependent children and the latter to those who have a disability. Rather than receive a social security benefit, the new arrangements allow for such individuals to receive a credit against the amount of income tax paid, the net result being that they pay less tax. In effect, the benefit is provided in the pay packet because there is a reduced amount of tax deducted from the recipient's gross wages. Those applicants whose income is below £90 per week (or £70 for single persons claiming disabled person's tax credit) will receive the maximum amount of credit, while those whose income is above this figure are subject to a 55% taper (similar, in principle, to housing benefit) whereby 55p in every pound above that amount is deducted from entitlement. An important consequence of these changes was outlined by Gordon Brown:

> 'Every working family will be guaranteed a minimum income...of...£200 a week, more than £10,000 per year...[Moreover, n]o income tax will be paid until earnings reach £235 a week. This is a tax cut available to 1.4 million families helping 3 million children.' (Budget Speech 9 March 1999)

While this may be the result of the deployment of the new tax credits, these two Bills, nevertheless, give a clearer insight into the evolving philosophy of the government towards social security. The focus on 'welfare to work' appears to necessitate a regime of compulsion on social security claimants, as exemplified by the increasing number of benefit claimants who will be required, under the Welfare Reform and Pensions Bill, to attend 'work-focused interviews'. Furthermore, the use of tax credits is a form of means testing whereby resources are channelled towards those who fall below a set level of income. It is difficult therefore, to avoid the conclusion that this is further avoidance of the government embracing a neo-right conservative model of social security, however it is dressed up. This is a clear political decision, rejecting other strategies such as basing social security provision on universal, non-means-tested benefits, largely funded by social insurance i.e. the social-democratic model. As Will Hutton further observes:

> 'The Brave New Worlds of giving tax credits...certainly has the advantage of helping the poor without using the dread words "increasing benefit", and of targeting funds where they are needed. But it also implies a wholesale and systemic increase in means-testing...In short these new tax credits...are not citizens' entitlements resulting from collective social insurance against risks we all confront. They are discretionary payments paid by the state because it considers the recipient deserving, and can be withdrawn and fiddled as the state thinks fit. It is an important redefinition of the Welfare State...[and] is a clear political choice...[with] the cost of re-establishing means testing as the core principle by which the disadvantaged qualify for help, while social security benefits have continued to dwindle in real terms.' (Hutton, 1999)

However, while this trend was unfolding, there was one policy that clearly distinguished this government from its Conservative predecessors. This was its commitment to introducing a national minimum wage.

## A national minimum wage

The previous 18 years of Conservative administration had seen government policy based on a refusal to intervene in regulating wages. As part of its philosophy of giving free rein to the market to determine the distribution of economic resources, this period witnessed a dismantling of most Wages Councils and Boards which had existed in a number of industries, e.g. agriculture, to set minimum wage rates for that industry. The Labour government which was returned in May 1997 had, in contrast, a manifesto commitment to introduce a national minimum wage and it moved speedily to implement that policy. In June 1997 it established the Low Pay Commission, under the chairmanship of Sir George Bain, whose tasks were to consider who should be covered by a national minimum wage and what the level of that wage should be. Its first report was presented in June 1998. During this period a National Minimum Wage Bill was also introduced in Parliament, and it received the Royal Assent on 31 July 1998. The National Minimum Wage Act 1998 establishes that workers in the UK over compulsory age qualify for the national minimum wage though some groups, such as the armed forces, share fishermen, volunteers and prisoners, are excluded. Unlike the Wages Councils and Boards, the national minimum wage establishes the same minimum wage for employees in all industries, occupations, regions and sizes of business in which they work. The Act does, however, allow people to be treated differently on the basis of age to the extent that those below the age of 26 can be subject to a lower national minimum wage.

The fundamental argument in favour of a national minimum wage is based on the notion of social justice while the arguments against it are essentially economic, based on the view that a national minimum wage has detrimental economic consequences. Having said that, arguments have been invoked to claim that its economic impact is not as detrimental as its critics claim and, in fact, it has certain economic benefits. The social justice argument for a national minimum wage is that a decent minimum wage is a basic right of all in a civilised society. Yet, for many, low pay has become a major source of poverty with it affecting some groups in society disproportionately than others:

> 'Over the past twenty years there has been a growth in earnings inequality. This has led to a substantial degree of in-work poverty and dependence on social security benefits to supplement low

wages...Low pay is more prevalent among certain groups of individuals, especially women and young people. It is closely associated with particular working patterns, such as part-time work and homeworking. And low pay is concentrated in certain business sectors – particularly in service industries, such as hospitality, retail, business services and social care – and in small firms.'(*National Minimum Wage*, First Report of the Low Pay Commission, June 1998, Cm 3976 pp.1 and 2)

The economic arguments against such a policy centre around the claim that it inevitably leads to an increase in labour costs which means that it leads to a loss of jobs as firms seek to reduce such costs or that firms become increasingly uncompetitive as a consequence of these increased costs. The impact on labour costs, runs the argument, is exacerbated by the issue of pay differentials whereby workers on higher rates of pay, on seeing the rate of the lowest paid workers rising to the level of a national minimum wage, will seek to maintain the differential between the lowest paid and themselves by pressurising for a similar rise in their wages. Economic arguments in favour of a national minimum wage include the view that competitiveness based on low pay leads to economic inefficiency. It allows firms that are inefficient in other aspects, such as failing to invest in up-to-date plant and machinery or not producing good quality products, to compete by paying its workers low wages. The argument is, therefore, that competition which is based on low wages rather than efficiency or quality of goods, produces an unstable business environment that ultimately leads to job losses rather than job creation. Further economic arguments against a national minimum wage, however, are that it can lead to increased prices for goods as firms pass on the additional costs to consumers while it is also claimed that it can have an inflationary effect. Many of the competing arguments were set out by the Low Pay Commission as follows:

'We had to form a judgment about the balance between a high National Minimum Wage, which would make a more substantial difference to the low paid, and the risk that jobs might be lost or that goods might become more expensive. A wide range of evidence – on pay differentials, business costs, competitiveness, inflation, employment and public sector finances – helped us to determine the most likely effects of the National Minimum Wage...

In a society which now has considerable inequalities in pay, a National Minimum Wage should secure greater equity in the workplace and provide for a more inclusive society. While setting a higher National Minimum Wage could make greater inroads into pay inequality, we are conscious that we will not help low-paid workers by recommending a rate which is so high that their jobs are put at risk, or they have to pay a lot more for everyday goods and services. Where to set the initial National Minimum Wage rate without risking damage to the economy is a matter of judgement. Such a new policy will take the labour market into largely uncharted waters and no one can predict its precise effect.' (*National Minimum Wage*, First Report of the Low Pay Commission, June 1998, Cm 3976, pp.4 and 89)

The upshot of seeking to balance the competing arguments in respect of a national minimum wage was that the Low Pay Commission recommended, inter alia, the following features of the national minimum wage:

- The appropriate hourly rate of pay should be £3.70 from June 2000 with an initial rate of £3.60 from April 1999.
- A lower 'development rate' of £3.20 should exist for 18–20 year olds from April 1999 rising to £3.30 in June 2000 and to those aged 21 or over during the first six months of a new job which involves accredited training.
- All those aged 16 and 17 as well as all individuals on apprenticeships should be exempt from the national minimum wage.

While the government accepted most of the Low Pay Commission's recommendations, there were a number of important modifications:

- The £3.60 per hour rate operates from April 1999 but the increase to £3.70 in April 2000 will not be automatic. The Low Pay Commission, given statutory powers in November 1998 to 'monitor and evaluate the introduction and impact of the national minimum wage...' will consider any future increase.
- The 'development rate' will extend to 18–21 year olds rather 18–20 year olds and will be paid, not at £3.20 per hour, but at £3.00 per hour, raising to £3.20 in June 2000 rather than £3.30.
- The 'development rate' for those within the first six months of a job will, therefore, apply to individuals aged 22 or over and will be paid at £3.20 per hour. However, the government refused to commit itself to increasing that rate to £3.30 in June 2000.

As a consequence, there are two development rates, as opposed to the Low Pay Commission's single rate for both young people and trainees.

With the National Minimum Wage Act 1998 being largely an enabling Act, it has delegated to the Department of Trade and Industry the power to introduce secondary legislation on such important matters as the various rates of the national minimum wage. These are contained in the National Minimum Wage Regulations 1999 and these regulations confirm the government's changes to the Low Pay Commission's recommendations. Regulation 8, per s.4 of the Act, establishes that the national minimum wage rate would be £3.60 per hour. Regulation 9(1) exempts workers under the age of 18 from the national minimum wage while reg. 9(2) exempts apprentices under the age of 26 during their first year of apprenticeship. Regulation 9(4) stipulates that a rate of £3.00 per hour will be the minimum wage for workers aged 18 to 21 (inclusive) and reg. 9(5) provides a rate of £3.20 for workers aged 22 or over who are in the first six months of employment with an employer where they are receiving training on at least 26 days of that period.

## Conclusion

As the previous discussion indicates, the first two years of the Labour government has seen a clear battle within that government between two competing philosophies towards the provision of social security and, as a consequence, towards the nature of social security reform. Frank Field was a victim of Gordon Brown's hostility towards the cost of his version of social democratic type reforms, though Field's reciprocal personal antipathy towards Harriet Harman did not help his (nor, in fact, her) cause. Reforms since Alistair Darling became Secretary of State for Social Security in July 1998, indicate that, despite the introduction of the national minimum wage in April 1999, a form of neo-right conservative model of social security, with a central role for means-tested benefits along with compulsory requirements for increasing numbers of claimants to engage in schemes to seek to obtain work, appears to be evolving.

### Bibliography

Burges, L. (1987) 'Does workfare work?' 68 *Poverty*.

Deacon, A. (1997) 'The case for compulsion', 98 *Poverty* autumn, quoting L. Mead, *The New Politics of Poverty*, Basic Books, New York, 1992, p. 172.

Hill, M. (1990) *Social Security Policy in Britain*, Edward Elgar.

Hutton, W. (1998) 'After the rhetoric, the reality', *The Observer*, 29 March.

Hutton, W. (1999) 'Now for Gordo's latest trick', *The Observer*, 14 March 1999.

*The Independent* (1998) 'Building a Modern Welfare State' A speech by Tony Blair, Prime Minister, in Dudley on 15 January 1998, reported 16 January.

Layard, R. and Philpott, J. (1990) *Stopping Unemployment*, Employment Policy Institute, London, 1990, quoted in Deacon (1997).

MacDermott, T., Garnham, A. and Holtermann, S. (1998) *Real Choices for Lone Parents and their Children*, Child Poverty Action Group.

Reith, L. (1998) 'Welfare Reform - a threat to disability benefits?', *Disability Rights Bulletin*, spring.

*The Times* (1998) 'Why Britain needs a new welfare state'. Tony Blair, 15 January.

Toynbee, P. (1998) 'Mind the iceberg', *The Guardian*, 1 April.

Vincent, D. (1991) *Poor Citizens: The State and the Poor in Twentieth Century Britain*, Longman.

Witcher, S. (1997) 'New Labour : thinking the unthinkable', 97 *Poverty*, summer.

# Appendix
# April 1999 Benefit Rates

## Means-Tested Benefits

### Income support and income-based jobseeker's allowance

*Personal allowances*

| Claimant | £ | p |
|---|---|---|
| *Single* | | |
| 16–17* | 30 | 95 |
| 18–24 (including some | | |
|    16–17 year olds*) | 40 | 70 |
| 25+ | 51 | 40 |
| *Lone parent* | | |
| Under 18* | 30 | 95 |
|   or | 40 | 70 |
| 18+ | 51 | 40 |
| *Couple* | | |
| Both under 18* | 61 | 35 |
| At least one aged 18+ | 80 | 65 |
| *Dependent children#* | | |
| For each child aged: | | |
|    under 11 | 20 | 20 |
|    11–15 | 25 | 90 |
|    16–19 | 30 | 95 |

* Under para 1 of Sch 2 of the Income Support Regulations and para 1 of Sch 1 of the Jobseeker's Allowance Regulations, the higher rate is paid to 16- and 17-year-old recipients of income support and JSA who fall into certain categories such as they qualify for a disability premium or, in certain circumstances, are living away from any parent. The higher rate is also used to calculate the entitlement of claimants for housing benefit.

# For the purpose of calculating dependent children allowances, a child is not treated as being 11 or 16 until the first Monday in September following the relevant birthday.

*Premiums*

|                                                        | £   | p  |
|--------------------------------------------------------|-----|----|
| Family premium                                         | 13  | 90 |
| Severe disability premium<br>   for each qualifying person | 39  | 75 |
| Disabled child's premium                               | 21  | 90 |
| Carer's premium                                        | 13  | 95 |
| Family premium – lone parent<br>   (for existing claimants only) | 15  | 75 |
| Disability premium                                     |     |    |
|    single                                              | 21  | 90 |
|    couple                                              | 31  | 25 |
| Pensioner premium (paid to<br>   those aged 60–74)     |     |    |
|    single                                              | 23  | 60 |
|    couple                                              | 35  | 95 |
| Enhanced pensioner premium<br>   (paid to those aged 75–79) |     |    |
|    single                                              | 25  | 90 |
|    couple                                              | 39  | 20 |
| Higher pensioner premium<br>   (paid to those aged those<br>   aged 80+ and to certain<br>   disabled pensioners) |     |    |
|    single                                              | 30  | 85 |
|    couple                                              | 44  | 65 |

N.B. Those premiums above the line are paid in addition to any other premium whereas, of those under the line, only one can be paid.

## Family credit/working families tax credit

|                                             | £   | p  |
|---------------------------------------------|-----|----|
| Adult credit                                |     |    |
|    (only *one* per family)                  |     |    |
|    until 4/10/99                            | 49  | 80 |
|    from 5/10/99                             | 52  | 30 |
| Premium if at least one parent works 30 hours or more per week | | |
|    until 4/10/99                            | 11  | 05 |
|    from 5/10/99                             | 11  | 05 |

Credit for each child
From birth to September after 11th birthday

| | | |
|---|---|---|
| until 4/10/99 | 15 | 15 |
| from 5/10/99 | 19 | 85 |

From September after 11th birthday to September after 16th birthday

| | | |
|---|---|---|
| until 4/10/99 | 20 | 90 |
| from 5/10/99 | 20 | 90 |

From September after 16th birthday to day before 19th birthday

| | | |
|---|---|---|
| until 4/10/99 | 25 | 95 |
| from 5/10/99 | 25 | 95 |

Applicable amount (threshold level)

| | | |
|---|---|---|
| until 4/10/99 | 80 | 65 |
| from 5/10/99 | 90 | 00 |

## Disability working allowance/disabled person's tax credit

| | £ | p |
|---|---|---|
| Adult credit | | |
| single | | |
| until 4/10/99 | 51 | 80 |
| from 5/10/99 | 54 | 30 |
| couple/lone parent | | |
| until 4/10/99 | 81 | 05 |
| from 5/10/99 | 83 | 55 |
| Premium for working 30 hours or more per week | | |
| until 4/10/99 | 11 | 05 |
| from 5/10/99 | 11 | 05 |

Credit for each child
From birth to September after 11th birthday

| | | |
|---|---|---|
| until 4/10/99 | 15 | 15 |
| from 5/10/99 | 19 | 85 |

From September after 11th birthday to September after 16th birthday

| | | |
|---|---|---|
| until 4/10/99 | 20 | 90 |
| from 5/10/99 | 20 | 90 |

From September after 16th birthday to day before 19th birthday

| | | |
|---|---|---|
| until 4/10/99 | 25 | 95 |
| from 5/10/99 | 25 | 95 |
| Disabled child's allowance | 21 | 90 |

Applicable amount (threshold level)

| | | |
|---|---|---|
| single | | |
| until 4/10/99 | 60 | 50 |
| from 5/10/99 | 70 | 00 |
| couple/lone parent | | |
| until 4/10/99 | 80 | 65 |
| from 5/10/99 | 90 | 00 |

## Housing benefit

The **personal allowances** and **premiums** for housing benefit are the same as for income supprot/income-based JSA except for the following:

|  | £ | p |
|---|---|---|
| Personal allowance for 16–24 year olds | 40 | 70 |
| Personal allowance for lone parent under 18 | 40 | 70 |
| Family premium – lone parent rate | 22 | 05 |

### *Non-dependant deductions*

Non-dependants in remunerative work whose gross weekly income is

| | |
|---|---|
| £255 or more a week | £46.35 per week is deducted |
| £204–£254.99 a week | £42.25 per week is deducted |
| £155 or £203.99 a week | £37.10 per week is deducted |
| £118 to £154.99 a week | £22.65 per week is deducted |
| £80 to £117.99 a week | £16.50 per week is deducted |
| Below £80 a week | £7.20 per week is deducted |

Non-dependants in non-remunerative work (including those in receipt of benefits) – regardess of income      £7.20 per week is deducted

A non-dependant deduction is made before any 'taper' is calculated.

## Council tax benefit

The **personal allowances** and **premiums** are the same as in respect of housing benefit except that there are no personal allowances for 16 and 17 year olds:

### *Non-dependant deductions*

Non-dependants aged 18 or over in remunerative work whose gross weekly income is

| | |
|---|---|
| £255 or more a week | £6.50 per week is deducted |
| £204–£254.99 a week | £5.40 per week is deducted |
| £118 or £203.99 a week | £4.30 per week is deducted |
| Below £118 a week | £2.15 per week is deducted |
| Others aged 18 or over | £2.15 per week is deducted |

*Second adult rebate*

| | |
|---|---|
| Second adult on income support/<br>    income-based JSA | 25% of council tax |
| Second adult's gross income<br>    under £118 | 15% of council tax |
|    £118–£154.99 | 7.5% of council tax |

# Non-Means-Tested Benefits

## Attendance allowance

| | £ | *p* |
|---|---|---|
| Higher rate | 52 | 95 |
| Lower rate | 35 | 40 |

## Constant attendance allowance

| | £ | *p* |
|---|---|---|
| Part-time | 21 | 65 |
| Normal maximum | 43 | 30 |
| Intermediate rate | 64 | 95 |
| Exceptionally severe cases | 86 | 60 |

## Contributory jobseeker's allowance

| | *Weekly amount* | |
|---|---|---|
| *Age of claimant* | £ | *p* |
| Under 18 | 30 | 95 |
| 18–24 | 40 | 70 |
| 25+ | 51 | 40 |

## Child benefit

| | £ | *p* |
|---|---|---|
| First child | 14 | 40 |
| Other child(ren) | 9 | 60 |
| First child | | |
|   – lone parent rate | 17 | 10 |

## Disablement benefit

| Extent of disablement | Amount Claimant aged under 18 and not entitled to an increase in respect of a dependant | | Amount All other claimants | |
|---|---|---|---|---|
| | £ | p | £ | p |
| 100% | 66 | 20 | 108 | 10 |
| 90% | 59 | 58 | 97 | 29 |
| 80% | 52 | 96 | 86 | 48 |
| 70% | 46 | 34 | 75 | 67 |
| 60% | 39 | 72 | 64 | 86 |
| 50% | 33 | 10 | 54 | 05 |
| 40% | 26 | 48 | 43 | 24 |
| 30% | 19 | 86 | 32 | 43 |
| 11–20% | 13 | 24 | 21 | 62 |
| 1–10% | 6 | 62 | 10 | 81 |

## Exceptionally severe disablement allowance

| £ | p |
|---|---|
| 43 | 30 |

## Disability living allowance

*Care component*

| Higher rate | £52.95 per week |
|---|---|
| Middle rate | £35.40 per week |
| Lower rate | £14.05 per week |

*Mobility component*

| Higher rate | £37.00 per week |
|---|---|
| Lower rate | £14.05 per week |

## Incapacity benefit

|  | Claimant under pensionable age | | Claimant of or over pensionable age | |
|---|---|---|---|---|
|  | £ | p | £ | p |
| **Short term** | | | | |
| *Lower rate* | | | | |
| claimant | 50 | 35 | 64 | 05 |
| adult dependant | 31 | 15 | 38 | 40 |
| eldest eligible child | – | 9 | 95 | |
| each other child | – | 11 | 35 | |
| *Higher rate* | | | | |
| claimant | 59 | 55 | 66 | 75 |
| adult dependant | 31 | 15 | 37 | 20 |
| eldest eligible child | 9 | 95 | 9 | 95 |
| each other child | 11 | 35 | 11 | 35 |
| **Long term** | | | | |
| claimant | 66 | 75 | – | |
| adult dependant | 39 | 95 | – | |
| eldest eligible child | 9 | 95 | – | |
| each other child | 11 | 35 | – | |

## Invalid care allowance

|  | £ | p |
|---|---|---|
| Claimant | 39 | 95 |
| Adult dependant | 23 | 90 |
| Child dependants | | |
| eldest eligible child | 9 | 95 |
| other children | 11 | 35 |

There is also a Christmas bonus of £10.

## Retirement pension

|  | Claimant £ per week | Adult dependant £ per week | Child dependant £ per week |
|---|---|---|---|
| Category A | 66.75 | 39.95 | 11.35 |
| Category B | | | |
| for a married woman | 39.95 | | 11.35 |
| for a widow | 66.75 | | 11.35 |
| for a widower | 66.75 | | 11.35 |

Category C
  for a person
    not a married woman  39.95           11.35
    for a married woman    23.90           11.35
Category D             39.85           11.35

Any amount for a child dependant is reduced by £1.40 if child benefit is received for an only or eldest child.

## Severe disablement allowance

|                      | £  | p  |
|----------------------|----|----|
| Claimant             | 40 | 35 |
| Adult dependant      | 23 | 95 |
| Child dependants     |    |    |
|   eldest eligible child | 9  | 95 |
|   other children        | 11 | 35 |

There is also an age-related addition which is paid dependent on the age of the claimant on the first day of the of the 196-day qualifying period:

| Age      | £  | p  |
|----------|----|----|
| Under 40 | 14 | 05 |
| 40–49    | 8  | 90 |
| 50–59    | 4  | 45 |

## Statutory sick pay

| £  | p  |
|----|----|
| 59 | 55 |

# Index